# BASEBALL COACH'S SURVIVAL GUIDE

## Practical Techniques and Materials for Building an Effective Program and a Winning Team

## Jerry Weinstein  Tom Alston

**PARKER PUBLISHING COMPANY**

West Nyack, New York 10994

**Library of Congress Cataloging-in-Publication Data**

Weinstein, Jerry.
    Baseball coach's survival guide : practical techniques and materials for building an effective
program and a winning team
    Jerry Weinstein, Tom Alston.
        p.    cm.
    ISBN 0-13-324948-4
    1. Baseball — Coaching.    2. School sports — Coaching.      I. Alston, Tom.
II. Title.
    GV875.5.W45    1998
    796.357'077—dc21                                                                        97-51514
                                                                                                CIP

Printed in the United States of America

10   9   8   7   6   5   4   3   2   1

ISBN 013-324948-4

---

### ATTENTION: CORPORATIONS AND SCHOOLS

Parker books are available at quantity discounts with bulk purchase for educational, business,
or sales promotional use. For information, please write to: Prentice Hall Career & Personal
Development Special Sales, 240 Frisch Court, Paramus, NJ 07652. Please supply: title of book,
ISBN, quantity, how the book will be used, date needed.

---

**PARKER PUBLISHING COMPANY**
West Nyack, NY 10994

A Simon & Schuster Company

On the World Wide Web at http://www.phdirect.com

Prentice Hall International (UK) Limited, *London*
Prentice Hall of Australia Pty. Limited, *Sydney*
Prentice Hall Canada, Inc., *Toronto*
Prentice Hall Hispanoamericana, S.A., *Mexico*
Prentice Hall of India Private Limited, *New Delhi*
Prentice Hall of Japan, Inc., *Tokyo*
Simon & Schuster Asia Pte. Ltd., *Singapore*
Editora Prentice Hall do Brasil, Ltda., *Rio de Janeiro*

# ABOUT THE AUTHORS

**Jerry Weinstein** has been Head Baseball Coach at Sacramento City College since 1985. He was also assistant coach for the 1996 and 1992 USA Olympic Baseball Teams, the USA Pan American Baseball Team in 1987 and has held coaching positions at University of Miami in Florida, Los Angeles Valley College, UCLA, Santa Monica High School and Pioneer High School in Whittier, California.

Coach Weinstein played varsity baseball for UCLA and earned a B.A. in physical education and history and an M.S. in kinesiology, both from UCLA. His writing credits include over 20 articles published in *Scholastic Coach* and *Athletic Director*, contributing author to *Major League Baseball Manual*, 1982, Doubleday & Co., Inc., and *USA Pitching and Catching Manual*.

His coaching highlights include 17 league championships or co-championships in 21 years at Sacramento City College, 246 drafted players and 126 pro signers, 19 of whom are playing or have played in the Big Leagues. He holds seven Sacramento Hall of Fame Coach-of-the-Year Awards and has been named California and National Coach of the Year. In addition, he has been in charge of player development of catchers for the Milwaukee Brewers minor league system, has managed other teams in the United States during the short season and conducted baseball clinics in Cuba and Italy. Coach Weinstein also spearheaded the building of a 2,000 seat, 3 million dollar stadium with no school or public funding.


**Tom Alston** has successfully executed the duties of pitching coach, JV head coach and Varsity head coach since 1989 when his high school coaching career began. His baseball career also includes a quarter of a century of directing AABC teams and organizations, Senior Babe Ruth, Babe Ruth, Little League and Bambino. Coach Alston has directed several coaches' clinics for Babe Ruth, Pony and Little League Coaches and has been one of the featured speakers at many clinics for players. During the summer months he has formed and operated leagues for training high school teams in a format that maintains high school rules and skill levels.

Tom Alston's "The Winning Pitch" column has appeared in every issue of *Collegiate Baseball* since the early nineties and has also appeared in select issues of *Amateur Baseball Magazine*. His selected writings have appeared in various other publications.

Formerly a retail business manager, he started Alston Industries, Inc., a manufacturer of race car chassis components, and after building it to multimillion dollars in annual sales, sold it in 1994. During that time, he wrote the book, *How to Go Drag Racing*, and co-authored *Chassis Tuning Manual*. He is currently doing marketing work for Associated Sales Tax Consultants, Inc.

# ACKNOWLEDGMENTS

First and foremost, I want to thank my wife Andrea, my daughter Amy, and my son Aaron for the sacrifices that they have made to allow me to further my career in baseball.

Secondly, I want to thank my Little League coach Murray Burke for getting me started in baseball and my college coach at UCLA, Art Reichle, who gave me the opportunity to learn and grow as a coach.

Finally, I'd like to thank all my assistant coaches and players with whom I have had the privilege of being associated, and from whom I have learned so much.

Special thanks to Tom Alston for encouraging me to pursue this project and transcribing all my notes.

I'd like to thank the following people who have shared their knowledge and have contributed to my development as a coach and teacher:

| | | | |
|---|---|---|---|
| Al Goldis | Ron Fraser | Dave Snow | Skip Bertmann |
| Butch Hughes | Wally Kincaid | John Herbold | Don Rowe |
| Ray Poitevint | Ron Squire | Paul Carmazzi | Kenny Myers |
| Dan Petta | John Noce | Tony Muser | Mike Stubbins |
| Dan Duquette | Joe Hicks | Ron Polk | Ken Ravizza |
| Marcel Lachmann | Dick Pierucci | Don Steele | Brad Kelley |
| Dan Mirsky | | | |

*Jerry Weinstein*

I want to thank my son Warren for enticing me to the edge of the lake of baseball; Joe Micallef, my closest friend, who pushed me into the water; to Gary Dreher, who before his death at the age of 47, for teaching me how to swim among the sharks. My special thanks to Jerry Weinstein for continuing my baseball education, and to my wife Cristina for standing by me through all the tough times and sharing the joy of the good times.

A special acknowledgment is sent out to Lou Pavlovich, Jr. of *Collegiate Baseball*, who has been important to my baseball writing career, and to Roderick Thorp, author of *The Detective* and *Die Hard*, who, as my mentor, is working hard to turn me into a novelist.

Finally, I want to thank Peggy Beasley for editing and transcribing all the raw interview data. I want to thank Fay Hansen for the countless hours poring over and editing this manuscript down to a workable size and to Tom Curtin for guiding it through the production process. My special gratitude goes to Connie Kallback, my editor on this book. Without her guidance and friendship, this would have never happened. She taught me about getting a manuscript ready, and I taught her more about baseball than she ever really needed to know.

*Tom Alston*

# ABOUT THIS RESOURCE

Imagine yourself as an expectant father waiting for your child to be born. You are nervous because you know that no written manual exists to help you along the way. Filled with love for the prospect of raising your son, you are willing to do whatever it takes to get the job done, but you know in your heart that you are not properly prepared.

Because you are committed to your offspring, you make the sacrifices of time and energy to raise him right. As he leaves your home to venture out in the world on his own, you wonder how he will turn out. After he drives out of sight, you sit in your suddenly silent living room and think about the years you spent in the process. You realize that if you had known when he was born what you know after he is grown up and gone, you would have had more control over the events. Your total life's experience has been gained and you have your degree in parenting now that you no longer need it. Something about this seems unfair.

To a small degree this happens in the life of every baseball coach. All of us have grown up and figured out how-to-do-it as we went. This *Guide* is a labor of love from the authors to all coaches. If we can make your life easier, and the game better by passing along some of our knowledge, we have accomplished what we set out to do.

Written with all high school and college coaches in mind, from new coaches to those with many years of experience under their belts, this *Guide* explains how to build and maintain a successful program from organization and recruiting to fund raising and scholarships. It also covers the nuts and bolts of teaching, drilling and developing your players by position.

The *Getting Started* section sets the foundation of what we do. Although we are competitors on the field and are very focused on winning every season, all games, each inning and every pitch, we know that one of the products we build is young men with character, ethics and integrity. The foundation of a student athlete is the student.

The communication portions of this section include contracts you can make with your players and evaluation forms for your performance, judged by the players. You have to be able to handle criticism if you're going to coach baseball. At times you will be misunderstood and may not always get the support you feel you deserve from your school, parents or community, but you must deal with it in a positive manner and focus on the game and the players.

You may find the pages on fund raising especially helpful as more and more sports are competing for the same athletic dollar.

*Recruiting and Tryouts*, section 2, suggests the proper sequence for notifying your prospective players as well as hints on how to quickly evaluate your talents.

A philosophical approach to preparing and executing a game plan is presented in section 3, *Game Control from Start to Finish*. It contains nearly 20 forms that the authors have successfully used over the years. They are provided in blank, ready-to-use form and also as filled-out samples to help you understand how to use or adapt them in your program. All are easily copied in 8 1/2″ × 11″ format and with special spiral wire binding that allows the book to lay flat on the copier.

The largest single topic in the resource deals with pitching and is divided into sections 4 and 5, *Pitching* and *The Pitches*. Beginning with an overview of the five most important pitching skills, *Pitching* takes you through mechanics, the pitching sequence, mechanical specifics for right and left handers, and control. *The Pitches* deals with types of pitches, the pitching plan, warming up, fielding techniques, and much more, ending with complete but concise advice on arm soreness.

The *Catching* section, with Coach Weinstein's special insight into the position, is the first of its kind. Most sources do not provide the in-depth strategy and technique for this position that is included here. It includes information on different kinds of stances, giving signals, techniques for receiving and throwing, with many extras such as charts to track the catcher's game performance.

Sections 7 and 8, *General Infield Play* and *Outfield Play*, provide drills and techniques as well as highly specialized positioning information.

*Defensive Strategy* and *Team Defense* are covered in sections 9 and 10. The highly specialized positioning charts—28 in all—are an invaluable resource and are, of course, reproducible.

Developed with the scrutiny of many years of practical experience, section 11 on hitting, also incorporates suggestions from major league coaches. It also includes nearly 20 specific drills to solve problems batters are facing or to improve certain skills.

Players who embrace the concepts in *The Short Game*, section 12, will improve their individual value to the team.

The authors are able to provide special insights in section 13, *Base Running*, since they have enhanced the effectiveness of their offensive game plans through the years by understanding the value-added nature of base running. This section is the "sleeper" in terms of how to win games. It can keep you out of rally-killing double plays as well as helping to create errors by the defense.

Section 14, *Offensive Strategy and Techniques*, will pique your interest as you see the game through one of the best offensive minds in baseball.

Evaluating scholarships and professional baseball is a timely and final section in the *Guide*. It includes an insight rarely spoken about when a young man is dazzled by the offer to sign a pro contract.

By reading and applying the guidance offered here, coaching will become a simpler task and will bring you closer to having a winning team. All you have to do is add:

Excitement

Countless hours

Tough love

Visions of success

Lost sleep

Happiness in seeing a player execute what you've been practicing

Hours away from your family

Tears of joy

Moments of annoyance

Personal moments with young men in times of stress

Feelings of satisfaction watching young men grow up

Moments of second guessing

Listening patiently while parents question your decisions

Wondering why stealing home seemed like a good idea at the time

Disciplining a team for something an individual did

Listening to your wife ask, "When are you going to get a real job?"

Fund raising money, then finding out the school has cut it out of your budget to give it to some other program because baseball "doesn't need it."

Having the character to not get angry when Title IX gives money to sports from a school budget that you had to raise privately

Final advice from the authors:

**Turn the page on the bad times.**

**Store all the good times in your heart.**

**Be able to recall all of them when you need to dispense wisdom.**


*Jerry Weinstein*
*Tom Alston*

# Contents

## Baseball Coach's Survival Guide

# GETTING STARTED

Coaching baseball can become a truly awesome task if you think seriously about the responsibility of coaching student athletes. You are investing in the future of the game when you coach budding players. It may seem trite to say you get out of it what you put into it, but it is, nonetheless, true. To take on the job of coaching, your dedication has to go beyond your love of the game. You have to like being around the players, enjoy the anticipation of helping them develop real skill and receive pleasure in watching them grow in the sport.

Your coaching philosophy likely takes it roots in the coaching skills you picked up from the most influential coach or coaches you had when you were learning the game. Their influence stayed with you because they took the time to teach the skills, or they taught you how to win, or they cared about you, or any number of other reasons, but their care, their skill, their knowledge and their enthusiasm for the game helped shape your coaching style today or what your coaching style will become if you're a new coach.

## SETTING GOALS

To help establish your philosophy or to make it clear to yourself or others, determine your goals as a baseball coach. Then go the extra step and actually write it down. Some of the coaches we know have mentioned these personal goals that they've adopted:

1. Creating an environment of fun for the kids.
2. Winning the state championships.
3. Helping just one player get to the major leagues.

One of our personal goals is to have our players become high school or college coaches.

The next step, and a rather logical one, is to develop an over-all team goal or mission. This kind of motivational step can help keep your program focused, but it's motivational only if it comes from a whole-team effort. One team developed this mission statement for its program: "To work intelligently to be as good as we can be on and off the field."

**Specific Team Goals.** Here are some of the goals or steps that can support a mission statement:

1. To finish the spring semester with a team GPA of 3.0 or higher, with a 2.5 or higher in academic classes.
2. To have no one dropped from class for nonattendance.
3. To make a total commitment to scoring runs.
4. To make a total commitment to stopping runs being scored against us.
5. To win the state baseball championship by playing every game pitch-by-pitch.
6. To have a team that enjoys the school and athletic experience.

**Key Concepts.** An integral part of goal development, key concepts, should also be established by the entire team if they're to be meaningful. The following examples show what some other teams have chosen as a focus:

1. All choices will be based on what is best for the team.
2. We will play our "best 9," not our "9 best."
3. We will not pout or transfer blame.
4. We will have "how to win awareness" (HWA).
5. Every time we fall, we will get up stronger.
6. Anything that we can vividly imagine, ardently desire, sincerely believe, and enthusiastically act upon must come to pass.

**Sample Phrases.** Key phrases, if established by the team as well, can become good motivators. These examples may help your team get started:

1. TEAM- Together Everyone Achieves More.
2. Practice and play hard.
3. If you're not early, you're late.
4. Best Speed!
5. What you do speaks so loudly, we can't hear what you say.
6. Failure to prepare is preparing to fail.
7. Intelligent hard work beats talent that does not work hard.

# ESTABLISHING STANDARDS

With your philosophy and goals in place, you'll want to set standards in all areas that affect your players. Here's a quick discussion of some of these areas you won't want to overlook.

*Grades.* It's important to track your athletes academically and hold them accountable for their grades. If you track them, you won't be surprised when you get notification of players who are ineligible for the playoffs. You don't want to depend on players who are not academically reliable.

What can you do to help kids along in those situations? If you are an on-campus coach and see a player in the hallway, you can make eye contact and talk with him: "Hey, how's it going in algebra? The teacher said you missed a couple of assignments." If you're an off-campus coach, you don't have the advantage of being able to talk to other teachers as easily, but you still can send around grade checks every two weeks or as often as necessary.

You also can track players' grades with grade reports, on a daily attendance basis or a two-week grade tracking system.

*Study Hall.* Have some type of study hall for players to attend who aren't performing well. It doesn't matter if the player's problem is being late or not going to class or not being prepared for class. The study hall is a way of communicating your strong belief in academics. You may need to bring in tutors if the player is doing everything he can but still doesn't understand the subject. Another player on the team who is more advanced in a particular area may be able to tutor that person or you can bring in an outside tutor. It's a total package of academics and athletics. This approach is positive from the standpoint of building community support for your program because you make it clear that you're concerned about the total student athlete.

*Discipline.* Some people may think discipline is a rod and a whip; some think it's handing the players a piece of paper and saying, "Take care of it yourself." A good coach takes charge. Be consistent. Have a set of rules and enforce them, even with your star players. A good coach does it with a sense of compassion because he knows that they are still kids. You'll want to hold them to the rules but give them a certain number of chances to earn their way back until they've used up all those chances.

Different kids need different kinds of responses. If you come down hard on player A, he may crumble and walk away. If you come down on player B, it may be just what he needs. Part of the psychology of coaching is knowing how to make sure that a player understands that he made a mistake, but that you still care about him.

***Structure.*** Kids want to have structure and rules. They don't want coaches, teachers, or parents who say one thing but don't apply it. They get confused. They want to know that if they're goofing around, the coach is going to call them on it. But they also want to know that when they do well, the coach is going to praise them. Then they can say to themselves, "Yeah, the coach yelled at me because he wants me to be the best I can be, not because he doesn't like me."

***Leadership.*** Leadership shows up in academics. It shows up in how often players miss school, and how seriously they take it. If they're allowed to goof around in classes and then come out to practice, you're in trouble. It starts tearing down the players' response to your leadership, and they may begin to believe that the program doesn't have a leader. Your success comes down to leadership.

***No Trash Talk.*** There is no place for trash talking in sports. It usually comes from immature students who don't know how to handle conflict. If the other team is winning, it's certainly inappropriate to be trash talking an opponent who is beating you. If the other team is losing, your players should avoid anything that might incite or motivate the opponent. Although it may seem to be the national pastime in professional sports, trash talk comes down to a lack of respect for opponents and a lack of respect for the game.

Players should learn when they are young that bullying their opponents to the point where they don't want to play anymore doesn't create a long-term win. It only creates a situation in which there is no game. In high school sports it can create situations where violence erupts. Remind your players that when they put on a uniform, they represent their school. Occasionally, there may be an outburst, but there's a difference between an occasional remark and a tirade.

***Positive Comments.*** There is a difference between bench jockeying and trash talking. Sometimes it is a very thin line. The best policy is to allow only positive comments to come from your dugout and your players. This allows for the release of positive emotion. If players treat their opponents the way they want to be treated, trash talking disappears.

***Standards.*** Ask your administrators for their minimum standards. Find out the school policy on alcohol, tobacco, and dress. Determine what types of rules the administration will support and which ones it can't.

Make it clear to your team that they are going to be under scrutiny because they are athletes. It's going to be easier to pick them out. If a player's face shows up five times in the paper and four times in announcements, it attracts negative attention and people will notice more when they get out of line.

# MAINTAINING POSITIVE RELATIONSHIPS

An important part of the coach's job is to build successful relationships with players, parents, school, and community.

***Interacting with Players.*** Being a players' coach—someone who thinks about the kids when they are off the field as much as on—adds a new dimension to success that wasn't common 10 or 15 years ago. Some players don't get that kind of connection anywhere else, and their coach becomes that connection in many respects.

In school, students learn because of who their teachers are and what they are taught. You can have the great lesson planned, but if your students don't really connect with you as a teacher, they may never reach their full potential. They may hold back. Likewise, kids play for you as a person because they like you, and they want to please you. If they know you care about them, they will perform better. You don't have to place them in other programs, but you can help them as much as possible. A players' coach usually gets more out of the kids.

***Marshmallows, Jellybeans and Rocks.*** The relationship you have with your players ultimately determines everything. This doesn't mean you treat them all equally. The true test of your ability as a coach is how you relate to everyone on your team as an individual. This focus on the individual produces the best team results. Some players need to be pushed; some need to be left alone; some need lots of encouragement. If you have a singular style and deal with everyone exactly the same, you will miss some incredible potential.

We've adopted a concept from John Scolinos. Think about this when you need help in dealing with your players. If you take a rock and hold it in a flame, its physical characteristics remain virtually unchanged. Hold a jellybean in a flame and it will hold its shape for a short period of time, but eventually it will melt. Put a flame to a marshmallow and it almost instantly begins to melt. Your team will always be made up of combinations of rocks, jellybeans, and marshmallows. If you can't find a way to get each of them to extend their reach and perform under pressure, you will fail them over the long run.

Don't fall into the trap of believing that people don't change either. Rocks can fall apart when their girlfriend breaks up with them before a big game. Jellybeans can become rocks as they gain confidence. Marshmallows can increase the amount of pressure they can deal with by gaining playing experience. It can change from one at bat to another at bat. It is your job to monitor those changes and respond to them.

All this doesn't mean you should try too hard to be your players' friend. They know you're older, more experienced and professional, and they want someone to respect and model.

***Interacting with Parents and Guardians.*** Coaches have to deal with parents' issues more often today and with more sensitivity than ever before. Parents' concerns and their abilities to challenge or question are much more intense than they were years ago.

A relationship problem that can commonly occur is in becoming too close to the parents. Just a fair warning: It's easier than you might believe to cross over into a relationship with parents that is too personal, especially if you're a new coach. Parents may think your friendship will change the way you handle your players. If they believe their son isn't getting exactly what they want, such as playing time or experience, coaching can become difficult.

A preseason meeting can set the tone for the way you will interface with parents. If a player is out there giving you several hours a day, five or six days a week, his parents have a right to ask questions. They may not get the answer they want, but they have the right to ask. They should be warned at the preseason meeting to avoid questioning the coach at inappropriate times, for example, after you just lost in the last inning.

Parents have a right to ask, "Why isn't my kid playing? What can he do better?" You have to be able to communicate. If a parent approaches you as an adult in a calm manner, you have the obligation to talk to them and tell them what you think about their kid. You can tell them, "He doesn't work the double play well," or "He doesn't go to his left," or "He doesn't swing the bat." If you are unapproachable, parents may well say, "Oh, you can never talk to the coach; he's not going to listen to you anyway."

There may be times when you have to handle irate parents. Listen to what they have to say; pay no attention to how they say it. Accept their criticism, then state your position. Don't get into coaching philosophies or coaching decisions. How you coach is up to you. All you have to do is explain why you coach that way. Then they have to deal with it. Give parents a forum where they can speak their minds in a peaceful, calm manner. In many cases, this alleviates later problems. If you're not approachable, parents may look for other parents who feel the same, and then you have a negative force working against you. If you deal with problems openly, you can resolve or eliminate most of them.

Here's something else that has changed the expectations of today's players and parents: People respond to professional athletes; kids and their parents may try to mimic them. Kids have better skills in many respects, and parents may believe that because their kids have better skills than they ever did, things should be different. What some parents don't realize is that all the players have better skills—not just their child. It's understandable that they want as much for their son or daughter as possible, in terms of scholarships, press, and recognition.

*Relationships with Others.* Be wary of trying to be validated by as many people as possible when you're first coaching. This can lead to giving out more information than is really necessary.

Also don't try to do everything at once. You can't be that complete coach the first year. The process takes longer than that. Getting sponsors from the community, building an alumni group, and creating a booster club are each projects in themselves and can't be accomplished all in one year. Just start putting some of the pieces together.

If you're balanced and organized you can focus on what you want the team to do and also take care of your other duties. If you have good organizing skills and clear priorities, you're on your way to establishing a strong foundation for your program.

*Components of Good Coaching.* The components of good coaching are basically the same as the components of good teaching: organization, teaching to an objective, modeling what you want kids to do, and having an activity that practices that model. All good coaches are great teachers, with or without a teaching credential. You will hear it from players; you will hear it from parents; and you will see it in how kids act. Have a practice plan that leads toward the goal you want to accomplish at the next game. Use an overall plan for each player that creates an opportunity for gradual development.

# COMMUNICATIONS

Use a three-copy form or Xerox copies when you communicate with a player. (See Figures 1-1 and 1-2.) Keep one copy for your permanent records. Give two copies to the player—one for him to keep and one for the parents to sign and return to you. That keeps everyone in the loop. If a parent complains, you have a record of what was said, and you can show that the parents acknowledged the communication. Avoid using the forms for criticism only. Include positive comments too.

If you encounter a player who still doesn't respond to this level of input, require a signed contract. (See Figures 1-3 and 1-4.) Spell out in writing the behavior he must eliminate and what the consequences will be if he doesn't. Make sure the player and the parent sign it. Then enforce your commitments. If you reach a level of ongoing negative contact with a player, make sure your supervisor has copies of what is going on so there are no surprises.

*Disciplining Players.* Make sure you document every conversation you have with your athletes when you are disciplining them. It is smart to have another coach or adult present when you reprimand or lay down the law. Don't expect your players to accurately communicate the facts of the situation to their parents. Call the parents in for a conference with the player present or at least call them or send them a note.

Figure 1-1: **BASEBALL COMMUNICATIONS FORM**

| Player's Name  Player's Signature | Date | Place |
|---|---|---|
| Coach's Name  Coach's Signature | | |
| Reason for communications notification: | | |

Acknowledgment: Player's Signature _____ Date _____

Acknowledgment: Parent's Signature _____ Date _____

Points of discussion (Coach):



Change in behavior expected:



Points of discussion (Player) (filled in by player at the time of interview):

Figure 1-2:  **BASEBALL COMMUNICATIONS FORM (SAMPLE)**

| Player's Name   *Tony Jones* | **Date** | **Place** |
|---|---|---|
| **Player's Signature** | *3/12/xx* | *Varsity Field* |

| **Coach's Name**   *Dick Brown* |
|---|
| **Coach's Signature** |

**Reason for communications notification:**

*Conduct detrimental to the team*

---

**Acknowledgment: Player's Signature** _____  Date _____

**Acknowledgment: Parent's Signature** _____  Date _____

---

**Points of discussion (Coach):**

*During two games last week Tony was reprimanded for using abusive language toward the other team and the umpires. He was warned at that time that his conduct violated the rules of the team, and the school. During Monday's game this week Tony called the umpire "Blind." I benched him immediately.*

*Tony is one of the best athletes on his team. He needs to realize that his performance is important for the team to meet all its goals. IF he gets ejected or benched, his behavior hurts the team and Tony.*

*Tony and his parents signed the preseason Team Rules form which prohibits this kind of activity.*

---

**Change in behavior expected:**

*If Tony violates this policy again, he will be suspended from the team for 3 games. If he continues after that, he will be removed for the rest of the season.*

---

**Points of discussion (Player)** (filled in by player at the time of interview):

*I felt the umpire was hurting me. I got mad because he could have cost us the game. It won't happen again.*

Figure 1-3:   **PERFORMANCE CONTRACT**

| Player's Name | Date | Place |
|---|---|---|
| Coach's Name  Coach's Signature | | |
| Reason: | | |

Acknowledgment: Player's Signature _____ Date _____

Acknowledgment: Parent's Signature _____ Date _____

**Terms of Contract**

**I agree to comply to the terms of this contract as a condition of remaining on the baseball team.**

Player's Signature _____ Date _____

Parent's Signature _____ Date _____

Figure 1-4:   **PERFORMANCE CONTRACT (SAMPLE)**

| Player's Name   *Billy Sheldon* | **Date** | **Place** |
|---|---|---|
| **Coach's Name**   *Dick Brown*<br>**Coach's Signature** | | |
| **Reason:**  *Disruptive behavior* | | |

**Acknowledgment: Player's Signature** _____  **Date** _____

**Acknowledgment: Parent's Signature** _____  **Date** _____

**Terms of Contract**

*From this date forward, Billy Sheldon agrees to:*

1. *Be on time for all classes.*
2. *Keep his overall GPA above 2.0.*
3. *Keep his grade in every individual class at or above a "C".*
4. *Be on time for practice.*
5. *Cooperate with teammates, coaches and umpires.*
6. *Comply with instructions from all coaches and teachers IMMEDIATELY.*
7. *Adhere to school policies, including those that relate to alcohol, tobacco, or drug use.*
8. *Follow team policies.*

*Any infraction may be grounds for dismissal from the team by the coach. No appeal of the coach's decision is allowed.*

**I agree to comply to the terms of this contract as a condition of remaining on the baseball team.**

**Player's Signature** _____  **Date** _____

**Parent's Signature** _____  **Date** _____

***Depending on Your Own Skills.*** If you're going to be a strong effective teacher, you have to have confidence in your own skills. You must be able to communicate content as well as the purpose for it. You need to motivate students. If you can get players charged up and excited, you will be more successful than a coach who can't.

Coaches use teaching skills—clear objectives, and detailed lesson plans or coaching plans. Coaches also need real goals—a goal for the team, a goal for the day, and a goal for each player. What kind of an experience do you want to create for your players? Are they having fun? Are they learning? Are they growing throughout the season? They may not have a lot of talent, but are they getting better and enjoying it from beginning to end?

# FIRST STEPS FOR A NEW COACH

Whether you are new to coaching, to a particular baseball program or to a school, awareness of the following items can help ease your way.

1. Find out how communications are sent and received on every level in your new school or community. Determine what is expected of a baseball coach.

2. Get in contact with every person that you will need. You must be able to purchase the supplies, schedule games, and find umpires.

3. You also want to have the support of the boosters, the parents, the school administration, and the players. It is your responsibility to get to know what they expect from a new baseball coach.

4. Try to meet supporters needs within the context of the priorities you set.

5. Keep up communications with all these people and expand your contacts to fulfill needs on a regular basis.

6. Maintain your communications on a long-term basis with your original group of contacts, but don't pass on unneeded information.

7. Improve what you are doing so that the results are more closely aligned to what is really wanted and needed. Continue to improve, and make sure all your contacts are aware of it.

Here are some examples of the kind of information you will need:

What district rules and requirements do you need to be familiar with?

What does your new school do about tutoring? In a high school, you've got to deal with grades because of the 2.0 rule.

When you go on a bus trip, what do you have to do?

What's the process for emergency cards? Do you have to have them with you at all times? Who should explain this to the parents?

The culture and organizational style of each school can be very different. Check with the other head coaches in the school to see how they deal with different issues in their program.

Try to get through this "orientation" process quickly so you can focus on baseball and building a program. Concentrate on taking players at any level of performance and helping them improve.

## A NOTE TO WALK-ON COACHES

In general, a walk-on head coach is hired by a program where it has been difficult to find teachers who are willing and qualified to be part of the sports program. If that's the case, your chances are enhanced because the program may be in chaos and the school may be perceived as undesirable by other teacher/coaches. This kind of situation can create a great opportunity for you to build a program the right way. You may find players who feel they have been abandoned, and who will respond to you quickly. You may find support from parents who were put off by previous staffs. If you apply discipline, organization, and high standards, you may turn an entire community around in regard to the baseball program.

Of course, the walk-on coach has a much tougher job at a high school than the on-campus teacher who also coaches baseball. It is harder to keep in contact with teachers or to build a comfortable relationship with them that can be helpful in working with your student athletes. On-campus coaches can ask teachers how their players are doing in class and request information if anyone is doing poorly. Some teachers respond positively to inquiries and will follow up. They also may connect with the kids a few more times in class by saying, "You know, Coach is really concerned about you." If a school values that, then they're more apt to contact you or be supportive of you. And if your players are gone during an important test time, teachers may be more willing to bend.

Here are a few suggestions for helping you get acquainted with the school's culture and its teachers: Talk to anyone who might be around during nonschool hours—teachers in charge of clubs or other recreational programs, parents waiting for their kids, janitors, or anyone familiar with the school who is friendly enough to impart information. It may help to have lunch at the school a few times if at all possible. You need to make sure that teachers know who you are.

A helpful tool in this respect is the Coach's Introductory Memo (Figure 1-5) that you can adapt to your own situation to send around to teachers. Attach a team roster so teachers can quickly scan the list to determine which players are in their classes. One creative coach used a form similar to this but Xeroxed a photo of himself so teachers could readily recognize him.

Figure 1-5: **COACH'S INTRODUCTORY MEMO**

Date: _____

To: All Classroom Teachers

Fr: Coach _____

As coach of the boys' _____ (freshman, JV, varsity) baseball team, I'm sincerely interested in my players' progress in each of their classes. Since I'm not usually in the building during the day, please leave comments about student players in my teacher box or leave me a voicemail message at _____ regarding any academic or behavioral problems that I should know about.

Also feel free to let players know that I'm concerned about them and that we are in communication about their progress. I want the players to understand that they are representatives of the baseball program whether they are in or out of uniform, on the field or in the classroom. It's just one of the things I can do to help students develop to their full potential. Feel free to use that emphasis, too.

Thanks in advance for your cooperation.

# EVALUATING YOUR PERFORMANCE

Make sure your athletic director or principal gives you specific feedback on your performance. If it's a matter of how you handled Situation A, an athletic director can model that behavior for you in a conference, and you can learn from it. If you have a problem with organization, not getting back to people, or poor scheduling, take the time to learn about time management.

***Post-Season Blind Surveys.*** At the end of each season ask the parents and players to complete post-season surveys. (See Figure 1-6.) If you run a complete program with a summer program, a winter program, and a high school season, do the surveys three times a year. Do a survey on each coach on your staff. Do them blind so the kids and the parents don't have to put their names on the survey. Get constant feedback so you can make course corrections. Have an open mind when you read the surveys because you may see comments about you and your staff that you don't agree with or don't like to hear. Use the data to improve your staff.

For long-term, on-going self-evaluation, periodically ask yourself the following questions:

- ◆ What do your players do after they finish school?
- ◆ Do they keep their commitments?
- ◆ Are they still involved in the game?
- ◆ Would they want you to coach their kids?
- ◆ Do they come back and thank you for preparing them for the next level of baseball or life after baseball?
- ◆ Do you have players who return to your program as coaches?

Performing well in these categories is what will keep you in the game over the long run.

***Winning.*** Winning is not the most important thing you do today with kids, but everybody enjoys the boost in school morale when you're winning. Over the long run, if you don't produce wins, the community may force the administration to replace you no matter how much the players like you. It is tough to get kids interested in a program that doesn't have a tradition of winning. Every coach walks the line between winning and producing a positive experience for his players. Although your success as a coach may be measured by the press in wins and losses, it may be measured by your school administration in an entirely different way.

Figure 1-6: **COACH EVALUATION FORM**

TO: Baseball Players

Please give an honest opinion of the coaching, teaching, and personal characteristics for each of your coaches.

COACH _____ TEAM _____ DATE _____

Grade this coach with a letter grade (A-,C+,D-, etc.) In each category:

Organization (practice, instruction, meetings, other) _____

Knowledge of baseball _____

His ability to communicate with you _____

Patience in dealing with you _____

Patience in dealing with the team as a whole _____

Good decisions in game situations _____

Ability to motivate you _____

Ability to motivate team _____

Overall leadership _____

Fairness _____

Team discipline _____

Ability to give positive comments when deserved _____

Overall coaching ability _____

Does this coach discipline players too much or not enough? Please explain. _____
_____
_____

What do you like about this coach? _____
_____
_____

What do you dislike about this coach? _____
_____
_____

What would you like to say to this coach? _____
_____
_____

Would you want your son to play for this coach? Why? _____
_____
_____

Playing baseball should be fun. Most players play in high school and that's the end of their career. It should be a positive, memorable experience. Winning creates positive feelings, but the way your players turn out as adults is the ultimate test.

# FUND RAISING

Do you have problems with equipment or facilities that money can fix? Are you tired of sewing patches on your kids' uniforms? Is your infield such a low spot on the grounds that it becomes a fish hatchery when it rains?

If you can say "yes" to any of these questions, we have a few suggestions.

First confront the fact that part of your job description as a baseball coach includes fund raising. But understand that accepting responsibility for it doesn't mean *you* have to do it. It means you are in charge of getting it done. Think about it coach—you don't play short, your player does. Treat fund raising the same way. Make sure someone does it, unless you want to do it yourself.

Begin by thinking about all the things you could improve in your program. The solution usually involves money. But if your program improves, your life improves. Get the money.

***Making Fund Raising the Players' Responsibility.*** Stress to your athletes that teamwork and taking responsibility for actions as a team are part of sports. So is fund raising. The players are the ultimate beneficiaries. Put some responsibility of getting the money on them. This is an important point. Put it on them, not their parents. This doesn't mean you don't take what mom and dad are willing to offer. Put the kids to work beyond what their parents will do. If you have ever complained that kids today have it too easy, become part of the solution. Demand that the athletes put back into the program as individuals.

Approach the job of fund raising in the same methodical organized manner you do teaching and playing the game. Don't accept minimal efforts. Raise your standards. If you have something to sell that supports the program, don't set a goal of five sales per kid and wait until mom and dad solve it for their son. Organize and attack the problem this way: How many households are in your community? How much does the program have if you get $10.00 from each?

# HOW TO DO IT

When your athletes were between six and puberty, how did they attack the neighborhood on Halloween night? If they thought they could get a month's supply of chocolate bars, they would knock on 500 doors to get it. Every player is an experienced door knocker when it comes to fund raising. Put their experience to good use.

Aggressively attack the problem—of no money—with an organized plan of action. If there are 5,000 houses in your community, and you are asking for $10.00, that means you have a $50,000 potential market. If you are only 10% successful, you'll get at least $5,000. Can you use it?

***Mapping It Out.*** Lay out a grid map of every street in your community. Drop off two players at the end of each corner and send one down each side. Drop two more players off at the next corner and send another pair on their mission. Continue until you have received so many donations you don't need any more money or until you have reached your goal.

***Supervision.*** Supervision is important—four or five people to a car with an adult. Go down each side of every street. When we started this program, it worked out well. We raised $350 an hour every time we did it. There was a small group of fifteen each time, but we raised more than $1,000 every three hours. Once we did it on a Saturday; another time, on a Sunday. One of the best times to do it though, in our experience, is in the evenings, especially in a community where both parents work because that's when they're home.

***Keeping Records.*** Make sure you keep good records of each address that donates or buys what you are selling. They will be your primary contacts the next time. Keep going to the well until it dries up. Continue to plow the addresses that didn't donate the first time. You'll always find some new customers. The plan will ensure that you have a future source of capital. If you get no buyers using this method, find something that will sell. It's your future.

Make enough copies of the Record of Contributions (see Figure 1-7) to give to your athletes, individuals or teams, who are collecting donations. The team may want to use these forms to create a database of contributors.

# OTHER WAYS TO RAISE MONEY

Look into many programs for ways to raise funds. Another type of fund raising program is a self-perpetuating program that continues to pay over time. Several new

Figure 1-7: **RECORD OF CONTRIBUTIONS**

| Date | First Name | Last Name | |
|---|---|---|---|
| Address | | City | |
| State | Zip | Phone | |
| Amount Paid | Cash ____ Check ____ | | |

| Date | First Name | Last Name | |
|---|---|---|---|
| Address | | City | |
| State | Zip | Phone | |
| Amount Paid | Cash ____ Check ____ | | |

| Date | First Name | Last Name | |
|---|---|---|---|
| Address | | City | |
| State | Zip | Phone | |
| Amount Paid | Cash ____ Check ____ | | |

network marketing programs, especially those with long distance telephone service, are great fund raisers. You could turn them over to a parent or a couple of people and just have them sit and make calls. Imagine a boiler-room operation where you have your players come in for one night during the week for two or three weeks during the year. They can be calling for season ticket sales if you have an inexpensive season ticket package, or use this system to sell whatever you have.

Another thing that's successful is the "throwathon" where athletes get pledges for how far they can throw. Create a schedule that allows the athletes to do the solicitation ahead of time.

***Program Ads.*** We sell booster ads using the canvassing method previously described. We call on people and tell them they can have their name listed in the program for $10.00. You may want to charge more for company ads because they take up more space.

The sponsor, whether a company or an individual, receives a program, and then we give them a little gift such as a sports bottle, key chain, snack clip, or another item with the team logo. This establishes an immediate return for their money. Don't wait until later to hand them out. The kids will load up their garages and never deliver them to the sponsors.

This checklist can help you, or a volunteer, organize a program ad fund raiser:

❒ Sell for $10.00 a name listing of an individual or company who wants to be listed as a sponsor.

❒ Sell space in the program for company ads and notes from parents to their kids or companies to the team.

❒ To enhance the sales of sponsors' ads, purchase some small promotional item for under $2.00 and hand it to the sponsor when he or she gives you the $10.00.

❒ Print photos for all players. Parents will want to be in the program if it has their son's picture.

❒ Establish an area for team records. Have team photos of all teams in the program. (Be sure to spell all the names correctly. Proofread, proofread, proofread!)

Keep a list of sponsors' names, addresses, and comments to be printed in the program.

***Fence Sign Program.*** Making fence signs and charging for advertising has been another successful program for us. The quality of the product has a direct bearing on how your sponsors feel about the program and whether they will come back next year. If you sell outfield signs, make sure the finished product is of high quality and is professional looking.

Here's an example of what costs might run and the money you can expect to make:

◆ Cost of a sheet of plywood - $20.00

◆ Cost of sign painting (professional) - $100.00

◆ Charge for one year, $300; two years, $550; three years, $750

The following tips help ensure that your fence-sign program runs smoothly:

◆ Take care of the sign. Take it down and put it inside during the winter months.

◆ If you have an unemployed parent in your community, put him or her in charge of the sign program and pay a commission. In this way, you can help your program and a parent.

◆ Have contracts printed up and make sure that the "sales force" and the customers understand all the terms.

◆ Don't extend credit. Get the money up front or you will be in the collection business.

***Newsletters.*** This is the single most valuable thing you can do, but it may also be the hardest because of its time-consuming nature. (Make sure you get paid to do the work, which includes postage, printing and time.) Then you are ready for the hard part—someone has to write it. Simple box scores, future schedules and league standing are the most basic columns to include.

This checklist of tips for producing a newsletter will help prevent overlooking something important:

❏ Determine how many newsletters you want to do during the season. Any for off-season to generate interest?

❏ Have volunteers for each of the columns turn in the information to the person who will produce the newsletter.

❏ Decide who will do the production. One of the easiest ways today is to have someone with a computer and laser printer do the keystroking, arrange it in columns and print out a master copy that would be suitable for copying at a copy center.

❏ Establish deadlines for each step.

❏ Get home addresses for sponsors. Have someone with a computer, other than the production person, maintain the list.

❏ Get a bulk rate postage permits to keep mailing costs down.

A newsletter can keep people without kids in the program attached to your team, but best of all, it can generate both financial and community support that is permanent.

See the newsletter layout format (Figure 1-8) for ideas for producing a newsletter on standard 8 1/2″ × 11″ paper.

*Joint Ventures.* Consider joint venture with the Parks and Recreation Department or with youth leagues such as Little League or Babe Ruth League or American Legion. They'll use your field when you're not if there are provisions for maintenance, upkeep and supervision to make sure the field remains in top shape.

*Grants.* It's incredible how much outside money is available for education. Look in the library to find out what's available in grants for developing your facility, for example.

Many foundations give money to educational institutions for various things. One of them happens to be athletics, and if you do your homework, you can write grants to one of those organizations to access some of their money. What's needed is preliminary letters to different foundations.

Visit the state library to find books on grants. Talk to grant writers because they earmark some of the grants specifically for youth baseball. The high schools have a better chance than the colleges because the colleges have gate receipts.

## OTHER CONSIDERATIONS IN FUND RAISING

Here are a few precautions and tips you won't want to pass over if you're serious about fundraising.

*Earmarking Funds.* It is vital that you have a specific goal for each year's fund raising. Declare the target in terms of time—the deadline—and also the product. Tell this year's players that when they raise their money, the program will build dugouts, for example. It keeps the players focused, and they will see the benefit of their work. It's motivating for the athletes to see the direct results of the money raised. They also need to be in the loop for the whole planning process.

It's important to have a meeting at the beginning of the year with all the athletes and their parents. Outline your needs and tell them what they're going to need, the plans to achieve it and where the money is going specifically. Be sure to check with the administration about where you can legally spend the money, and also make sure it benefits the entire program. If you decide to buy shirts for just the JV team, for instance, you'll have problems on your hands.

Figure 1-8: **NEWSLETTER TEMPLATE**

# BASEBALL TODAY

## VARSITY WINS EASTER TOURNAMENT
### HOBBS LATE INNING HOMER PUSHES VARSITY TO WIN

Aaa aaa aaaa aaaaa aaaaa aaaaaaa aaaaa aa a aaa aaaaaa a aa aaa aaaa aaaaa a aaa aaaa aaaaa a aa aaa aaaa aaaaa aaaaaa a aa aaa aaaa aaaaa aaaaa aaaaaa aaaaaaa a aa aaa aaaa aaaaa aaaaaaa aa aaa aaaa a aaaaa aaaaaa a aa aaa a aaaa.

Aaa aaa aaaa aaaaa aaaaa aaaaaaa aaaaa aa a aaa aaaaaa a aa aaa aaaa aaaaa a aaa aaaa aaaaa a aa aaa aaaa aaaaa aaaaaa a aa aaa aaaa aaaaa aaaaa aaaaaa aaaaaaa a aa aaa aaaa aaaaa aaaaaaa aa aaa aaaa a aaaaa aaaaaa a aa aaa a aaaa.

Aaa aaa aaaa aaaaa aaaaa aaaaaaa aaaaa aa a aaa aaaaaa a aa aaa aaaa aaaaa a aaa aaaa aaaaa a aa aaa aaaa aaaaa aaaaaa a aa aaa aaaa aaaaa aaaaa aaaaaa aaaaaaa a aa aaa aaaa aaaaa aaaaaaa aa aaa aaaa a aaaaa aaaaaa a aa aaa a aaaa.

Aaa aaa aaaa aaaaa aaaaa aaaaaaa aaaaa aa a aaa aaaaaa a aa aaa aaaa aaaaa a aaa aaaa aaaaa a aa aaa aaaa aaaaa aaaaaa a aa aaa aaaa aaaaa aaaaa aaaaaa aaaaaaa a aa aaa aaaa aaaaa aaaaaaa aa aaa aaaa a aaaaa aaaaaa a aa aaa a aaaa.

Aaa aaa aaaa aaaaa aaaaa aaaaaaa aaaaa aa a aaa

aaaaaa a aa aaa aaaa aaaaa a aaa aaaa aaaaa a aa aaa aaaa aaaaa aaaaaa a aa aaa aaaa aaaaa aaaaa aaaaaa aaaaaaa a aa aaa aaaa aaaaa aaaaaaa aa aaa aaaa a aaaaa aaaaaa a aa aaa a aaaa.

Aaa aaa aaaa aaaaa aaaaa aaaaaaa aaaaa aa a aaa aaaaaa a aa aaa aaaa aaaaa a aaa aaaa aaaaa a aa aaa aaaa aaaaa aaaaaa a aa aaa aaaa aaaaa aaaaa aaaaaa aaaaaaa a aa aaa aaaa aaaaa aaaaaaa aa aaa aaaa a aaaaa aaaaaa a aa aaa a aaaa.

### CRAB FEED DINNER TO RAISE FUNDS FOR SUMMER PROGRAM

Aaa aaa aaaa aaaaa aaaaa aaaaaaa aaaaa aa a aaa aaaaaa a aa aaa aaaa aaaaa a aaa aaaa aaaaa a aa aaa aaaa aaaaa aaaaaa a aa aaa aaaa aaaaa aaaaa aaaaaa aaaaaaa a aa aaa aaaa aaaaa aaaaaaa aa aaa aaaa a aaaaa aaaaaa a aa aaa a aaaa.

Aaa aaa aaaa aaaaa aaaaa aaaaaaa aaaaa aa a aaa aaaaaa a aa aaa aaaa aaaaa a aaa aaaa aaaaa a aa aaa aaaa aaaaa aaaaaa a aa aaa aaaa aaaaa aaaaa aaaaa aaaaa

### Freshman Lefty throws no-hitter for JV team

Aaa aaa aaaa aaaaa aaaaa aaaaaaa aaaaa aa a aaa aaaaaa a aa aaa aaaa aaaaa a aaa aaaa aaaaa a aa aaa aaaa aaaaa aaaaaa a aa aaa aaaa aaaaa aaaaa aaaaaa aaaaaaa a aa aaa aaaa aaaaa aaaaaaa aa aaa aaaa a aaaaa aaaaaa a aa aaa a aaaa.

Aaa aaa aaaa aaaaa aaaaa aaaaaaa aaaaa aa a aaa aaaaaa a aa aaa aaaa aaaaa a aaa aaaa aaaaa a aa aaa aaaa aaaaa aaaaaa a aa aaa aaaa aaaaa aaaaa aaaaaa aaaaaaa a aa aaa aaaa aaaaa aaaaaaa aa aaa aaaa a aaaaa aaaaaa a aa aaa a aaaa.

***Setting a Time Limit.*** Remember that fund raising is a concentrated effort. It's not done long term. It's a one-shot deal, so do what you need to do in as little time as possible. Fund raising year round gets old because it wears the coaches down, and it wears the athletes down.

But don't leave it up to the kids. Set tight deadlines. Weekly goals for each player will get more results than one 30-day goal for the program. In the absence of a tightly run schedule, most athletes go home and wait for their parents to give them the money. You're going to get that money anyway, so gather the players, create a big map of your community and take them out to get the money.

Besides being a short-term effort, fund raising should also be set up for a specific period so it doesn't drag on. We do it in January before high school season starts. A side benefit is that you've got more players because you haven't made your cuts yet. This also gives you daily contact and control over the kids a month early. If your season starts February 1, start fund raising on January 1.

***Thinking Big.*** Don't be one of those coaches who doesn't think big enough. Don't ask for dimes when you can ask for dollars, and don't ask for dollars when you can ask for hundreds. Set your goals high. It's just as easy for people to say "no" to a dollar as it is to a higher number. You save yourself much solicitation if you get people to say yes to $100.

As tough as the economic times have been, we still have been able to go out in the streets and bring in money. In fact, we completely rebuilt the infield on the varsity diamond. If we can do it, you can too!

# RECRUITING AND TRYOUTS

Out of quantity comes quality. This axiom is certainly true when it comes to baseball. Try to get as many players out for your team as possible. To be a good recruiter in a high school setting, take these steps:

1. Go to the physical education classes.
2. Be aware of who played on the freshman and JV teams in past years.
3. Be aware of the students who played in the youth leagues but are no longer playing.
4. Be aware of the basketball and football players who could be baseball players.
5. Get involved in the community and build a network of people so you can evaluate everybody who has a chance to be a player.
6. Sell the program.
7. Display signs around the buildings.
8. Have enough teams to accommodate all the athletes.

## ANNOUNCING THE TRYOUTS

Potential players should be prepared for the tryouts. If they're not, you're going to get a lot of players who aren't in shape or who injure themselves trying out. Set up an informational network to all students who intend to try out. (See Figure 2-1 for a form you can use.) Communicate how tryouts will be conducted. Give them some basic guidelines including the skills they'll have to demonstrate and how they will be evaluated. For further efficiency, you can reproduce the tryouts notice to announce the date and time for the preseason meeting. (See Figure 2-2.)

Potential players need to be in throwing shape and in running shape. If possible, make some recommendations in terms of a particular physical education class that they might want to be enrolled in, or some basic conditioning techniques that they should use to prepare themselves for the tryouts.

Have all potential candidates fill out a basic questionnaire before the tryouts so you know something about them before they demonstrate their skills. (See Figure 2-3

Figure 2-1: **PREPARATION CHECKLIST FOR BASEBALL TRYOUTS**

To maximize your chances of making the baseball team, be prepared in the following areas for trying out:

**Throwing:** To be in throwing shape, practice throwing for 30 days prior to the beginning of tryouts.

**Running:** You also need to be in running shape. We test in sprints. You will be timed in the 60-yard and 40-yard dash. We check overall endurance with long distance running. Put yourself on a stretching and running program for at least 30 days before tryouts.

**Conditioning:** Get into weight training. Stronger is always better.

Before you attend tryouts, you must meet with me at the time listed below:

**Date** _____

**Time** _____

**Room** _____

At this meeting, you will fill out a questionnaire about yourself. Bring a pen or pencil.

All baseball players will be expected to participate in fund raising and field work.

This is high school baseball, a competitive sport. What's most important is your performance now, not what you've done in the past. The whole purpose of the program is to build players who can perform on the varsity level.

After the tryouts, we will meet with players, parents, and guardians to explain our program philosophy.

Figure 2-2: **TRYOUTS FOR HIGH SCHOOL BASEBALL**

*MANDATORY PRE-SEASON MEETING*

DATE

TIME

Pick up the information sheet to prepare for the tryouts.

Figure 2-3:   **PRE-SEASON BASEBALL QUESTIONNAIRE**

Name_____ Grade_____ Phone_____

Address_____ City_____ Zip_____

Date of Birth_____ Parent's or guardian's name _____

Which team are you trying out for?   Frosh_____   JV_____   Varsity_____

Which positions can you play at the varsity level?_____

Are you willing to be part of the team even if you don't get a lot of playing time? Explain

_____

_____

_____

_____

What do you see for yourself as a future baseball player here in high school?

_____

_____

_____

Describe your performance in baseball last year. _____

_____

_____

_____

What role would you like to play this year?_____

What other sports do you play?_____

What were your grades in the previous quarter? _____

What emotion do you associate with baseball? _____

What emotion do you associate with baseball coaches?_____

Fill out the names, positions and batting order of your team in its most important game
this year if you were the head coach.

          name                    position

1.

2.

3.

4.

5.

6.

7.

8.

9.

Is there anything else you want the coaches to know that may help you make the team?

_____

_____

_____

for another reproducible form you can use.) After you select your team, have a team meeting and a parents' meeting. Getting the parents involved helps them understand the guidelines for your team, meet other parents, and understand your total program and what's expected of the players. It also helps them realize that their kids are in a competitive situation, not Little League, Pony League, or Colt League.

## DEVELOPING AS MANY ATHLETES AS POSSIBLE

The more athletes you have in your program and the more you are able to help them develop, the better the chance you have for a finished product, especially at the varsity level. On the freshman, JV level, you want to have as large a squad as you can carry. The difference between a 13- or 14-year-old and a 18-year-old is gigantic. Even the difference between a 14-year-old and 15-year-old can be significant. Every kid should have a chance to develop.

Coaches don't always see the possibilities for how a certain player can help the team. Then a year later, when the player is several inches taller or twenty pounds heavier, incredible things happen. Tom Siever out of high school was just an average guy. He wasn't even a drafted player. Then he went into the military. Look what happened to him!

People don't mature at the same time, so the key is not to give up on anybody, especially not on the basis of their physical ability. But kids can also change their attitudes. If you have a problem with someone, don't close them out. Give them another chance the next year. Never reduce the number of opportunities you have to use a player.

## THE PLAN FOR TRYOUTS

The key is to have a broad base for tryouts and evaluations. Obviously you want players who want to be on the teams, but in your initial screening, include anyone who is even remotely interested. You never know what will happen once they have a little bit of success. They may develop confidence and become more motivated. Healthy attitudes develop just like skills.

The longer the period you have for the tryouts, the better. Initially potential players may be nervous and won't perform up to their basic abilities. Evaluate their basic skills for running, throwing, fielding, and hitting. Here are considerations for each of those areas.

*Running.* The most important tool in baseball for position players is running speed. Running speed indicates that there are some fast twitch muscle fibers, which are essential for success. Whether it's in arm speed or bat speed, hand speed or running speed, there's a real correlation between those fast twitch fibers and success. Run them first. Use a 40 or 60-yard dash. The average major league runner is a seven flat runner for the 60-yard. You can evaluate against that, or 4.9 for the 40-yard-dash.

*Throwing.* Another basic skill you test for in tryouts is arm strength. You can test arm strength with long distance throwing or with a radar gun if you have access to one.

*Fielding.* Evaluate potential players for their ability to field ground balls. Put all your infielders at shortstop and make them throw across the diamond. Put your outfielders in the outfield and have them throw from right field. See how long it takes them to throw the ball 270 feet. An average big league player will throw 270 feet in approximately three seconds.

*Hitting.* The only fair way to evaluate hitting is under game conditions. You can make certain evaluations from machine work and a batting practice situation. If that is all you have time for, make the best of it.

*Evaluations.* After you see some players run and throw, you know that they don't have the basic minimum baseball skills. You need to run them through the whole tryout, see them field ground balls, and then watch their swing. You may have to tell some of them right away that their skills are not good enough. Every player is entitled to an evaluation.

If you have told any players that they're not good enough to be on the team, they may say, "I want to be on the team. What can I do to be on this team?" Ask them, "Are you willing to be a team manager? Are you willing to be a stat man? Are you willing to be on the field crew? Are you willing to announce the games?"

Also let them know that there are many schools and camps, and refer them to the best camps for the skills they need. Be honest. You have to tell them what you see and what you think. Be positive, but realistic.

*Allowing Enough Time for Tryouts.* The number of players you have will determine how many days tryouts will take. If time permits, do a soft toss drill, then try to evaluate all the pitchers separately. Let them throw to a catcher or a net screen so you can look at their mechanics. Evaluate arm strength. Bring the pitching machine out and evaluate people against higher speed hitting skills, then play an intersquad game. The ideal time to do a fair evaluation is an off season league. Having a summer and winter program is the fairest way to evaluate your players under every condition. If you limit yourself to four weeks of tryouts, you risk missing the players with character, work ethic, and a passion for the game.

Every player is entitled to an evaluation. Don't post lists up on the door. Potential players who take the time to come out are entitled to four or five minutes of your time to tell them what you saw. Give a written evaluation to each athlete, then tell them what they need to work on if you're going to cut them.

## KEEPING LARGE ROSTERS

Even players who are slow can be part of the program. They can help you with fundraising and with networking and bringing more people into the program to play or for support. They may have a friend or relative who's a baseball player and may want to be involved because they had a positive experience in your program. Keeping large numbers from the tryouts in your program is beneficial to the total program as long as each person understands their role.

***Staff and Facility Requirements.*** You must have adequate coaching staff to handle your teams. The more teams you have, the better, even if you have a ninth-grade team that doesn't play other teams in your league. Maybe they will play teams on the outside, or maybe they will play like a farm team. The number of players you can keep is based on facilities. You can double up, and the JV can practice with the varsity if you have the right kind of facility.

***Players Who Aren't Playing.*** Everyone's responsible for their own attitude once they're on the team. They have a specific role. You have to designate that role and talk with them about it.

You may need to tell a player, "You're the 20th person on this team. Chances are you're not going to play in any games. You're going to catch in batting practice, you're going to catch in the bullpens, and you're going to get a uniform. You're going to travel with us, but you may not play at all. You'll have a chance to make yourself better. This is your role, this is how you can help the team, and if you accept that role, you're on the team." These athletes can be support people. When you're working on offense, they can be on defense. When you're working on defense, they can work on offense. They can throw in batting practice, or they can shag. They should be treated with respect.

In some high school programs, there isn't money for extra uniforms. You may have to ask parents to buy them or do more fundraising to support extra players and their equipment and uniforms. Just remember that somewhere down the line, these players are going to pay off if they have a positive experience on your team.

# PLAYER DEVELOPMENT

Playing time is based on performance to a large extent, but in the lower level (JV and freshman) teams, the emphasis is on player development and not so much on winning. The lower level should get players ready to go up to the varsity and be performers. This may mean that you're going to ask players to take on roles that do not necessarily reflect their strengths or help win games, but will help players develop. The whole scheme of the program is to build people who can perform on the varsity level. Communicate this to athletes and parents so everybody knows the ground rules before the season starts.

You might have a policy on your freshman team that they throw only fast balls and change-ups, no breaking balls, until they can throw a change-up with command for strikes. You have to identify what each individual needs to work on to become a better player. For example, a player who's a right-hand hitter and who can really run, but is unlikely to be big in stature, may become a switch hitter.

In the ball games, your emphasis may be on hitting the ball on the ground and bunting. Maybe some athletes aren't good left-hand hitters but need to play in the games. They may not be very successful, but if they're going to be productive players on the varsity and utilize their basic skills, they'll have to try. They may have to fail to succeed. They may even have to get worse to get better. That's what it means to have the patience for player development.

## THE COACHING STAFF

When you're focusing on development, the wins may take a beating. You have to make sure your entire staff knows you are a single baseball staff. You need to rotate coaches through the whole system so that one year a coach coaches freshman, the next year he coaches JV, and then he becomes a varsity assistant. At the end of the year for the play-offs, every assistant, all the JV, frosh and varsity assistants are with the varsity for the play-offs. It is great when they get to see the effects of their work from the year before. You can rotate them so they stay with the same group of kids, or you can rotate against it.

Rotate coaches from freshman to varsity, and then back down, or rotate up. It's worthwhile to see a group of coaches grow and mature, and it provides a better perspective on player development. Your projection skills will also improve as you go along.

## AVOIDING LEGAL PROBLEMS

We don't want to emphasize legalities, but you should be aware of the most common legal problems baseball coaches encounter. We've provided a checklist for avoiding legal problems (Figure 2-4) that contains the most important legal considerations on one page. Be sure to take a look at it.

Another safeguard is a form that athlete's parents or guardians sign to release the program and the school from liability and assumption of risk for any harm or danger the student may incur while playing. Most districts have such a form and will want you to make it a prerequisite for students to play baseball. Be sure you have these forms on file with required signatures before your first day of practice.

## Figure 2-4: AVOIDING LEGAL PROBLEMS CHECKLIST

Here are five major ways to help avoid legal problems:

1. ***Proper conditioning.*** Make sure your athletes are in excellent physical condition to participate. Conditioning your players for your sport is basic common sense and a legal necessity.

2. ***Proper supervision.*** Always be present and actively supervise your athletes. The failure to be present is the most often cited reason for litigation against coaches. If situations arise that may involve the use of force, always use the prudent and reasonable action approach in restraining athletes.

3. ***Safe equipment and facilities.*** Make sure your equipment and facilities are safe. Check and recheck everything used by your athletes. Report immediately any discrepancies or safety hazards. Place the safety and welfare of your athletes above all else.

4. ***Adequate instructions.*** It is your responsibility to make sure your athletes are taught the basic fundamentals and rules for your sport. Teach the appropriate techniques in a progressive manner. You must not only teach what to do, but also what **NOT** to do. For example, baseball players must be taught to **NOT** swing a bat without making sure the area is clear.

5. ***Full warning.*** Failure to explain to young athletes the potential dangers of the sport they are playing is the most neglected aspect of any safety program. It is most important to explain to your players why they need to be in good condition and why they must learn the proper skills and techniques of the sport. You must warn and remind your athletes of the potential injury problems of your sport as often as possible.

In short, a coach must condition, supervise, offer proper equipment and facilities, teach the skills of the sport in a progressive and proper manner, and warn of the potential risk of injury associated with the sport. Anything short of this places you and the School District in legal jeopardy.

# GAME CONTROL FROM START TO FINISH

Before you discuss the specifics of game control, you need to establish a philosophical basis that will help explain the reasons for the system.

## WINNING

One of your goals is to win. The nature of baseball offers you an opportunity to win more often, against superior physical opposition, than in any other team sport. You need to look no further than the big leagues to see fragile, nonphysical, left-handed pitchers turn over change-ups and sink fast balls at 80 mph or less. They screw powerful big-league hitters into the ground, and win games against 95 mph power pitchers and muscular hitters. For this reason, it is realistic to win every day if you do your job.

## CONTROLLING THE SITUATION

You should adhere to the concept of "playing against the game." Basically, what this means is to control the situation and not let the situation control you. You have to believe that you control your own destiny. You determine your success or failure, not your opponent, the umpire, the weather, or any of the multitude of other variables that affect the game. Once the ball leaves the pitcher's hand, the fielder's hand, or the bat, each player must make the adjustments necessary to be successful. Too much time and energy is wasted by players and teams worrying about what the other team is doing and adjusting their game to try to do things that they can't have success doing. "Playing against the game" helps eliminate the emotional highs and lows that are so often associated with the positives and negatives in athletics.

Many times, these highs and lows are caused by the "rally hat mentality"—rallies can't be generated unless you have your hats turned inside out. You should have your "rally hats" on every inning without having to turn your hats inside out. This can be carried further to apply to the bad pregame infield or the lack of chatter being the cause for a loss. The list goes on and on. Those runs in the first seven innings count just as much as those scored in the eighth and ninth innings. No one ever got hits or made great fielding plays because they talked it up. Teams that took poor pregame infields have won lots of games. Too often coaches lament that their team doesn't seem to get anything started until the seventh or eighth inning, and many times that's too late. This late inning pattern is a result of the "rally hat" mentality of emotional highs and lows over things that are not important factors in winning. Beat the ball. Throw it accurately, catch it, hit it hard, and outrun it.

**Synergy.** Another important aspect in winning that relates to the team concept is "synergy." This is a scientific term that has real application to team sports. Synergism is the action of two or more substances which cannot achieve a desired result alone, but together can produce the desired result. With this concept in mind, you need everyone's 100% investment into the competition. Synergy allows for no "hold outs."

**Positives.** Positives create the best environment for winning. Coaching too much through intimidation and negatives many times causes players to try to keep from failing rather than try to succeed. Harassed players tend to tune out and miss all the good things that coaches have to say and perceive only *how* they say it. Most coaches try to be positive, but their voice or body language belie them. If you let the situation control you as a coach, it will control your players. This falls into the category of maintaining control and coaching to win, as opposed to just coaching.

Some athletes need to have the hammer dropped on them, but not all athletes and not all the time. This is not to say that you have to fall all over yourself complimenting or consoling your players, but if you strike a balance, it will help team performance. Doing nothing is also all right. Doing nothing gives athletes a chance to learn to control their own energizer in reacting to the successes and failures associated with athletics. There are a lot of down times and failures built into a sport like baseball. But there are a lot of hitters in the Baseball Hall of Fame who failed 70% of the time. They had to get up off the mat lots of times to win. They realized that they didn't have to be perfect to win.

The good players learn to differentiate between what matters and what doesn't matter. You can take a bad pregame, deal with a late bus, forget equipment, strike out, make errors, and walk people, and still be in a position to win, as long as you keep things in perspective. You must be in the right mental set to be able to perform at your best when the game is on the line.

**Responsibility.** The real key to winning is that you have good athletes who accept responsibility for their actions and development and are able to push their own "hot buttons." You need to develop or find the self-starters who can work independently to develop their skills. These athletes not only hate to lose, but they also find ways to win games not imagined by players who wait for someone else to motivate them. The poor self-starter is usually wasting lots of time and energy putting off work or fixing blame for personal failures.

**Basic Skills.** To simplify these concepts and to relate them directly to baseball, you must be able to do five basic things to the best of your ability to be in a position to win:

1. Play high-level catch.
2. Throw quality strikes.
3. Pressure the defense by running the bases aggressively and intelligently.
4. Pressure the defense by putting the ball in play.
5. Have great team spirit while playing against the game.

# PRACTICE

Practice management and organization are the keys in developing the abilities to execute the five basics. Practice must be competitive. This is another word for the importance of game-like practices. Practices must be organized to win, not just to be organized. It doesn't matter how many repetitions you get. If they are not game-like, they are a waste of time. It's like a computer: garbage in—garbage out! If you take 30 good swings and 10 bad swings in practice, sometime during the game, those 10 bad swings will surface and you can't necessarily determine when.

The goal is to have team members practice as intensely as they can and have fun doing it. Do almost all of your technique coaching during practice, scrimmages, and intra-squad games. Technique coaching just before games or during the game muddies the water. Practice, fall games, and summer league is the time for the players to work on new development. This is not to say that there are no opportunities to work on weak areas given the right game situation at any time during the season.

# INDIVIDUAL PRACTICE GOALS

Individual practice goals will vary according to the time available for experimentation and new skill development. Players need time to work on skills such as switch hitting, the short game, a new pitch or pattern of pitching, shallow outfield play, and many other new skills. But don't ignore their strong areas. The point is to expand your total game. Practice is a trial-and-error time for players and coaches to identify and establish each player's role on the team, as well as determine what skills they'll take into the regular season.

During the season, don't gamble once the game starts. Over the long haul, if your athletes can't execute a skill in practice, they won't be able to do it in a game. There may be some new skill development during the season, but the main emphasis is on maintaining strong skills at their highest level.

# SCHEDULES AND GOALS

Players should pick up a practice schedule each morning before they start school so they are prepared and ready for practice, and you don't have to waste time explaining what you are going to do. See Figure 3-1, Practice Plan, for a completed sample.

On the bottom of your practice schedule, you may want to provide a space that asks each player to write down two goals for practice on that day, as well as expected

Figure 3-1: **PRACTICE SCHEDULE**

Daily Practice Plan for _____
(date)

**12:15** Early groundballs/Outfield fundamentals/Catchers frame, block, throw & catch pens
Pens - changeups + curveballs (names): Bowe, West, Rogers, Scott, Brown, Bert, Day

**12:50** Comebackers/cover 1st/tweeners

**1:00** Stretch

**1:15** Form run/Pit arm stretch

**1:20**

| Position Players | Pitchers |
|---|---|

| Position Players with Hitting Coach<br>1) circle swing<br>2) cage hit (eyes on curve balls)<br>3) knee on ground sac bunt<br>4) knee to ground sac bunt<br>5) FBH technique | L & Balance<br>90/120 warm up<br>  & long catch<br>75/60 change ups<br>Basic 7<br>Spin curves | Pen guys<br>2 Man Pepper |

**3:30**
Hitting Coach    1) spoke
        2) butt up
        3) fake break
        4) bid-tarp
Running Coach    1) primary leads 2b
        2) secondary leads 2b
        3) give & take leads
**4:00** Mile 4 time

Pitchers fielding practice (10 min ea)
1) balk moves 1b
2) 2 fungo combackers (cb) to 2b
3) cb 1b/home/scramble
4) cover home
5) short balls/squeeze flips

**Post Practice:** Shortstops & Second Basemen with Infield Coach

**5:30** Bar B Q at Hughes - Must attend

**7:00** Mtg in Hughes—Coaches, Players, Parents

(If you need a parking pass for your parents, see me.)

*Pen Wed 12:00 All catchers + Bish, New, Call, Daffin, Morris, Moses, Nunes
*If you have a class conflict, let me know Tues.

level of performance in achieving those goals. An example might be to execute 20 base hit bunts to third base, with the expected results being to bunt 15 balls on the dirt between the foul lines and the grass. The key is to set measurable goals with realistic expectations. This goal setting is just another way of putting the responsibility back on the team and individual players for their performance and development.

Occasionally, you may set a practice schedule and no coaches will be in attendance, or you'll let the players run their own intra-squad games. This puts the responsibility to make things work on the group as a whole and helps players get a coach's perspective on what it takes to have a successful practice. You should also have certain preannounced practice days where the individual offensive or defensive segment is unplanned. Each player will have to submit his own practice plan for that segment, along with goals and expected results. You are trying to develop the concept that the players are responsible for their actions and that you trust the players to do what is best for the team and themselves.

# GAME DAY

Game day and pregame preparation starts with the game sheet, which is basically a schedule for the day, outlining everyone's role and responsibilities from batting practice and pregame infield assignments to game duties. See Figures 3-2 and 3-3. The Game Day Timetable in Figures 3-4 and 3-5 lists all pregame events by time. You want everyone to know their role before the game so that they can prepare to perform mentally and physically. The first thing you do on game day is familiarize yourselves with the field, especially if you are playing away. This involves a quick walk around to check conditions such as the infield slope, mounds, background, distances, the playing surface, the fences, the backstop, and the sun and wind.

Your pregame routine should be similar to your daily practice routine. Make sure that pregame batting practice involves a combination of execution, stroke development, swings, and live base running. Hit in the same order you will use in the game, so base runners can react to the same hitters they will be reacting to in the game when they are on base. Pregame batting practice is a time for positive reinforcement. Don't do technique instruction during batting practice because you want clear-minded players who "see it and hit it" in the game, and you don't want to get into an "analysis paralysis" situation before the game. Because you want the hitters to feel good about themselves after batting practice, save your best balls for pregame batting practice and make sure that you have both a lefty and righty available to throw good "get it in there" strikes, even if they have to move up to 55 feet or so.

On the defensive side, during batting practice your infielders take at least 50% of their grounders off the bat. Make sure that the infielders make throws with all ground balls off the bat or fungo, rather than just returning them to the fungoer or shag man. The outfielders should play most of the balls off the bat to get used to the sun, wind, and background. If you are faced with an unusual fence configuration or height, mix in some fungo work with your outfielders as well.

Pregame infield is an obligatory show for the fans and scouts more than anything else. You've already taken enough ground balls during batting practice to have famil-

## Figure 3-2: GAME DAY ASSIGNMENT CHART

| Opponent: | Place: | Date: |
|---|---|---|

**Pre-Game Assignments**

| Meeting: | Jog & Stretch: | Warm-up: |
|---|---|---|

**Field BP Format:**               **Cage BP Format:**

| BP Pitchers | | Group 1 | |
|---|---|---|---|
| BP Catchers | | Group 2 | |
| Buckets | | Group 3 | |
| Shag Lf Foul | | Fungos | |
| Shag Rf Foul | | SS/1B | |
| Shag left | | 2B/3B | |
| Shag center | | Catch 1b | |
| Shag right | | Catch 2b | |

**Pre-Game Infield:**

| Infield | | | | | | | Cover 1st | |
|---|---|---|---|---|---|---|---|---|
| Fungo to Left | | Catch | | 1/2 way | | | RF line | |
| Fungo to Right | | Catch | | 1/2 way | | | LF line | |

**Game Duties**

| Pen Cat. | | Stander | | Cat. Bet.Inn | | W/U OF | | Inf. Ball: | |
|---|---|---|---|---|---|---|---|---|---|
| 1B Coach | | | 3B Coach | | | Bullpen Coach | | Pos OF/INF: | |
| Pitchers Charts and Gun | | | | | | Looks Chart: | | Catchers Chart: | |
| Scouting: | | | Pitchers Tendencies: | | | | | Scoreboard: | |
| Scorebook: | | | Watch: | | Video: | | | Announcer: | |
| Shag LF: | RF: | | Stands: | | Back: | | | Eye in Sky: | |

**Starting Line-up:**

| Order: | vs. RHP | vs. LHP | Pitchers Rotation | Pitchers Cond. | Pos.Players Work outs |
|---|---|---|---|---|---|
| 1 | | | Long: | | |
| 2 | | | | | |
| 3 | | | | | |
| 4 | | | Middle | | Pit. Workouts: |
| 5 | | | | | |
| 6 | | | | Players Cond. | |
| 7 | | | | | |
| 8 | | | Short | | |
| 9 | | | | | |
| Pitcher | | | | | |

Figure 3-3: **GAME DAY ASSIGNMENT CHART (SAMPLE)**

| Opponent: TIGERS | Place: VALLEY HIGH SCHOOL | Date: 2/27/XX |
|---|---|---|

**Pre-Game Assignments**

| Meeting: 9:15 | Jog & Stretch: 9:30 | Warm-up: 9:45 |
|---|---|---|

**Field BP Format:** 10:00     **Cage BP Format:**

| BP Pitchers | BOLTON WIRIK McKAY | Group 1 | Willis VOPATA ERWIN PRYOR |
|---|---|---|---|
| BP Catchers | ROGERS CULMO | Group 2 | BLANDFORD BOGGS SPINK WHITLEY |
| Buckets | DONOVON | Group 3 | JOSEPH ROGERS KIRTLAN OWENS |
| Shag Lf Foul | HONEYCUTT | Fungos | McKAY CARMAZZI PORT |
| Shag Rf Foul | McCANN | SS/1B | HEDLEY |
| Shag left | EASTLICK | 2B/3B | GROVES |
| Shag center | ADGE | Catch 1b | LUDINGTON |
| Shag right | BARRY | Catch 2b | FUJIWARA |

**Pre-Game Infield:** 11:10

| Infield | PORT (BASHORE, CULMO, GONGWEAR) | | | | | Cover 1st | McCANN |
|---|---|---|---|---|---|---|---|
| Fungo to Left | WIRIK | Catch | Ludington | 1/2 way | DONOVON | RF line | BARRY |
| Fungo to Right | McKAY | Catch | CRAIG | 1/2 way | FUJIWARA | LF line | GROVES |

**Game Duties**

| Pen Cat. ROGERS | Stander BOGGS | Cat. Bet.Inn BOGGS | W/U OF THOMAS | Inf. Ball: THOMAS |
|---|---|---|---|---|
| 1B Coach McKAY | | 3B Coach PORTY | Bullpen Coach BARIANTI | Pos OF/INF: CARMAZZI |
| Pitchers Charts and Gun GOLMAN → ADGE HONEYCUTT | | | Looks Chart: 2-MAN | Catchers Chart: French |
| Scouting: HORTON | | Pitchers Tendencies: CHANDLER | | Scoreboard: SIMONELLI |
| Scorebook: HEDLEY | | Watch: GROVES | Video: PETE ALTMAN | Announcer: SIMKO |
| Shag LF: GROVES | RF: EASTLICK | Stands: DONOVON | Back: CRAIG | Eye in Sky: GURLEY |

**Starting Line-up: vs.** TIGERS

| Order: | vs. RHP | vs. LHP | Pitchers Rotation | Pitchers Cond. | Pos.Players Work outs |
|---|---|---|---|---|---|
| 1 | Willis 8 → | | Long: Ludington CULMO Gongwear FUJIWARA | Med. Ball 5 YDRS | — |
| 2 | VOPATA 5 → | | | | |
| 3 | ERWIN 2 → | → DH | | 3×50 SITUPS | |
| 4 | PRYOR DH | SPINK 3 | Middle | | Pit. Workouts: |
| 5 | SPINK 3 | McLAUGHLIN 9 | BASHORE | | PENS: HEDLEY GROVES |
| 6 | PFEIFER 7 → | | | Players Cond. | |
| 7 | McLAUGHLIN 9 | Kirtlan 2 | | | NO THROWING: EASTLICK HONEYCUTT Adge DONOVON CRAIG |
| 8 | Whitley 6 → | | Short: Welch BREWER | — | |
| 9 | OWENS-BRAGG 4 → | | | | |
| Pitcher | BERGER | | | | |

Figure 3-4: **GAME DAY TIMETABLE**

DATE:_____ VS.:_____

| : - |
| --- |
| : - |
| : - |
| : - |
| : - |
| : - |
| : - |
| : - |
| : - |
| : - |
| : - |
| : - |

NOTES:

Figure 3-5: **GAME DAY TIMETABLE (SAMPLE)**

DATE: _4-27-xx_ VS.: _(opponent team)_

| |
|---|
| 9:15 - Meeting |
| 9:30 - Jog & stretch |
| 9:45 - Warm-up |
| 10:00 - Batting practice - home team |
| 10:30 - Batting practice - away team |
| 11:00 - Clear the field |
| 11:10 - Home infield |
| 11:25 - Away infield |
| 11:40 - Field prep |
| 11:55 - National Anthem |
| 12:00 - Game Time |
| : - |
| : - |
| : - |

NOTES:

iarized yourselves with the field and readied yourselves for the game. Make sure that the infield is game-like and that you keep the infield short.

You may be able to create a game-like, carry-over value from your pregame infield that helps you win a game. For example, in one of our games, we finished our infield with a force play at home from the second baseman to the catcher, who arm faked to first base and then reversed the ball to third base. We worked on that play only in pregame infield. Late in another game, with the bases loaded, we reversed a force play at home, and got a double play to get out of the inning. We ended up winning 4-3 and got to the regional.

# SCOUTING

Discuss your scouting information the day before you play. Focus on positioning the hitters, identifying the runners and bunters, discussing their pitchers' tendencies, and going over any special defensive plays that your opponents may use. See the blank opponent's scouting chart and completed sample in Figures 3-6 and 3-7. Spend little or no time discussing how you are going to pitch the hitters because most of the pitch decisions are initiated in the dugout. Going over the hitters too much may distract from your strengths and force you into pitching too fine. Scout during pregame and during the game to supplement and reconfirm the material you have.

You can learn a lot by watching and listening at pregame batting practice, infield, pregame pitcher's warm-up, and pitcher's warm-up between innings. Use the stopwatch extensively in your scouting to evaluate arm strength, pitcher and catcher release times, and running speed. Be particularly concerned with the opposition's pitching patterns during the game, as well as a pitch count and velocity readout on your pitchers to help give you an early indicator when your pitcher is tiring.

This opponent's pitcher tendencies chart in Figures 3-8 and 3-9 is used to record each pitch that the other pitcher throws. From this chart, you can determine if the pitcher has any consistent pitching patterns, such as throwing first-pitch fast balls, or 2-0 change-ups. Write the hitter's name in the first column, the first pitch thrown in the second column and follow the count across to the right side of the page. Chart each pitch under the appropriate count. On the far right, total up the number of each different pitch thrown to the individual hitter during that at-bat. On the bottom of the chart, total up the results of each count, and briefly describe the pitcher in the space provided.

# THE GAME

The actual game should be a repetition of what the team has done in practice and pregame. The game is similar to taking a test in a class. It should be an enjoyable and challenging experience that is a measure of how well the team has prepared. If everyone has done his job in practice, there will be no new material or surprises in the game.

Figure 3-6:  **OPPONENT'S SCOUTING CHART**

| NAME | BAT | POS. | # | POSITIONING | PITCH | BUNT | RUN | EXECUTION |
|------|-----|------|---|-------------|-------|------|-----|-----------|
|      |     |      |   |             |       |      |     |           |
|      |     |      |   |             |       |      |     |           |
|      |     |      |   |             |       |      |     |           |
|      |     |      |   |             |       |      |     |           |
|      |     |      |   |             |       |      |     |           |
|      |     |      |   |             |       |      |     |           |
|      |     |      |   |             |       |      |     |           |
|      |     |      |   |             |       |      |     |           |
|      |     |      |   |             |       |      |     |           |
|      |     |      |   |             |       |      |     |           |
|      |     |      |   |             |       |      |     |           |
|      |     |      |   |             |       |      |     |           |
|      |     |      |   |             |       |      |     |           |
|      |     |      |   |             |       |      |     |           |

NOTES:

Figure 3-7:   **OPPONENT'S SCOUTING CHART (SAMPLE)**

| NAME | BAT | POS. | # | POSITIONING | PITCH | BUNT | RUN | EXECUTION |
|---|---|---|---|---|---|---|---|---|
| Jones | L | 8 | 23 | RF- straight  Inf.-St. CF- SL. OPP.+ UP LF. " " " | Away mostly FB's | yes | yes | will bunt to 2B v 3B |
| Smith | R | 4 | 5 | OF. – straight Inf. – pull | work up In the zone FB's IN | yes | yes | lots of execution in all situations |
| Black | S | 6 | 22 | OF. – pull + Inf. – Pull | OFF SPEED Early, Try to Jam | NO | yes | very little, may hit v run |
|  |  |  |  |  |  |  |  |  |
|  |  |  |  |  |  |  |  |  |
|  |  |  |  |  |  |  |  |  |
|  |  |  |  |  |  |  |  |  |
|  |  |  |  |  |  |  |  |  |
|  |  |  |  |  |  |  |  |  |
|  |  |  |  |  |  |  |  |  |
|  |  |  |  |  |  |  |  |  |
|  |  |  |  |  |  |  |  |  |
|  |  |  |  |  |  |  |  |  |
|  |  |  |  |  |  |  |  |  |

NOTES:

Figure 3-8: **OPPONENT'S PITCHER TENDENCIES CHART**

| HITTER | PITCH FIRST | PITCH SECOND A | B | 1-1 | AHEAD 0-2 | 1-2 | 2-2 | BEHIND 2-0 | 2-1 | 3-0 | 3-1 | 3-2 | F | C | CW | S | O |
|--------|-------------|----------------|---|-----|-----------|-----|-----|------------|-----|-----|-----|-----|---|---|----|----|---|
| TEAM | PITCHER | | | | NUMBER | | | THROW | | | | | DATE | | | | |
| 1 | | | | | | | | | | | | | | | | | |
| 2 | | | | | | | | | | | | | | | | | |
| 3 | | | | | | | | | | | | | | | | | |
| 4 | | | | | | | | | | | | | | | | | |
| 5 | | | | | | | | | | | | | | | | | |
| 6 | | | | | | | | | | | | | | | | | |
| 7 | | | | | | | | | | | | | | | | | |
| 8 | | | | | | | | | | | | | | | | | |
| 9 | | | | | | | | | | | | | | | | | |
| 10 | | | | | | | | | | | | | | | | | |
| 11 | | | | | | | | | | | | | | | | | |
| 12 | | | | | | | | | | | | | | | | | |
| 13 | | | | | | | | | | | | | | | | | |
| 14 | | | | | | | | | | | | | | | | | |
| 15 | | | | | | | | | | | | | | | | | |
| 16 | | | | | | | | | | | | | | | | | |
| 17 | | | | | | | | | | | | | | | | | |
| 18 | | | | | | | | | | | | | | | | | |
| 19 | | | | | | | | | | | | | | | | | |
| 20 | | | | | | | | | | | | | | | | | |
| 21 | | | | | | | | | | | | | | | | | |
| 22 | | | | | | | | | | | | | | | | | |
| 23 | | | | | | | | | | | | | | | | | |
| 24 | | | | | | | | | | | | | | | | | |
| 25 | | | | | | | | | | | | | | | | | |
| 26 | | | | | | | | | | | | | | | | | |
| 27 | | | | | | | | | | | | | | | | | |
| 28 | | | | | | | | | | | | | | | | | |
| 29 | | | | | | | | | | | | | | | | | |
| 30 | | | | | | | | | | | | | | | | | |
| 31 | | | | | | | | | | | | | | | | | |
| 32 | | | | | | | | | | | | | | | | | |
| 33 | | | | | | | | | | | | | | | | | |
| 34 | | | | | | | | | | | | | | | | | |
| 35 | | | | | | | | | | | | | | | | | |
| 36 | | | | | | | | | | | | | | | | | |
| 37 | | | | | | | | | | | | | | | | | |
| 38 | | | | | | | | | | | | | | | | | |
| 39 | | | | | | | | | | | | | | | | | |
| 40 | | | | | | | | | | | | | | | | | |
| TOTALS | | | | | | | | | | | | | | | | | |

Describe (Movement, Velocity Location, Command)

F-

C-

CH-

SL-

O-

How does he hold runners (Break Time Moves, Tempo (Quick, Slow Varied)

Figure 3-9: **OPPONENT'S PITCHER TENDENCIES CHART (SAMPLE)**

| HITTER | PITCH FIRST | PITCH SECOND A | B | 1-1 | AHEAD 0-2 | 1-2 | 2-2 | BEHIND 2-0 | 2-1 | 3-0 | 3-1 | 3-2 | F | C | CH | S | O |
|---|---|---|---|---|---|---|---|---|---|---|---|---|---|---|---|---|---|
| TEAM — PITCHER MORGON   NUMBER #27   THROW LHP   DATE 2/27| | | | | | | | | | | | | | | | | |
| 1 Willis | F | C | | | F | | | | | | | | 2 | 1 | 0 | | |
| 2 VOPATA | F | | F | F | | | | | | | | | 3 | 0 | 0 | | |
| 3 ERWIN | C | | F | | | | | CH | F | | | | 2 | 1 | 1 | | |
| 4 PRYOR | C | C | | | F | F | | | | | | | 2 | 2 | 0 | | |
| 5 SPINK | F | C | | | | | | | | | | | 1 | 1 | 0 | | |
| 6 PFEIFER | F | | CH | | | | | F | | CH | | | 2 | 0 | 2 | | |
| 7 McI. | F | | F | | | | | F | | | | | 3 | 0 | 0 | | |
| 8 WHITLEY | F | C | | | F | | | | | | | | 2 | 1 | 0 | | |
| 9 OWENS | F | | CH | C | | F | F | | | | | C | 3 | 2 | 1 | | |
| 10 | | | | | | | | | | | | | | | | | |
| 11 | | | | | | | | | | | | | | | | | |
| 12 | | | | | | | | | | | | | | | | | |
| 13 | | | | | | | | | | | | | | | | | |
| 14 | | | | | | | | | | | | | | | | | |
| 15 | | | | | | | | | | | | | | | | | |
| 16 | | | | | | | | | | | | | | | | | |
| 17 | | | | | | | | | | | | | | | | | |
| 18 | | | | | | | | | | | | | | | | | |
| 19 | | | | | | | | | | | | | | | | | |
| 20 | | | | | | | | | | | | | | | | | |
| 21 | | | | | | | | | | | | | | | | | |
| 22 | | | | | | | | | | | | | | | | | |
| 23 | | | | | | | | | | | | | | | | | |
| 24 | | | | | | | | | | | | | | | | | |
| 25 | | | | | | | | | | | | | | | | | |
| 26 | | | | | | | | | | | | | | | | | |
| 27 | | | | | | | | | | | | | | | | | |
| 28 | | | | | | | | | | | | | | | | | |
| 29 | | | | | | | | | | | | | | | | | |
| 30 | | | | | | | | | | | | | | | | | |
| 31 | | | | | | | | | | | | | | | | | |
| 32 | | | | | | | | | | | | | | | | | |
| 33 | | | | | | | | | | | | | | | | | |
| 34 | | | | | | | | | | | | | | | | | |
| 35 | | | | | | | | | | | | | | | | | |
| 36 | | | | | | | | | | | | | | | | | |
| 37 | | | | | | | | | | | | | | | | | |
| 38 | | | | | | | | | | | | | | | | | |
| 39  FB-7 | 0 | 3 | 1 | 3 | 2 | 1 | | 2 | 0 | 1 | 0 | 0 | 20 | | | | |
| 40  CB-0 | 4 | 0 | 1 | 0 | 0 | 0 | | 0 | 0 | 0 | 0 | 1 | | 8 | | | |
| TOTALS  CH-2 | 0 | 2 | 0 | 0 | 0 | 0 | | 1 | 0 | 1 | 0 | 0 | | | 4 | | |

14 (by row 4/5)
32 (by row 9/10)

Describe (Movement, Velocity, Location, Command)

F- STRAIGHT 84-86 IN TO LHH
C- Downer 71-73 LOTS OF STRIKES
CH- GOOD MOVEMENT 75-78
SL-
O-

How does he hold runners (Break Time, Moves, Tempo)
(Quick, Slow, 51

1.31 WITH FB

1.36 WITH CB, CH

NO SLIDE STEP → BASIC MOVE → NOT GOOD

LOTS OF PICK @ 2B

During the game, you should be able to put things on automatic pilot and let them happen, and make adjustments when necessary. Use your game card (also called a score card), which has your lineup as well as all your extras listed with their roles. This is especially important if you have reentry in your league. It also gives you a chance to use players who don't have complete skills but can perform specialized tasks to help the team win. Your game card should also have a space for your opponents' lineup, subs, and pitchers, as well as defensive positioning. Keep a simplified running score sheet on your game card, with emphasis on what your opponents do and what pitch they hit. This helps to amend your positioning and pitching patterns if necessary. Figure 3-10 shows an example of a blank and filled-in game card. For another sample filled-in score card, front and back, see Appendix B.

# OFFENSIVE SIGNALS

All your offensive signals should be given from the dugout. The main function of your base coaches is to get pitches and to help your base runners when necessary, which is generally less than 10% of the time. Try not using base coaches in the off season if you want the base runners to learn to recognize the situations and coach themselves. Your base coaches should have simple rules. With no outs, the runners advance to third or home only if they can be safe without sliding. With one out, they advance to third or home if it takes a perfect play to throw a runner out, unless you are down by two or more runs. With two outs, you have to make third without a slide (the only exception being with a pitcher who throws a lot of balls in the dirt, where your chances of scoring from third with two outs are increased)—and everyone scores from second on a ball through the infield if you are tied, down one, or ahead. Occasionally make adjustments and stop runners at third on hits through the infield, based on the next hitter. However, the runner from second wants to score from second, so stop only if necessary.

Believe in a signal system, rather than a random or arbitrary set of signals, or two or more sets of signals. Use a simple and flexible system, that allows you to effect a signal in more than one way and change during a game or from game to game.

# SAMPLE SIGNAL SYSTEM

The system we use for both our offensive and defensive signals is a starter-stopper system. In this system, you must assign a number value to all your offensive techniques. For the sake of simplicity, let's consider steal as #1, hit and run as #2, and bunt as #3. We arrive at these numbers by establishing a start counting sign, a stop counting sign, and a release sign. For example, the belt could be the starter, the hat could be the stopper, and clapping could be the release, which tells the base runner and/or hitter that it is okay to look away. If we wanted to put the steal on, we could touch the belt, the arm, and the hat; or we could touch the belt, the ear, and the hat. The possibilities are endless, without changing the basic concept.

Figure 3-10:  **GAME CARD**

| LEAD OFF | BID | H+R | BHB | SAC | INNINGS SCORED | 2 OUT RUNS | SB | SCORE R @3B | BB/HBP |
|---|---|---|---|---|---|---|---|---|---|

OPPONENT TRIPS:

STOPPER:

## Your
## Team
## Logo

| | # | B | P | STARTER | SUBS. | L | HITTERS | R | L | PITCHERS | R |
|---|---|---|---|---|---|---|---|---|---|---|---|
| 1 | | | | | | | | | | | |
| 2 | | | | | | | | | | | |
| 3 | | | | | | | | | | | |
| 4 | | | | | | | | | | | |
| 5 | | | | | | | | | | | |
| 6 | | | | | | | | | | | |
| 7 | | | | | | | | | | | |
| 8 | | | | | | | | | | | |
| 9 | | | | | | | | | | | |
| P | | | | | | | | | | | |

| | 1 | 2 | 3 | 4 | 5 | 6 | 7 | 8 | 9 | 10 | 11 | 12 | 13 | 14 | 15 | TOTAL |
|---|---|---|---|---|---|---|---|---|---|---|---|---|---|---|---|---|
| PITCHES | | | | | | | | | | | | | | | | |
| | | | | | | | | | | | | | | | | |
| | | | | | | | | | | | | | | | | |

- - - - - - - - - - - - - - - - - - - - - - - - - - - - - - - - - - - - - - - - - - -

| ERRORS | RUNS | DP'S | WP/PB/SB | BB | PICKS | 1ST OUT | BUNT D | C+R'S | 2 OUT RUNS |
|---|---|---|---|---|---|---|---|---|---|

CITY TRIPS:

## OPPONENT

| | # | B | P | STARTER | # | B | SUBS. | 1 | 2 | 3 | 4 | 5 | 6 | 7 | POSITIONING |
|---|---|---|---|---|---|---|---|---|---|---|---|---|---|---|---|
| 1 | | | | | | | | | | | | | | | |
| 2 | | | | | | | | | | | | | | | |
| 3 | | | | | | | | | | | | | | | |
| 4 | | | | | | | | | | | | | | | |
| 5 | | | | | | | | | | | | | | | |
| 6 | | | | | | | | | | | | | | | |
| 7 | | | | | | | | | | | | | | | |
| 8 | | | | | | | | | | | | | | | |
| 9 | | | | | | | | | | | | | | | |
| P | | | | | | | | | | | | | | | |

| # | B | SUBS. | # | B | SUBS. | # | T | PITCHERS | # | T | PITCHERS |
|---|---|---|---|---|---|---|---|---|---|---|---|
| | | | | | | | | | | | |
| | | | | | | | | | | | |
| | | | | | | | | | | | |
| | | | | | | | | | | | |
| | | | | | | | | | | | |
| | | | | | | | | | | | |
| | | | | | | | | | | | |

Figure 3-10a: **GAME CARD (SAMPLE)**

| LEAD OFF | BID | H+R | BHB | SAC | INNINGS SCORED | 2 OUT RUNS | SB | SCORE R @3B | BB/HBP |
|---|---|---|---|---|---|---|---|---|---|

OPPONENT TRIPS:

STOPPER: hat

Your
Team
Logo

| | # | B | P | STARTER | | SUBS. | | L | HITTERS | R | L | PITCHERS | R |
|---|---|---|---|---|---|---|---|---|---|---|---|---|---|
| 1 | 24 | R | 8 | Seever | 5 | | | | New | | | Gill | |
| 2 | 3 | R | 7 | Bell | | | | | Miller | | | Leese | |
| 3 | 8 | R | 4 | Correa | 3 | 7 | Straw | | | Teen/Miles | | | Daffin | |
| 4 | 15 | R | DH | Hartman | | | | | Carl | | | Morris | |
| 5 | 11 | R | 5 | Veronie | 1 | | | | Maher | | | M/R | |
| 6 | 35 | R | 3 | Flournay | 4 | | | | Straw | | | | |
| 7 | 22 | R | 9 | Graham | | 6 | Carlson | | Hanks | | | Bern | |
| 8 | 12 | R | 2 | VanHorn | 2 | 8 | | | Hickman | | | Moses | |
| 9 | 16 | R | 6 | Lekse | | | | | | | | Bowe | |
| P | 28 | R | 1 | Woodards | | | Gill | | | | | Scott | |

| | 1 | 2 | 3 | 4 | 5 | 6 | 7 | 8 | 9 | 10 | 11 | 12 | 13 | 14 | 15 | TOTAL |
|---|---|---|---|---|---|---|---|---|---|---|---|---|---|---|---|---|
| PITCHES | 8 | 16 | 27 | 38 | 50 | 61 | 69 | 77 | | | | | | | | |
| Solano | 0 | 0 | 0 | 0 | 0 | 0 | 0 | 0 | 2 | | | | | | | |
| SC | 1 | 0 | 0 | 0 | 0 | 3 | 1 | 1 | | | | | | | | |

----------------------------------------

| ERRORS | RUNS | DP'S | WP/PB/SB | BB | PICKS | 1ST OUT | BUNT D | C+R'S | 2 OUT RUNS |
|---|---|---|---|---|---|---|---|---|---|

CITY TRIPS:

**OPPONENT**

*Verbal-*
*"good w/2 strikes"*
*=pitch out?*

| | # | B | P | STARTER | # | B | SUBS. | 1 | 2 | 3 | 4 | 5 | 6 | 7 | POSITIONING |
|---|---|---|---|---|---|---|---|---|---|---|---|---|---|---|---|
| 1 | 6 | R | 6 | Lewis | 1st | | | f-9 f2 | f-7 f3 | 5-3 f2 | 1g8 c2 | | | | jam |
| 2 | 8 | L | 5 | Glosser | | | | 3u f3 | k f1 | 4-3 f1 | f8 | | | | jam |
| 3 | 10 | R | 3 | Xandel | | | | 5-3 | 6-3 | f9 | f8 | | | | jam ladder |
| 4 | 33 | L | 8 | Horsemann | runner 1st | | | f8 f4 | kc cu | L8 f2 | 1 f9 ch2 | | | | away 4fb ladder bb in |
| 5 | 29 | R | 9 | Kimball | 1st | | | sl7 f8 | bb | 6-3 f4 | | | | | bb/fb away |
| 6 | 32 | L | DH | Wilcox | 1st | | | f7 | f2 f6 | 4-3 f3 | | | | | jam ladder |
| 7 | 7 | R | 4 | Pridemore | | | | f4 f5 | 6-3 f2 | f9 f5 | | | | | strikes |
| 8 | 11 | R | 2 | Braun | | | | 1-3 f2 | k c1 | kc c1 | | | | | |
| 9 | 2 | R | 7 | Roberts | | | | k c1 | k c1 | kc c2 | | | | | strikes away? |
| P | 21 | | 1 | Jimenez | | | | | | | | | | | |

| # | B | SUBS. | # | B | SUBS. | # | T | PITCHERS | # | T | PITCHERS |
|---|---|---|---|---|---|---|---|---|---|---|---|
| | | | | | | | | | | | |
| | | | | | | | | | | | |
| | | | | | | | | | | | |
| | | | | | | | | | | | |
| | | | | | | | | | | | |
| | | | | | | | | | | | |

You can conceal your signals by doing something before you touch your starter or after your stopper by adding on a wipe-off signal or an activator. A possible activator example: Signals can be given only when you are standing still; any signals given on the move mean nothing. You can change your starter and/or stopper at any time, and expand or simplify the number of signals depending on what you want to do offensively. The more sophisticated you get, the more you'll need to add little extras for details such as fake break, first and third offense, and delay steal. You can include verbal signals, but you can't rely on verbals as the only method of giving signals because of crowd noise.

No matter what signal system you use, make sure that the players are looking when you are giving signals. Too often, you have to get the hitter's and/or the base runner's attention to give a signal. This should not be necessary if your hitters look on every pitch until they get a release, and if you wait for the base runner to stand on the base before you start your signals. The only exception would be after a foul ball, when the base runners should look for signals as they are returning to the base. This will cut down on the number of enemy eyes on your signal process. You don't have to drag out the signals in obvious situations when nothing is on, but it is important that the hitter and base runner are conditioned to look before every pitch. A simple release sign is enough to tell the hitter and base runner that nothing is on.

## GETTING THE PLAYERS INVOLVED IN OFFENSE

Give your hitters and base runners latitude in putting on or suggesting their own offense. This is one of the real advantages to giving your signals from the dugout. It allows you the chance to talk with your hitters in the dugout or in the on-deck circle directly to get a feeling for what they feel confident in executing in a given situation. It also helps you prepare those players for what you want. Have your players tell you what they want to do to effect a certain action, because there is nothing worse than asking a player to advance a runner with a sacrifice bunt who believes that swinging the bat or base hit bunting will be more successful. Similar situations change drastically from game to game, or at bat to bat, depending on who is pitching. You may feel better about executing one skill over another from day to day and against different pitchers. Give your hitters the opportunity to suggest their own offense while they are at bat. If you think that the situation is correct, then put on the play after receiving the hitter's recommendation.

This eliminates the need for offensive conferences and allows for a change of tactics as the situation changes with the count and how the hitter is being pitched. It also gives the coach and player more confidence in picking the best play for the situation. With a runner on second base and no one out, occasionally we'll give the hitter an option as to how to advance the runner from second to third—by sacrifice bunt, base hit bunting, or hitting the ball to the right side.

If your base runners are free to steal any time, you can add the "don't run" sign. This gives them the flexibility to run when they get their best jump. The only guideline is that they must have their best jump, which means that you'd rather have them picked leaving too early, than thrown out at the advanced base. These rules also apply when you put on "must steal" sign from the dugout. Especially in your quest to develop aggressiveness in timid base stealers, you'll need to give a "must steal" sign, whether they get their best jump or not. This should not be confused with the hit and run. It is used with players who are afraid to run and must be forced to run to find their limits.

***Recording Results.*** The chart in Figure 3-11, Home to First Running Time Chart, and its accompanying completed sample in Figure 3-12, provide an efficient way to record the running time of each hitter from home to first base. Use this during the game to get the most realistic picture of performance. The watch should start when the hitter's hands begin to move forward on the swing, and stop when the runner touches first base. If the runner takes a turn at first base, the charter should put a "T" next to the time. If the runner bunted the ball, put a "B" next to the time.

Another helpful pair of charts, Figures 3-13 and 3-14, can be used during the fall to record the offensive results of hitters.

## WHEN TO WORK ON SIGNS

Work on signals primarily in intra-squad games. Let the players put on their own signals — it helps reinforce them. Assign partners so players can test each other on the signals. Pair up players who are shaky with those who know the signals. The real key to signal recognition is anticipation. The players need to know the offense and their role in the offense, so that they can anticipate what you will ask them to execute. During a game, you can prepare a player for an upcoming signal by putting it on and then wiping it off early in the count, and then putting it on later in the count. After all this preparation, the rule is still, "when in doubt, ask." Many teams will use an acknowledgment for each signal, but this involves too much overt communication and makes it too easy for your opponents to pick signals.

## GAME NOTES

In general, don't do technique coaching during the game. You can take game notes with a small tape recorder. This allows you to stay with the game. Go over your notes the next day at practice or in a meeting before a game. Any technique corrections made during a game are usually in terms of end result performance. For example, a pitcher may be rushing his body ahead of his arm and be consistently high and inside with his fast ball. Instead of making one of the many possible physical adjustments to correct this rushing problem, it's better to talk in terms of making a location adjustment and miss low and away. For many pitchers, especially young ones, adjusting in terms of performance to correct a physical problem is much easier and more successful in games than trying to make kinesthetic or feel-type mechanical adjustments.

This is not to say that you can't make a physical adjustment with some players to effect a change in performance, as long as you have been successful doing it in practice. Just be careful not to give too much coaching input during the game. The best performers seem to let it happen, rather than make it happen. This is especially true with

Figure 3-11: **HOME TO FIRST RUNNING TIME CHART**

Team Name _____

| OPPONENT | | DATE | PERIOD COVERED | |
| --- | --- | --- | --- | --- |
| | | | MONTH | YEAR |

| HOME ☐  AWAY ☐ | CLUB: |
| --- | --- |
| WEATHER | TIMER SIGNATURES |

| NAME | 1 | 2 | 3 | 4 | 5 | 6 | 7 | TIMES TO 1st BASE BEST | WORST |
| --- | --- | --- | --- | --- | --- | --- | --- | --- | --- |
| | | | | | | | | | |
| | | | | | | | | | |
| | | | | | | | | | |
| | | | | | | | | | |
| | | | | | | | | | |
| | | | | | | | | | |
| | | | | | | | | | |
| | | | | | | | | | |
| | | | | | | | | | |
| | | | | | | | | | |
| | | | | | | | | | |
| | | | | | | | | | |
| | | | | | | | | | |
| | | | | | | | | | |
| | | | | | | | | | |
| | | | | | | | | | |
| | | | | | | | | | |
| | | | | | | | | | |
| | | | | | | | | | |
| | | | | | | | | | |
| | | | | | | | | | |
| | | | | | | | | | |
| | | | | | | | | | |

Figure 3-12: **HOME TO FIRST RUNNING TIME CHART**

Team Name _____

| OPPONENT | | | | DATE 3/27/xx | | PERIOD COVERED MONTH 3/27/xx YEAR | | | | |
|---|---|---|---|---|---|---|---|---|---|---|
| HOME ☒  AWAY ☐ | | | | CLUB: (your team) | | | | | | |
| WEATHER Dry → No wind | | | | TIMER SIGNATURES Dox GPorr | | | | | | |
| NAME | 1 | 2 | 3 | 4 | 5 | 6 | 7 | TIMES TO 1st BASE | |
| | | | | | | | | BEST | WORST |
| Willis | 4.21 | 4.41T | 4.10B | 4.29 | | | | 4.10B | 4.41T |
| Vopata | | | | | | | | | |
| Erwin | | | | | | | | | |
| Pryor | | | | | | | | | |
| Spink | | | | | | | | | |
| Pfeifer | | | | | | | | | |
| Mclaughlin | | | | | | | | | |
| Whitley | | | | | | | | | |
| Owens-Bragg | | | | | | | | | |
| | | | | | | | | | |
| | | | | | | | | | |
| | | | | | | | | | |
| | | | | | | | | | |
| | | | | | | | | | |
| | | | | | | | | | |
| | | | | | | | | | |
| | | | | | | | | | |
| | | | | | | | | | |
| | | | | | | | | | |
| | | | | | | | | | |
| | | | | | | | | | |

Figure 3-13: **OFFENSIVE RESULTS CHART**

GAME DATE:

| | 1 | 2 | 3 | 4 | 5 | 6 | 7 | 8 | 9 | 10 | 11 | 12 | 13 | 14 | 15 | 16 | 17 | 18 | R | H | E | LOB | BB | K |
|---|---|---|---|---|---|---|---|---|---|---|---|---|---|---|---|---|---|---|---|---|---|---|---|---|
| V | | | | | | | | | | | | | | | | | | | | | | | | |
| H | | | | | | | | | | | | | | | | | | | | | | | | |

| PLAYER | POS | AB | R | H | 2B | 3B | HR | RBI | SB | E | SAC | 2ND | 3RD | K | BB | COMMENTS ON GAME |
|---|---|---|---|---|---|---|---|---|---|---|---|---|---|---|---|---|
| | | | | | | | | | | | | | | | | |
| | | | | | | | | | | | | | | | | |
| | | | | | | | | | | | | | | | | |
| | | | | | | | | | | | | | | | | |
| | | | | | | | | | | | | | | | | |
| | | | | | | | | | | | | | | | | |
| | | | | | | | | | | | | | | | | |
| | | | | | | | | | | | | | | | | |
| | | | | | | | | | | | | | | | | |
| | | | | | | | | | | | | | | | | |
| | | | | | | | | | | | | | | | | |
| | | | | | | | | | | | | | | | | |

GAME NOTES:

Figure 3-14: **OFFENSIVE RESULTS CHART (SAMPLE)**

GAME DATE: 10-15-

| | 1 | 2 | 3 | 4 | 5 | 6 | 7 | 8 | 9 | 10 | 11 | 12 | 13 | 14 | 15 | 16 | 17 | 18 | R | H | E | LOB | BB | K |
|---|---|---|---|---|---|---|---|---|---|---|---|---|---|---|---|---|---|---|---|---|---|---|---|---|
| V CSM | 0 | 0 | 2 | 0 | 0 | 0 | 0 | 0 | 1 | 0 | 0 | 0 | 0 | 0 | - | - | - | - | 4 | 8 | 1 | 13 | 2 | 12 |
| H SCC | - | 1 | 0 | 0 | 4 | 1 | 0 | 0 | 2 | 1 | 0 | 0 | 0 | 2 | - | - | - | - | 13 | 19 | 1 | 16 | 9 | 6 |

| PLAYER | POS | AB | R | H | 2B | 3B | HR | RBI | SB | E | SAC | 2ND | 3RD | K | BB | COMMENTS ON GAME |
|---|---|---|---|---|---|---|---|---|---|---|---|---|---|---|---|---|
| SMITH | 8 | THL I | III II | II | - | - | - | - | II | I | - | - | I | - | - | PLAYED VERY HARD - Great 2 strike ab's |
| BLACK | 4 | THL | - | III | I | - | I | III | - | - | I | I | 0 | I | I | 2 Two out RBI Base hits |

GAME NOTES:
1) Too many MISSED SIGNS    2) Drive Bunt Defense - Pitcher is pitching through "Fake open glove" from the SS.
3) 3B - The lead off hitter of any inning can not bale hit bunt against you. 4) First Baseman's need work on balls in the dirt. 5) Infielders - Great job of creating a throwing lane during rundowns.
6) Our pitchers need to be more aggressive going to catch pop-ups in the infield.

hitters, who must react, not think. You can make the players aware of situations that will help the team win. You want players to know the pitches whenever you can get them. Chart the pitching patterns to every hitter separately, so that your hitters can make an educated guess as to pitch and location when they have less than two strikes.

# CHARTING THE PITCHER'S PROGRESS AND PERFORMANCE

The following charts and forms, designed to track the pitcher's progress and performance, range from charts to be used during games or practice to self-evaluation forms and questionnaires for the pitcher himself to fill out. We include them here with the suggestion that you use or adapt the ones most suited to your program. They may be copied as many times as needed for individual coaches or players. You will find the ten reproducible charts and their accompanying filled-out samples on page 62 immediately following discussion of all the charts.

*Pitcher's Performance Chart.* Figures 3-15 and 3-16 represent an all-encompassing, pitch-by-pitch chronicle of the game—a detailed pitch-by-pitch scorecard. Every pitch is recorded as to ball and strike, location, type of pitch, the result of each pitch that is swung at, the direction of all contact, and an evaluation of the type of contact.

During the game, pitchers, catchers, and coaches can look at this chart to make adjustments and plan for ensuing at bats.

Under the ball and strike column for each hitter, the type of pitch is entered by numbers. (See the key in the upper right hand corner of the chart.) If the hitter swings at the pitch, put a check in the "B" column that represents that particular pitch. Locate the pitch in the zone provided in the middle of the square provided for that at bat. Mark the number sequence (i.e., first pitch is 1, second pitch is 2, etc.) in or out of the strike zone. If the ball is hit, indicate where it is hit and how it is hit (i.e., G 6-3 is a regular ground ball to shortstop, HG 4-3 is a hard hit ground ball to the second baseman, 1F7 is a fly ball single to left field, 2L 8/9 is a line drive double to right center field). Additionally, draw a line in the direction that the ball is hit and evaluate the type of contact by putting a dot in the column to the right (hard or soft contact). If the pitch is non competitive (a pitch so far out of the strike zone that the hitter recognizes immediately that the pitch is an obvious ball—i.e. a fifty foot curve ball or a fast ball way up and out of the strike zone) dot that into the non competitive column to the right.

After each inning summarize the pitcher's statistics for that inning (balls and strikes for each particular pitch, total balls and strikes, runs, hits, walks, and strike outs). When the pitcher finishes his outing, summarize his effort including hard contact, soft contact, and non competitive pitches. There is room beside each hitter's line of at bats to make comments as to defensive positioning and recommended pitching patterns.

**Pitch Location and Count Chart.** This chart, as shown in Figures 3-17 and 3-18, is used during bullpens, batting practice, or during games. If you use it during games, you can keep a cumulative chart as well as a separate chart for each inning to monitor the pitcher's adjustments as well as correlate performance with location and pitch counts. The purpose of this chart is to keep track of pitch counts, (total and for each pitch) locations, and first pitch efficiency and tendencies.

The chart, which is self explanatory, is charted from the pitcher's view point. The pitcher will use some of the information on this chart for his summary chart.

**Pitcher's Velocity Chart.** The velocity chart in Figure 3-19 is self explanatory. In the sample chart, Figure 3-20, swings are checked and pitches out of the stretch are circled. Comparing stretch and wind up velocities allows you to evaluate the efficiency of your stretch move. Charting the pitches in order lets you see if there is a drop off in velocity later in the inning due to fatigue or lack of focus. Charting inning by inning allows you to spot fatigue before it shows up on the performance side. Differentials between high and low end velocities for each pitch gives the pitcher a chance to reflect back on the mechanics that allow, for example, a seven-mile-per-hour difference in velocity between two pitches. If it is not changing speeds by design, a differential of five miles per hour or more is cause for inspection. Breaking balls and change up velocities indicate proper or improper mechanics and allow for adjustment during the game. For example, if the pitcher's optimal speed differential between his change up and fast ball is 11 miles per hour (as a result of past performance) and on this day it is only six miles per hour and hitters are making solid contact, it may indicate that he has to loosen his grip to slow the change up down.

There is also space to insert break times to the plate with a runner on first base as well as a runner on second base.

The velocity chart is also a good indicator for a pitcher recovering from an injury to show if he has fully recovered, is in the process of injuring his arm, or requires more rest before his next start.

**Pitcher's Questionnaire.** The pitcher should complete the Pitcher's Questionnaire, Figures 3-21 and 3-22, without the benefit of his game chart, location chart, and velocity chart. This forces him to focus and replay the game and not just regurgitate what the summary chart or any other chart tells him. We prefer to have this questionnaire completed before the next day when we give him all of his charts. We want to know first how he thinks rather than what the charts tell him. This helps him better prepare for his next outing.

Questions one through seven are obvious. Questions eight and nine are key in developing a game plan for the pitcher's practice time before his next outing. We want the drills and or goals to be specific, measurable, and behavioral in nature. Rather than say that he is going to work on controlling his fast ball, we would expect a goal like, "In my pens on Tuesday and Friday, I am going to throw ten fast balls to one location (low and away) with nine of the ten ending up in the one quadrant." This plan and goal could be more detailed and specific, but the key is that it is behavioral (doing something) and measurable. The drills and goals must be challenging but also realistic and attainable.

Questions 10 through 18 address the mental game and how the pitcher dealt with the stress inherent in the game.

You may want to copy the Pitcher's Questionnaire on the other side of the Pitcher's Summary Chart for the efficiency of a one-page handout.

***Pitcher's Summary Chart.*** Figures 3-23 and 3-24 represent a compilation of all the charts—the final product of the pitching effort. Not only does it paint a picture of the pitching performance, but it also gives the coach and the pitcher a chance to evaluate that effort and develop a plan for maintainance or improvement.

After the questionnaire is filled out, the pitcher gets all of his charts and fills out his summary chart. He uses his location chart to dot in the location of every pitch. As a result of plotting the location of each pitch in its individual strike zone, he can see if he is too one sided (fast ball) or identify mechanical or point of aim problems with all pitches. For example, a lot of arm side high fast balls and breaking balls may indicate a rushing problem where the body is gliding to the plate before proper separation. Arm side high change ups may indicate lack of trust with less than fast ball arm speed. The key to the location zone is that the players can diagnose potential problems. The location chart also gives the total number of each pitch as well as the ball/strike ratio for each pitch. First pitch strike tendencies are also detailed. Any pitch that is thrown less than 15% of the time is not a usable pitch. The minimum acceptable strike/ball ratio for each pitch is 60% and the minimum first pitch strike percentage is 55%.

The summary chart is our primary informational chart. With it, the pitcher can review his performance in its entirety. From this chart, we can compute the following:

Middle chart (obvious information not included)

1. First pitch strike percentage by pitch.
2. Pitches hit for outs which can indicate that the pitcher is under or over using a pitch.
3. Hard hit balls.
4. Non competitive pitches.
5. Pitches used for strike outs.
6. 1-1 pitches and 1-1 strikes (key pitch, 2-1 =.290 and 1-2=.180)
7. Pitches thrown on 2-0, 3-0, 3-1, and 3-2 counts (goal is less than 1 per inning)
   Upper chart
1. Lead off men out – the key hitter each inning.
2. First and second pitch strikes – the first tenant of our pitching plan – throw the first or second pitch for a strike
3. Pitches per inning – goal is 15 or less. Remember that stuff and command suffer after the 16th pitch and we want our best to be pitching late in the game.
4. The less information we put into the hitter's computer, the greater our chance of success. Also, the fewer pitches we throw, the faster the inning, and the better defense.

5. Runs/earned runs – This is a measure of mental toughness. Some pitchers tend to give up runs when they are not earned runs because they can transfer the responsibility to someone else.

6. Two out runs – This is another mental toughness gauge. The good pitchers can elevate their effort when they need to. Most games are determined by three or four pitches.

7. Four pitch at bats – Our goal is less than 50% four plus pitch at bats. Pitches per hitter does not tell you this especially if there is lots of hitting action early in the count.

When the pitcher finishes his summary chart, he turns it in to the coach or pitching coach who makes comments and returns it to the pitcher. Both the coach and the pitcher keep the charts in their folders.

***Pitcher Delivery Checklist.*** The pitcher delivery checklist in Figures 3-25 and 3-26 is a chart we use to monitor the progress of the pitcher's attention to his mechanics. It can be used like a diary to evaluate progress and to document where the pitcher is, relative to expectations. The chart is self explanatory.

***Pitcher's Self Evaluation Chart.*** Figures 3-27 and 3-28 is another chart that is used to evaluate progress. The pitcher can use it to see where he is at present, where he is going, and how he is going to get there. The chart is basic and self explanatory.

***Work Progress Chart.*** The chart in Figures 3-29 and 3-30 is a diary of what the pitcher has done to improve himself. It is filled out after every attempt to correct a problem. Designed for mechanical adjustments within the pitching delivery, it can be used for any coaching area—defense, the mental game, or just about anything.

***31-Day Pitch Count Chart.*** Using Figures 3-31 and 3-32, you can monitor the number of pitches that an individiaul pitcher throws over a 31 day period. Our chart monitors games, pregame bull pens, bull pens, and batting practice. Simply record the number of pitches thrown on that day, for that specific activity.

***31-Day Pitching Schedule Chart.*** The chart in Figures 3-33 and 3-34 is used to schedule the pitcher's throwing routine.

Figure 3-15: **PITCHER'S PERFORMANCE CHART**

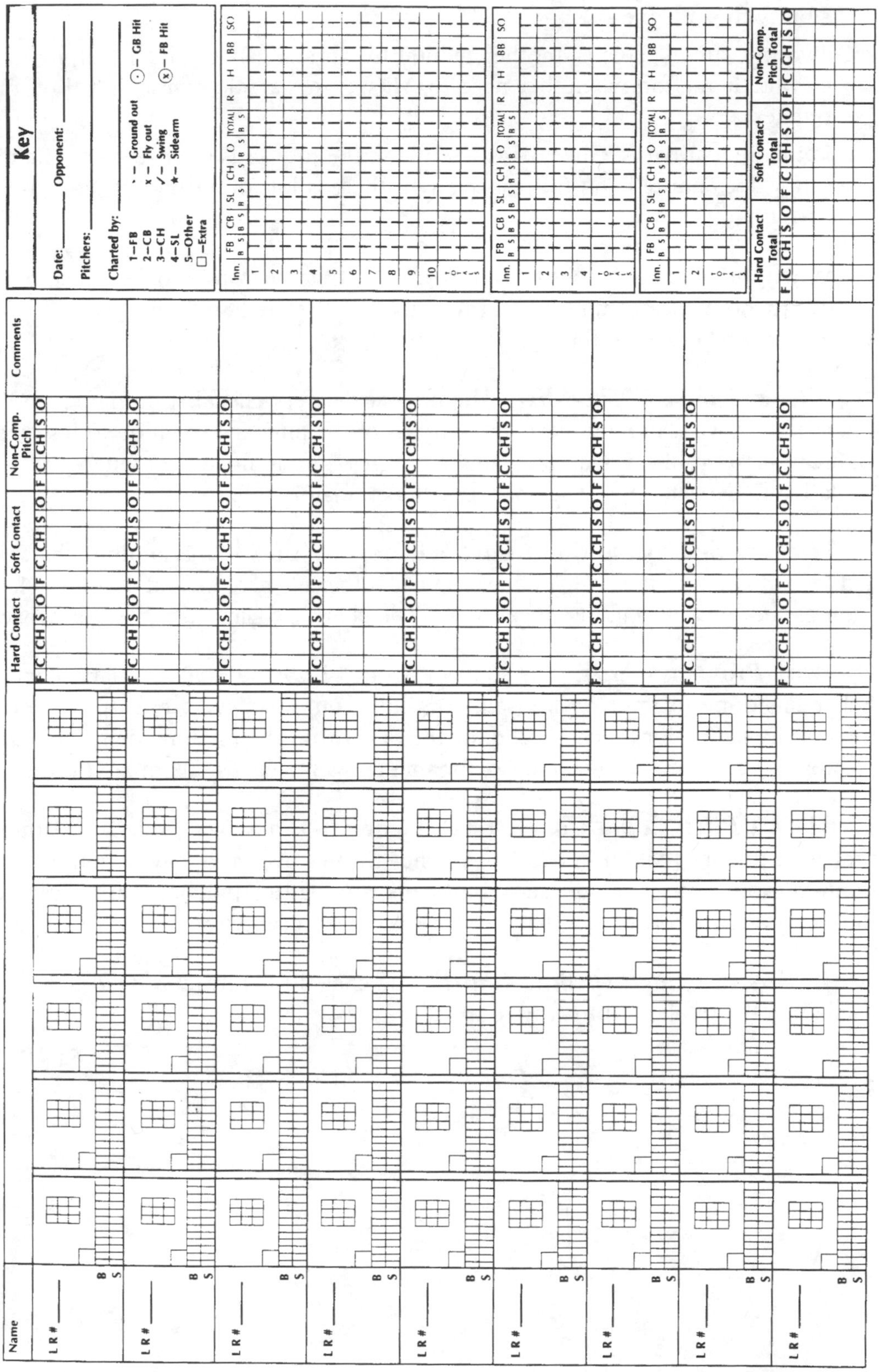

Figure 3-16: **PITCHER'S PERFORMANCE CHART (SAMPLE)**

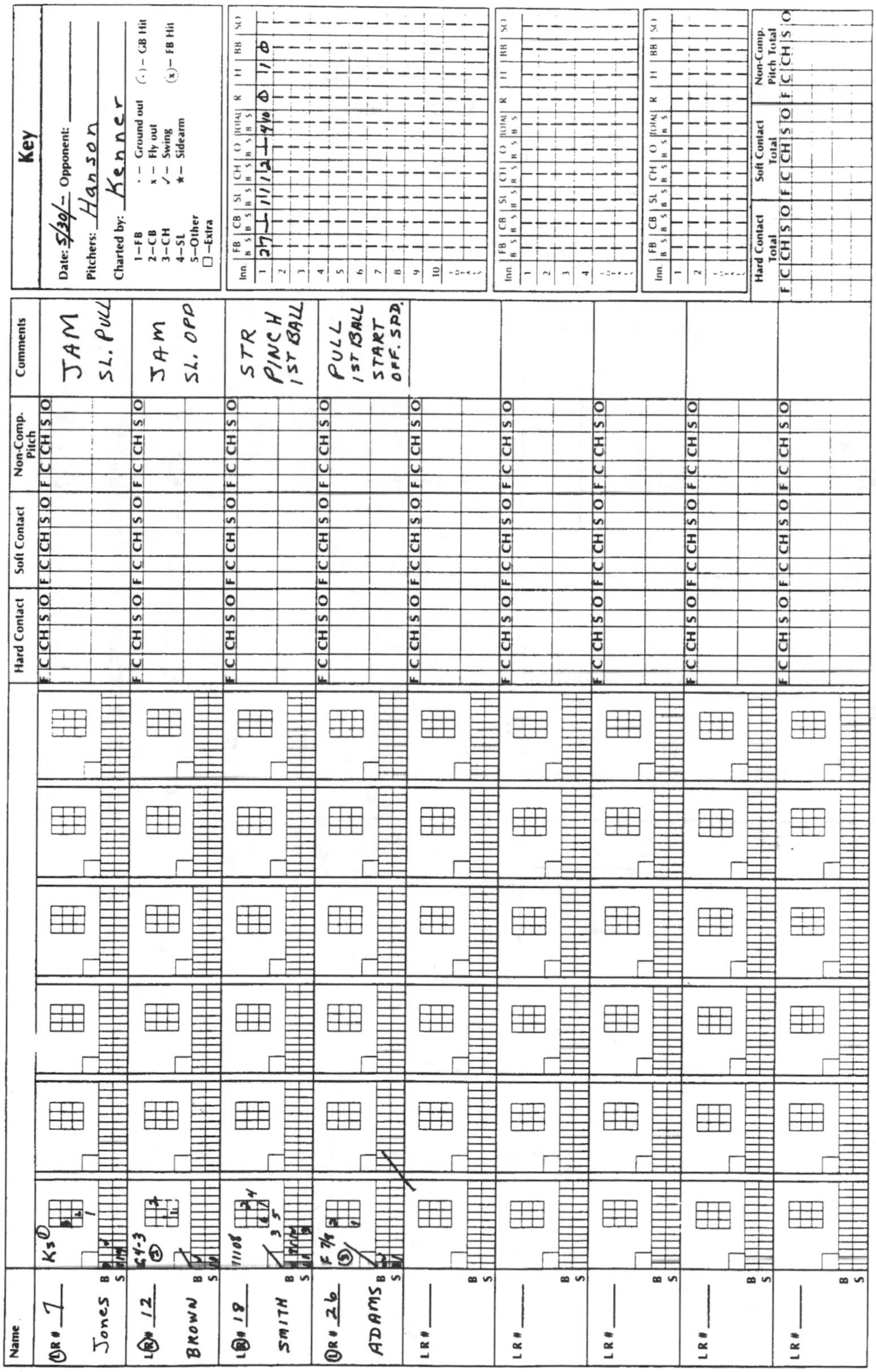

Figure 3-17: **PITCH LOCATION & COUNT CHART**

DATE _____          NAME _____
                            Charted By _____

                                        - BP -
FB   S _____                          - B -
     B _____                          - G -

| 1  | 31 | 61 | 91  | 121 |
| 2  | 32 | 62 | 92  | 122 |
| 3  | 33 | 63 | 93  | 123 |
| 4  | 34 | 64 | 94  | 124 |
| 5  | 35 | 65 | 95  | 125 |
| 6  | 36 | 66 | 96  | 126 |
| 7  | 37 | 67 | 97  | 127 |
| 8  | 38 | 68 | 98  | 128 |
| 9  | 39 | 69 | 99  | 129 |
| 10 | 40 | 70 | 100 | 130 |
| 11 | 41 | 71 | 101 | 131 |
CB   S _____
     B _____
| 12 | 42 | 72 | 102 | 132 |
| 13 | 43 | 73 | 103 | 133 |
| 14 | 44 | 74 | 104 | 134 |
| 15 | 45 | 75 | 105 | 135 |
| 16 | 46 | 76 | 106 | 136 |
| 17 | 47 | 77 | 107 | 137 |
| 18 | 48 | 78 | 108 | 138 |
| 19 | 49 | 79 | 109 | 139 |
| 20 | 50 | 80 | 110 | 140 |
| 21 | 51 | 81 | 111 | 141 |
| 22 | 52 | 82 | 112 | 142 |
CH   S _____
     B _____
| 23 | 53 | 83 | 113 | 143 |
| 24 | 54 | 84 | 114 | 144 |
| 25 | 55 | 85 | 115 | 145 |
| 26 | 56 | 86 | 116 | 146 |
| 27 | 57 | 87 | 117 | 147 |
| 28 | 58 | 88 | 118 | 148 |
| 29 | 59 | 89 | 119 | 149 |
| 30 | 60 | 90 | 120 | 150 |

SL   S _____                    S _____
     B _____              Total
                                  B _____

1st Pitch

     S _____          LETTERS
                        BELT
     B _____            1. Circle last pitch each inning
                          2. Locate 1st pitch with letters
                             (F, CB, SL, CH, FK)
                          3. Add individual totals and
                             total pitches
                        KNEE

Figure 3-18: **PITCH LOCATION & COUNT CHART (SAMPLE)**

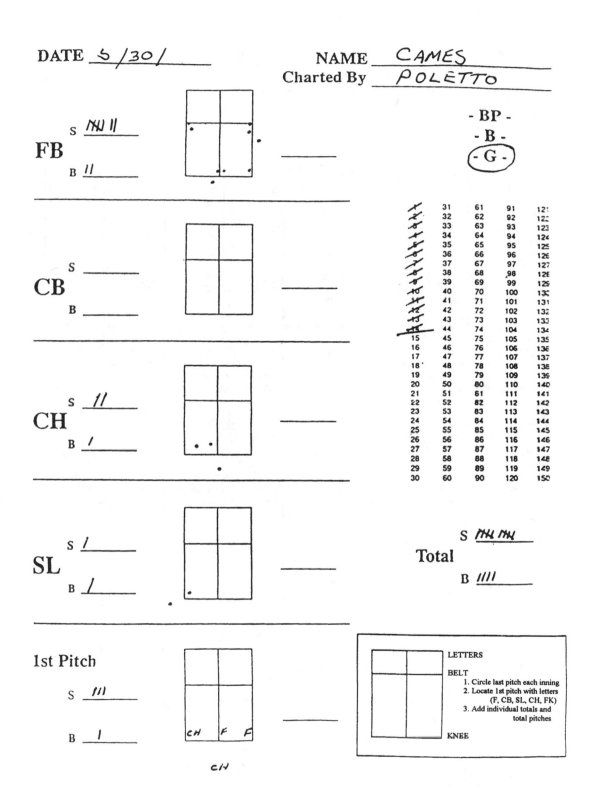

DATE 5/30/      NAME CAMES
Charted By POLETTO

FB   S |||||||      B ||

- BP -
- B -
- G -

CB   S _____      B _____

CH   S //      B /

SL   S /      B /

Total   S ||||||||||      B ////

| | | | |
|---|---|---|---|
| 31 | 61 | 91 | 121 |
| 32 | 62 | 92 | 122 |
| 33 | 63 | 93 | 123 |
| 34 | 64 | 94 | 124 |
| 35 | 65 | 95 | 125 |
| 36 | 66 | 96 | 126 |
| 37 | 67 | 97 | 127 |
| 38 | 68 | 98 | 128 |
| 39 | 69 | 99 | 129 |
| 40 | 70 | 100 | 130 |
| 41 | 71 | 101 | 131 |
| 42 | 72 | 102 | 132 |
| 43 | 73 | 103 | 133 |
| 44 | 74 | 104 | 134 |
| 15 | 45 | 75 | 105 | 135 |
| 16 | 46 | 76 | 106 | 136 |
| 17 | 47 | 77 | 107 | 137 |
| 18 | 48 | 78 | 108 | 138 |
| 19 | 49 | 79 | 109 | 139 |
| 20 | 50 | 80 | 110 | 140 |
| 21 | 51 | 81 | 111 | 141 |
| 22 | 52 | 82 | 112 | 142 |
| 23 | 53 | 83 | 113 | 143 |
| 24 | 54 | 84 | 114 | 144 |
| 25 | 55 | 85 | 115 | 145 |
| 26 | 56 | 86 | 116 | 146 |
| 27 | 57 | 87 | 117 | 147 |
| 28 | 58 | 88 | 118 | 148 |
| 29 | 59 | 89 | 119 | 149 |
| 30 | 60 | 90 | 120 | 150 |

1st Pitch   S ///      B /

CH   F   F

CH

LETTERS

BELT

1. Circle last pitch each inning
2. Locate 1st pitch with letters
   (F, CB, SL, CH, FK)
3. Add individual totals and
   total pitches

KNEE

## Figure 3-19: PITCHER'S VELOCITY CHART

OPPONENT/DATE:  
PITCHER:  
INNING #  
CHARTER:

OPPONENT/DATE:  
PITCHER:  
INNING #  
CHARTER:

| FB | CURVE | CH | SL | FB | CURVE | CH | SL |
|---|---|---|---|---|---|---|---|
| 1 | 1 | 1 | 1 | 1 | 1 | 1 | 1 |
| 2 | 2 | 2 | 2 | 2 | 2 | 2 | 2 |
| 3 | 3 | 3 | 3 | 3 | 3 | 3 | 3 |
| 4 | 4 | 4 | 4 | 4 | 4 | 4 | 4 |
| 5 | 5 | 5 | 5 | 5 | 5 | 5 | 5 |
| 6 | 6 | 6 | 6 | 6 | 6 | 6 | 6 |
| 7 | 7 | 7 | 7 | 7 | 7 | 7 | 7 |
| 8 | 8 | 8 | 8 | 8 | 8 | 8 | 8 |
| 9 | 9 | 9 | 9 | 9 | 9 | 9 | 9 |
| 10 | 10 | 10 | 10 | 10 | 10 | 10 | 10 |
| 11 | 11 | 11 | 11 | 11 | 11 | 11 | 11 |
| 12 | 12 | 12 | 12 | 12 | 12 | 12 | 12 |
| 13 | 13 | 13 | 13 | 13 | 13 | 13 | 13 |
| 14 | 14 | 14 | 14 | 14 | 14 | 14 | 14 |
| 15 | 15 | 15 | 15 | 15 | 15 | 15 | 15 |
| MPH | MPH | MPH | MPH | MPH | MPH | MPH | MPH |
| W | W | W | W | W | W | W | W |
| S | S | S | S | S | S | S | S |
| AVE MPH | AVE MPH | AVE MPH | AVE MPH | AVE MPH | AVE MPH | AVE MPH | AVE MPH |

BREAK TIME 1ST      /      /      /      BREAK TIME 1ST      /      /      /  
BREAK TIME 2ND      /      /      /      BREAK TIME 2ND      /      /      /

OPPONENT/DATE:  
PITCHER:  
INNING #  
CHARTER:

OPPONENT/DATE:  
PITCHER:  
INNING #  
CHARTER:

| FB | CURVE | CH | SL | FB | CURVE | CH | SL |
|---|---|---|---|---|---|---|---|
| 1 | 1 | 1 | 1 | 1 | 1 | 1 | 1 |
| 2 | 2 | 2 | 2 | 2 | 2 | 2 | 2 |
| 3 | 3 | 3 | 3 | 3 | 3 | 3 | 3 |
| 4 | 4 | 4 | 4 | 4 | 4 | 4 | 4 |
| 5 | 5 | 5 | 5 | 5 | 5 | 5 | 5 |
| 6 | 6 | 6 | 6 | 6 | 6 | 6 | 6 |
| 7 | 7 | 7 | 7 | 7 | 7 | 7 | 7 |
| 8 | 8 | 8 | 8 | 8 | 8 | 8 | 8 |
| 9 | 9 | 9 | 9 | 9 | 9 | 9 | 9 |
| 10 | 10 | 10 | 10 | 10 | 10 | 10 | 10 |
| 11 | 11 | 11 | 11 | 11 | 11 | 11 | 11 |
| 12 | 12 | 12 | 12 | 12 | 12 | 12 | 12 |
| 13 | 13 | 13 | 13 | 13 | 13 | 13 | 13 |
| 14 | 14 | 14 | 14 | 14 | 14 | 14 | 14 |
| 15 | 15 | 15 | 15 | 15 | 15 | 15 | 15 |
| MPH | MPH | MPH | MPH | MPH | MPH | MPH | MPH |
| W | W | W | W | W | W | W | W |
| S | S | S | S | S | S | S | S |
| AVE MPH | AVE MPH | AVE MPH | AVE MPH | AVE MPH | AVE MPH | AVE MPH | AVE MPH |

BREAK TIME 1ST      /      /      /      BREAK TIME 1ST      /      /      /  
BREAK TIME 2ND      /      /      /      BREAK TIME 2ND      /      /      /

Figure 3-20: **PITCHER'S VELOCITY CHART (SAMPLE)**

OPPONENT/DATE:  
PITCHER:  
INNING # 1  
CHARTER: Hauser

OPPONENT/DATE:  
PITCHER:  
INNING #  
CHARTER:

| FB | CURVE | CH | SL | FB | CURVE | CH | SL |
|---|---|---|---|---|---|---|---|
| 1   88 | 1 | 1   77 | 1   80 √ | 1 | 1 | 1 | 1 |
| 2   88 | 2 | 2   78 √ | 2   81 | 2 | 2 | 2 | 2 |
| 3   87 | 3 | 3  ⟨77⟩√ | 3 | 3 | 3 | 3 | 3 |
| 4   88 √ | 4 | 4 | 4 | 4 | 4 | 4 | 4 |
| 5   89 √ | 5 | 5 | 5 | 5 | 5 | 5 | 5 |
| 6   87 | 6 | 6 | 6 | 6 | 6 | 6 | 6 |
| 7   86 | 7 | 7 | 7 | 7 | 7 | 7 | 7 |
| 8   88 | 8 | 8 | 8 | 8 | 8 | 8 | 8 |
| 9  ⟨87⟩√ | 9 | 9 | 9 | 9 | 9 | 9 | 9 |
| 10 | 10 | 10 | 10 | 10 | 10 | 10 | 10 |
| 11 | 11 | 11 | 11 | 11 | 11 | 11 | 11 |
| 12 | 12 | 12 | 12 | 12 | 12 | 12 | 12 |
| 13 | 13 | 13 | 13 | 13 | 13 | 13 | 13 |
| 14 | 14 | 14 | 14 | 14 | 14 | 14 | 14 |
| 15 | 15 | 15 | 15 | 15 | 15 | 15 | 15 |
| MPH | MPH | MPH | MPH | MPH | MPH | MPH | MPH |
| W  87.62 | W | W  77.5 | W  80.5 | W | W | W | W |
| S  87.00 | S | S  77.0 | S  — | S | S | S | S |
| AVE 87.55 MPH | AVE MPH | AVE 77.33 MPH | AVE 80.5 MPH | AVE MPH | AVE MPH | AVE MPH | AVE MPH |

BREAK TIME 1ST          /      /      /     BREAK TIME 1ST          /      /      /  
BREAK TIME 2ND       /      /      /        BREAK TIME 2ND       /      /      /

OPPONENT/DATE:  
PITCHER:  
INNING #  
CHARTER:

OPPONENT/DATE:  
PITCHER:  
INNING #  
CHARTER:

| FB | CURVE | CH | SL | FB | CURVE | CH | SL |
|---|---|---|---|---|---|---|---|
| 1 | 1 | 1 | 1 | 1 | 1 | 1 | 1 |
| 2 | 2 | 2 | 2 | 2 | 2 | 2 | 2 |
| 3 | 3 | 3 | 3 | 3 | 3 | 3 | 3 |
| 4 | 4 | 4 | 4 | 4 | 4 | 4 | 4 |
| 5 | 5 | 5 | 5 | 5 | 5 | 5 | 5 |
| 6 | 6 | 6 | 6 | 6 | 6 | 6 | 6 |
| 7 | 7 | 7 | 7 | 7 | 7 | 7 | 7 |
| 8 | 8 | 8 | 8 | 8 | 8 | 8 | 8 |
| 9 | 9 | 9 | 9 | 9 | 9 | 9 | 9 |
| 10 | 10 | 10 | 10 | 10 | 10 | 10 | 10 |
| 11 | 11 | 11 | 11 | 11 | 11 | 11 | 11 |
| 12 | 12 | 12 | 12 | 12 | 12 | 12 | 12 |
| 13 | 13 | 13 | 13 | 13 | 13 | 13 | 13 |
| 14 | 14 | 14 | 14 | 14 | 14 | 14 | 14 |
| 15 | 15 | 15 | 15 | 15 | 15 | 15 | 15 |
| MPH | MPH | MPH | MPH | MPH | MPH | MPH | MPH |
| W | W | W | W | W | W | W | W |
| S | S | S | S | S | S | S | S |
| AVE MPH | AVE MPH | AVE MPH | AVE MPH | AVE MPH | AVE MPH | AVE MPH | AVE MPH |

BREAK TIME 1ST          /      /      /     BREAK TIME 1ST          /      /      /  
BREAK TIME 2ND       /      /      /        BREAK TIME 2ND       /      /      /

## Figure 3-21: PITCHER'S QUESTIONNAIRE

1. What was your best pitch? Why?

2. What pitch did you use in clutch situations?

3. Did you pitch with a specific pattern in mind?

4. Was the same first pitch used too often?

5. What pitch was hit the hardest?

6. If you had trouble with command, which pitch and where?

7. Look to see if each pitch was thrown where you wanted.

8. What adjustments will you make between now and the next time you practice or pitch?

9. Drills and goals for next week:

10. What were your stresses for today's game?

11. How did you experience the stress before the game?

12. How did your pregame bullpen go for you?

13. How did your stress level affect your actual pitching performance? i.e., rushed, hoped pitch would be a strike, etc.

14. How much self-control did you experience before your pitches?

15. What did you do to regain control when you felt that you were not where you needed to be?

16. What did you learn from today's performance?

17. How was the support that you received from your coach and teammates?

18. Anything else you want to say?

Figure 3-22:  **PITCHER'S QUESTIONNAIRE (SAMPLE)**

1. What was your best pitch? Why?
   *Fastball. Good location, movement, and velocity.*

2. What pitch did you use in clutch situations?
   *Fastball, I was able to locate it all day.*

3. Did you pitch with a specific pattern in mind?
   *I was trying to tilt as much as I could.*

4. Was the same first pitch used too often?
   *No, I was able to mix it up.*

5. What pitch was hit the hardest?
   *None of my pitches were hit very hard.*

6. If you had trouble with command, which pitch and where?
   *A lot of curve balls in the dirt.*

7. Look to see if each pitch was thrown where you wanted.


8. What adjustments will you make between now and the next time you practice or pitch?
   *I need to focus on my curve ball. I will focus on locating it. Specifically, I need to get it up more. Release point emphasis.*

9. Drills and goals for next week:
   *Adjust my target in the bullpen, try to throw curveballs for strikes. 60% strikes in the pen.*

10. What were your stresses for today's game?
    *I had played a lot of the other guys in high school.*

11. How did you experience the stress before the game?
    *Talking to the scout down in the pen.*

12. How did your pregame bullpen go for you?
    *Very average.*

13. How did your stress level affect your actual pitching performance? i.e., rushed, hoped pitch would be a strike, etc.
    *I caught my mind drifting towards results and not staying with the process.*

14. How much self-control did you experience before your pitches?
    *Very good, I was able to recognize and release.*

15. What did you do to regain control when you felt that you were not where you needed to be?
    *Stepped off the rubber and inhaled slowly through my nose.*

16. What did you learn from today's performance?
    *There are not a lot of hitters who can hit a good fastball in.*

17. How was the support that you received from your coach and teammates?
    *Outstanding.*

18. Anything else you want to say?
    *I want to talk to you about maybe taking more time to throw in the pen. I did not feel completely loose until the second inning.*

Figure 3-23:   **PITCHER'S SUMMARY CHART**

PITCHER: _____  CATCHER: _____  OPPONENT: _____  PLACE: _____  DATE: _____

| INNINGS PITCHED: | NUMBER OF HITTERS: | LEAD OFF MEN OUT: | PITCHES PER INNING: | RUNS: / E RUNS: | STRIKEOUTS: | 4 PITCH + AT BATS: | WIN LOSS NO DECISION SAVE BLOWN SAVE | STOLEN BASES AT 2ND: 3RD: |

| # OF PITCHES THROWN: | 1ST PITCH STRIKES: | 1ST/2ND PITCH K'S: | PITCHES PER HITTER: | 2 OUT RUNS: | BB'S: | BREAK TIME AT 1B 1) 2) 3) | WILD PITCH: HIT BATTERS: | PICKS AT 1B: 2B: 3B: |

| PITCH | # OF PITCH | % OF TOTAL PITCH | # OF STRIKES | # OF BALLS | STRIKE % | VLCTY W. | VLCTY S. H. L. | 1ST PITCH BALLS | 1ST PITCH K'S | PITCH HIT FOR OUT: | HARD HIT BALL | NON COMP. PITCH | PITCH FOR K'S: | 1-1 K'S: | 2 0 | 3 1 | 3 2 |
|---|---|---|---|---|---|---|---|---|---|---|---|---|---|---|---|---|---|
| FB | | | | | | | | | | | | | 1 | 1 | | | |
| CB | | | | | | | | | | | | | | | | | |
| CH | | | | | | | | | | | | | | | | | |
| SL | | | | | | | | | | | | | | | | | |
| O | | | | | | | | | | | | | | | | | |
| TOTAL | | | | | | | | | | | | | | | | | |

FAST BALL

CURVE BALL

CHANGE UP

SLIDER

OTHER

Figure 3-24: **PITCHER'S SUMMARY CHART (SAMPLE)**

| PITCHER: CAMES | CATCHER: HORTON | OPPONENT: Braves | PLACE: home or away | DATE: 5/30/XX |
|---|---|---|---|---|

| INNINGS PITCHED: | NUMBER OF HITTERS: | LEAD OFF MEN OUT: | PITCHES PER INNING: | RUNS: / E RUNS: | STRIKEOUTS: | 4 PITCH + AT BATS: | WIN (circled) LOSS / NO DECISION / SAVE / BLOWN SAVE | STOLEN BASES AT |
|---|---|---|---|---|---|---|---|---|
| 9 | 33 | 8 | 12.55 | 1 / E RUNS: 1 | 11 | 12 | WIN | 2ND: 0 3RD: 0 |

| # OF PITCHES THROWN: | 1ST PITCH STRIKES: | 1ST/2ND PITCH K'S: | PITCHES PER HITTER: | 2 OUT RUNS: | BB'S: | BREAK TIME AT 1B | WILD PITCH: / HIT BATTERS: | PICKS AT |
|---|---|---|---|---|---|---|---|---|
| 113 | 26 | 31 | 3.43 | 0 | 1 | 1) 1.12 2) 1.18 3) 1.16 | WILD PITCH: 0 HIT BATTERS: 0 | 1B: 1 2B: 0 3B: 0 |

| PITCH | # OF PITCH | % OF TOTAL PITCH | # OF STRIKES | # OF BALLS | STRIKE %: | VLCTY. W. S. | VLCTY. H. L. | 1ST PITCH | 1ST PITCH K'S | PITCH HIT FOR OUT: | HARD HIT BALL | NON COMP. PITCH | PITCH FOR K'S: | 1-1 | 1-1 K'S: | 2-0 | 3-0 | 3-1 | 3-2 |
|---|---|---|---|---|---|---|---|---|---|---|---|---|---|---|---|---|---|---|---|
| FB | 71 | 62.8 | 51 | 20 | 71.83 | 86.77/86.41 | 90/85 | 16 | 13 | 9 | 3 | 6 | 7 | 5 | 4 | 1 | 1 | 3 | 1 |
| CB | — | — | — | — | — | — | — | — | — | — | — | — | — | — | — | - | - | - | - |
| CH | 26 | 23.0 | 19 | 7 | 73.07 | 77.1/76.91 | 80/76 | 10 | 8 | 4 | 2 | 2 | 1 | 3 | 3 | 1 | - | 2 | 3 |
| SL | 16 | 14.2 | 10 | 6 | 62.05 | 79.2/79.3 | 81/77 | 7 | 5 | 2 | 1 | 2 | 3 | 2 | 1 | - | - | - | 1 |
| O | — | — | — | — | — | — | — | — | — | — | — | — | — | — | — | - | - | - | - |
| TOTAL | 113 | 100 | 80 | 33 | 70.80 | — | — | 33 | 26 | 15 | 6 | 10 | 11 | 10 | 8 | 2 | 1 | 5 | 5 |

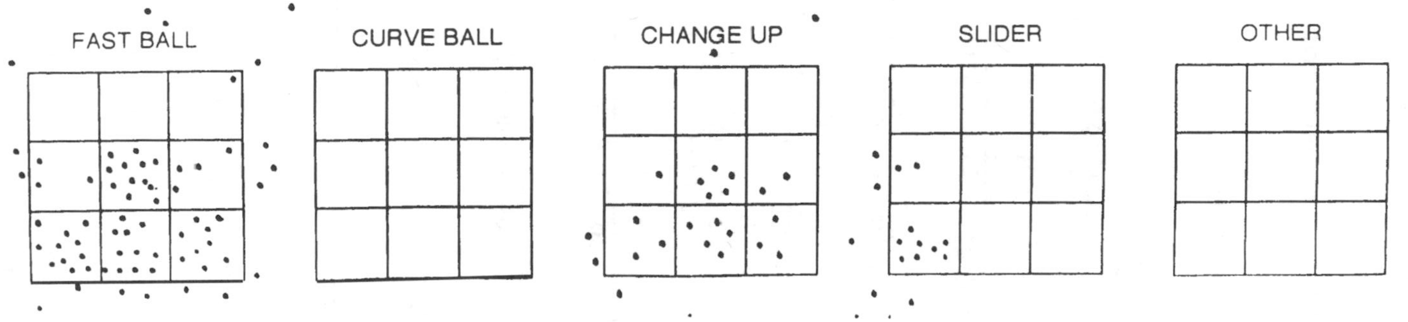
FAST BALL
CURVE BALL
CHANGE UP
SLIDER
OTHER

Figure 3-25: **PITCHER DELIVERY CHECKLIST**

| | |
|---|---|
| Name: | Date: |

**Rubber Position (RT MD LT):**

**Rocker Step (length and direction):**

**Hand Pump (over head, under chin) Head Over Rubber:**

Balance Point:
>    A.  **Lift Leg Height:**
>
>    B.  **Foot Position:**

Ball glove / Separation:

Lead Arm Action:

Arm Length In Back:

Glide To Power Position:

Direction Towards Plate:

Foot Position Landing:

Head Position Landing:

Arm Slot:

Extension (Alignment Of Hand, Arm, And Shoulders):

Finish (Arm Length, Long side, Relaxation, And Recoil):

NOTE: Please include any additional comments on the back of this paper.

Figure 3-26:   **PITCHER DELIVERY CHECKLIST (SAMPLE)**

Name: JOHN BLACK                                      Date: 5/1/95

Rubber Position (RT MD LT):
RIGHT SIDE OF THE RUBBER → Angled toward the 3B SIDE

Rocker Step (length and direction):
SHORT, 6 to 8 INCHES, At A 45° ANGle to home plate

Hand Pump (over head, under chin) Head Over Rubber:
HANDS go over the head, possibly too far behind Ahead?

Balance Point:
A. Lift Leg Height: SLIGHTLY HIGHER THAN parrallel to the ground

B. Foot Position:  Toe is Pointed down And back.

Ball glove / Separation:
Separation is late. THIS MAY be A result of the extreme
hand pump over the head.

Lead Arm Action:
Alignment is outstanding. — Might be more Aggressive with the
lead Arm in an Attempt to Accelerate throwing Arm.

Arm Length In Back:
Tends to wrap the ball Around his back. Make sure the
ball comes straight out and that the hand is on top of the ball.

Glide To Power Position: THE HEAD IS STARTING ~~too~~ TO FLY OFF the
target to compensate for the late separation.

Direction Towards Plate: POOR — THE HEAD IS Pulling the body off of
the target and towards the 1B SIDE.

Foot Position Landing:
Alignment between the plate and the instep of the pivot foot
is good. FIGHT FOR A FIRM LANDING

Head Position Landing: THE HEAD + EYES ARE TILTED TOWARDS the
1B SIDE. Fight to keep the head and eyes parrallel to the ground

Arm Slot:  3/4

Extension (Alignment Of Hand, Arm, And Shoulders):
NOT ENOUGH extension with throwing Arm.

Finish (Arm Length, Long side, Relaxation, And Recoil):
Too SHORT. NEEDS A longer finish with less effort.

NOTE: Please include any additional comments on the back of this paper.

Figure 3-27: **PITCHER'S SELF EVALUATION CHART**

| NAME: | DATE: |
|---|---|

What are your strengths as a baseball pitcher?

What do you think you need to work on to reach your potential?

What is your plan to improve in these areas?

How long do you think it will take?, Why?

GRADE YOURSELF ON A SCALE OF 1-10 IN EACH OF THESE SKILL AREAS AND MAKE A FEW COMMENTS AS TO WHY YOU HAVE GIVEN THE GRADE YOU HAVE.

Delivery: (Wind up, balance, arm action, landing foot, follow through, etc.)
Grade:

Holding Runners: (Stretch effectiveness, moves to 1st/2nd, break time as it relates to stuff)
Grade:

Situation Pitching: (With runners on base, score, inning, etc.)
Grade:

Setting Up Hitters: (Game situations, hitters' weaknesses, location, changing speeds. etc.)
Grade:

Fielding: (Comebackers to 1st/2nd, bunts and bunt D's, backups, covering 1st/home, etc.)
Grade:

Command:
Grade:

| Grade Each Pitch | Overall Physical Development (Grade/Comment) |
|---|---|
| Fast Ball: | General Condition: |
| Curve Ball: | Speed: |
| Slider: | Strength/Power: |
| Change Up: | Flexibility: |
| Other : | Diet: |
| | Vision: |
| | The Mental Game: |

NOTE: Please include any additional comments on the back of this paper.

Figure 3-28: **PITCHER'S SELF EVALUATION CHART (SAMPLE)**

| NAME: JOHN BLACK | DATE: 5/2/95 |
|---|---|

**What are your strengths as a baseball pitcher?** My velocity + my slider are my strengths. I love to pitch and I am very competitive on the mound.

**What do you think you need to work on to reach your potential?** My mental approach and my mechanics are very erratic. When I lose my good mechanics, I struggle.

**What is your plan to improve in these areas?** I need to do a better job with my shadow work, and make a choice to take responsibility for my mental game

**How long do you think it will take?, Why?** I don't know. I have never realy concentrated on these areas.

GRADE YOURSELF ON A SCALE OF 1-10 IN EACH OF THESE SKILL AREAS AND MAKE A FEW COMMENTS AS TO WHY YOU HAVE GIVEN THE GRADE YOU HAVE.

**Delivery:** (Wind up, balance, arm action, landing foot, follow through, etc.)
Grade: C+ | Some days, my mechanics are great. I have to work to be more consistent. My performance is directly related to my mechanics.

**Holding Runners:** (Stretch effectiveness, moves to 1st/2nd, break time as it relates to stuff)
Grade: C- | Runners always get great jumps off of 2nd base. I do a much better job of holding runners on 1st base. My stuff usually does not suffer out of the stretch.

**Situation Pitching:** (With runners on base, score, inning, etc.)
Grade: 8 | The only situation that bothers me is a bases loaded. I become very aware of walking the hitter or hitting him.

**Setting Up Hitters:** (Game situations, hitters' weaknesses, location, changing speeds. etc.)
Grade: 8+ | I usually pitch to the pitching plan very well.

**Fielding:** (Comebackers to 1st/2nd, bunts and bunt D's, backups, covering 1st/home, etc.)
Grade: A- | I do a great job in this area. The reason that I did not give myself an A+ is because I break down on bunt D's only in a while

**Command:**
Grade: B | When my command suffers, all of my fast balls are high and inside on my arm side, the slider is up and long/loopy.

| Grade Each Pitch | Overall Physical Development (Grade/Comment) | |
|---|---|---|
| Fast Ball: 8 | General Condition: Good | 7 |
| Curve Ball: — | Speed: Poor | 4 |
| Slider: 7 | Strength/Power: Good | 7 |
| Change Up: 6 | Flexibility: O.K | 6 |
| Other : — | Diet: Poor | 4 |
| | Vision: I have not had my vision checked | ? |
| | The Mental Game: Poor | 3 |

NOTE: Please include any additional comments on the back of this paper.

Figure 3-29:   **WORK PROGRESS CHART**

| PLAYER: | | | |
|---|---|---|---|
| DATE:<br>INSTRUCTOR: | MECHANICAL<br>PROBLEM: | DRILL/METHOD FOR<br>CORRECTION: | PROGRESS: |
| | | | |
| | | | |
| | | | |
| | | | |
| | | | |
| | | | |
| | | | |
| | | | |
| | | | |
| | | | |
| | | | |
| | | | |
| | | | |
| | | | |

NOTE:  Please include any additional comments on the back of this paper.

Figure 3-30:   **WORK PROGRESS CHART (SAMPLE)**

| PLAYER: JOHN BLACK | | | |
|---|---|---|---|
| DATE:<br>INSTRUCTOR: | MECHANICAL<br>PROBLEM: | DRILL/METHOD FOR<br>CORRECTION: | PROGRESS: |
| 2-10-95<br>WEINSTEIN | POOR BALANCE - TOO MUCH DRIFTING | BALANCE CATCH K-BOARD /BEAM WORK | GOOD - Found that my weight was on my heal |
| 2-25-95<br>WEINSTEIN | My glove hand arm is pulling me off of my target. | SHADOW AND mirror work with focus on lead Arm Alignment. | - THUMBS down separation is a key for me |
| | | | |
| | | | |
| | | | |
| | | | |
| | | | |
| | | | |
| | | | |
| | | | |
| | | | |
| | | | |
| | | | |
| | | | |

NOTE:  Please include any additional comments on the back of this paper.

Figure 3-31: **31-Day Pitch Count Chart**

PITCHER: _____

MONTH: _____

| DAY OF THE MONTH | 1 | 2 | 3 | 4 | 5 | 6 | 7 | 8 | 9 | 10 | 11 | 12 | 13 | 14 | 15 | 16 |
|---|---|---|---|---|---|---|---|---|---|---|---|---|---|---|---|---|
| GAMES | | | | | | | | | | | | | | | | |
| PRE GAME BULL PENS | | | | | | | | | | | | | | | | |
| BULL PENS | | | | | | | | | | | | | | | | |
| BATTING PRACTICE | | | | | | | | | | | | | | | | |
| DAY OF THE MONTH | 17 | 18 | 19 | 20 | 21 | 22 | 23 | 24 | 25 | 26 | 27 | 28 | 29 | 30 | 31 | |
| GAMES | | | | | | | | | | | | | | | | |
| PRE GAME BULL PENS | | | | | | | | | | | | | | | | |
| BULL PENS | | | | | | | | | | | | | | | | |
| BATTING PRACTICE | | | | | | | | | | | | | | | | |

Figure 3-32: **31-Day Pitch Count Chart (Sample)**

PITCHER: ROBERTS

MONTH: MARCH

| DAY OF THE MONTH | 1 | 2 | 3 | 4 | 5 | 6 | 7 | 8 | 9 | 10 | 11 | 12 | 13 | 14 | 15 | 16 |
|---|---|---|---|---|---|---|---|---|---|---|---|---|---|---|---|---|
| GAMES | | 87 | | | | | | | 92 | | | | | | | 80 |
| PRE GAME BULL PENS | | 36 | | | | | | | 37 | | | | | | | 36 |
| BULL PENS | | | | | | 52 | | | | | | | 45 | | | |
| BATTING PRACTICE | | | | | | | | | | | | | | | | |

| DAY OF THE MONTH | 17 | 18 | 19 | 20 | 21 | 22 | 23 | 24 | 25 | 26 | 27 | 28 | 29 | 30 | 31 | |
|---|---|---|---|---|---|---|---|---|---|---|---|---|---|---|---|---|
| GAMES | | | | | | | 102 | | | | | | | | | |
| PRE GAME BULL PENS | | | | | | | 38 | | | | | | | | | |
| BULL PENS | | | | 42 | | | | | | | | | | | | |
| BATTING PRACTICE | | | | | | | | | | | | | | | | |

Figure 3-33: **31-DAY PITCHING SCHEDULE CHART**

MONTH: _____

| PITCHER | 1 | 2 | 3 | 4 | 5 | 6 | 7 | 8 | 9 | 10 | 11 | 12 | 13 | 14 | 15 | 16 | 17 | 18 | 19 | 20 | 21 | 22 | 23 | 24 | 25 | 26 | 27 | 28 | 29 | 30 | 31 |
|---|---|---|---|---|---|---|---|---|---|---|---|---|---|---|---|---|---|---|---|---|---|---|---|---|---|---|---|---|---|---|---|
| | | | | | | | | | | | | | | | | | | | | | | | | | | | | | | | | |
| | | | | | | | | | | | | | | | | | | | | | | | | | | | | | | | | |
| | | | | | | | | | | | | | | | | | | | | | | | | | | | | | | | | |
| | | | | | | | | | | | | | | | | | | | | | | | | | | | | | | | | |
| | | | | | | | | | | | | | | | | | | | | | | | | | | | | | | | | |
| | | | | | | | | | | | | | | | | | | | | | | | | | | | | | | | | |
| | | | | | | | | | | | | | | | | | | | | | | | | | | | | | | | | |
| | | | | | | | | | | | | | | | | | | | | | | | | | | | | | | | | |
| | | | | | | | | | | | | | | | | | | | | | | | | | | | | | | | | |
| | | | | | | | | | | | | | | | | | | | | | | | | | | | | | | | | |
| | | | | | | | | | | | | | | | | | | | | | | | | | | | | | | | | |

G=GAME          PG=PRE GAME BULL PEN          BP=BULL PEN          P=BATTING PRACTICE

# Figure 3-34: **31-Day Pitching Schedule Chart (Sample)**

MONTH: MARCH

| PITCHER | 1 | 2 | 3 | 4 | 5 | 6 | 7 | 8 | 9 | 10 | 11 | 12 | 13 | 14 | 15 | 16 | 17 | 18 | 19 | 20 | 21 | 22 | 23 | 24 | 25 | 26 | 27 | 28 | 29 | 30 | 31 |
|---|---|---|---|---|---|---|---|---|---|---|---|---|---|---|---|---|---|---|---|---|---|---|---|---|---|---|---|---|---|---|---|
| Jones | | G | | | BP | | | | G | | | BP | | | | G | | | | | | | | | | | | | | | |
| Smith | | | G | | | BP | | | | G | | | BP | | | | G | | | | | | | | | | | | | | |

G=GAME    PG=PRE GAME BULL PEN    BP=BULL PEN    P=BATTING PRACTICE

# DEFENSIVE SIGNALS

Defensively, initiate all pitches from the dugout. Send in pitches through the catcher. You can include the location with the pitch. Pitchers are free to change the pitch and/or location anytime they want. It is important for pitchers to have confidence in the pitch they throw, so your dugout pitch is merely a suggestion. When the pitcher changes a pitch or location, you want to be able to do it as rapidly as possible without going through all the pitches and locations. This can be done by a simple wipe system where the pitcher wipes up or down the chest with the glove to add or subtract one or more numbers from the number pitch first given by the catcher.

Don't use location with all your pitchers because they don't all have good enough command, and when you locate in or out, they get too fine and don't throw enough strikes. You will locate for your catcher, but the catcher may not signal the location to the pitcher, other than set up the body position and/or target in the preferred location. Your pitching philosophy is to make the hitter swing the bat so you are not pitching very fine, especially early in the count, unless the situation dictates pitching fine. Allow your catcher to change the suggested pitching location because the catcher has a better view of the hitter's position in the batter's box. This occurs only infrequently, and primarily with the fast ball.

# CALLING THE PITCHES FROM THE DUGOUT

Two major criticisms of calling the pitches from the dugout are that it slows the game down and it takes the game away from the players. First, it is important to have a simple and changeable system that you can get to your catcher as soon as the ball goes back to the pitcher. It is the catcher's job to get the signal to the pitcher before the hitter gets back in the box. You want a quick tempo from your pitchers and they should be ready to pitch before the hitter gets into the box. Calling pitches from the dugout will not be a deterrent to the learning process if you allow your pitchers to control what they throw and if you review the pitching charts with the pitchers and catchers after the game. You can let the catchers call all the pitches for parts of certain games, so that you can evaluate their development and prepare them for the future when they are on their own.

There are four major advantages to calling pitches from the dugout:

1.  It takes a lot of pressure off catchers and especially your pitchers. Many pitchers who have to decide their own pitch or rely on an inexperienced catcher to call the pitch waste a lot of energy worrying whether they are about to throw the right pitch. Calling the pitches from the dugout allows these pitchers to focus their concentration and energy on throwing the pitch as well as they can.

2.  It allows for better pitcher development. Most pitchers and catchers, especially inexperienced pitchers, will become one-pitch pitchers when calling their pitches alone. When that pitch deserts them during the game or in a future game, they are painted into a corner. The usual scenario is mostly fast balls, especially on the first pitch and when behind, and breaking balls on the second pitch after a fast ball strike or when way ahead in the count. The change-up is rarely thrown.

When we call pitches from the dugout, it allows us to suggest pitches that the pitcher would not usually consider, which gives the pitchers a chance to develop their second and third pitches and the confidence necessary to throw them in clutch situations, or when their number-one pitch is not in the strike zone or is not getting the job done.

3. It enables you to stop the running game, especially from first to second. You can orchestrate the number of throws to first, the type of pick, the quick stop off to see if the runner flinches and is therefore running, the type of delivery to the plate—quick set, slide step for LHP, or long hold—and the pitch-out. This is especially helpful on the pitch-out because the catcher is looking on every pitch, and you don't have to get the catcher's attention except when you want to put on a pitch-out. It also helps your infielders in positioning themselves for a potential pick and rundown, as well as all the possibilities in a first and third situation. Although most moves to first are coming from the dugout, it does not preclude the pitchers from moving to a base on their own.

4. It allows you to alert align your defense before the pitch. You know what the pitch is going to be, or if the pitcher changes the pitch to one that is not compatible with your defensive alignment, you have enough time to get the pitcher to step off so that you can realign the defense.

Having the potential to control the game from the dugout does not take the game away from the players any more than a football staff takes the game away from their players by controlling the offensive plays and defensive alignments. There are a lot of parallels between football and baseball. The quarterback audibles at the line of scrimmage, and the pitcher changes the pitch. The football defense changes in response to the offensive formations, and the baseball defense adjusts to changes in count and situations. The football coach is prepared to control any situation on the field, and baseball coaches have the same opportunities. Spontaneity, creativity, and athletic reactions to situations are still keys to success in athletics no matter what comes in from the dugout or sideline. The key factor in baseball is that you have a system to control the situation if and when you feel that it is necessary.

# DEFENSIVE ALIGNMENT

Discuss your defensive alignments and shades in practice and post them in the dugout before the game. If you do not have positioning information before the game, watch batting practice carefully or position according to your pitcher. When in doubt, start the hitter off the lines at first and third, bunch the shortstop and second base, play the center field straight, and play the left field and right field in the alleys. From there, you can adjust to the pitch and the count. Whether you have previous scouting or not, as the game progresses, you can change your positioning.

Most importantly, the first responsibility for positioning the hitter falls upon the players. Position your players, especially outfielders, by simply pointing and gesturing, or by the numbers. For example, in positioning your left fielder, number one would be shallow towards the line, two would be shallow and straight away, and three would be shallow toward the alleys. Four, five, and six represent medium depth; and seven, eight, and nine are deep. How deep or shallow depends largely on the game situation and the skill of the outfielder. If you played a hitter "775," he'd be pull and deep in left and center, and medium and straight in right field.

Infield alignment with a runner on third base goes from the dugout to the middle infielders, who pass it on to the corner infielders. Your first and third defense goes from the dugout to the catcher, who relays it to the pitcher and infielders. All bunt defenses go from the dugout to the catcher, who passes it on to the pitcher and the rest of the infielders. The focus is that everyone is on the same page and is aware of their roles. Finally, you want to be able to initiate picks through either your infielders, catchers, or pitchers.

# POSTGAME

Postgame is a brief time for any important announcements, a few positives from the game even in a losing effort, and pitchers' conditioning. It is best, in most cases, to condition your pitchers after the game so that they are fresh for the game. Also, it's better to make corrections on poor performance the next day when you can look at things more objectively and analytically, and less emotionally. This is also the time to evaluate your game goals and reinforce the positives.

# PITCHING

A baseball team can't compete at a high level without quality pitching. Other games, such as slow-pitch softball, de-emphasize the value of a pitcher. But in baseball, the pitching function is extremely important. If you watch all the transactions made in professional baseball, you will discover that a very high percentage of the trades involve pitchers. Forty percent of the major league active rosters are pitchers. The majority of the "stretch run" trades involve pitchers.

Although statements like "pitching is 90% of the game" may be unprovable, the above facts are undeniable. Consequently, if you glean only one thing in your entire coaching career, make sure you come to an understanding that "you win on the bump." If you don't make sure your pitchers spend time pitching every day, all the ground balls and hitting drills will never get you over the top.

## OVERVIEW OF THE
## FIVE MOST IMPORTANT PITCHING SKILLS

Defense starts with pitching and good pitching requires a number of different skills—throwing with accuracy, velocity, movement, quickness, and refining the quality of pitches, such as the sharpness of the breaking pitch. The skills we regard as the five most strategic in pitching are discussed here with the most important at the top of the list.

*Hitting the Target.* The absolute number one goal of pitching is hitting the target. If you think of it in very simple terms, pitching is really nothing more than target practice. Everything else is secondary. But you truly have a fighting chance when your pitcher gets the ball where you want it to go. That is, in fact, the only thing a pitcher has control over—where to throw the ball. After that, he has very little control over what happens.

*Changing Speeds.* The ability to change speeds is a second factor in refining the pitching process. Changing speeds creates a timing problem for the hitter. Hitting is timing, and pitching is destroying the hitter's timing. If the pitcher can do that, he's another step on the way to success.

***Creating Movement.*** The third factor is the ability to create some movement on the baseball. The most desirable movement is a two-plane type of movement where the ball moves horizontally and vertically as in the fast ball, change-up, or breaking ball. The ability to throw a ball with this kind of movement is advantageous for all pitches.

***Maximizing Velocity.*** The ability to generate velocity creates a situation in which the hitter has less time to react to the pitch. A pitcher can become more effective by cutting down the hitter's reaction time. Mechanically it's the result of the whole body working together at high speed in the right sequence.

***Working Fast.*** A fast tempo adds to the pitcher's edge. He should get the signal before the hitter gets into the batter's box. Teach him to change pitches and location with wipes rather than going through all the pitches and wasting time. One of the things that really kills the tempo of games is a pitcher walking down off the rubber at the edge of the grass. Teach him to get the ball back from the catcher while he is near the rubber. Fast tempo pitching takes the hitters out of their routine.

The pitcher should slow the tempo only when he needs to regain composure to pitch effectively. Sometimes the hitters will slow him down, but if he is ready, the umpires will push the hitters to get into the box. Even if the umpires don't force the tempo, the pitcher is ready to pitch immediately after the hitter gets ready, which makes the hitter feel rushed. If the pitcher forces the hitter back into the box quickly after a bad swing, some neural carryover lends itself to another poor swing.

A quick tempo does not mean quick pitching to the hitter. The pitcher should let the hitter get set in the batter's box, but put pressure on the hitter to get into the box rapidly.

***Review.*** Here are the five pitching skills in a reminder list for your pitchers:

1. Hit the target.
2. Change speeds.
3. Create movement.
4. Maximize velocity.
5. Work fast.

Keep in mind that efficient mechanics give a pitcher a chance to have the most consistent ability to hit the target because they lead to a repetitive delivery with a consistent arm slot and release point. Good mechanics also give the best possible chance to maximize arm strength and arm speed and to reduce the chance for injury. Pitchers with good mechanics can maintain their stuff for a longer period, which allows them to pitch later in the game.

# DOWNHILL PLANE—THE GOAL IN MECHANICS

The objective in good pitching mechanics is to create a downhill path to the plate with the pitch. The way to achieve this is by throwing overhand or three quarters to high three quarters. Overhand throwing is not the natural way the arm works, but to pitch effectively, the pitcher has to create a downhill plane, so overhand throwing is really imperative.

The pitchers who drop down on their rear leg and drive to the plate often over-stride or pitch with a low elbow. They must be aware of over-striding because it will destroy their downhill plane. Don't hesitate to continually remind them of the concept of downhill plane to the plate. Show them that they need to create an acute angle to the plate for the hitter. The hitter is swinging down and up into the ball. The pitcher is coming down from ten inches above home plate and somewhere between 12 inches and 18 inches above his head, into a strike zone 2'-3' over home plate. The downhill angle is somewhere between 7 and 13 degrees depending on the height of the release point, the height of the pitcher, the height of the mound, and the position of the pitch in the strike zone.

The greater the downhill plane your pitcher has coming to the plate, the more his arm and hand work down through the line of sight. Even without any sink or side-to-side movement, the ball is moving down through the strike zone. It forces the hitter to be more precise and accurate with his swing.

When the pitcher's arm goes horizontal, the ball stays on the bat longer. The trajectory is flatter so the hitter has a better chance of making solid contact. Horizontal arm action is caused by going into rotation too early in the delivery. Effective downhill pitching has a long linear component and a late rotational component.

The way to get the downhill plane is by getting the arm up early. One reason that you see so many tall pitchers and very few pitchers under six feet in the big leagues is because the taller pitchers create a more downhill angle to the plate. In the 1960s when pitching dominated the game, the rules committee reduced the height of the mound from 15 inches to 10 inches to infuse more offense into the game. Less downhill plane was the reason.

It isn't that pitchers can't get people out by throwing a low three-quarter side arm or submarine, but most consistently they're going to get hitters out in a high three-quarters or overhand motion that creates a downhill plane to the plate. This plane will benefit all pitches. It allows the change to move down and toward the arm side and breaking ball down and away from the arm side. This two-plane breaking ball and change-up movement induces more swings and misses and off center contact.

# THE PITCHING SEQUENCE

The pitching sequence involves a number of motions from starting position to landing. Each is discussed here in detail.

***Starting Position.*** A right-handed pitcher should start on the right-hand side of the rubber and left-handed pitchers on the left-hand side of the rubber. This creates a mechanical advantage because the pitcher's angle coming at the hitter is more critical. From the right-hand side of the rubber the right-hand pitcher is almost throwing from behind the right-hand hitter. When the hitter is in a direct line with the flight of the pitch, it is tough for him to judge the speed and movement of the ball.

The fear factor also enters the equation when the right-handed hitter is presented with this angle from the right-handed pitcher. It makes it tough for the hitter to see the release point with both eyes. Against a left-handed hitter, the pitcher hides the ball with the upper part of his body when he's on the right-hand side of the rubber. Therefore, the ball gets to the hitter a little bit faster because he can't react as soon to the release point.

Hitters do not start to hit until they see the ball, just before the point of release. You hear about pitchers being sneaky fast or that hitters don't react to a pitcher well because he hides the ball. What they're talking about is that they don't see the ball leave the pitcher's hand as well when the pitcher is on the right or left-hand side of the rubber. The fact that the pitcher's release point is closer to home plate also creates this effect.

There are exceptions. Fernando Valenzuela was a left-handed pitcher with a screw ball. Pitching off the right-hand side of the rubber gave his ball more room to get into the strike zone. Many sinker ball pitchers who continually miss arm-side-in off the plate need to move to the opposite side of the rubber.

A pitcher should find one spot on the rubber where he is the most effective and stay there. He should stand tall with his shoulders angled toward the baseline closest to his arm side (1/4 turn to the third base for right-handed pitchers or 1/4 turn to first base for left-handed pitchers.) (PHOTO 4-1)

His head and eyes are aimed straight to the plate. The 1/4 turn starting position out of the windup makes it easier to get to the balance position. Many pitchers who start square tend to swing their stride leg back, which forces them to tilt their upper half and rush to the plate. As he takes the sign, the glove is pointed north and south with the ball in it.

***Rocker Step.*** The pitcher can start the motion by reaching into the glove, gripping the ball with the throwing hand palm facing the hitter, and taking a short rocker step toward eight o'clock, then raising his hands over his head. The rocker step takes

Photo 4-1

Photo 4-2

the weight off the pivot foot, and allows him to turn the pivot foot in front of the rubber and parallel to the rubber. He should keep his head centered over the rubber as he takes the rocker step.

***Reaching a Balance Position.*** As the pivot foot turns parallel to the rubber, the pitcher brings the stride leg knee toward the throwing arm chest side. (The knee is lifted to two o'clock and pointed somewhere between three and four o'clock as the hips turn.)

The stride foot should be toe down, under the knee and pointed slightly back. His weight should stay balanced over the ball of the pivot foot while standing tall. (PHOTO 4-2) As the stride leg is reaching the top of its lift, the hands start down and back after separating somewhere near the middle of the chest. As previously mentioned, some pitchers tend to swing their leg back rather than lifting with the quad. This tilts their upper body to the plate before the arm is ready. This forces the arm into a side to side horizontal plane which does not allow for a good power position and a downhill plane to the plate.

***The Balance Position.*** To reach the balance position, the pitcher should be in a tall, upright position, not leaning back on his heels, and his center of gravity over the ball of his pivot foot. The stride leg toe is down and pointed slightly back so the front hip is closed. If the stride leg toe is up, it forces the weight back on the heel of the pivot foot. Don't let your pitcher pick the stride leg up so high that it puts him back on his heels. Certain pitchers will pick their leg up higher, especially more overhand pitchers, and then they will duck their head a little bit. Nolan Ryan did that. He would pick his stride leg up very high, almost up to his chest, then duck his head down. Keeping his balance point out over the ball of his pivot foot, he would counter balance the high leg lift by ducking his head.

The true balance position looks like this:

1. The pitcher's leg is lifted where his thigh is about parallel to the ground, and the throwing hand is starting to reach back.

2. His weight is balanced over the ball of his pivot foot.

This balance position also keeps his front side closed, which allows for more power at the point of release. Skip Bertman, the baseball coach at Louisiana State University and the 1996 Olympic Head Coach, talks about "biting your shirt" on your front shoulder to help keep the front side closed while in the balance position.

***Hand Separation.*** It is helpful if the pitcher brings his hands up over his head before he picks the stride leg up. His hands should be up so that when his stride leg comes up, his hands can separate easily in sync with the leg lift. This gives him time to get his arm up into a power position as he glides to the plate and before the stride foot hits the ground. Many no windup pitchers tend to be tight in their chest and shoulders. The wind up loosens the chest and shoulders and coordinates the hand separation with the leg lift. It is important to be loose and relaxed throughout the delivery. For a no windup pitcher, or a modified no windup pitcher, the key is that the hands separate down, or start down to separate, while the stride leg is lifting. The hands are not lifting while the leg is. When that happens, the hands are going to be late so that when the stride foot makes contact with the ground, the body won't be in a good power position.

The thumbs point down on the separation. This type of vertical separation lends itself to a long arc which produces a loose down, back, and up arm swing with the hand on top of the ball. A little shoulder tilt during separation as a result of thumbs down separation of the hands also helps keep the backside loaded and the shoulders in line with the target. This shoulder tilt also prevents rotating off the target and aids in a downhill release. He must tilt uphill to throw downhill. It is kind of a cartwheel arm and shoulder action that also allows for a longer and more closed stride that promotes good leverage at release. Three-quarter arm to low three-quarter arm pitchers tend to have less tilt and more rotation.

***Thumbs Down Separation.*** The thumbs down separation also leads to better throwing arm action. It keeps the throwing hand on top of the ball and the throwing arm in a flexed position that is not easily wrapped behind the back. This wrapping arm action is seen in a slinging horizontal arm swing where the shoulder blades are often overly pinched together. However, this pinching action with the elbow up and cocked and not horizontal is often in evidence with the harder throwers because the distance from the end of the back swing to the release point is a factor in velocity. Moderation is the key. If the shoulder blades are too pinched together, a lot of stress is placed on the anterior shoulder. A pitcher also risks having his arm late and flat at the point of release.

Some pitchers have a flatter take away as they separate their hands. They don't create as long an arc with their arm at the bottom of their arm swing. Sometimes the pitcher's mechanics require the flatter take away because it allows them to get their arm up faster. One danger in this is that young pitchers tend to tighten up when they take it away too flat. They also tend to get underneath the ball with their elbows. They look like waiters or pie throwers just before the point of release. (PHOTO 4-3). The high elbow delivers the hand to the release point at a higher speed. The faster hand speed will increase the arc of the arm and the result will be better velocity. If they're flat and they get their elbow up into the power position, it is not a problem as long as they are relaxed. Tight muscles react slowly and loose muscles react quickly. The pitcher needs arm speed to create velocity in pitching.

Photo 4-3

***The Glide and Stride to Home Plate.*** The glide to the plate starts when the pitcher's leg reaches the top of its leg lift. The pitcher should stay away from the lift and drift to the plate action as the leg starts to lift. The hands separate and the throwing hand reaches back. As the pitcher glides (stride) home, the stride foot stays closed with the bottom of the foot going to the plate (the bottom six cleats of his shoe.) The six cleat (knee to knee) stride keeps the front side closed and allows for maximum leverage for the pitch. He should ride his back leg as long as he can." There is going to be some flex in his rear leg and some straightening from his stride leg just before he glides. This serves to keep his weight back and fosters acceleration to the plate.

Pitchers who aggressively push off the rubber get into a disadvantageous mechanical position because they push their body ahead of their arm. They end up firing the back leg too soon and fly open with their head and lead shoulder. When they fly open, the back leg is up and they look like a "dog over a fire hydrant." (PHOTO 4-4)

***Stride Leg.*** The stride leg, in a piston-like action, reaches as far to the plate as possible without affecting the pitcher's downhill plane. This usually produces a stride very close to the pitcher's body height. There are notable exceptions. Nolan Ryan strides considerably further than his height with excellent results. The longer stride advances the release point closer to home plate, which cuts down on the air resisting the ball in flight. The forward movement of the pitcher's arm starts when the foot plants.

***Pitching Is Like Closing a Door.*** The hinges of the door are on a pitcher's front side. He closes the door from the back

Photo 4-4

side, as opposed to the hinges of the door being on the throwing arm side where many pitchers swing open with their front shoulder and close the door back away from the hitter. This causes lack of extension and leverage at release. When the front foot hits, it's critical that his direction side, the lead side, is going toward home plate. You want all his energy going toward the target, which is somewhere within the 17-inch rectangle above home plate.

Stepping too far left of the line created from the instep or toe of the pivot foot causes the pitcher to open his front side—making much of his energy go away from the target and losing the mechanical advantage. It's also easier for the hitter to see the ball because the pitcher loses some deception. The farther to the right of the midline the right-handed pitcher steps, the straighter the foot has to be. Some pitchers step too close and block their throwing arm with their hips. This forces the arm to flatten out, losing the downhill plane. Ideally, he should step right on the midline with the front toe slightly closed.

The stride foot should be slightly closed and the leg should be firm to allow a consistent release point as a result of a solid foundation. This also gives the ability to stop the lower half and transfer all the energy to the throwing arm, which allows for maximum acceleration of the arm and hand. Think of a car coming to a quick stop. If the passengers did not have the shoulder harness part of their seat belts on, the top part of the body would snap forward towards the dash. This is precisely what you want your pitcher's top half to do as a result of the firm leg and foot plant. The same phenomenon is evident in the pole vault. The vaulter sprints down the runway and plants his pole in the vault box. The pole comes to a sudden stop and all the energy is transferred to the pole which flexes and helps to propel the vaulter over the bar.

When the front foot hits, the pitcher's arm is in a power position. In the power position the stride foot toe is slightly closed and the toe of the stride foot is on a line to home somewhere from the instep to the toe of his pivot foot.

***Landing.*** In the landing the weight is on the entire front foot with the weight toward the inside of the ball of the landing foot, not way up on the toe nor back on the heel. The stride leg foot is planted firmly on landing. Avoid spinning out or fanning out the stride leg foot. The stride leg is flexed and firm but not stiff. The front shoulder and hip are pointed to home plate and the pitcher's glove hand is into the chest or slightly in front of it, with the glove above the elbow. The throwing arm approximates an "L" position with the throwing arm elbow at or slightly above shoulder level with the fingers pointing up. The eyes are level and he stands tall with the back knee slightly flexed.

# THE PITCH

The pitcher starts to pitch when the front foot hits. When he starts to throw, he will rotate to a position where the shoulders are square to the plate and the trunk is extended (arched). As the hand starts forward, the trunk is flexing and the hand is moving at a very high rate of speed. The ball is released at or slightly in front of the head with the arm and hand at full extension. The shoulders, arm, and hand form a straight line. (PHOTO 4-5)

Photo 4-5

On release, the fingers are behind the ball on fast balls, inside on change-ups (depending on the type of change) and over the ball on breaking balls. The sequence is hand first, head second and then belly button or chest over the stride leg. His eyes should be parallel to the ground at the time of release. His lead side is his direction side as well as a linear accelerator to home plate. He shouldn't spin his upper body as a result of an overly aggressive and horizontal lead arm.

He must pull down and in with his lead elbow under control. If he is too aggressive, he tends to roll his lead shoulder and head out. But if he is too passive he can decelerate his throwing arm. If his lead arm goes horizontal he will lose direction to the plate. When he pulls with the lead arm, the glove should pull no further than the glove side hip. It should not end up extended behind his back which usually indicates out of control over throwing.

***Rolling the Laces.*** Throwing extension starts by rolling the laces of his pivot down. As his throwing hand extends to the target, his head follows, and then his belly button finishes out over the stride leg knee and then his back heel rotates up and out. He should be focused on throwing the ball through the target.

***Follow Through.*** The pitcher decelerates his throwing arm as his throwing arm shoulder finishes across his stride leg, somewhere between his knee and hip. The distance the throwing hand finishes outside the stride leg is about the same as the distance between the head and the release point. His head's going to roll out of the way during the follow through. The side of his throwing arm is much longer than his glove hand or directional side as he finishes his delivery. He must extend as much as possible after release to allow for a longer arc to decelerate the throwing arm.

How violent his release is will determine what happens in his follow-through. Make sure at completion that there is not a violent recoil of his throwing arm. The lead leg should be slightly flexed because it gives more time to decelerate the arm under control. After he lands, he should try to make an adjustment to get himself in the best position to field. Make sure he decelerates his arm before getting into a fielding position.

***Pitching out of the Stretch.*** Pitching out of a windup and pitching out of the stretch are the same thing except when pitching out of a stretch, the pitcher starts from closer to his balance position, from a position where he's already taken his rocker step

and made his turn. The six cleat action really comes into play here because he's got to
keep himself loaded on his back side and
still be quick to home plate. In the wind up
he lifts the leg and separates the hands. In
the stretch it is important to separate his
hands first and then lift his leg. The same
things apply as in the wind up. He glides to
the plate when he gets to the bottom with
his hand and the top with his leg.

The emphasis on being quick to the
plate has been so critical for most people
that they use a slide step to the plate. This
causes pitchers to jump off their back side.
They don't keep their back side loaded, so
they lose miles per hour and risk injury.
Think about the six cleat action as staying
loaded on the back side with a knee-to-
knee action when bringing the front knee
to the backside knee and showing the bottom six cleats to the hitter. Then he can
achieve the same things he's achieved out of
the wind up. (PHOTO 4-6)

Photo 4-6

# RIGHT HANDER'S STRETCH MOVE

Refer to the Summary Chart of Mechanical Check Points—Right Handed Pitcher in
Figure 4-1 for the entire pitching sequence, proper mechanics and possible problems.

A right hander sometimes closes up a little bit (left heel lined up with right toe)
so that he can pick the knee up toward his throwing-arm shoulder without having to
rotate back. He should avoid rotating back before he starts his six cleat action to the
plate. He picks the quad straight up but not very high and goes six cleat as he's going
to the plate.

Closing up a little bit and changing the angle makes it a little tougher to go to first
base. However, it makes him more efficient going to the plate. The number one priority is to be efficient going to the plate. He gives the catcher a better chance to throw the
runner out and gives himself a better chance of getting the hitter out because he'll have
better stuff to the plate.

If his team is going to throw the runners out, and he's relying on his pick-off move
to keep the runner close, chances are he's not efficient going to the plate. If that happens, the base stealer is not going to take a long enough lead to get picked because he
knows he can run on your pitcher's slowness to the plate and still be safe.

Figure 4-1: **SUMMARY CHART OF MECHANICAL CHECK POINTS - PITCHERS**

| Sequence | Proper Mechanics | Fault | Resulting Problem |
|---|---|---|---|
| Starting Position | Upright & relaxed. Glove north and south. Quarter turn arm side. | Bent over & tense. Glove east and west. Shoulders square to home plate. | Lack of free & easy delivery. 1st or 3rd base coaches can read pitches. Inability to get to efficient balance position. |
| Rocker Step | Short & toward 8 o'clock (rhp.) Weight centered over rubber. | Big rocker step with back arched. | Weight goes on heels & inability to get to balance position with weight centered over ball of pivot foot. All of the above creates direction problem with lead side opening prematurely. |
| Leg Lift to Balance | Lift quad with toe down & pointed back slightly. Lift stride leg knee toward throwing arm shoulder. | Picking up stride leg straight & toe up. Swinging leg up with foot wide. Open thigh or over rotates into balance position. | Poor balance & inconsistent arm slot & release point. Lack of downhill plane. Inconsistent stuff. |
| Balance position | Tall position balanced over ball of pivot foot on firm rear leg. Head, hips & shoulders are level. | Weight on heel of balance leg. Weight does not stay over rubber. Balance leg overly flexed. | Body rotates open prematurely producing horizontal arm. Trouble maintaining stuff & wild high in the zone. |
| Separation | Thumbs point down on separation & move vertically down middle of body. Separation starts before body glides to the plate. | Separation after body glides to plate. Separation behind mid line. Hand doesn't stay on top of ball. | Late arm with low elbow and horizontal arm. No downhill plane. |
| Glide | Retains weight balanced over rubber until leg reaches top of lift & throwing arm starts to reach back. Linear to the plate with shoulder, hip, & foot closed to plate. Stride leg straightens as glide to the plate is initiated. | Premature push from balance leg. Lead arm pulling on horizontal plane. Stride leg thigh opens to plate. | Early rotating with body ahead of arm. Lack of downhill plane. Loss of velocity & lacking endurance. |

| | | | |
|---|---|---|---|
| Stride | In a down & out action the foot steps on a line from toe instep of pivot foot to home plate. Length of stride is approximately body height. Land toe in on "flat" of foot with knee slightly flexed, but firm. | Stirde is too open or closed. Unstable foot plant. Stride leg knee too flexed. Stride too long, preventing head & shoulders from extending over stride leg knee. | Direction problem early or retarded rotation of trunk. Upper body recoils. |
| Power Position | Stride foot slightly closed with firm stride leg & foot. Lead shoulder and hip pointed to home. Glove is above elbow. Throwing arm approximately an "L" at or above the shoulder with the fingers pointing up. Eyes, hips and shoulders are level. Posture is tall. | Open front side. Head leading elbow low and wrist laid back. | Loss of leverage at release. Loss of downhill plane. |
| The Pitch | Hand starts forward when stride foot plants as a result of laces of pivot foot turning down to ground. Trunk goes into rotation and goes from extension to flexion after hips & shoulders square up to plate. Hand above head at release & shoulders in nearly straight line. Knee of balance leg drives forward & inward with balance leg heel turning up and out. The leg is approximating a "V." | Trunk rotates open with stride. Stride leg too soft & body drifts forward after stride foot plants. Lack of backside drive after stride foot plants. Fingers on side of ball or pronate early. | Lack of velocity. Elbow & forearm problems. Poor control. |
| Follow Through | Long arc of deceleration in front of body. Arm finishes between hip and knee of stride leg. Back is near flat and arm is relaxed. Throwing arm side in longer than glove side. | Short arc in front of body. Arm cuts across body or finishes down & into body. Arm is tight & recoils from finish position. Arm & shoulder stops short of glove side thigh. | Posterior cuff strain. Loss of velocity & inconsistent release point. |

# LEFT HANDER'S STRETCH MOVE

The basic delivery to the plate for a left hander should be a leg lift just like out of the windup. This gives him the best chance of coordinating the top and bottom half and eliminating rushing to the plate. The starting position for the left handed pitcher should find the feet narrower than shoulder width and the feet staggered. The right heel should be lined up with the left toe. This makes it easier to get to the balance position because he just lifts with the quad to get to his balance position. No rotation is required to load the back side.

The pivot foot can be slightly angled with the heel away from the rubber to move the 45 degree line down the mound and increase the deception of the move to first. The pitcher starts with his head looking directly at first or half way between the plate and first base. This is the starting point for his pick as well as his pitch. The hands should be coupled somewhere between his chin and belt. This is open to individual preference and comfort.

As his leg lifts, his hands lift slightly or separate. The key is to separate his hands before he glides to the plate. Everything must be the same with all body parts on the pitch as well as the pick to first.

The left hander can use the six cleat action also as a change of pace for the base runner and a change of pace for the hitter. It can be the basic move to home for some left handed pitchers.

In the bullpen pitchers should work more out of the stretch than the windup since most of their big pitches in the game are going to be out of the stretch. This is especially true for relievers.

# CONTROL

The essence of pitching is the ability to hit the target. If he can hit his target, most likely he can get by with one pitch, if that pitch is good enough. This is true on almost any level. He develops control by being precise in everything he does. All his mechanics are important. Every time he picks up the ball to play catch, he's pitching. He is not just warming up to play catch; he is warming up to pitch every time he throws the ball.

*Target Orientation.* The pitcher needs to be target oriented and have a fine visual center on his target from the time that he's in his balance position until the ball gets to the target. The more detail he gets out of the target, the better chance he has of hitting his target. The smaller the target, the better the chance of improving control. He can take a soft center focus when he's in his windup, but once he gets to the balance position, he needs to have a really detailed fine center focus on his target. The target can be the inside of the glove, or it could be anything, but it needs to be small. Some pitchers don't look into the target as they strike a balance position. They may have a picture of the target in the mind's eye without really looking at it. Most pitchers can't do this, but we can think of two who could: Luis Tiant, who played for the Boston Red Sox and other teams, and Fernando Valenzuela, pitcher for a number of teams including the Los Angeles Dodgers and the San Diego Padres.

***Pitcher Charts.*** *Ten comprehensive charts to track pitcher performance and progress as well as some self-evaluation forms are located in the last half of section 3, "Game Control from Start to Finish."*

# THE PITCHES

## FASTBALL

The most important pitch in baseball is the fast ball. A pitcher must possess the ability to throw the fast ball to both sides of the plate and hit his target consistently.

*Four Seam.* The first fast ball is the four seam fast ball. (PHOTO 5-1) That is the basic fast ball because that's the easiest one to control. It can probably be thrown for the most velocity because there's less movement and more seams rotating against the air. It should be the first fast ball the pitcher learns. The four seam fast ball is thrown across the horseshoe, with the horseshoe pointed in or out. He puts his fingers together in the center of the ball with his thumb underneath. Spreading the fingers too much tends to tighten the wrist and forearm. It is okay to tuck the thumb a little bit if it allows for a more secure grip. Generally, the pitcher sets the thumb between the index finger and middle finger, but there are variations: Some will tuck the thumb underneath so there's less resistance against the fingers so they can put more backspin on the ball. Other pitchers will slide the thumb inside the ball to get more tail and or sink.

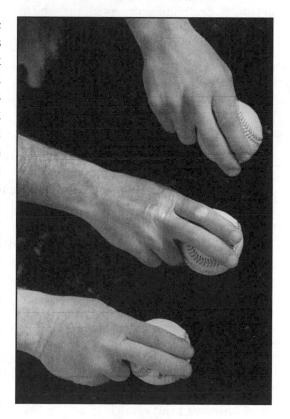

Photo 5-1

*Choking the Ball.* The pitcher shouldn't choke the ball in his hand. He needs some space between the backwards "c" of his hand and the backside of the baseball. The ball should be away from the palm of his hand. Too much hand and finger contact

99

creates drag, which slows the ball down. A pitcher with short fingers needs to hold the ball a little bit deeper. Ideally it should be out as far in the fingers as possible to still allow a firm enough grip on the ball. The grip at release should be firm enough so the ball will not pivot in his fingers. A periodic grip check with your pitchers will ensure the proper grip.

The four seam fast ball is thrown when the pitcher needs to throw a strike. This is the fast ball he should throw most often when he pitches inside on his arm side. This is also the fast ball he throws most often when he pitches in to lefthanders away from his arm side. This is the fast ball to use when he wants to put a hitter away, down and away, because it has a little better velocity. It's probably going to have a little more spin on the ball and the more spin on the ball, the smaller the ball looks to the hitter. It is also used with pitching up in the zone.

***Two Seam Fast Ball.*** The second fast ball is going to either be a two seam across the narrow seam fast ball, or a two seam with the seam fast ball.

***Two Seam Across.*** On the two seam across fast ball, the pitcher can adjust finger placement and come off a little bit more on the inside of the ball with the middle finger and wrist and move the thumb over a little bit. The wrist must stay firmly inside the ball to get more sink on the two seam across fastball. The movement on this pitch is two plane. It's going to move in and down on his arm side, so it leads to ground balls. This pitch has more movement and probably less velocity than his four seam fast ball. If he can throw it away from his arm side and get movement, he can back door right hand hitters because it starts off the plate and runs back on the corner. Right hand hitters tend to give up on this pitch. He can also gap left hand hitters with this pitch. They will back off the plate thinking the pitch will be in, and it tails back over the plate.

***The Two Seam with the Seam Fast Ball.*** The two seam, with the seam, fast ball has less down movement than his two seams across, but it's going to have more run to it. It can start over the plate and run in on a righthander's hands or start on the outside half and run away from a lefty. The tendency is more tail. If thrown to left hand hitters, it may run back over the inside corner ala Greg Maddux. Left hand hitters often buckle on this pitch because it starts in off the plate.

# MOVEMENT AND VELOCITY

Make sure that the pitcher doesn't give up too much velocity to get movement and that his four seam, two seam across and two seam with, are all thrown with the same mechanics and the same arm angle. Make sure he doesn't end up adjusting his grip so much that he loses velocity to the plate. But keep in mind that there's a fine line between movement and velocity. Sometimes it's beneficial to lose velocity and create movement.

Every pitch is thrown off fast ball arm speed. That's why the fast ball is the most important pitch, but arm speed shouldn't change whether it's fast ball, curve ball or change-up. When changing pitches, the only thing that changes is the part of the ball that's thrown and the grip:

- On the fast ball, the pitcher throws the back of the ball;

- with a curve ball, the front of the ball;

- the change-up, the back inside of the ball; and

- with a cutter, the top outside of the ball. All are thrown with fast ball arm speed.

# CHANGE-UP

The second pitch in importance is the change-up, which is a change-of-speed pitch. It destroys the hitters timing and it's easy on the pitcher's arm. A pitcher can pitch in the big leagues with a fast ball and a change-up. Mario Soto did it. Greg Maddux and Tom Glavine of the Atlanta Braves feature the fastball and the change up. The change-up is a fast ball that's a foot slower than a normal fast ball. It's a pitch that the pitcher wants the hitter to make contact with. It forces the hitter to wait a little bit longer and makes his fast ball appear faster, especially if he can throw the fast ball inside for strikes. In essence the change-up takes bat speed away from the hitter.

If a pitcher has an effective change-up, it increases the relative velocity of his fast ball because the hitters can't start as soon. The velocity varies depending upon the pitcher, movement, and amount of deception in the delivery. Look at the hitter, and the hitter will tell you if it's the right speed. If the batter double clutches and hits the change-up or takes it, it's probably too slow; and if he's right on the change-up, it's probably too fast.

If there's a differential of about ten miles an hour, that's sufficient because you want the hitter to hit the ball. If the pitcher throws it on the inside part of the plate, you expect the hitter to pull it foul. Over the middle of the plate, expect a pop up or a weak ground ball. If the pitcher throws it away, expect the hitter to swing and miss or cue if off the end of the bat. Pitching is all about making the hitter hit the ball poorly.

The pitcher should throw a change-up when the hitter is looking for a fast ball. If he's a first pitch fast ball hitter, or if he's behind in the count, the change is a good pitch. Again, there are no "always" and "nevers" when to throw any pitch. Generally speaking, whatever the pitcher feels is the right pitch at that time is the right pitch to throw.

***The Grip.*** When he throws his change-up the pitcher should use fast ball arm speed, and try to create some two-plane movement. There are many different ways to throw the change-up, but the key is a loose grip. The looser the grip, the slower the pitch. He can use his regular fast ball grip and just hold the ball looser and deeper in his hand, and that will do it. He just throws the back inside of the ball from a power position and gets extension. Holding the ball deeper in the hand will also slow the pitch.

The circle or OK grip is also effective. Make a circle with the thumb and index finger and set the ball in the palm of the hand. The narrow seams should be inside the circle formed by the thumb and index finger. Keep the circle created by the thumb and index finger going at the middle of the plate. (PHOTO 5-2)

Many left-handed pitchers have success with a three-finger grip with the index and middle and ring finger resting on top of the ball. (PHOTO 5-3) Again the key is a loose deep grip and fast ball arm speed while throwing the back inside of the ball.

***Velocity of the Change-Up.*** The tendency for young pitchers is to worry about throwing the change too hard. In the early stages of the change-up, it is better to throw too hard than too soft. Young pitchers throw their change-up by slowing their arm speed down when they worry about the change being too fast. Pitchers who worry about the change being too fast will drop their elbow out in front of their body and push the ball up to the plate. They look more like dart throwers. The key is to emphasize elbow up and extension of the hand to the plate.

A pitcher must throw this pitch from his power position and stay inside the ball, throwing the back inside of the ball as opposed to starting behind the ball with his fingers and turning it over at release. Those who go from a fast ball with the fingers on top of the ball and then turn it over tend to have problems in their elbows and their shoulders. A pitcher should stay inside the ball, throw a fast ball and finish more palm out than palm up as on his fast ball.

When pitchers worry about the change-up getting hit, they throw it in the dirt. A change-up in the dirt has done nothing, because the batter is not going to swing at it because it has fastball trajectory and when it is in the dirt it is an obvious ball right out of the pitcher's hand. The pitcher who has a lot of two plane sink may get some swings and misses on the change-up down. In the early stages of the development of the change-up, pitchers should miss up in the strike zone. The change-up should be up rather than in the dirt. If it's up, the hitter will swing.

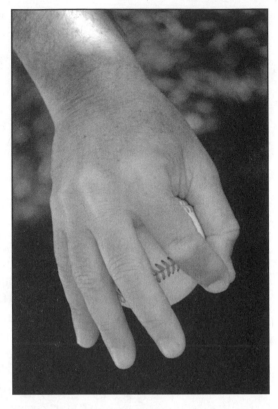

Photo 5-2

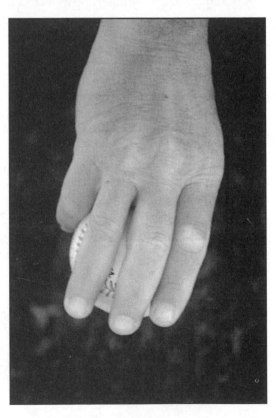

Photo 5-3

If the pitcher has done the job with the change-up in terms of change of speed and gets a hitter out in front, the hitter won't be able to hit the high change that well anyway. It's a fly ball or swing and miss because the pitcher has him out on his front foot. The pitcher has destroyed the batter's timing.

***Learning the Change-Up.*** The best way to learn how to throw the change-up is by throwing it:

1. Every day playing catch.
2. In bullpens by alternating it with the fast ball to carry fast ball arm speed over to the change-up.
3. Repetitively in pens to learn how to adjust the release point.
4. Most importantly, by throwing it in games.
5. In the off season pitch with the fast ball and change-up only. No breaking balls until the pitcher can throw the change-up for strikes at least 60% of the time. If the pitcher misses with the change-up, he has to come back with it until he throws a strike.

The key is for the pitcher to learn to trust his body to do the right thing. Other reminders for the pitcher:

◆ Use a loose deep grip,

◆ stay inside the ball with fast ball arm speed, and

◆ hit his target.

# CURVE BALL

The curve ball is a change-of-movement pitch. The goal is quick, late, down, or down-and-across action—a down-and-across or slurvey-type break that is three-quarters rather than straight down. A three-quarter curve ball gives the pitcher all 17 inches of the plate to work with and may buckle the hitter on his arm side by forcing him to give ground or flinch. The rotation is from one o'clock to seven o'clock or two o'clock to eight o'clock for a right-handed pitcher. This diagonal or tilted curve ball is hard for the hitters to pick up because the trajectory is more like the fast ball than the curve ball.

The downer or 12:00 o'clock to 6:00 o'clock curve ball tends to go up out of the pitcher's hand, making it easier for the hitter to read the trajectory. It is tough to get it called for a strike if it is the least bit loopy. However, the short, hard downer that has tight spin is exceptionally hard to pick up because it spins on the same axis as the fast ball. Also, it is equally effective to both left and right-handed hitters.

***Breaking Ball Grip.*** The breaking ball is gripped along the wide seam with the horseshoe facing the palm of the hand. The thumb and middle fingers should be on or

Photo 5-4

just behind the seams with space between the palm of the hand and the ball. (PHOTO 5-4) The index finger is placed loosely next to the middle finger and can be straight or bent. It can also be knuckled down on the ball to create the "spiked curve ball" grip. The bent or knuckle down position of the index finger puts emphasis on pressure from the middle finger. (PHOTO 5-5)

The thumb may be bent and tucked, but it should not be held too tight because that destroys wrist flexibility and looseness. This grip gives him four seams working against the air, and the more seams, the more spin and quickness to the break. The arm action and arm speed of the breaking ball is the same as the fast ball. The exception would be a slight inward turn of the hand at the power position. This puts the side of the hand at the hitter. He must be careful not to hook the wrist before or after the power position. (PHOTO 5-6) The wrist and the hand should be in a relatively straight line. Wrist hooking tightens the forearm and could cut down arm speed. However, with youth league pitchers, hooking the wrist on release may be easier on their arms because it retards the vigor-

Photo 5-5

Photo 5-6

Photo 5-7

ous arm snap associated with the breaking ball and prevents rotation in the elbow joint that can also cause physical problems.

Depending on the angle of the break, the fingers are pointed somewhere between nine and eleven o'clock. Ten and 11:00 produce a down-and-across break, and nine o'clock produces a straight down break.

***Throwing the Breaking Ball.*** A pitcher should throw the front outside (slurve) or the front of the ball (downer) with fast ball arm speed, emphasizing hand speed out in front. It is similar to throwing through a doorway. The hand works from the upper right-hand corner of the doorway to the lower left-hand corner.

The correct way to throw the breaking ball is with the elbow up and forward, with the focus on extension of the hand and throwing arm. (PHOTO 5-7) Even though the release of the breaking ball is somewhere by the ear, the thought process is to throw it nose out, with emphasis on extension and pulling from the bill of the cap down and in to the belt. The bill of the cap can be a reference point for the release point of the breaking ball. The line of sight of the eyes can also serve as a reference point for the breaking ball. It should be thrown somewhere between the eyes or through the far eye, depending upon the angle of break he wants.

Unlike the fast ball, which finishes outside the stride leg thigh, the breaking ball is finished more toward the waist. The breaking ball should be thrown from the middle of the plate out to the hitter on his arm side. It may be thrown back door, away from the hitter, towards his arm side. Care must be taken when he back doors the breaking ball not to throw it over the plate. It's easy for the hitter to pick it up as it comes right into his swing. The back door curve ball is effective if he has some diagonal tilt to his breaking ball because the offside hitter tends to give up on this pitch. It also can be wrapped around the back foot of the hitter, away from the arm side.

The true downer breaking ball, 12:6, is thrown over the middle of the plate. The pitcher must be careful not to get underneath with the elbow below the shoulder or throw the outside of this pitch because it ends up too flat with no downhill plane, and most hitters can really identify this pitch early. The flat curve ball stays on the plane of their swing.

# OTHER BREAKING PITCHES

Here are the techniques with advantages and disadvantages for throwing other breaking pitches—knuckle curve ball, split, cut fast ball and the knuckle ball.

***Knuckle Curve Ball.*** Another breaking ball that a pitcher can throw is the knuckle curve ball. This is for pitchers who don't have wrist flexibility and don't have a feel for a breaking ball. This falls in the same category as the split. The pitcher holds the ball with the knuckles or nails of the index and middle fingers on or just across the wide seams. It's thrown like the four-seam fast ball.  The emphasis is on a strong wrist snap at release. It has fast ball arm speed and fast ball trajectory because it's thrown with a knuckle ball grip. The ball loses spin and goes down hard at the end. It's a tough pitch to control, but for a pitcher who doesn't have feel for the breaking ball, the knuckle curve ball is a viable pitch. He can use one or two fingers. If he throws the top of the ball, he will get the tumbling action.

***Split.*** The other option is the split. It acts similar to the knuckle curve ball but has fast ball trajectory. There is no up and down action. A pitcher has to experiment to get the proper grip and can start by throwing the two seam with the seam fast ball grip and gradually keep spreading his fingers. He throws the split like his fast ball and emphasizes staying over the ball with his fingers and resist or retard the natural pronation at release. If the pitch has too much spin and doesn't break down hard at the end, the ball is not wedged deep enough between the fingers. If it knuckles and floats up to the plate, then it is wedged too deep. If this happens, the finger spread should be narrowed or the ball should be moved out toward the finger tips.

The pitcher needs to have the thumb off to the side to get down action, without a lot of push from the thumb. (PHOTO 5-8) Some pitchers will push with their thumb slightly against left-handed hitters (RHP) to get more down and away action. Even though the speed is less than the fast ball, it gives quick late and down break from both the split and the knuckle curve.

***Cut Fast Ball.*** Before young pitchers begin to use the split or knuckle curve ball, have them try to throw a cut fast ball (short slider) because the chance of throwing it for strikes is better. The pitcher throws the top outside of the ball with a fast ball or slightly off center grip.

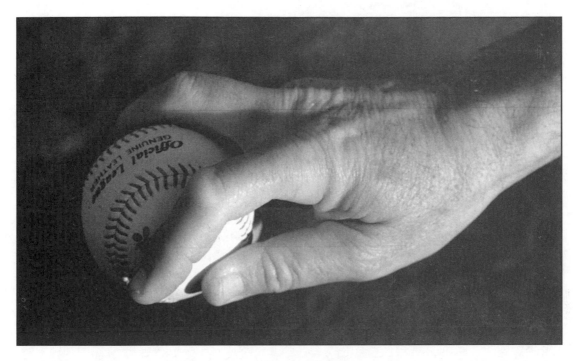

Photo 5-8

There are a couple of grip options. He can use his four seam fast ball grip with the horseshoe out and just work off the outside of the ball closer to the "c" of the horseshoe, or he can come off the two seams and turn his fingers to the right (RHP), and run his index finger right on the seam. (PHOTO 5-9) When he throws the cutter, he tries to work his fingers over the ball on release. This creates a short down-and-across break. The ball comes off the first joint of his index finger and middle finger. The pitchers who have problems with the cutter or slider come around the ball because they are trying to make the ball break too much.

The short slider is a put away pitch that is thrown down and away from a right-handed hitter (from a RHP) and up and in to a left-handed hitter (RHP) or down at the left-handed hitter's back foot. It is thrown with a short down and across break (3"- 4".) The pitcher can throw a longer breaking slider as a "get it in there" pitch. The long slider has an earlier longer break and is thrown on a less downhill plane than the short slider. On the long slider the pitcher is working more to the outside of

Photo 5-9

the ball with his fingers and throwing the pitch at the hitter and having it end up over the plate. He generally throws this pitch early in the count with a RHP against a RHH, but he can occasionally throw it off the plate to a LHH (RHP) and have it break on the corner (back door).

Most pitchers either throw a curve ball or a slider. Generally if they try to use both they'll end up with two mediocre pitches because they don't have enough game or practice time to work on both. The curve ball and the slider release points overlap which will produce one average or below average pitch. Those few pitchers who throw both the curve ball and slider generally throw the curve to LHH (RHP) and the slider to RHH.

*The Knuckle Ball.* A lot of young people like to throw the knuckle ball. They are either knuckle ball pitchers or they're not, throwing all knuckle balls or none at all. Young players with decent arms should learn how to throw the fast ball, breaking ball, and change-up. Then as they move up, if they aren't accomplishing what they need, they can try to trick people and use the knuckle ball. The knuckle ball is thrown with a stiff wrist and a low elbow and is pushed to the plate. This is not for young arms. The knuckle ball is an adjustment for not being able to get hitters out with the other three pitches.

# THE PITCHING PLAN

The pitching plan is a strategy to get hitters out. It is a specific pattern of pitching that is adjusted to the individual abilities of every pitcher and the situation. Much of this plan has been developed in conversations with Don Rowe, Pitching Coach of the Milwaukee Brewers.

*Strikes Early in the Count.* The number one goal is to throw the first or second pitch for a strike. Too much emphasis on first pitch strikes tends to put excessive pressure on that first pitch and leads to low quality strikes and a high percentage of balls. The goal of a first or second pitch strike keeps the pitchers in a better comfort zone. Also, the 0-0 count batting average of the big leaguers is near 300. The pitcher with two pitches at command for strikes on the first or second pitch, is in a more advantageous position. It comes down to throwing his highest percentage strike pitch or pitches to his highest percentage location on the first or second pitch. The situation will dictate variation in this plan. Obviously with runners on second and third (RHP) and a good left handed hitter at bat, but a weaker right-handed hitter coming up will dictate the situation changes in the plan. The general plan is always open for adjustment.

*The 1-1 Pitch.* The second part of this plan is dealing with the 1-1 pitch. The most important pitch in baseball is the 1-1 pitch because the difference between batting average between two and one (.290) and one and two (.180) is 110 points if you take all the big leaguers over the course of a season. The pitcher has to throw that pitch for a strike and needs to pay attention to that 1-1 pitch in terms of location and type of pitch to give the best chance possible to throw that 1-1 pitch for a strike. Every pitch is important because the game is played one pitch at a time, but the difference in offensive productivity between 2 & 1 and 1 & 2 is large. It is imperative to throw two of the first three pitches for a strike.

**The 0-2 and 2-0 Pitch.** The third part of the plan deals with the 0-2 and 2-0 counts. When he is behind in the count (1-0, 2-0, 2-1, 3-1, 3-0) he should box the next pitch. He should throw his highest percentage strike pitch on a downhill plane, over the middle of the plate, in an area above the knees to the waist. More advanced pitchers will go mid-thigh to knees. The more proficient pitchers can half-box in these situations and throw the ball knees to waist or mid-thighs, in and out, and not just over the middle. The 0-1 count is a prime time to half-box for some pitchers.

**Boxing and Tilting.** The boxing technique can be used on any count based on the abilities of the pitcher, command stuff, and situations. When the count is 0-2 or 0-1 for some pitchers, he should tilt. This involves going up and in on the hitter and then down and away. The up and in pitch should be a fast ball thrown at the hitter's hands just below his front elbow. In general he wants to throw this pitch with four seams, but it could be thrown along the narrow seams and have it run into the hitter on his arm side or back over the inside corner to a hitter away from his arm side. The slider could also be used away from his arm side to get the ball in on the hands. This up and in pitch can be thrown off the plate to move the hitter's feet. This takes the hitter out of his comfort zone. It can also be thrown on the inside corner for a strike. The hitter, pitcher, and situation will determine whether he should try to throw this up and in pitch for a strike or not.

The second part of the tilt technique is to throw the ball down and away for a strike. When thrown to the hitter on his arm side, this can be a four-seam fast ball or a two-seam fast ball that tails back on the corner, or a breaking ball. This is difficult because it's hard to get tailing action away from his arm side. When thrown to the hitter away from his arm side, (right-handed pitcher versus left-handed hitter), this pitch can be a two or a four-seam fast ball, a change-up that tails, or occasionally, a back door breaking ball, which is a breaking ball that starts off the plate and breaks on the corner. Hitters tend to give up on this pitch but care must be taken so that the pitch does not break over the middle of the plate.

Tilting, especially when a pitcher can establish the hand-high inside corner of the plate for strikes, makes the hitters more inside conscious and gives the pitcher the entire 17" of the plate to work with. In reality if he can command the inside and the outside of the plate, he has 22" of plate because the ball's diameter is 2-1/2", and adding that in and out to the 17" plate makes 22". Also, the umpires will add width to the plate for pitchers who work fast and throw lots of strikes.

The pitcher can also reverse the tilt and start low and away and then go up and in for strikes. This keeps the hitters from gearing in to one pattern. Another possibility in the 0-1, 0-2 situation is to double up on pitches, throwing two in a row to the same spot to keep the hitters from adjusting to the tilt pattern.

**Doubling.** Doubling up is a technique that keeps the hitter from anticipating a tilt pattern. Many experienced hitters dive into the plate after a pitcher goes in on them. To combat this, the pitcher can double up and throw consecutive pitches in on the hitter. The first may be in off the plate, and the second for a strike. It is important to throw in off the plate to "move the hitter's feet" and take them out of their comfort zone. The pitcher's goal is to give the hitter an "uncomfortable at bat." For hitters away from his throwing arm side, right-handed pitcher versus left-handed hitter, the pitcher can go in off the plate with a fast ball and then wrap a breaking ball around a hitter's back foot.

Another variation of this two-pitch put away is working up and down to cause an eye switch, which keeps the hitter from gearing in to the ball down only. This is especially effective for pitchers who throw a down breaking curve ball or a split that goes down. Hitters will swing at fast balls up, thinking that they are downer curve balls or splits because the rotation is on the same axis. The curve is 12:6 and fast ball 6:12. The downer curve ball starts high and ends up down in the strike zone. The hitters swing at fast balls up thinking that they are curve balls or splits that are about to break down into the zone.

**One Pitch Put Away.** The final technique in the pitching plan is the one pitch put away. This is the two-strike pitch with which the pitcher is going to finish off the hitter. The put away pitch is a fine strike or a high pitch in the hitter's chase zone. The fine strike with the fast ball can be in on the hitter's hands, a four-seam fast ball right at the hitter's hands, or a two-seam fast ball that runs on in the hitter's hands, or knee-high pitch on the black of the plate away. The pitcher throws this pitch four-seams away from his arm side and either two or four-seam on his arm side.

The chase zone fast ball is a four-seam fast ball up out over the plate or up and away from the hitter. This "up-the-ladder" pitch is especially good against hitters who are trying to lift the ball but chase balls up in the zone. The put away breaking ball is thrown low and away for a strike and the chase zone breaking ball is thrown in the dirt. The one-pitch put away can be the hitter's pitch that's just out of his effective hitting zone. Generally speaking, this is the 0-2 pitch or 1-2 pitch.

The pitcher should treat the 2-2 pitch like a 3-2 pitch. He should be able to throw the same pitch 2-2 as he would throw 3-2. Young pitchers try to trick hitters 2-2 by throwing too fine or throwing breaking balls, then they struggle to throw strikes on 3-2, and they rarely throw the breaking ball.

**Pitch Counts.** The overall pitching plan goal is to get the hitter out on as few pitches as possible. The more pitches the hitter sees, the more information goes into his computer, and the fewer innings any pitcher will be effective. Control really drops off after 16 pitches in an inning. The ideal is to average less than four pitches per hitter. A notable goal would be "on or out in three pitches."

Young pitchers with suspect command can't waste pitches. They tend to give the hitters too much credit anyway. These pitchers may have to box all their pitches. As you progressively work through their bullpens, you work finer and finer until they develop better control by forcing them to have more specific, smaller targets. The best hitters fail seven out of ten at bats. This means that strikes, even low quality strikes get most hitters out.

***Pitcher's Strengths.*** In critical situations a pitcher should go with the pitcher's strength against the hitter's strength. For example, the pitcher's and the hitter's strength is the low fast ball. If the pitcher can throw his low fast ball a little lower than the hitter's effective hitting zone, chances are he'll get that hitter out. If he doesn't do this, the tendency is to get behind the hitter with his second or third pitches and then the hitter has count leverage and gets his pitch anyway and then hits it. The hitter who doesn't have count leverage and gets the pitch in his location is out much of the time anyway, especially if the pitcher has a good downhill plane to the plate.

There is no defense against the base on balls. It ensures 100% occupancy of first base. Sixty three percent of all fairly hit balls in the big leagues are outs. Again, the score, inning, outs, hitter, base runners, and on-deck hitter will dictate how the pitcher will approach each hitter. In general, though, the more the pitcher pitches around people and the more total runs you give up, the more big innings he creates.

***Side Work.*** Side work is critical in developing mastery of the pitching plan. Each hurler must practice boxing, tilting, and put always. Having a hitter stand in is also beneficial, especially for the younger pitchers. The more experienced pitcher is zeroed in visually on the inside of the glove or whatever his target is. The young pitchers get distracted by the hitter, so having the hitter stand in gives the young guy a chance to work on not being distracted. A good baseball and the catcher in full gear is also a must.

## IDENTIFYING HITTERS AND ATTACKING THEIR WEAKNESSES

The ability to identify hitter's strengths and weaknesses can give the pitcher an important edge. Here are six prime opportunities to assess hitters before the pitch:

1. ***Study batting statistics.*** The hitters attempting to steal the most bases are usually the best runners and attempt to bunt for a base hit more often. In general, these hitters have less power and pull fewer balls. Weaker hitters usually have the lowest batting averages. Batting statistics on fast balls versus off speed pitches, two strikes and less than two strikes, runners in scoring position versus no one on, and right handed pitchers versus left handed pitches will also help the pitcher attack the hitter. Hitters who have a lot of strike outs usually have more power, swing at the first pitch, and chase balls in the dirt and fast balls up. Hitters who have lots of walks take more pitches and don't swing at the first pitch as often.

2. ***Look at scouting charts.*** More than anything, they tell the pitcher where the ball will be hit in certain situations. It allows him to be aware of positioning so he can pitch accordingly. Our number one positioning rule is to position the pitcher first. The scouting chart should provide hard and soft contact zones by pitch count and situation to help the pitcher establish a pitching plan.

3. ***Observe early batting practice.*** This reveals hitters who are struggling. Regular batting practice helps identify stances and swings and it may give some leads on strong and weak zones. The short game and execution type hitters will usually identify themselves by their focus or extra work in those areas.

4. ***Watch the hitters during the game.*** This is the best venue for assessing hitters. The pitcher should compare his command with the pitcher who is pitching so he can develop a realistic approach based on his skills. In particular, the pitcher should observe the hitter's position relative to the plate—on the plate, off the plate, back in the box, up in the box, open stance, square stance, or closed stance.

   Next he should watch the hitter's first movement—straight in, or out. This will help him establish potential weaknesses in and out. (Specifics are covered later in this section).

   The pitcher should also look for strong and weak hitting zones by pitch, chase zones, first pitch tendencies, out pitches, situational adjustments (two strikes and less than two strikes), strike out candidates, and match ups (right or left handed hitters and hitters he matches up well against and those hitters he doesn't). He should note their position in the batting order. For example, the one, two, and nine hitters usually run better, have less power, and bunt more. The four, five, and six hitters tend to have more power, pull more, and be more aggressive. The seven and eight hitters are often the weaker hitters. Obviously this changes from team to team and is intended only as a starting point to prepare the pitcher for his outing.

5. ***Watch the arc of the bat of the hitter in the on deck circle.*** If he uppercuts, he could be a low ball hitter. If he swings down, he may be a high ball hitter. If he has a long arc, his bat may be slow; a short arc may show bat speed. If he is a nervous type, he may be overly aggressive and undisciplined.

6. ***View videotapes.*** The pitcher who has the luxury of seeing, before pitching, the hitters he will face can really break down their swings. Caution him not to over analyze or give hitters too much credit and pitch them too carefully. Some pitchers, after seeing videos of good hitters, pitch too fine and attack the hitters with their secondary pitches. The key is for the pitcher to get hitters out with his strengths and attack hitters' weaknesses when he is ahead as long as he isn't going away from his strengths.

The chart, Pitching Approach Guidelines in Figure 5-1, presents general guidelines based on the hitter's swing or stance. It is by no means an absolute formula to get hitters out. Hitters will make adjustments. This is especially true when they are continually exploited in a particular way. Pitchers also need to be sensitive to these adjustments, which can occur from one game to another or from one at bat to the next. The chart identifies hitter's stances and swing characteristics along with some general approaches to getting those hitters out. When in doubt of how to attack a hitter, the pitcher should start the hitter away and work off the hitter's reaction to that pitch. This is especially true late in a close game.

## Figure 5-1: PITCHING APPROACH GUIDELINES

| CHARACTERISTIC | APPROACH |
|---|---|
| Upper cutter (Lift to swing) | 1) Fast balls up<br>2) Balls down below the solid contact zone and within the chase zone<br>3) Away |
| Extreme down arc (chop swing) | 1) Down<br>2) Off speed |
| Slow bat | 1) Hard stuff inside |
| Pulling out    (Stride away from plate)<br>or (opens front shoulder and hip prematurely) | 1) Away, especially off speed pitches |
| Over swinging | 1) Off speed, balls in the chase zone |
| Dives into the plate<br>(Strides towards the plate) | 1) Hard stuff inside<br>2) Off speed away and play opposite |
| Pulls head before contact | 1) Away, especially with off speed pitches |
| Commits weight to front foot on stride | 1) Off speed pitches<br>2) Fast balls up |
| Long swing (sweeps bat) | 1) Hard stuff in on the hands |
| Inside out swing | 1) Down and in<br>2) Pitch away and play opposite |
| Takes a lot of pitches | 1) Strikes |
| Free swinger with undisciplined strike zone | 1) Off speed in chase zone<br>2) Fast balls in chase zone |
| Pull hitter | 1) Fast balls in off the plate<br>2) Off speed pitches away |
| Opposite field hitter | 1) Hard in<br>2) Away and play opposite |
| **STANCE CHARACTERISTICS** | |
| Flat bat | 1) Down |
| High hands and or high back elbow | 1) Hard inside, especially up |
| Deep crouch | 1) Up |
| Upright with stiff legs | 1) Down |

| STANCE CHARACTERISTICS *(continued)* | |
|---|---|
| Bat wrapped behind head | 1) Hard stuff inside<br>2) Breaking balls away |
| Close to the plate | 1) Fast balls inside<br>2) Away if this hitter has bat speed (dependent on first move action after pitch) |
| Off of the plate | 1) Away if the hitter does not dive into the plate with the stride - play opposite<br>2) Inside if the hitter shows a slow bat |
| Hands close to the body (back elbow not visible to the pitcher) | 1) Jam |
| Open stance | 1) Away if he strides away from the plate<br>2) Inside if he strides towards the plate (distance from the plate also is a factor) |
| Closed stance | 1) Away if he strides away from the plate<br>2) Inside if he strides towards the plate (distance from the plate also is a factor) |
| Hands way away from the body | 1) Jam |
| Narrow based stance (feet close together) | 1) Off speed<br>2) Fast balls up |

# WARMING UP

How a pitcher warms up to get ready to pitch in a game is critical. He needs to have a specific set routine, adjustable to climate and how he feels on that day. In general, pitchers warm up too early, throw too many pitches, and try to be perfect in the pen. Emphasis in the bullpen is on hitting the target and getting mind and body ready to pitch. There is no great connection between good or bad pregame bullpens and good or bad games. This is especially true with experienced pitchers. Keep pregame instruction to a minimum.

The following sample warm up plan is summarized in Figure 5-2 "Check-list for Warmup" on page 118. You may want to make copies for pitchers and other coaches on the team. The person in charge of bullpen equipment will find Figure 5-3 helpful too.

Photo 5-10

***Sample Warm-Up Plan.*** The pitcher should start by jogging until he breaks a sweat, 3-5 minutes, depending on heat and humidity. Then he goes through his stretching routine. Before he starts throwing he should go through 10 reps of light resistance with surgical tubing for each of these:

1. arm circles (PHOTO 5-10)
2. internal rotation (PHOTO 5-11)
3. external rotation (PHOTO 5-12)
4. biceps curls (PHOTO 5-13)
5. triceps extension (PHOTO 5-14)
6. front raise (PHOTO 5-15)
7. side raise (PHOTO 5-16)
8. bent over raise (PHOTO 5-17)

These exercises increase the blood flow to the pitching muscles and reduce the number of warmup pitches needed in

Photo 5-11

Photo 5-12

Photo 5-13

Photo 5-14

Photo 5-15                    Photo 5-16

Photo 5-17

Figure 5-2:  **CHECKLIST FOR WARM-UP**

☐  Jog 3-5 minutes.

☐  Stretch.

☐  Surgical tubing.

☐  Long toss, flat ground, 10-15 at approximately 120 feet.

☐  Four-seam fast ball out of balance position.

☐  Two-seam fast ball across, in and out, windup, stretch.

☐  Two-seam fast ball with in and out, windup, and stretch.

☐  Four-seam fast ball in and out windup and stretch.

☐  Catcher sideways two or four-seam fast ball at hands.

☐  Catcher right-hand side sideways, throw fast ball at front shoulder windup.

☐  Catcher right-hand side sideways two or four-seam fast ball at hands. Stretch.

☐  Catcher left-hand side, sideways throwing the fast ball at front shoulder in the stretch.

☐  Balance position box three change-up.

☐  Box fast ball and change up windup and stretch.

☐  Bring catcher to 30 feet and spin Breaking Ball.

☐  Go behind mound and spin Breaking Ball out of stretch.

☐  Move catcher back and throw Breaking Ball out of balance position.

☐  Throw Breaking Ball out of the windup and stretch.

☐  Tilt set versus right-hand hitters.

☐  Tilt set versus left-hand hitters.

☐  Put away versus right and left-hand hitters.

☐  Pitch out, modified pitch out and intentional BB to each side.

Figure 5-3:  **CHECKLIST FOR BULLPEN EQUIPMENT**

❑  Surgical tubing

❑  Pitcher's ball bag for playing catch

❑  Game balls-minimum four

❑  Catcher in full gear and a stander with a helmet

❑  Towels

❑  Rosin bag

❑  Spike cleaner for wet days

❑  A 60' 6" measuring tape

the pen. Keep warm up pitches under 40. The fewer pitches the pitcher throws in the pen, the more he has left for the game. After the tubing, the pitcher should play long catch on flat ground. The trajectory of this long catch, up to 120 feet, is the same as the trajectory of the pitch. The pitcher can crow hop or step behind his stride foot or a combination of the two before he throws. This will keep his front shoulder from flying open. The long catch will take about three minutes, 10-15 throws.

Don't count these into the total warmup count. Then the pitcher goes to the bullpen and throws three or four four-seam fast balls away from his arm side from the rubber and from the balance position to the catcher in full gear in the up or down position. The focus is on separating the hands before gliding to the plate. Then he throws a two-seam across the seam fast ball in and out, a two-seam with the seam fast ball in and out, and a four-seam fast ball in and out, alternating windup and stretch with each pitch. The goal is to define the outer limits of the strike zone.

Have the catcher standing sideways in the right-hand batter's box and hold his glove up, hands high on the inside corners. The pitcher throws a two or four-seam fast ball to the glove and then a four-seam at the catcher's front shoulder. Next he does the same to the catcher in the left-hand hitter's box, mixing windup and stretch throughout.

Next the pitcher boxes (knees to waist) three change-ups out of the balance position, then alternates boxing four seam fastball and change 2-4 pitches. Then he brings the catcher up to approximately 30 feet in the down position and spins his breaking ball from the no-stride position. Don't count these pitches. Next he moves behind the mound and works out of the stretch, steps uphill and throws his breaking ball. This forces him to release the breaking ball more in front on a downhill plane. Again, don't count these.

Now move the catcher back to the 60' 6". Try to have a hitter stand in. The pitcher throws three breaking balls out of the balance position, two breaking balls out of the windup, and two out of stretch. He finishes the warmup by tilting to a right-hand and left-hand hitter (working from up and in to low and out) and throwing a couple of put away pitches. The final pitches are a pitch out, modified pitch out, and an intentional walk pitch to each side, none of which count in the total number.

It is best to warm up the same direction as the mound on the field. However it's not a huge factor unless it's really windy. The pitcher can warm up on the mound and finish up off the flat ground to get used to pitching with or against the wind or with a cross wind to especially assess the effect it's going to have on his breaking ball. Make sure the catcher is in full gear and that you have a couple of good balls for the pen. The distance must be correct. Have a 60' 6" tape ready, have a stander available, and a home plate. Some people like to have "string targets" in their pen. Modify the warmup plan to meet each pitcher's needs. However, each pitcher should know the warmup plan and monitor the number of pitches he throws. If a pitcher needs more pitches to warm up, it may be an early warning of some arm problems.

***After Warm-Up.*** After the pitcher warms up, give him enough time to towel off and rest before he pitches. Three or four minutes is usually sufficient. If he's a guy who really sweats, let him change into a dry shirt then or sometime during the game when he stops sweating.

Before an inning starts, the pitcher should throw all his pitches at least once, and the last pitch out of the stretch. Demand quality pitches between innings. Don't allow him to just flip it up there. Make him stay close to five pitches between innings because those pitches count against his total available.

When he's in the dugout between innings, the pitcher should stay off his feet, wear a coat if necessary, towel off, and replace lost fluids. He should sit with the catcher, review the last inning, plan for the next one, and use the charts when necessary. This also keeps him from experiencing emotional highs and lows of the offensive part of the game. He needs to focus on pitching. Obviously, if your pitcher is in your line-up, this applies only to the innings when he doesn't hit.

**Rough First Innings.** Pitchers who always have rough first innings, should do the warm up twice. Make them warm up and then sit down for about five minutes and then throw again before the first inning so it's almost like having pitched the first inning. It's a mental thing more than anything else. Usually it happens because a pitcher has convinced himself that he always has a tough first inning, and it becomes a self-fulfilling prophecy. Warming up twice is one way of psychologically creating the second inning.

Some first inning reminders:

◆ Have a disaster plan for the first inning.

◆ Don't give up unnecessary runs.

◆ Call pitches that are your pitcher's strengths.

◆ Don't get stuck on one pitch if it's not in the strike zone.

◆ Keep it simple.

The goal is to get out of the first inning without giving up unnecessary runs.

**Warming Up Relievers.** Relievers need to warm up in a hurry. They don't have the luxury of being able to throw 30+ pitches and take their time. Sometimes the game gets out of hand in a hurry and a reliever has to play quick catch.

Don't let them start with a windup—it takes too long. The reliever should get two of his pitches game-ready; one, if there's not time. Long and short relievers should loosen up a little bit to get the kinks out before the game and during if necessary to be prepared. Some young players warm up too much and throw too many pitches down in the bullpen.

They need to pay attention to the game and know how to warm up rapidly. A reliever should stretch every inning to avoid sitting around for five or six innings and having to warm up without being stretched out. A reliever can jog a little and stretch every inning but not necessarily do any throwing. He can also shadow his throwing so he's ready to go. If he does these things, he should be able to get ready in two hitters.

Try to give your relievers a general idea of their role and how you will use them on a particular day. Anytime you get a guy up three times, either get him in the game or don't use him on that day. It is important to keep count of how many pitches relievers throw in the pen and the effort level, even if they don't throw in the game.

Many pitchers press when they are pitching, and people are warming up behind them. They have to learn to focus on the game pitch by pitch and to ignore those things they can't control.

Give relieved pitchers a choice: Let them wait for the reliever to come out and hand the reliever the ball or hand the ball to the coach and jog off the field. If they need it, let them take some time to sit down and reflect and then get treatment as soon as possible. Sometimes pitchers get frustrated when they get relieved and blow off their stretching and treatment by the trainer. Try to prevent this by reminding pitchers that once they're done pitching on that day, they are starting to prepare for the next outing.

## FIELDING TECHNIQUES FOR THE PITCHER

A pitcher should be effective to the plate and then become a fielder. He must not sacrifice effectiveness to the plate: Velocity, location, and movement are most important. Landing in a good fielding position is also important, but secondary to the other three factors. After he finishes the pitch, he can square up to the hitter.

When the pitcher fields a ball, he becomes an infielder. This calls for short-arm throwing. He takes the ball out of the top of the glove to reach the power position. He should take the ball out of his shirt pocket to throw to help develop a quick release, which he needs to throw out good runners. This is an adjustment for most pitchers because most pitching requires longer and slower arm action.

***Come Backers.*** The pitcher should expect every low, and especially low and away, fast ball to be hit back to him. If it is hit hard at him or to his left, he should jog to first base and dart it to the first baseman rather than stop and wait for the first baseman to reach first. This leads to fewer errant throws because pitchers are used to rhythm throwing and don't function well from a dead stop at a short distance. This technique also provides for better rhythm and greatly cuts the distance of the throw. The throw can be underhanded to the first baseman.

If the ball is hit a short distance to the pitcher's right, he should keep his hands together and shuffle until the first baseman arrives at first. If the ball is hit way to his right or softly in front of him, he should take short, choppy, controlled steps going after the ball—-especially on wet days when the footing is not good. The pitcher should field these short balls with the instep of his pivot foot perpendicular to the direction of the throw.

On slowly hit balls, especially toward the third base line, the pitcher has to get it and throw it in one movement—no crow hops, no wasted movement. On slower runners, he may have time to take a little crow hop or shuffle step. This is pre-pitch preparation—he knows his runners.

The pitcher fields the ball with his glove whenever possible. If the ball has stopped rolling, he should grab it from the top rather than try to pick it up from the side or underneath. He should call loud and clear for all balls he is going to field—"Ball! Ball!" or "I got it!"

Both the hard come backer to the first base side and the short ball have to be over-practiced. Soft rag balls or Incrediballs are excellent for hard come-backers, providing for good reaction time work without the risk of injury. Short balls can be practiced by setting a number of balls down the third base line in front of home plate and down the first base line. The pitcher should step inside as he fields this one so he doesn't end up throwing through or over the runner.

Line your pitchers up on the mound, and one by one have them shadow a pitch, break hard, but under control to one of these balls, and make the play to first. This can also be done with a short toss to a fungo man which forces the pitcher to read and react to short balls off the bat.

On come-backers with a runner on first, runners on first and second, or first and third (one out, and certain zero out situations), pitchers should throw to second base. Young pitchers have to be constantly reminded to throw to second with runners on first and second before they pitch because they tend to want to throw to third. It's approximately a 35-foot shorter double play when they go via second base.

In most cases, the shortstop will be covering second unless the ball is to the pitcher's right, in which case the shortstop will have a break for the ball. When the shortstop is toward third base and the second baseman is up the middle, the second baseman will take the feed.

When the pitcher is throwing to a middle infielder, he should lead the shortstop to the base, and if the second baseman is covering, throw it straight to the second base bag after the second baseman arrives at the base. Hopefully, the second baseman and shortstop are not both breaking for the base at the same time. The middle infielder who is not covering should stop, kneel down, and point to the second base.

The pitcher should know who is covering before the pitch. When he has the time, he should catch the come backer in a sideways position with his momentum moving toward second, much like an infielder relaying a throw from an outfielder. He should throw the ball chest high over the base. Because he's an infielder, he should shorten his throw by taking the ball up out of the glove. When the ball is hit hard, and he doesn't have the time to take it sideways in the step-catch-throw mode, he just turns and throws.

There will be times when he fields a hard come backer and the infielder is late covering. He should keep his hands together at his chest under his chin, shuffle toward second and throw when the infielder arrives at second. This prevents him from separating his hands too early and being out of rhythm because he started, stopped, and then restarted his throw.

A good drill to practice come-backers to second is to have a pitcher in the middle of two fungo men and a catcher for each fungo man. It starts with a fungo to the pitcher, who catches it sideways, and wheels and throws to the catcher for the fungo man behind the pitcher. Just as the pitcher releases the ball to the catcher behind him, the fungo man behind him hits another come backer, and the process continues.

Work on come backers to home and with runners on first and third, none out, in a close game. Later in a close game, the pitcher reads the runner on third base. If he goes, the pitcher either has to run at him or go home. If he does not run when the pitcher checks him, the pitcher throws to first or second, depending on the situation, speed of the runners, and speed of the batted ball.

**Pop-Ups.** Pitchers should go after pop-ups until they are called by an infielder. In our system, the pitcher has priority over the catcher, but the pitcher should not run the catcher off a ball that he is camped underneath. Too often, pitchers vacate the mound when the ball goes off the bat and nobody catches the ball. This is especially true on low pops and pops right on the mound. If two infielders are simultaneously calling for the ball hit near the mound and a collision is imminent, call the position of the infielder you want to catch the ball and grab the other one.

**Covering First Base.** Encourage the first baseman to get as many balls as he can on the right side of the diamond. The pitcher should bounce off the mound toward first on any balls hit to his left with the exception of the infield in. No runner ever got tagged out running by the mound.

For balls hit to the first base side when the pitcher is covering first base, have the pitcher tell the first baseman when he's ready for the ball. He can say either, "Now," or "Ball, ball," so that he receives the ball before he gets to the base. He should catch the ball, look up at the base, and step on the base. As soon as he hits the base, he bounces off to the inside, gets the ball up out of his glove, and gets ready to make another play. The first baseman should tell the pitcher to turn around so that he doesn't run down the line or run across the line.

The slower the ball is hit and the further it is hit away from first base, the more direct route the pitcher has to take to first base. The closer it is hit to first base, the more of a loop he can take where he runs parallel to the first base line. In general, he should not run to the cut of the grass up the first base line.

If the ball is hit to the second baseman and the first baseman goes for it, the pitcher makes a big loop so his shoulders are square with the infielder making the throw. This facilitates catching the ball. When he runs straight to the base and the ball is coming from the second baseman, the angle is too critical for him to catch the ball consistently.

For any ball hit slowly to his left that he fields as a pitcher, he should assume that the first baseman is going for it, too. The pitcher is going to have to intercept it and take it all the way to the base. He can't stop and look for the first baseman to be there to accept the throw.

For any ball hit to the pitcher's left that he can't get, he should call, "Take it." The first baseman also needs to know when the pitcher has a ball that's hit to his left. If it's hit down the first base line, the pitcher has to let the first baseman know he's got the ball. The pitcher should always use a verbal in that situation. He should yell "Ball, ball," or "I've got it," so the first baseman knows to cover first.

The pitcher should never trail or chase the ball when it's hit to his left. He should just continue to the base to receive the throw from the first or second baseman. When the pitcher practices covering first, always include the second baseman in the drill.

***Backing Up Bases.*** The pitcher has a place to go on every play:

◆ With a runner on second and any number of outs, he must break to back up first base on all infield ground balls, especially those hit to the second baseman. The catcher must stay at home, and many times the second baseman cannot get there. Care must be taken not to obstruct the batter-runner going from home to first.

◆ On base hits with no one on base, or base hits with a runner on third base, the pitcher must back up second base.

◆ On fly balls with a runner on third, or a base hit with a runner on second, the pitcher must back up home plate with his back against the backstop. This is always true when backing up a base. He should get as much depth as possible. This means the pitcher must run hard. After he has given up a hit or is about to give up a run, many times a pitcher may fail to hustle in backing up a base.

◆ With a runner on first and a base hit, the pitcher will back up third base.

◆ On an extra base hit with a runner on first, first and second, or the bases loaded, a base hit with runners on first and second or the bases loaded, or a fly ball to the outfield with runners on second and third or the bases loaded, the pitcher will break to a halfway position between third and home to react to the direction of the throw. He should keep his head on a swivel and watch the outfielder.

◆ Ground ball base hits to the right side are especially difficult because the pitcher breaks to cover first base first, then he must put the brakes on and sprint to his backup position.

◆ On an attempted stolen base of second base, the pitcher must break to back up third base in case the catcher's throw ends up in center field. In all backup situations, pitchers must have their heads on a swivel to follow the action of the ball to ensure that they will be in the proper position.

All backups need to be practiced. You can do this in a team situation with or without live runners and a coach fungoing. Backups can also be practiced with pitchers only breaking off a mound and reacting to a coach setting the situation. Enhance this drill by putting a coach by the mound and having the pitcher break between third and home while looking back at the coach, reacting to his hand signal, and then backing up third or home.

***Covering Home Plate.*** The pitcher's first job in covering home plate is to direct the catcher to the ball. The pitcher should yell "front," "back," "feet," "one," or "three" to tell the catcher which side it's on rather than saying left or right, because sometimes there's confusion as to whose left and whose right. Also, he should point to the ball in case the catcher does not hear him. Next, he should get to the plate. He should stay out of the base line to avoid injury and protect his legs. He tags straight down and shows the umpire the ball. When he shows the umpire the ball, he's making an out sign—he's giving a subliminal message to that umpire. He's got to sell the tag.

# CONTROLLING A KNOWN FIELDING SITUATION

On intentional walks, the pitcher must make sure before he pitches that the catcher has both feet in the catcher's box. The pitcher should come up to a definite stop, check the runner, and throw a firm, four-seam fast ball, chest high, to the opposite batter's box. This has to be practiced so that pitchers are conditioned to throw the ball with confidence and trust rather than just pushing it up to the plate. Have your pitcher practice this situation every time he finishes up in the bull pen during his warm-up before the game.

# HOLDING RUNNERS ON BASE AND IDENTIFYING RUNNING SITUATIONS

A key to stopping the running game is to identify running situations. The first clue is to identify the players who have speed. This is not a real problem if you have played the team before. If you have not seen the team play, check the stat sheet for stolen bases and stolen bases attempted. If you do not have access to stats, then you can expect the center fielder, shortstop, and second baseman to be the best runners. The same goes for the one, two, and nine hitters.

Watch batting practice. Which players work extra on their base hit bunt technique? They tend to be better runners. Watch infield and batting practice to identify the players who run without effort and the ones with first step quickness. Once you have identified the runners and non-runners, you have to identify the situation in which both will run.

The plus-runners like to run early in the count, first or second pitch, especially with two outs, and most always run with three balls on the hitter. They will run more in close games.

Even guys with poor running ability will attempt to steal in certain situations. Poor runners will run mostly with three balls on the hitter (with the emphasis on three balls and two strikes). Poor runners will run in 2-2, two-out situations when the pitcher is throwing a high percentage of strikes on that count. The poor runners try to pick breaking ball counts to run on. (The time difference between a fastball and a breaking ball is one one-hundredth of a second for each mile per hour. An 85 mph fastball is 1.2 to home and a 65 mph breaking ball is 1.4 to home.) The poor runners will delay steal more, especially with left-handed hitters up.

***Long Hold and Step Off.*** One technique to predict whether a runner is going to steal on a pitch is the long hold and step off. The pitcher should hold it long enough to create tension in the base runner, but not long enough for the hitter or umpire to call time. Just before he is about to call time, the pitcher should take an aggressive step back with his pivot foot. Often the runner will flinch or break toward second as a reaction to the pitcher's quick movement.

The key to the long hold is that the pitcher must appear as if he is going home. He should not eyeball the runner, but look right to home plate. It is important that the pitcher does not separate his hands before he steps off and that he does not open up his front shoulder. He must be ready to pick at first in case in the runner starts to break to second and tries to scuffle back to first.

***Hold Until Time Called.*** A second technique to identify if the runner is going to run on a pitch is just to hold the ball until the hitter or umpire calls time. Again, the coach and the catcher observe the runner. If he looks anxious or the right leg is quivering, then there is a good chance that he wants to run on that pitch. Keep in mind also that he may change his mind once he realizes that you have identified his intent.

These two techniques and the pick at first also help identify if the batter is bunting. Teams generally do not bunt and run simultaneously. This is especially true with the sacrifice bunt. The position of the hitter in the batter's box will also give away steals. Hitters tend to be deeper in the box when runners are stealing. They intend to take the pitch and push the catcher farther away from second base. They are up on the front of the box more when they are bunting. Many runners give away their intent to steal. They set up differently when they are stealing; for instance, after they receive the signal, they adjust their helmet or look to second base. Because most base runners will do something to indicate that they are stealing, the pitcher must be a good observer.

## BASIC HOLDING SITUATIONS

Here are more than half a dozen holding situations to review with your team:

***Right-Handed Pitchers Holding Runners on Base.*** It's common to see pitchers practice their pick-off moves to first base, but it's also important for them to practice moves to home. They have to develop an efficient stretch move to the plate.

An excellent technique is the six-cleat action or knee-to-knee action. Before the pitcher glides to the plate, he loads up his backside and shows the cleats of his stride foot to the hitter. In the six-cleat stretch move, he should start separating the hands just before he starts his leg lift, so his arm can reach the power position as the stride foot plants. He should start with 80-90% of his weight on his back leg.

This is much better than the slide step where the pitcher jumps off the back side and dead legs his lead leg to the plate with a really low slide step to home. This technique will put a lot of stress on the arm and shoulder because it rushes the body ahead of the arm, and it can greatly reduce throwing velocity.

The pitcher should attempt to get the ball to the plate in 1.2 seconds from his first move with his hands until the ball hits the catcher's glove. The breakdown on the stolen base with a 12-foot lead for an average runner is approximately 3.5 seconds. An average-throwing big league catcher throws 2.0 and it takes a tenth of a second for a tag. The pitcher has to factor in his catcher's release time, the break time of the pitcher, and then add them all up to see if he has a chance to throw a runner out. That's assuming the runner gets a good jump so that his break is at or before the pitcher's first move, which often is not the case.

If a pitcher has an effective move to first base, it will also slow the base runner. He needs to hold runners on first to slow the running game. But more important, he needs to be effective to the plate in terms of velocity and location to get the hitter out. Any inability to get the hitter out because he over-focused on the runner will hurt him more than a stolen base.

The coach should use his radar gun and pitching charts to tell him if his pitching is less effective in the stretch. If the stretch move is more than three miles per hour slower than the windup, then mechanical adjustments need to be made. This is true if there is a big disparity between the windup and stretch as they relate to ball/strike ratio or hard contact average.

Even though it is preferable to have one stretch move to home, there are times when the pitcher can alter his delivery to load up the back side a little better, such as when it is not a running situation or he is unconcerned about whether the opposition will run or not.

Another technique to stop the steal of second against the right-handed pitcher is the long hold and pitch. When a pitcher holds the ball, the base runner tends to get antsy. His front leg starts to quiver, his body gets tense, and he does not run. The long hold has to be long enough to create muscle tension in the runner but not long enough for the umpire or hitter to call time out.

It's advantageous to stop the running game without throwing to first base because there is risk involved every time the pitcher picks. This is especially true in the amateur game. Excessive picks also take away from the total pitching and defensive focus. Remember, every pick is just like a pitch.

The pitcher can also mix in a quick set-and-pitch pattern once he has established that long set-and-pitch pattern. The key here is that he starts his stride leg just as or slightly before his hands change direction in the stretch position.

Right-handed pitchers have four options to stop the running game without picking to first: 1) long hold; 2) long hold step off; 3) long hold and pitch; and 4) quick set and pitch.

***Right-Handed Pitcher's Pick to First.*** Our right-handed pitchers have two picks at first—a slow jump pivot or a quick jump pivot. The pitcher uses the first one to let the runner know he will pick at first. It can cause a runner to shorten his lead. It is also good for the pitcher with an erratic quick pick to reduce the possibility of throwing balls away. A quick pick is used to keep the runner close, as well as pick the runner off.

Both moves are executed with jump and pivot turn action. The pitcher should not bend his knees before jumping, but start with knees flexed in the stretch position to facilitate the jump turn. As he initiates the jump pivot, he uses a short arm action with the ball coming up out of the glove to the power position. The emphasis is on lots of wrist and forearm action on the throw. It's a very short arm throw.

The pitcher should throw it around the corner to first. He should not open up past first base. His front shoulder should point at first or somewhere between first and the start of the running box at first base.

He should step toward and gain ground to first base so that he is not called for a balk. He needs to jump low and quick, turning his head toward first. A good drill is to shadow the quick foot action to first and then quickly jump back to the starting position. This drill fosters a quick foot action and low jump pivot that leads to a good move.

In the stretch, the pitcher sets his hands at or slightly above his chest in a tension-free position. He does this for two reasons:(1) it facilitates getting the ball out of the glove for the pick; and (2) it gives him time to accelerate his arm to get in the power position. Pitchers who are late with their arm out of the stretch end up throwing horizontal or underneath the ball. They can move their hands down so they have a shorter distance, or take the ball flatter, back out of the glove. Again, everything depends on the individual and should be determined through trial and error. Videotaping is an important aid to identifying problem areas.

The pitcher should pick somewhere in the tag zone in front of first base. The throw should be higher rather than lower because it's easier for the first baseman to handle. We have more problems with throws, knees and down, where the first baseman gets tied up with the runner, especially if the ball sinks.

For the runner who tries to get momentum or walking leads at first base the pitcher should pick when the runner crosses his feet or gets extended past the point of return. Once we identify this type of runner, the catcher can signal the pick at first by letting his glove drop forward. If the runner starts moving late, the first baseman can call in a pick or have the pitcher step off. Also, a move with the hands on the way up or on the way down is effective against those base runners who try to get moving leads.

The move to first base is sometimes used to change the tempo of the game. If a pitcher is pitching poorly to home plate, call for a pick, which forces an eye switch. That may clear the negative picture out of his mind and give him a fresh start. The switch also can be very distracting to the hitter.

Multiple picks can wear base runners down and stop them from running. However, you need to be careful that you do not destroy your own positive tempo and your players' and pitcher's focus at the same time. You may also be sending a subtle message to your catcher that you do not trust his ability to throw runners out.

The move to first base is also used to buy some time for the relief pitcher who is warming up.

**Pitchout and Modified Pitchout.** The pitchout and the modified pitchout are techniques that can help stop the running game.

Don't have the pitcher pick at first before pitching out. Give the runner good pitching tempo to run on. Remember, you want him to run when you throw a modified pitchout or a pitchout, and a long hold discourages the attempted steal.

The pitchout is a four-seam fastball thrown to the opposite batter's box. On the modified pitchout, we have the catcher set up with his nose on the outside corner and the pitcher throws an eye-high four-seam fastball just off the plate. This serves the same purpose as a pitchout, but requires less movement by the catcher. It conceals the fact that it is a pitchout, which keeps the base runner from reading the catcher and not stealing or running in a hit-and-run situation. If it is a hit-and-run, and the hitter does swing, chances are it will be a swing and miss or pop-up to the location of the pitch.

If you have your opponent's signals and you use a modified pitchout as opposed to a pitchout, there is less chance that the opposition will suspect that you have their signals. It is also used against teams who read pitchouts well and do not run. This is especially true on the hit and run. The modified pitchout is thrown eye high just off the outside corner.

You want the delivery to home to be the same as the normal six-cleat action. Good base stealers will choke off their attempt to steal if you suddenly quicken delivery. There is some value to a quicker delivery in a hit-and-run situation or left-handed pitchers. However, it really isn't that critical because the runner's not running with his best jump.

# LEFT-HANDED PITCHERS HOLDING RUNNERS ON FIRST

The left-handed pitcher should have a great move to first base. He should stop the running game better than right-handers by getting more out on picks to first. However, because most players don't run against lefties, left-handed pitchers have a tendency not to develop their move to first on their delivery to the plate.

Our basic left lift move for the left-handed pitcher is a predetermined move. He is predetermining whether he will pitch or pick depending on the situation and the runner. The key is that all the actions of the pitch and the pick are the same so the base runner has no key for an early read.

Starting with the head position, the pitcher should put it at first base or somewhere between first and home on both the pitch and pick so that he doesn't get that "look to first and throw home, or look home and throw first" patterns that most lefties have. He should minimize the amount of head movement and keep it simple.

He keeps his shoulders on a parallel line between the mound and home plate. Some base runners key the back shoulder. If it rotates away from first, then the pitcher is closing up to throw to first. He keeps the shoulders level. Many left-handed pitchers lean back to throw to first and scrunch over to pitch to home.

Consistent leg action is also important. Many left-handers will open their thigh to pick and close it to pitch. The lead foot must not pass the front edge of the rubber. This commits him to pitch or pick at second. The video is the only sure-fire means of identifying differences in the move to first and the move to home. Lefties must learn to judge the 45 degree line to first.

The pitcher can stretch the 45-degree line by jogging to first after every pick so the umpires can't establish his actual path. Angling his pivot foot so that his heel is a few inches off the rubber will also help him stretch the 45-degree angle closer to home, creating the illusion that he is pitching home when you are picking. This allows him to step more towards home and still have daylight between his legs when he picks to first. Many plate umpires call balks when there is no daylight between his legs when he steps. It also makes it easier to throw to first without rotating the hips or shoulders.

It doesn't hurt to have lots of footprints on the mound going toward first.

The pitcher can have different levels of moves to first. A real honest straight move to first is one in between first and the 45-degree line, and one on the 45-degree line.

Establish early in the game that the pitcher will throw to first three times consecutively. Many base stealers will run on the lefty's first move after the second pick.

Throwing three times consecutively early in the game keeps the pitcher from having to throw over to first later in the game.

It is beneficial to have an anti-first move technique. On this move the pitcher can just pick his foot up and pick to first so the base runner can't steal on his first move.

Another leg lift technique for the lefty is the "read" technique. It is very effective, but he needs to be very skilled in terms of body control, and it takes lots of practice because it is not a predetermined move. It requires a quick eye switch and change of focus. Without proper balance, this is not possible.

Again, he needs a relatively narrow base with the feet spread about shoulder width and the toes on line to home or slightly closed (right foot closer to first). The pitcher looks directly at the runner on first. While looking at the runner, he uses his quadriceps muscle to pick up his stride leg with the toe pointed down to get to a balance position with the thigh parallel to the ground and the heel of the stride foot even with and close to the knee of the back leg. While in the balance position, he reads the runner at first. If the pitcher thinks the runner is going to run, he throws to first. If the pitcher does not think he is going to run, he looks home and throws home. This really stops a runner from running on his first move. If he does, the pitcher has to cut his leg short and step quickly to first.

If the runner waits until the pitcher looks home to run, it is too late because the elapsed time is under 1.0 seconds.

The pitcher can mix in a predetermined move where he looks to first on his leg lift, looks home, and then throws to first. This is a change of pace in a hit-and-run situation. It also gives him a chance to pick the runner at first when he is not running because the runner becomes so conditioned to starting his secondary lead when the pitcher looks home.

When the pitcher throws to first, he should cut the 45-degree mark as close as possible, and as soon as his stride foot hits, jog to first base.

***Six-Cleat Move.*** The toughest move to run on against a left-hander is the six-cleat move. It's virtually impossible to get a good jump on a left-hander who six cleats. It is similar to the six-cleat action by the right-handed pitcher.

The pitcher sets up with his feet no wider than shoulder width and the stride foot heel in line with the pivot foot toe. He brings the knee of the stride leg to the knee of the pivot leg, turns the bottom six cleats of the stride foot to the hitter, and glides low to the plate. This gets the ball to the plate in 1.1 or 1.2 seconds. Base runners can't start towards second until they read the first move by the pitcher, so the position of the pitcher's head must be consistent. He should either look at first or look at a 45-degree angle between home and first when he initiates his delivery.

The pitcher can pick to first off the six-cleat action with a quick low step to first. The six-cleat move is so quick that the runner has no time to get a read or jump.

In a hit-and-run situation, it gives the pitcher a chance to field a ground ball and still force the runner at second. It is also effective after the pitcher has made three moves to first base and the runner is planning to run on the pitcher's first move. The quick six-cleat move does not allow the runner to guess and run on the pitcher's first move.

The six-cleat move also has an effect on the hitter, especially when the pitcher's basic move is a leg lift. The six-cleat gets on the ball on the hitter faster because he is anticipating that the pitcher will lift his leg to initiate the pitch.

This technique can also be used with a runner on second because of the change of tempo effect it has on both the hitter and base runner. The negative aspect of the six-cleat move is that some pitchers lose effectiveness to the plate because they can't load the back side adequately or their arm drags because they don't have enough time to get it up to a power position.

A left-handed pitcher also needs to have a step-off move so that the runners with plus-speed can't get an extended lead and run on his first move and beat the first baseman's throw to second after he picks. A step-off move calls for the left-handed pitcher to take a short step back toward second with his pivot foot and, in one movement, throw to first. The pick requires a flatter, more horizontal arm action.

Slightly closing the lead shoulder right as he steps off allows the pitcher to get better leverage and more on the ball. He can feature more than one speed step-off to set the base runner up for a quick step-off pick.

**Holding Runners on Second.** In all cases, the primary factor in holding runners is the specific situation. Is it a running situation? If not, then you don't want your pitcher to divide his focus, expend energy, and cut down his defensive coverage by holding the runner. The pitcher should not give the runner third unless it's a non-factor. The scoreboard will generally tell him what to do.

If it's a running situation, the key is that the shortstop, second baseman, and pitcher coordinate their look package. The shortstop and second baseman must know how many looks the pitcher is going to make before he pitches to the plate so that they're not breaking to second base while the pitcher is pitching to the plate.

The pitcher should vary the tempo of his looks to second. For example, you call for two looks at second. On the first look, he looks at second and holds the look for a few counts. On the second look, he looks quickly at second, looks home, and throws home.

He should look home and throw home. Some pitchers can look to second and throw home, especially if they have a clear visual picture of the target in their mind's eye.

If there are multiple looks, the pitcher, shortstop, and second baseman need to know who's going to be breaking toward the base to hold the runner, so if they go open glove to pick the runner, the pitcher's looking at the right infielder. He should focus on one of them. Too often, a pitcher is not aware of who is holding the runner—he looks at the shortstop, and the second baseman will break to second base with an open glove to pick the runner.

Any time the runner at second is walking or has momentum to third base, the pitcher should keep looking at the runner. Hopefully, the shortstop or second baseman will break with an open glove so he can pick the runner. If the runner at second has momentum, and one of the middle infielders does not break to pick, the pitcher should step off, hold the ball, or bluff a pick at second. On the other hand, if the runner at second has a short lead or is going back to second on the pitcher's last look, the pitcher should quickly look home and throw home.

The hitter dictates who's going to hold the runner. Is he a right-handed pull hitter? Chances are the second baseman's going to have the primary responsibility. If this is an overpowering pitcher, and nobody pulls the ball, the shortstop's going to hold the runner. If the pitcher is throwing a breaking ball, there are many factors that he has to consider. This is all communicated before the pitcher gets on the rubber or the pitch is called.

When the shortstop is responsible for holding a runner on second, you want him to start right on the runner's backside, as opposed to way off the runner and running a distance to hold the runner. This cuts down the runner's primary lead, and the shortstop can get better positioning on each pitch, because he doesn't have to run to the base, stop to shift his momentum, and race back to his position.

There are two types of moves to second: the reverse pivot and the inside move.

1. The reverse pivot is much like the jump pivot to first, except that it's a 180-degree turn as opposed to the 90-degree turn to first. The emphasis is on getting the head turned to second with a low jump turn. The ball is taken up into the power position during the turn. Care must be taken not to over-rotate toward third base.

2. The inside move is a clockwise move to second. The inside move must look like the move to home plate with the emphasis on the same leg lift and long arm action as on the pitch. It is a slow move that allows the runner to initiate his secondary lead. The pitcher starts with the heel of his pivot foot closer to home plate to facilitate the inside turn to second. When the pitcher is picking with an inside move, he looks at the runner as soon as he turns so if the runner breaks to third base, the pitcher can cut his inside move off and throw to third base.

**Holding Runners on Third.** If the pitcher needs to hold a runner on third, he should pitch out of the stretch. It cuts the runner's lead down and makes it tougher to squeeze, as well as score on an infield ground ball. It also greatly reduces the chance of balking or stealing home. With multiple runners on base, it is imperative to pitch out of the stretch to make it tougher to score from second and to allow for the double play by way of second base if the bases are loaded.

If the pitcher can't get the hitter out by pitching out of the stretch, he needs to practice more out of the stretch until he has an equal amount of confidence and ability out of the stretch. Until he develops the stretch skills, he can pitch out of the windup. Make sure he looks the runner back at third after he gets the signal and before he starts the windup.

# ARM SORENESS

Arm soreness is a very general term to describe mild to severe arm pain. You need to address all instances where the pitcher has concern about the health of his arm. The pitcher has to feel comfortable with and have trust in his coaches and trainers. If he does not have trust in them in the area of arm problems, a minor physical problem can develop into a severe physical problem over time. A minor physical problem can also cause mental stress, which could prevent the pitcher from pitching up to his capabilities.

***Communicating the Problem.*** The key to developing this trust is communication. The coaches and trainers need to communicate and convince the pitcher that it is the coaches and trainer's responsibility to ensure that the pitcher is healthy so that he can pitch as well as he is physically able to. The coaches and trainers are there to protect the best interest of the players, not to penalize the pitcher by taking pitching time away from him. Pitchers low in trust are afraid that he will lose playing time because of injury.

Pitchers are also afraid to find out that they are injured. They try to bulldog their way through and pretend that they don't have a problem. This is fine if there is no problem. But if there is a problem, this will generally exacerbate it.

Every pitcher is going to experience arm soreness at some time during his career. It's common to have some discomfort accompanying most performances. Some pitchers have a very low pain tolerance and panic the first time they feel anything. They can't pitch. It affects them psychologically as well as physically. A pitcher should not baby his arm so much that he never builds up the strength and endurance that's necessary to be a competitive pitcher, but he should learn to differentiate between post-game arm soreness, which results from metabolite buildup, and arm soreness resulting from arm injury.

***Types of Arm Soreness.*** Pitchers and coaches need to be aware of common types of arm soreness.

1. The first and most prominent is general arm or muscle soreness that develops from throwing one hundred pitches in a game. It generally lasts one or two days after pitching.

2. The second type of muscle soreness we term "muscle ache." It is a more specific and localized soreness and/or tightness that lasts more than two days. This "muscle ache" often is with the pitcher even when he is not pitching. Many times it is indicative of a strain, a weakened muscular state, muscle fatigue, or something more serious. Pitchers may alter their motion or release point to avoid discomfort, which can lead to a serious long term injury.

   Usually this condition requires intervention by a trainer, physical therapist or team physician. Treatment may be in the form of rest or may involve muscle stimulation, ice massage, or other massage. Most likely it will involve some stretching and strengthening to rehabilitate the problem and prevent its recurrence. Occasionally anti-inflammatory drugs are prescribed to help speed the recovery.

3. The third type of soreness is termed "muscle pain." It is a more intense localized soreness that can also radiate from the point of the tender spot. It is a lasting soreness that prevents the pitcher from throwing without pain and should be assessed and treated immediately. This muscle pain can be caused by a moderate to severe muscle strain, tendinitis, muscle tears or joint impingement, associated with a grinding or popping sensation in the joint. Often, only a physician can detect the cause of these problems, especially if they persist over a time or are recurrent after rest and treatment by the trainer.

Arm problems are caused by many things: Lack of strength, lack of flexibility, overuse and poor mechanics rank near the top.

***Conditioning for Arm Soreness.*** Proper conditioning is the best way to avoid arm problems. Strength, flexibility and building a gradual throwing base are critical ingredients in the conditioning process. Be sure pitchers use the correct type of strength program. The wrong type of strength program will over develop certain shoulder muscles that can cause a decrease in proper circulation. The strength building process is not limited to the upper body. It is even more critical to build abdominal, gluteal and leg strength. The person who is stronger has better circulation and stronger, thicker tendons that help combat the stresses of out of range or awkward out of sync deliveries. When a pitcher throws one hundred or more pitches in a game, he is bound to throw some pitches out of rhythm with his arm down, front shoulder out, or with a recoiling action. However, repeated bad deliveries will cause problems no matter how strong and flexible the pitcher is.

***Overuse.*** Overuse is a prime culprit in arm soreness. Focus on how many pitches the pitcher warms up with and how many he throws in a game. Also monitor velocity in the game, either visually or with a radar gun. If you don't have a radar gun, compute the velocity with a stop watch. Time from the release until the ball hits the catcher's mitt. Loss of velocity usually suggests fatigue. When a pitcher is tired, his mechanics break down. Fatigue and bad mechanics lead to:

1. Arm problems.
2. Loss of control, especially loss of control up in the zone.
3. A low pitching elbow at the time of release.
4. An increase in the time a pitcher takes between pitches.
5. An increase in the number of picks.

Every pitcher is different so there is no set number of maximum pitches. However, with a proper training base, one hundred and twenty is the maximum that most pitchers can pitch effectively and remain healthy. There are exceptions, but it is always safer to err on the conservative side and throw too few pitches than too many. The worst problem may be the pitcher himself. Don't ask how he feels because he will pitch until you drag him off the mound. Young guys generally will stay in until they are hurting, and it's too late then. Overuse may show up in the next start or soon thereafter as some type of arm soreness associated with loss of velocity, loss of control or possibly a change in mechanics.

# POST-PITCHING ARM EXERCISES

As soon as the pitcher leaves a game he is starting to prepare for his next outing. The first thing the pitcher does after pitching is light weight resistance work with surgical tubing to help flush the metabolites and release the tension out of the shoulder, back and arm. This involves 15 repetitions with each of the following exercises:

1. **External rotation-light tubing.**
2. **Internal rotation-light tubing.**

3. **Humeral depression front-medium tubing.** (PHOTO 5-18) Depress the humerus with non-throwing hand by holding the throwing-arm shoulder down and pulling with throwing hand from a position facing the fence and above the head straight down to throwing-arm side. The throwing arm is straight throughout this exercise.

4. **Humeral depressions side-medium tubing.** (PHOTO 5-19) Same as above except stand sideways with throwing arm next to fence. Depress shoulder with non-throwing hand and pull down from above the head to the side (palm facing side of body).

5. **Rotator cuff flush (30 reps)-light tubing.** (PHOTO 5-20) Face the fence with arms extended and tubing in both hands. Pull hands in (palms facing) until elbows are bent at 90 degrees. Next, raise the backs of the hands to approximately shoulder height (elbows will be bent to approximately 45 degrees).

Next the trainer will statically stretch the arm and shoulder to help promote circulation. Finally, the trainer will apply ice to the shoulder and elbow for twelve to fifteen minutes to further promote circulation and reduce post-exercise muscle soreness.

The post-pitching protocol is not for all pitchers. A lot depends upon how many pitches the pitcher throws. Everyone is different; by trial and error you usually find out what best meets the needs of the individual pitcher. The trainer or coach needs to check out the pitcher the next day and each day after that to see if any problems surface.

**Photo 5-18**

**Photo 5-19**

Arm problems are an inevitable byproduct of overhand throwing. The goal is to reduce these problems through proper conditioning, proper mechanics, proper use, proper post game treatment and proper rehabilitation when injured. (See also Figure 5-4).

**Photo 5-20**

Figure 5-4:  **HOW TO CARE FOR DIFFERENT PARTS OF THE ARM**

### GENERAL CARE

#### Muscles
1. Pump massage muscle to relax tension in muscle, increase blood flow, and to re-nourish the area. Also decreases muscle spasm.
2. Ice cup massage.
3. Electrical muscle stimulation.
4. Anti-inflammatories* if necessary.

#### Tendons (tendinitis)
1. Cross-friction massage perpendicular to decrease scar tissue and increase nutrient flow.
2. Ice cup massage.
3. Ultrasound in post-acute stage.
4. Anti-inflammatories* if necessary.

#### Ligaments (sprain with laxity)
1. Rest.
2. Strengthen musculature around joint to increase stability of capsule. No stretching until stable.
3. Ice bag/ice cup.
4. Cross-friction.
5. Ultrasound in post-acute stage.
6. Anti-inflammatories* if necessary.

#### Nerve (without damage)
1. Stretch dural sheath to clear the neural pathway and to keep the sheath from binding the nerve. This also helps to relax the surrounding masculature. (This treatment is indicated as long as the nerve problem is not the result of any injury to another area, e.g., ulnar nerve problem as a result of medical elbow tendonitis.)

### SPECIFIC AFFECTED AREAS

#### Total Shoulder
POSSIBLE CAUSES
1. Hand and elbow too low with hand too wide.
2. Elbow too low with hand too high.
3. Arm and/or wrist hooked.
4. Rushing the body ahead of the arm.
5. Excessive body tilt away from the arm.

TREATMENT
1. Rest.
2. Narrow the problem and treat accordingly. X-ray and/or MRI if necessary.
3. Strengthen posterior and scapula-thoracic musculature.
4. Anti-inflammatories* if necessary.
5. Gradually resume thowing.

MECHANICAL ADJUSTMENT TO PREVENT RECURRENCE
1. Emphasize an upright and balanced position over the rubber without swinging the stride leg back. Limit hip rotation away from home plate. Increase lumbar and lower extremity flexibility.

**Elbow and/or Forearm**

POSSIBLE CAUSES

1. Over-extension of the elbow (especially on breaking balls).
2. Early and excessive pronation of the hand.
3. Supination of the hand (when breaking ball is too lateral).
4. Excessive external rotation of the shoulder with late internal rotation.

TREATMENT

1. Rest.
2. Treat ligament problems.
   a. X-ray and/or MRI.
   b. Ice cup massage.
   c. Cross-friction.
   d. Ultrasound.
   e. Strengthen forearm, flexors, extensors, and ulnar deviators.
   f. Anti-inflammatories*.
3. Treat tendon problems.
   a. Ice cup massage.
   b. Cross friction massage.
   c. Ultrasound.
   d. Stretching, including pronators.
4. Treat nerve problems.
   a. Neural sheath stretch.
   b. Consult physician.
5. Treat muscle problems.
   a. Ice cup massage.
   b. Pump massage.
   c. Stretch and strengthen wrist extensors.
   d. Anti-inflammatories* if necessary.
   e. Gradual throwing program.

MECHANICAL ADJUSTMENT TO PREVENT RECURRENCE

1. Insure that the elbow is at or above shoulder height in a power position. Also, make sure that the elbow is up and forward before release on breaking balls. Stride leg must be firm and flexed at and after release. Early separation is key to prevent early hip rotation (opening up).

**Posterior Rotator Cuff**

POSSIBLE CAUSES

1. Short arm action in front of body.
2. Throwing arm not finishing across stride leg.
3. Recoiling action of arm, shoulder or body.
4. Lack of loose wrist action.
5. Stiff stride leg on release.
6. Throwing too far across the body.

TREATMENT

1. Rest (depending upon severity).
2. Anti-inflammatories* (depending upon severity).
3. Manual therapy.
   a. Ice cup massage.
   b. Cross-friction massage (if tendon problem).
   c. Pump massage (if muscle problem).
   d. Free weights and/or surgical tubing.
   e. PNF (Proprioceptive Neuromuscular Facilitation).
4. Gradual throwing program depending on time away from throwing.

MECHANICAL ADJUSTMENT TO PREVENT RECURRENCE
1. Focus on extension after release with throwing arm shoulder finishing in a relaxed position across the stride leg knee.
2. Emphasis on lower extremity stretching.

### Anterior Shoulder

POSSIBLE CAUSE
1. Early or excessive external rotation of the throwing shoulder.
2. Hand and/or elbow too low in power position or hand too close to the head.
3. Wrist collapsed with the hand underneath the ball.
4. Premature and/or excessive rotation of the lead side.

TREATMENT
1. Rest (depending upon severity).
2. Anti-inflammatories* (depending upon severity).
3. Treat muscle problems.
   a. Ice cup massage.
   b. Deep soft-tissue massage.
   c. Door stretch for right pectoral minor.
4. Treat tendon problems.
   a. Ice cup massage.
   b. Cross friction massage.
   c. Ultrasound.
   d. Stretching.
5. Strengthening and gradual throwing program depending upon time away from throwing.

MECHANICAL ADJUSTMENT TO PREVENT RECURRENCE
1. Separate hands while balanced over the rubber to allow for a linear route to the target and to prevent premature rotation.
2. Focus on high elbow power position with the ball above the hand.

### Biceps (usually a form of tendinitis)

POSSIBLE CAUSE
1. Overuse or throwing when fatigued
2. Lack of recovery time between work
3. Lack of strength. Muscle atrophy due to lack of rest and or a lack of a strength maintenance program.

TREATMENT
1. Rest.
2. Ice cup massage.
3. Cross friction massage.
4. Strengthen external rotator cuff.
5. Anti-inflammatories* if necessary.
6. Gradual throwing program if there was a prolonged period of rest.

MECHANICAL ADJUSTMENT TO PREVENT RECURRENCE
1. Strength building and/or strength maintenance is the issue here, especially in the external rotators of the shoulder. Also, external hip rotators (piriformis) need to be stretched.

### Lateral Shoulder (swollen supra-spinatus tendon noticeable with shoulder joint at or above 90-degree extension)

POSSIBLE CAUSES
1. Overuse leading to an impingement
2. Poor lower body mechanics
3. Weak or fatigued external rotators

TREATMENT
1. Rest.
2. Ice cup massage.
3. Cross friction massage with shoulder in extension.
4. Ultrasound.
5. Pump massage supra-spinatus.
6. Anti-inflammatories* if necessary.
7. Gradual throwing program if period was prolonged.

MECHANICAL ADJUSTMENT TO PREVENT RECURRENCE
1. Inefficient lower-half mechanics usually associated with striding too far across the body. Focus should be on a more efficient stride direction to home plate while emphasizing rolling the laces of the pivot foot.
2. Strengthen the shoulder to stabilize the shoulder in the glenoid fossa.

---

* Anti-inflammatories should be avoided in players with ulcers or allergies to the chosen drug. Common anti-inflammatories include:
ASPIRIN (Ecotrin, Bayer, generic); IBUPROFEN (Motrin, Advil, Nuprin, Rufen, generic); INDOMETHACIN (Indocin, Indomed); and NAPROXEN (Naprosyn, Aleve).

# CATCHING

The catcher is the focus of attention for every play. All members of the team look to him for leadership. The catcher must set the example; he can't let down. When he's on defense, he must be on defense, and he must make sacrifices to get the maximum out of his pitcher.

The primary skill a catcher must have is to catch, but he must also throw accurately and be able to block the ball in the dirt. On the amateur level, good throwing is less important. If he can't catch, he will give up too many free bases, so the stolen base is almost beside the point. The ability to throw people out becomes more critical as players move into higher levels of baseball.

A pitcher senses security in his catcher based on how the catcher handles the ball. If the catcher is sloppy behind the plate, it will undermine the pitcher's confidence in him. Everything the catcher does to help the pitcher, no matter how small, makes a difference in the game. The catcher's job is, essentially, to create an environment where the pitcher is totally focused on the execution of his pitches.

Photo 6-1

## SIGNAL STANCE

Catching starts with a proper signal stance: the catcher should be up on his toes with his heels close together. His legs are close together, pointed a bit more toward third base than first base so that the glove hides the signals from the third base coach. His legs must be close together to funnel the signals to the pitcher so that the first and third basemen can't see the signals. (PHOTO 6-1)

Photo 6-2

If they can see them, a first or third base coach or a runner at first may see them. The catcher should ask the first and third basemen to let him know if he's too open.

The catcher should make sure his fingers don't drop below his thighs where someone from behind or to the side can see the fingers. (PHOTO 6-2) He should also check that the fingers are not so far away from his legs that the sun casts a shadow of the digits on the shin guards or feet. When giving signals, he should rest his throwing arm forearm on his thigh; after giving the signals, he should bring the glove to the signal hand so that signals aren't dragged out. (PHOTO 6-3)

## GIVING SIGNALS

The catcher should be decisive with his signal giving and body language. It will affect the quality of the pitch. He should use his runner-on-second signals, with or without a runner on base, so the pitcher doesn't

Photo 6-3

have to adjust to two sets of signals and so it's harder for a base runner on first to pick the pitch. You can suggest that he wear a long sleeved shirt to conceal his elbow position and forearm movement. He should also avoid taps to show location. They are too easy to read and generally show that the pitch is going to be a fast ball.

The catcher and the pitcher should review signals before the game and between innings if necessary. Have them sit next to each other on the bench between innings. Discourage meetings on the mound before an inning starts.

You need a system to hold runners. You need signals for a step off, long hold, and different kinds of moves to the bases and to home, for example, a slide step, long hold and pitch, short hold and pitch. You also need a sign for a wheel pick (an inside move at second base), and for a fake third pick at first or fake first pick at third.

## GOING FROM SIGNAL TO RECEIVING STANCE

The catcher must get into the receiving stance the same way on all pitches, making sure that he's close to the hitter after he comes out of the signal stance. He should be able to reach out with the glove and touch the hitter's back elbow. (PHOTO 6-4) He must not be so close to the hitter that he's called for catcher's interference. However, he needs to be close enough to avoid getting chewed up on foul tips or balls in the dirt. Being close to the hitter allows him to cut the ball off closer to the impact point.

Setting up too far away from the hitter is a problem on a breaking ball. (PHOTO 6-5) If the catcher is too far away, the pitcher will be throwing the breaking ball to the catcher, and it ends up being up over the plate to the hitter. The catcher must

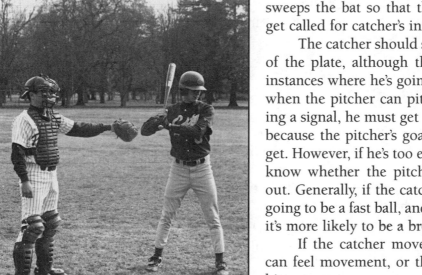

Photo 6-4

be aware of the isolated hitter who really sweeps the bat so that the catcher doesn't get called for catcher's interference.

The catcher should sit over the middle of the plate, although there will be some instances where he's going to sit in and out when the pitcher can pitch fine. After giving a signal, he must get the target up early because the pitcher's goal is to hit the target. However, if he's too early, the hitter will know whether the pitcher is going in or out. Generally, if the catcher sits inside, it's going to be a fast ball, and if he sits outside, it's more likely to be a breaking ball.

If the catcher moves early, the hitter can feel movement, or the coach, on-deck hitter, or runner on second base can relay the location to the hitter. The catcher can avoid this by setting up in the signal stance a little bit off the center of the plate if he wants the ball in or out, or by sliding into position late when it's too late for the hitter

Photo 6-5

to make an adjustment. If the pitcher is not able to consistently throw in or out, it is better to sit over the middle and just target in and out off the catcher's knees. This prevents the excessive reaching that leads an umpire to call a ball when it should have been a strike.

## RECEIVING STANCE

In the receiving stance, with no one on base, the catcher has some options. He needs to get in the stance that gives the pitcher the best target and produces the best outcome for that particular pitch. He can get down on one knee or both knees. (PHOTO 6-6) When there is no one on base, and less than three balls or two strikes on the hitter, the catcher should use the stance and target that is best for the pitcher. The only way he finds that out is by communication and experimentation.

Generally, the catcher needs to be in an up position. Make sure that his elbows are outside or above the knees and his arms are flexed. (PHOTO 6-7) The glove should not be too close to his face. (PHOTO 6-8) His feet should be a little bit wider than shoulder width, and his toes pointed out at approximately a forty-five degree angle. (PHOTO 6-9) This facilitates the setup to throw. It also eases the catcher's ability to move laterally because he doesn't have to open up his hips to move side to side.

Photo 6-6

Photo 6-7

Photo 6-8

Photo 6-9

The catcher needs a little more weight on the left foot so he can move better to the right. This allows him to move more easily away from the glove-hand side, where most catchers have less range. Make sure that he's on the soles of his feet, with the weight inside up toward the balls of the feet. He must stay off his toes to avoid putting himself off balance and falling forward. This causes him to lose lateral range. He should keep his buttocks up, but not so high that it forces his head down. His head should be above the shoulders and his hips below for balance. The hips must be high enough so as not to force the weight on his heels.

Allow your catcher to catch one-handed with his bare hand behind his back when no one is on base. (PHOTO 6-10) If he catches with his bare hand next to his glove, he should set it open with his thumb tucked behind his index finger and his hand behind the web of the glove. (PHOTO 6-11)

When the catcher is in this position, if the ball is fouled off and he gets hit on the hand, the ball will hit the palm of the hand or the fingers without hitting straight on. This shouldn't happen if he stays on the same level as the pitch because balls are fouled up or down. The loose fist exposes the knuckles or the ends of the fingers because a catcher tends to extend from the loose-fist position. A two handed targeting catcher also has the option of sliding his bare hand up his elbow as he catches the ball to protect his throwing hand. (PHOTO 6-12)

**Photo 6-10**

Photo 6-11

Photo 6-12

# RECEIVING TECHNIQUES

Here are several different techniques that can help the catcher improve his skills in receiving the ball.

1. ***Framing Technique.*** If no one is on base, the catcher should catch the ball close to the plate. The closer to the plate he receives the ball, the easier it is to recognize a strike as a strike. He's not trying to get balls called strikes—he's trying to get every strike called a strike. The objective is to catch the ball with a smooth-handed action and with a minimum of body movement. He should not jerk or pull any pitches into the strike zone. Good framing technique will usually get the more marginal pitches.

   The catcher is not trying to put one over on the umpire, only to give strikes the best possible showcase. If the catcher isn't smooth, the umpire will feel that he's trying to take advantage of him by pulling pitches into the zone. This may cause the ump to take pitches away from your team. It is important for the glove to beat the ball to the spot. If the glove arrives late, the ball will carry the glove out of the strike zone.

2. ***Low Balls.*** The low ball is a fast ball at or slightly below the knees or a breaking ball at or slightly above the knees. The catcher should catch a low ball with the fingers up. If he turns his glove over and catches the ball palm up, most umpires won't call these low balls strikes (PHOTO 6-13). The only exception is a

Photo 6-13

Photo 6-14

hard-throwing sinker ball pitcher where the catcher may have to turn his glove over or backhand a lot of his sinkers. (PHOTO 6-14)

3. **High Balls.** The high ball is a fast ball just above the belt or a breaking ball at or slightly below the belt. The catcher should knock the high pitch down. He should catch the top half of the high pitch with the pocket of the glove facing down because he has a 13-inch glove from the heel to tip and the pitch looks 13 inches higher than it really is if he catches the ball with the fingers up. (PHOTO 6-15)

4. **Backhands.** The catcher should backhand the outside pitch up to the plate in the web of the glove. This keeps the ball in the strike zone if he catches it firmly. (PHOTO 6-16) The low/mid pitch that must be backhanded can be brought toward the body by hooking the wrist as he catches the ball. (PHOTO 6-17) This keeps the catcher from knocking the low ball down and out of the strike zone.

5. **Glove Side.** The technique here is to surround the pitch to the glove side and catch it close to the plate with the glove faced into the plate. He should avoid catching it squarely with most of his glove outside the strike zone or backhanding it and taking it out of the strike zone. (PHOTOS 6-18, 6-19, 6-20, 6-21)

6. **Letting the Close Pitch Sit.** In a non-running situation, it is critical to let the close pitch sit. Too many catchers rise up prematurely to return the ball to the pitcher or third baseman on a third strike. If the umpire is unsure about whether

Photo 6-15

Photo 6-16

Photo 6-17

Photo 6-18

Photo 6-19

Photo 6-20

a pitch is a ball or a strike, and the catcher bounces up, there is a tendency to call the pitch a ball. Conversely, if the catcher lets the pitch sit, the umpire may call it a strike. If he doesn't call it a strike, he may call the next one a strike.

In letting the ball sit, timing is critical. The catcher should hold the pitch long enough for the umpire to have a good clear look at it, but not so long that he feels the catcher is trying to force him into calling a strike. If umpires want to take more time calling pitches, don't rush them by picking up too soon. If they're rushed, they'll call a strike a ball before they call a ball a strike. Let the close pitch sit with no runners on base.

In running situations, the priority is on throwing people out; the framing aspect is secondary. Instead of catching the ball close to the plate, the receiver should catch the ball back into his body so it's easier to load and throw.

Photo 6-21

Photo 6-22

***Expanding the Strike Zone.*** Remind the catcher not to shift on balls within the strike zone. A good receiver must have his body as still as possible. He can expand or shrink the strike zone with his hands and a minimal amount of body movement. The umpires will tend to call pitches balls when the catcher sways or moves around a lot. The umpire is basically guessing on the outside pitch, so movement by the catcher can make a strike look like a ball.

On the outside pitch in a non-running situation, the catcher can set up on the corner and turn his body into the plate slightly. (PHOTO 6-22) This opens up a lane for the ump to see the pitch better, and it enables the catcher to catch the ball closer to the plate. This technique is best used when the pitcher is working away from his throwing arm side so the umpire can track the pitch better (right-handed hitter and right-handed pitcher). When the pitcher is throwing to his arm side, the ball does not cross the umpire's line of sight (left-handed hitter and right-handed pitcher). In this situation the umpire is really guessing on the pitch. If the catcher doesn't open up and sets up a little off the plate and catches the ball out of the strike zone without movement, many times it will be called a strike. He must be sensitive to the umpire's strike zone. The tendency is to expand the strike zone in and out (especially out) rather than up. The catcher should keep pushing the envelope to see how much off the plate or down (even up) that the umpire is going to give his pitcher on that day.

***Keeping the Tempo.*** When there is no one on base, the catcher must get the ball back to the pitcher quickly to maintain a quick tempo. Try to get this progression instilled in the catcher's brain: Catch the ball, drop to the knees, and throw it back. You don't want him to walk the ball to the pitcher or stand up to throw. It throws the tempo off and forces the umpire to reset after each pitch. You want the ump to get in his stance and stay there as long as possible because his concentration and focus will be better.

## REMEDIES FOR DROPPING PITCHES

Dropped pitches are often a result of these different actions by the catcher:

◆ Blinking as the ball arrives at the plate. Consciously blinking as the pitcher releases the ball can overcome this.

◆ Ducking the head as the hitter swings. You can help them remedy this by videoing them during batting practice.

◆ Not picking up the ball at the point of release. This happens when the catcher gets to the point of release too early and focuses behind or in front of the point of release so he doesn't actually see the release. Fine centering visually on the release point for too long also affects the vision negatively. The catcher should soft focus (relaxed) on the pitcher's front shoulder until it closes to the plate then move to a fine focus (more intense) at the release point.

◆ Not relaxing the glove hand sufficiently. The catcher shouldn't put his hand too deep into the glove because this makes his wrist stiff and tight. (First pose in PHOTO 6-23) The hands will be rigid and move slowly. He must have enough hand in the glove so that he can control it. He should have the heel of his hand exposed from the glove. (Second pose in PHOTO 6-23) He can use a heel of the hand protector to protect him when he's blocking or gets hit by a foul tip.

Maintaining a loose, relaxed wrist will help the catcher stay more flexible and catch more pitches. He can relax his glove hand by pointing it down slightly at the time of the pitch. (PHOTO 6-24) Some people like to break their hands open a quarter turn to the left. (PHOTO 6-24) This is okay, but breaking straight down puts the hands in a more neutral position.

If the catcher drops a pitch and it's a strike or near the strike zone, and there's no one on base, make sure he keeps his glove in the strike zone and don't let him retrieve the ball. If the umpire doesn't see that the catcher dropped the ball, and the catcher leaves the glove in the strike zone, the umpire may call it a strike. If the catcher goes to get the pitch, the umpire is going to call it a ball. Umpires are conservative and tend not to call dropped pitches as strikes. This is an occasional technique and should not be overdone. It's better to catch the ball.

Photo 6-23

## THROWING

There are two hard-and-fast rules for throwing runners out. First, the catcher must have a clear throwing lane. Second, he must have momentum going in the direction of the throw. His head is a good indicator of whether he has proper momentum.

Photo 6-24

**Photo 6-25**

**Photo 6-27**

His eyebrows should be level at the time of release and the head should follow the flight of the ball until the start of the follow-through. (PHOTO 6-25)

The catcher should modify his basic up stance that he uses with no runners on so that he sits a little higher and his throwing hand is behind his glove. (PHOTO 6-26)

Running situations are based on the scoreboard (inning, outs, count and score) and the personnel. It's the catcher's respon-

**Photo 6-26**

sibility to anticipate that the runner is going on every pitch. It's not the first baseman's responsibility to tell the catcher that the runner is going.

In a running situation, the catcher must catch the ball closer to his body than in a non-running situation. By catching the ball deeper, the catcher will be able to get the ball out of the glove quicker and into a throwing position. (PHOTO 6-27) The ball

Photo 6-28

should be taken out of the top of the glove in front of the body and taken to a power "L" position. (PHOTO 6-28)

If he is too extended when he catches the ball, it takes too long to get the ball back into the power throwing position. The ball is going to move faster than his hands, so when he catches the ball deeper, it is a shorter load to the power throwing position. This is especially true on pitches that he doesn't need to reach for.

When the stride foot hits the ground, the throwing arm starts forward from the power "L" position. Rolling the laces of the pivot foot initiates the start of the throw. The hand leads the throw, the head follows, and the chest finishes above the stride leg knee. The stride leg foot is slightly closed, and the stride leg is slightly bent but firm. The lead arm remains on the left chest or slightly below because of the action of the lead arm elbow pulling down and in to the lead side.

The catcher must avoid leading with the head, which pulls him off target and forces him to fire his legs too soon. This leaves him little leverage or power. An overly aggressive or horizontal lead arm takes him off the linear path to second and forces early rotation and a low three-quarter to side arm throw. (PHOTO 6-29)

## STEP-CATCH-THROW TECHNIQUE

Since all throwing techniques to third base involve the step-catch-throw technique, and since the jump-pivot-step-throw as well as the rock-back-and-throw techniques all require the catcher to step-catch and throw, at times, the focus here is on the step-catch-throw technique.

Everything is initiated with the right foot. It's a short shuffle step that is started just before the catcher catches the ball. The longer the catcher steps with the right foot, the longer it takes to get his left foot down. He can't throw until the left foot hits. He must release most throws with the left foot behind home plate. If he ends up on, or in front of home plate, it usually indicates that the shuffle step was too long. Stepping on the plate is dangerous because it is easy to slip.

The catcher must stay down as he is moving through the ball and gradually rise up to throw. He should take the ball up out of the glove, and try to get a four-seam grip across the horseshoe. However, taking extra time to get a four seam grip is counterproductive. If he can't get a four-seam grip, it's okay as long as he has the ball above his fingers at release. A slight spread between the index and middle fingers with the thumb underneath between the middle

Photo 6-29

Photo 6-30

Photo 6-31

and index finger is best. The inside side of the thumb grips the seam underneath the index and middle fingers. The thumb should be firm enough so the ball does not rotate to either side on release. This ensures the 6-12 rotation. His grip should not be so tight that he loses flexibility in the wrist. The ring finger also serves as a guide to ensure 6-12 backspin rotation. (PHOTOS 6-30, 6-31)

Players must always throw to a target. The catcher keeps his eyes on the target until the ball arrives. Many catchers just look at the base and use it as a target. This is a problem, especially at second since most catchers don't have enough arm strength to throw down on the base and carry the ball to the base. The target will vary depending on arm strength on that day and conditions such as wind or rain. During infield or while warming up, he should check his arm strength for that day, and check again between innings while he is establishing his target and throwing to second base.

Photo 6-32

## THROWING RUNNERS OUT AT SECOND

The following techniques for ball handling will help the catcher throw runners out at second base. The situations are for right- or left-handed hitters.

***Right-Handed Hitter Up.*** The ball inside to a right-handed hitter is surrounded by the glove with a sweeping or raking motion as the body is gaining momentum toward second. (PHOTO 6-32) When the ball is away from a right-handed hitter, he steps up and out to try to catch the ball off the left shoulder with his head on the first-base side of the ball. This is particularly true on balls way up and out. It requires a bigger step, and he should gain ground toward second as he lands with the pivot foot between a 45 degree and 90 degree angle to second base. (PHOTO 6-33)

When the catcher doesn't step up and out on a ball away, his body will tilt to the right and will force him to throw across his body. This forces his arm down to a 3/4 or side arm position which lacks power and produces sinking or tailing throws. (PHOTO 6-34)

If the ball is on the outside corner or slightly farther out, he can throw without a shuffle step. If the ball is low and on the outside corner to a right-handed hitter, he must roll his head to the left to get the arm up so he can throw with back spin (6-12 rotation). (PHOTO 6-35) If he doesn't roll his head, the arm will be down. This leads to a lateral side-to-side throwing action which also leads to throws that tail and lack carry.

Photo 6-33

***Left-Handed Hitter Up.*** With a left-hander up, the receiver has to delay a little bit, on balls inside, catch the ball back-handed and then step up and out toward the plate with the right foot to throw. That's one of the reasons it's tougher to throw with a left-handed hitter at the plate. He's not

Photo 6-34

Photo 6-35

Photo 6-36                                          Photo 6-37

allowed the luxury of gaining early momentum on the ball in to the left hand hitter. On the right-handed hitter, he can rake the inside pitch and throw right to second base. On the ball in to the left-handed hitter, he has to delay, so it's a catch-step-throw, rather than a step-catch-throw. The only exception would be when the left-handed hitter gives ground on balls way in or is knocked down and the throwing lane is open.

## THROWING RUNNERS OUT AT THIRD

To throw runners out at third base, the catcher must be clear of the hitter. He shouldn't throw through or over the hitter. He must clear behind the hitter on balls inside to the right-handed hitter and clear in front on balls away from the right-handed hitters. When he clears behind the right-handed hitter, he starts with the right foot. He can lead step (PHOTO 6-36) or drop step. When he drop steps, he drops his right foot behind his left foot and throws. This action gets his body away from the hitter and creates more of a throwing lane. (PHOTO 6-37) It also closes his front side which ensures good direction on the throw.

The lead step gets him closer to third with more momentum but does not give him as much lane, and he has to close his front shoulder to throw. He has the option to clear in front or behind on balls over the middle of the plate. (PHOTOS 6-38, 6-39)

When the ball is low and away, and he's tilted to the right, he just rolls his shoulders and gets his head out of the way to throw. This will get the ball above the hand at release. He aims to the foul side of third base. This helps compensate for the body tilt, which leads to throws that tail and end up way to the third baseman's left.

Photo 6-38

## SITUATIONAL THROWING

Here are some additional specific situations with our recommendations for throwing.

***Ball in the Dirt, Runner Stealing.*** If the ball is in the dirt and the runner is stealing, the receiver should short hop the ball on the move if it is not a deep backstop. The cutoff point is approximately 45 feet, depending on the speed of the runner and the game situation. If the catcher has pre-determined that he is going to pick the ball, he should try to step inside the ball with his right foot and catch the ball on the glove-hand side. (PHOTO 6-40)

If he can't get around the ball, he can pick it to his backhand side. (PHOTO 6-41) This technique takes lots of practice and is a case of do or die. Just make sure that the runner can't go to third if he misses the pick.

Photo 6-39

Photo 6-40

***Drawing Batter's Interference.***
Anytime the batter's swing brings him near or across the plate, it is important to throw through the hitter rather than around him. The catcher must make aggressive contact with the hitter. Really sell the contact. (PHOTO 6-42) If he makes contact, the umpire will call batter's interference. When an umpire calls batter's interference, you get an out 100% of the time. If the catcher dodges the batter who has illegally taken away the throwing lane, chances are you will throw out a low number of the runners stealing and batter's interference will not be called. The batter's intent has nothing to do with whether it is interference or not. The hitter can be called out even if he has both feet in the box.

***Throwing in a First and Third Situation.*** Many first and third defenses call for the catcher to look the runner back

Photo 6-41

at third base before his throw to second. The catcher looks for a raised glove by the third baseman or reads the runners body language and distance off third base. (PHOTO 6-43) If the glove is up, he arm fakes to second, jump pivots, and throws to third. With a LHH up he can throw straight to third. If the glove is not up, he continues the throw to second. He can practice this during infield any time he throws to second, as well as between innings when he throws to second after the last warmup by the pitcher.

## CATCHER'S PICKS

Catcher's picks are best after swings and misses or missed bunt attempts. On missed bunts picks should be automatic. Another good time to pick is on balls that the catcher picks cleanly out of the dirt. Runners are being taught to run on balls in the dirt so they are vulnerable when the ball is caught cleanly out of the dirt. The receiver and his infielders need to have a prearranged system for catcher's picks other than on missed swings or bunts.

You can utilize a delay pick system at first and third base for runners who put their head down and loaf back to the base at third or first. This is also effective for runners who start to look for their signals before they reach the base. The catcher loads up and goes to his left knee just like he's going to throw the ball back to the pitcher and then throws to third base as he pops the left knee down. (PHOTO 6-44) When he throws to third base, he needs to make sure he has a throwing lane by setting up outside and throwing in front of the right-handed hitter or inside and throwing behind the right-handed hitter. It's easier with a left-handed hitter because he has a

Photo 6-42

Photo 6-43

**Photo 6-44**

natural throwing lane. A great time to pick at third is right after a triple when the base runner's legs are a little dead.

The catcher can do the same thing to first base. The key is to drive the left knee straight to where he is throwing. He should always throw behind the left-handed hitter on picks to first.

## BLOCKING BALLS IN THE DIRT

A good receiver blocks the ball in the dirt; he doesn't try to catch it. His blocking technique is passive, not aggressive. He has a soft body when he blocks the ball, with his shoulders rounded and chin tucked. As he tucks his chin, his thumbs should be out so he has soft forearms or biceps instead of an angular elbow exposed to the ball. This reduces the risk of injury. He'll get a bruise rather than a fracture.

To block the ball that is going straight on, the catcher just folds his knees straight down and cuts the ball off as close to the impact point as possible. He must assume a semi-upright position with the shoulders just rolled slightly forward and the toes pointed out, not straight back. His buttocks are low, resting on his heels. (PHOTO 6-45)

Don't let him kick his feet back. Many catchers aggressively block balls into the ground and drive their chest down on the ball. By kicking their feet back, they are driving the ball farther away from the impact zone in a hard body action. If the catcher rejects the ball too far away, runners will advance. Runners are learning to read balls in

**Photo 6-45**

the dirt. The catcher will have a tough time throwing them out if he does not keep balls in the dirt close to his body. Kicking his feet back keeps him higher and more angular. It opens up more holes for the ball to get through and creates more angles and deflections. It also exposes the tips of his shoulders to balls that kick high.

He must get his hips around the inside and the outside pitch and lead with the knee closest to the ball. (PHOTO 6-46) He shouldn't lead with his glove. When he leads with his glove to his throwing arm side, he opens up his shoulders and it kicks the ball away at a critical angle. (PHOTO 6-47) He should move out and up to the ball right or left at a 45-degree angle and turn it back into the plate.

He also must adjust between the fast ball and breaking ball. The breaker tends to back up toward the pitcher's arm side after it hits. He needs to block the ball as close to the impact point as possible because it gives it less room to elude him. It is also at this point that the ball is moving the slowest, close to the ground where it's cushioned.

## TAG PLAYS AT HOME PLATE

The catcher must stay low so the runner can't knock him down. He shows the runner the plate especially on throws from center and right so he can avoid a collision. He receives throws sideways like a middle infielder. He must block the plate with his left shin guard while he is fielding the ball. The shin guard and foot should point directly at the runner. (PHOTO 6-48) He lets the ball get to him and goes straight down with a tag. Whenever possible, he gets the ball in his bare hand and keeps a little space

Photo 6-46

between his bare hand and the glove. (PHOTO 6-49) He lets the runner slide into the back of his glove and then gets the glove ball and bare hand out of the tag zone. He doesn't reach for the ball.

**Showing the Umpire the Ball.** The catcher then quickly shows the umpire the ball and looks for another out. (PHOTO 6-50) He makes an out call as he shows the umpire the ball, which is a subliminal suggestion to that umpire that the runner is out. He should keep his mask on for protection. If he's going to get the ball late and expects the base runner to try to run him over, he drops to both knees as he catches the ball and drives the runner over the top with his arms. Both feet should be pointed to the same side so his body

Photo 6-47

Photo 6-48

Photo 6-49

**Photo 6-50**

can move with the tag and avoid injury. (PHOTO 6-51) If he gets the ball with lots of time, he goes up the line and sidesteps the runner and tags him on the back. If the runner tries to run him over, the catcher makes him pay by tagging him high and hard. A smart catcher avoids collisions whenever possible and rolls away from contact when he is standing tall.

# CATCHING EXTRAS—
# RECEIVING THROWS

Your catchers will appreciate having these tips for receiving throws.

*Dropped Third Strikes.* Whenever possible the catcher should run the ball into the infield so he gets an angle to throw to first base. If it's way to the outside, then he throws from foul territory. Do not let him throw dropped third strikes with first base occupied and less than two outs, even

**Photo 6-51**

if the runner tries to steal second on a pitch. Remember that a ball in the dirt that he catches is still considered a dropped third strike.

***Backing Up First Base.*** The catcher should try to beat the runners to first base when he backs up first. He backs up first base on all base hits with no one on base. He gets in line with the middle infielder's or outfielder's throw in case they throw behind the runner at first.

***Force Play at Home Plate.*** The catcher positions himself in front of the plate with his right foot on the front edge of the plate. He anticipates a bad throw by keeping his knees flexed, and stays soft. (PHOTO 6-52) On a potential double play ball, he squares his shoulders to the fielder and waits to see the path of the throw. He steps to the ball with his left foot, then jump pivots to clear both the third and first baselines to get his momentum going to first base. (PHOTO 6-53)

Photo 6-52

Photo 6-53

If there is no chance for a double play, he is a first baseman. He stays soft and sees the flight of the throw and steps to the ball with his left foot, making sure he stays on the plate. This is especially important on balls to the side. He can cheat a little bit on balls thrown straight to him. If there is no play at first, he arm fakes and looks for runners rounding third base.

## CATCHING EXTRAS—HIT BALLS

Give your catchers these tips on hit balls.

**Bunts.** The catcher blocks a rolling ball with the glove. (PHOTO 6-54) He tries to circle the bunt down the third baseline with his back to first base, especially if it gets off the dirt. (PHOTO 6-55) If it's still in the dirt, he doesn't have to circle the ball. He doesn't have to get rid of his mask if it does not hinder his movement and vision.

**Pop Ups.** Pop ups around the plate will drift back to the infield. The higher the pop up, the greater the drift. Generally a ball thrown on the right side of the plate will be fouled right and those to the left will be fouled left. The catcher doesn't run directly to the ball; he goes down the foul line and waits for it to come to him. He must have his shoulders parallel with the base lines. On a ball out in front of the plate, he turns so that the ball is coming right to him rather than moving away. He can keep his mask on if it's a low bunted pop up.

The pitcher has priority over the catcher so he doesn't have to go very far to catch pop ups. He must find the pop up before he goes after it; when he finds the ball he hustles to it then walks under it. He runs on his toes and catches the ball "on his nose."

Photo 6-54

The catcher should catch the ball at eye level with the palms up whenever possible or with the fingers up at shoulder level. (PHOTO 6-56) The ball drifts depending upon the height of the pop up, the wind, and the height of the stands. Often when the ball gets above the stands and there's any wind, it will have much more drift. After the catcher locates the ball, he casually throws his mask in the opposite direction.

## CATCHER'S GAME PERFORMANCE

The catcher's chart in Figure 6-1 is an efficient game-time tool for evaluating the catcher. It is accompanied by a filled-out sample in Figure 6-2. Either or both of these can be copied as many times as needed for your team.

This information will help you, or any other charter, use the form.

Each pitch is charted by location: I=In, O=Out, U=Up, D=Down, UO=Up & Out, DO=Down & Out, and DI=Down & In.

A plus sign next to the location of the pitch indicates that the pitch was caught properly. UO+ represents a pitch up and out caught properly. Blocked balls are recorded in the lower left hand corner of the chart. Dd would represent a down ball that was dropped. A score is recorded at the end of each inning; 9/11, for example, would show that the catcher caught nine of eleven balls properly.

The charter should put a dot under the corresponding description in the second section. Properly caught balls are recorded under the + section. Throwing times are recorded in the bottom right corner of the chart. The accuracy of each throw is recorded with a + or a − sign.

Photo 6-55

Photo 6-56

Figure 6-1: **CATCHER'S CHART**

NAME:     DATE:     OPPONENT:

| INNING | SCORE | PITCHER |
|---|---|---|
| 1 | | |
| 2 | | |
| 3 | | |
| 4 | | |
| 5 | | |
| 6 | | |
| 7 | | |
| 8 | | |
| 9 | | |
| 10 | | |

KEY:   +=GOOD EXECUTION   D=DROP   BM=BODY MOVEMENT   NE=NO EXTENSION   PU=PICKS UP
      J=JERKY FRAME   NF=NOT FIRM   B=BOXED   BB=BAD BLOCK

| LOCATION | + | D | BM | NE | PU | J | NF | B | BB | EXECUTION |
|---|---|---|---|---|---|---|---|---|---|---|
| OUT (RHH) | | | | | | | | | | |
| IN (RHH) | | | | | | | | | | |
| UP | | | | | | | | | | |
| DOWN | | | | | | | | | | |
| TOTALS: | | | | | | | | | | |

BLOCKING:   +

COACHING NOTES:

PLAYER'S NOTES:

GOALS:

  –

| THROWING TIMES | |
|---|---|
| BETWEEN INNINGS | GAMES |
| 1. + - | + - |
| 2. + - | + - |
| 3. + - | + - |
| 4. + - | + - |
| 5. + - | + - |
| 6. + - | + - |
| 7. + - | + - |
| 8. + - | + - |
| 9. + - | + - |
| 10. + - | + - |

Figure 6-2: **CATCHER'S CHART (SAMPLE)**

NAME: ESPINOSA  DATE: 5/21/93  OPPONENT: MODESTO

| INNING | | SCORE | PITCHER |
|---|---|---|---|
| 1 | I+ DI+ O+ U+ O+ D+ DO+ | 6/7 | BREWER |
| 2 | U+ U+ I+ O+ DI+ DO" DM I+ O+ | 7/9 | '' |
| 3 | O+ I+ O+ D+ DO+ DI+ U+ O+ | 8/9 | '' |
| 4 | O+ I+ D+ OII I+ O+ O+ B+ D+ U+ I+ DI+ DO+ | 12/13 | '' |
| 5 | U+ O+ I+ I+ I+ I+ O+ O+ DO+ | 8/8 | '' |
| 6 | O" ISM U+ O+ O+ D+ D+ | 7/9 | '' |
| 7 | U+ U+ O3 I+ O+ U+ D+ O+ | 9/10 | '' |
| 8 | O+ O+ O+ I+ U+ D+ | 6/6 | ADGE |
| 9 | D+ D+ U+ OD I+ I+ O+ U+ D+ DI+ O+ | 9/11 | '' |
| 10 | | | |

KEY: +=GOOD EXECUTION  D=DROP  BM=BODY MOVEMENT  NE=NO EXTENSION  PU=PICKS UP
J=JERKY FRAME  NF=NOT FIRM  B=BOXED  BB=BAD BLOCK

| LOCATION | D | BM | NE | PU | J | NF | B | BB | EXECUTION |
|---|---|---|---|---|---|---|---|---|---|
| OUT (RHH) | 24....4 | 0 | 0 | 0 | .1 | 0 | 0 | ..2 | 24/31 |
| IN (RHH) | 18 | .1 | 0 | 0 | 0 | 0 | 0 | 0 | 18/19 |
| UP | 14 | 0 | 0 | 0 | 0 | 0 | 0 | 0 | 14/14 |
| DOWN | 16 | 0 | 0 | 0 | 0 | 0 | .1 | .1 | 16/18 |
| TOTALS: | 72 | 4 | 0 | 0 | 1 | 0 | 1 | 3 | 72/82 |

THROWING TIMES

| | BETWEEN INNINGS | GAMES |
|---|---|---|
| 1. | ⊕ - 2.06 | + - |
| 2. | ⊕ - 2.11 | + - |
| 3. | ⊕ - 2.18 | + - |
| 4. | + ⊕1.98 | + - |
| 5. | ⊕ - 1.99 | + ⊕2.04 |
| 6. | ⊕ - 2.23 | + - |
| 7. | + ⊕2.01 | + - |
| 8. | ⊕ - 2.16 | ⊕ - 2.06 |
| 9. | ⊕ - 2.19 | + - |
| 10. | | + - |

BLOCKING: + ‖‖‖‖ ‖‖‖‖ ‖   − ‖‖‖   .878   11/14  78.6%

COACHING NOTES: 1) MOST DROPS WERE ON BREAKING BALLS AWAY.
2) NEED WORK THIS WEEK ON BREAKING BALLS IN DIRT TO THROWING ARM SIDE.

PLAYER'S NOTES: I am having trouble on the breaking ball, especially the breaking ball. I am going to toe out more with my right foot and put more weight on my left foot.

GOALS: 1. Improve my ability to catch and block the breaking ball to my right.
A) Catch 25 breaking balls on the outside daily - Goal - catch 24/25
B) Block 20 breaking balls to my right daily - Goal - keep 18/20 within the 6' (radius) circle

# GENERAL INFIELD PLAY

Infield play is nothing more than a game of high-level catch, and it starts with the right kind of prepitch preparation and setup. Prepitch preparation determines where the players will position themselves before the pitch is made. Prepitch is the movement a fielder makes as the pitcher is delivering a pitch.

## POSITIONING

A straight away position for the first and third baseman means about seven steps off the line and seven back. For the shortstop and second baseman, straight away is 11 steps off second base (approximately 27 feet) and 16 steps back (approximately 35 feet). The key factor here is not the distance but the fact that your basic positioning is always being taken off the base, which is going to be the same on every field. Too often, infielders work off the cut of the infield, which can be different on every field. They should adjust according to many factors. They shouldn't play so deep that they outplay their arm strength.

Young infielders, especially shortstops, have a tendency to play the cut of the infield. This allows them to catch more balls but does not allow them to throw runners out. The ball takes more time to get to them, and they don't have enough arm strength to make up for the increase in distance. Young third basemen tend to play too shallow, which cuts down on their range. Another factor in prepitch positioning is the infielder's ability to move laterally. If he moves better in one direction than another, he may cheat his positioning to his weak side.

**Situational Positioning.** The game situation affects the basic positioning. Pitchers tend to have balls hit in certain areas, especially when they throw specific pitches to specific locations. Steve Carlton, who was an overpowering left-handed pitcher with the Phillies and Cardinals, had a great slider that he threw down and in to right-handed hitters. When they hit it, they either pulled it foul or hit it fair down the third base line. Mike Schmidt, third baseman for the Phillies, had to be aware when this pitch was being thrown so he could anticipate balls down the line. The type of hitter and his running speed will affect your basic positioning. This is true when your pitcher is not adept at locating the ball within the strike zone, so the hitter gets his pitch more often.

Hitters tend to pull more when they are ahead in the count and go the other way when they are behind in the count, especially with two strikes. The inning, outs, score, and location of the base runners will dictate changes in your basic straight away positioning. Field conditions like long grass, a wet field, sun and wind (wind can slow down ground balls) will affect positioning. Your emphasis is on making the routine play at all times. The outstanding play takes care of itself.

**Setup Position.** The infielder's setup position is critical. Allow for individual differences; but, in general, you want your infielders in a fairly upright position with the feet spread no more than shoulders' width. They should get the weight on the balls of their feet by flexing the ankles and centering flexed knees over the balls of the feet. It is best to get 60% of their weight on their strongest leg or "power leg," rather than balanced 50/50 where they have to load up one side or the other to move laterally. The 50/50 balance position tends to put too much weight forward where the infielder is falling to the plate. This really cuts down on the ability to move side to side or back.

The trend is toward a lot of momentum in the form of walking in or bouncing before or when the ball enters the contact zone. This is done to overcome inertia. It produces inefficient first steps to the ball because the infielder is moving before he reads the ball off the bat. That little bounce or set step, like the tennis players use, moves his eyes up and down at the critical point of contact. This is analogous to the hitter jumping in the air at the time the pitcher releases the ball. There can be some leaning before contact as a result of reading the hitter and his bat or body position, but the real read comes when the ball comes off the bat. The ball will tell the player where to go.

When an infielder sets 60% of his weight on his power leg, no weight shift is necessary to push off that leg. For example, if his power leg is his right leg, which is the case for most right-handed throwers, and the ball is hit a fair distance to his right, he must pivot on the ball of his right foot, cross over with his left foot, and go get the ball. If the ball is hit to his left, he will push off his right foot, and take his first step with his left foot leading. With a 50/50 setup, most infielders would shift the weight to the foot closest to the ball, cross over with the other foot, and go get the ball. If he shifts his weight after the ball is hit, it retards his movement to the ball. The player should take a positive step to the ball as soon as it is hit, and keep his eyes on the same level as the set up position. Rapid changes in eye height distort his perception of bouncing balls in flight. The player finds his power leg by performing a one-leg long jump with each leg. The longest jump identifies the power leg.

If the player sets up with the weight on his toes instead of the balls of his feet, or if he is not set but moving forward on the pitch, balls that he has to give ground on or move laterally on will lead to inefficient first steps. If he is balanced correctly, he will naturally react to balls that he has to move in or back up on. It is important that all infielders expect the ball to be hit to them on every pitch.

**Tracking the Ball.** There is more visual flow when your middle infielders track the ball from the pitcher's hand into the plate. It's like a ribbon of white going into the plate, and then a ribbon of white coming off the bat. When the player hard focuses only on the point of impact, the ball explodes into his visual field and causes a kind of a startled response that produces lots of false steps. The player must also read the hitter's body and bat position as he initiates his swing. The count, type of hitter, type of pitch and pitcher, and the situation also factor into his anticipated path to field the ball.

Your corner infielders will soft focus on the hitter to see any subtle changes in his bat angle, foot position, or position in the batter's box which might indicate bunt or intended direction of contact. Your middle infielders also need to pay attention to these keys. The corner infielder's focus is on the contact zone once the ball is in flight. The angle is too critical to track the ball from the pitcher's hand, and the player can't get an early enough read on the bunt.

***Reacting to the Ball.*** An infielder must read the ball off the bat and move aggressively to the ball. He should widen his base as he gets to the ball and keep his momentum through the ball. As the player fields the ball, he is moving forward. As a right-hander, the player would step with his left foot, then a short little shuffle step with his right foot, and he steps with his left foot to throw. His rhythm is left field, right-left throw. The stride with his right foot should be a low, short, shuffle, not a high, long, time-consuming stride.

Whenever possible, he should play around the ball and be moving toward the base to which he's throwing. It is best to field the ball off his left instep, just to the left of the middle of his body. If the player can't get around the ball to his right and it is not a full-fledged backhand play, the player can sweep the glove around the ball in a backhand position with the glove parallel to the ground. This should be done with the momentum moving to first.

The player should get the ball at the top of the bounce where it's moving its slowest, or at the bottom so that it's cushioned off the ground. Teach him to field the ball aggressively and play through the ball with his hands and body. He should slightly cushion the ball while he's catching it, but play up through the ball when he catches the bottom half of the ball. He should separate his hands out in front when he's throwing. It's almost like the player's taking the ball out of his shirt pocket to throw. (PHOTO 7-1)

***Hand Position.*** The infielders should keep their hands thumbs up, with the arms bent at approximately 45 degrees. Much like a boxer in a defensive stance, this is a neutral relaxed position that allows the infielder to move freely. Many infielders start with their hands—especially the glove hand—straight out in front of the body with the palm up. In order to move, they have to bend the elbows. The palm up, thumb rotated out position will stiffen the shoulders, forearms, and wrists, and make for stiff, hard hands and a slower take off.

***Glove Position.*** The approach is an offensive approach to defense; an aggressive approach. Your infielder is going to go get the ball. When he's fielding the ball, his glove is at a 45 degree angle to the ground with his glove hand at 7 o'clock and his bare hand at 1 o'clock. (PHOTO 7-2) If the player gets his glove too parallel to the ground, the ball will roll through his glove. If he gets his glove too much toward a 90 degree angle,

Photo 7-1

then the ball gets back too deep in the fingers of his glove and under his body. The glove is like a dustpan, and he's stopping the ball with his glove and securing the ball with his throwing hand.

He should field the ball out in front of his body and separate his hands in front of his body to initiate the throw. The 1 and 7 relationship of the hands (right-handed thrower) helps keep the hands soft and quick reacting. The 7 o'clock glove position exposes the most usable part of the glove to the ball. The web, index finger, and middle finger are the usable parts of the glove. Balls that make initial contact with the part of the glove that houses the little finger and ring finger usually do not get caught. When the glove hand approaches 6 o'clock, especially when it is in the center of the body, it locks out and tightens the hands and wrist, which makes for hard hands, and too many drops and ricochets. The

Photo 7-2

throwing hand at 1 o'clock allows for a natural transfer of ball from glove to hand, and can be used to protect the fielder's face in case the ball takes a bad hop and jumps up on the last hop.

# FIELDING THE HIT

The following techniques demonstrate how to catch balls to the backhand or glove-hand side and how to handle other specific kinds of balls.

**Backhands.** On balls hit to his backhand side, the infielder should catch the ball in the web of his glove, with his glove hand extended away from his body, and his throwing arm foot perpendicular to the direction of his throw. (PHOTO 7-3) If he tries to catch the ball too close to his body, the ball will hit in the palm of his hand and he will drop the ball. He then lands with his throwing arm foot forward, so that he can just plant and throw. If he's dealing with a slow base runner, the player may be able to take a "skip step" (crow hop) before he throws; but, in general, he wants to be able to plant and throw without any extra steps. There are going to be occasions when the stride foot is closest to the glove, and the player has to take an extra step with his throwing arm foot so that he can set up to throw. His step to the backhand side may be a crossover or a lead step, depending on which foot is his power foot. The angle of the step is dependent upon how hard the ball is hit. The harder the ball is hit, the deeper his first step must be to give him time to get to the ball.

Photo 7-3

***Glove Side.*** Balls hit to his glove-hand side can also be reached with an initial crossover or lead step, depending upon which foot is his power foot. Again, the depth of the first step is dependent on how hard and how far the ball is hit to his glove-hand side. The harder and/or farther away from him, the deeper the first step. Once he catches the ball to his glove-hand side, he must close his shoulders so that he can add direction and power to his throw. Sometimes, he's not afforded the luxury of being able to close up and throw because of the hitter's running speed, the speed of the batted ball, and his arm strength. In those cases, he just gets rid of the ball the best he can. Sometimes, when the ball is hit way to the shortstop's or second baseman's left (glove-hand) side, he will be forced to reverse pivot (turn toward his glove-hand side) to throw to first base. On balls to his glove-hand side that force the player to extend, if he steps to the ball with his throwing arm foot, he can get closer to the ball than if he reaches with his stride leg foot and drops his throwing arm foot behind.

***Slow Roller.*** When fielding a slow roller, players should use the following technique: The player fields the ball while his left foot is forward, and he makes the throw as soon as his right foot comes forward in the next step. It is all one motion. Whenever possible, he should throw the ball over the top so it won't tail or sink. In this case it is best to field the ball on his glove-hand side with one hand. He should bare hand a slow roller only when there's no other way of throwing the runner out. If the ball has stopped rolling, he should press down on top of the ball, and use the ground as a glove. If the player cannot get around the ball and his momentum is not headed toward where he is throwing, he'll be throwing across his body and have to start to throw three or four feet to the inside of the line. Anytime he is throwing, especially with a slow roller, he should take the ball up out of the glove. The exception would be the second baseman who is close to first and throwing from low three quarter or sidearm. He should keep the initial arc of the throw very short so that he can prepare himself early to throw.

***Arm Fakes.*** On all bobbles, where there is not a play, the player should fake a throw and look for runners rounding bases. There are chances for more than one out in every play. When a player boots the ball, always have him bare hand it in order to fake a throw. The player should also arm fake when there are runners on base and the ball is hit too slowly to complete the play.

***Throwing.*** In throwing, a player is working for quick release. He's throwing the ball from the position he catches it, using the wrist, forearms, hips, and legs. He must separate out in front, and get the ball out of the top of the glove as soon as possible, making that transfer with his bare hand on top of the glove. When the ball leaves his hand, it should be above his hand to ensure 6-12 rotation. He should work for a four-seam grip during the transfer, have his index finger and middle finger across the wide seam, and his thumb underneath. Short-arm action will elicit a quick release. Don't let him drop his arm below his waist to throw—he should throw out of his shirt pocket. He should also:

♦ Keep his momentum going toward his target whenever possible.

- ◆ Keep his knees bent, and use his legs and feet.
- ◆ Keep his eyes on the target.
- ◆ Avoid watching the ball in flight.

**Diving Catches.** Diving and catching balls is a skill that is developed through practice. Start the infielder with the ball in his glove and on one or both knees, preferably on the grass. From this one or two-knee position, the infielder dives to either the fore or backhand side, and pops up by using the hands, hips, and feet. It is a combination push-up and jump pivot. From this athletic landing position, the infielder throws to the base. He should make every effort to get the front shoulder turned to the target. There are situations where there is not enough time to get to his feet to throw runners out, so the player also has to practice throwing from his knees. This drill can be carried a step further by starting on his feet and diving. The next step in the progression would be soft toss, and then the fungo. Separate two infielders on the grass and try to fungo balls between them where they both have to dive to catch them. One infielder is diving to his forehand side and one to his backhand side, after which they switch. (Be careful to stagger the infielder so that they are not on a collision course.)

# THINKING IN THE FIELD

Here are some tips regarding the mental and verbal part of the game, another important aspect.

**Verbal Communication.** Verbal communication is a must on defense. It helps the player and his teammates to be alert and aware of situations before they happen. They must know the pitcher and catcher signs, and how they will work the hitters. It is a good practice to get in the habit of saying something to another infielder every other pitch.

**Making Friends with the Field.** Another form of preparation is called "making friends with the field." It involves walking the field before the game to find out the individual characteristics of that field. This checklist offers some of the questions you'll want to answer.

❐ Will the ball stay fair or roll foul at the foul lines?

❐ Is it a fast field or slow field?

❐ Is it a smooth field or bumpy?

❐ What is the distance of the perimeter fencing and outfield fencing so the player can avoid injuries and preplan his route on extra base hits?

❏ Where will the sun be at different times in the game and where can the player get a read on the wind (trees, flag)?

❏ What is the background like behind home plate?

*Being in the Defensive Zone.* When he's in the field, a player must be on defense. He should forget about the strikeout his last time at bat. Let him know that's history. Physical errors happen. Each player should create a defensive circle for himself. When he steps into that circle at the time of the pitch, he should focus totally on the flight of the ball and the strike zone out in front of the plate. He can't be in an offensive mode at that time. He can step out of the defensive circle in between pitches, but once the pitcher is ready to pitch, he needs to step inside.

He also has to be a grounds keeper. When he's playing on a bad surface, he should repair the divots that are taken out of the infield. Remind him that when he's on a bad surface, he has to play more aggressively and field more short hops.

# DRILLS TO DEVELOP GROUND BALL SKILLS

Most young players tend to take too many ground balls with not enough focus. They're better off taking fewer ground balls with quality than taking many.

When your players practice taking ground balls, make sure they incorporate a throw to a base. Just taking a ground ball off a fungo and throwing back to the fungo man is generally not a good practice situation because fielding and throwing is a one-part technique. Make your practice as close to game situations as possible by having players get as many balls off the bat as possible. Off the fungo, when they're not working on a specific area, have the fungo man randomly mix it up.

*Bare Hand.* Start working from the setup position, with no glove, and roll the ball to the fielder, who, in turn, moves to the ball, plays through it, and throws to his target. The emphasis is on technique, especially the hand position and the exchange of the ball from the glove hand to the throwing hand in front of the body. This drill isolates the hands and eliminates the body movement. Use of tennis balls also enhances the hand factor in fielding. Fungoing tennis balls and baseballs can also be done without a glove. All no-glove drills point out the importance of using the correct part of the hand (glove) to stop the ball (middle finger, index finger, and thumb).

*Paddle Glove.* A small glove or paddle glove is also a good training aid when working on improving glove and hand position, as well as transfer out in front. One-handed fielding with the glove hand only is another good glove position drill. It isolates the glove hand and can be done with rolled or fungoed balls.

*Shadow Drill.* Shadow fielding is a drill done with a pitcher and hitter. The pitcher shadows his delivery and the hitter swings the bat in response to the pitcher. The infielder works on the timing of his setup, and then reacts to the body position and bat angle of the hitter. The infielder will play through the ball, move laterally, or play it as a slow roller, depending on how he reads the hitter.

**Backboard.** Playing balls off a handball or tennis backboard is a great drill for working on technique. This can be done solo by just throwing the ball off the backboard and playing through it. Better yet, the infielder can set up facing the wall and his partner, who is behind him, can throw the ball off the wall, forcing the infielder to move in different directions at different speeds without predetermining his first step. This partner drill is excellent in forcing the infielder to gather information quickly before taking his first step.

**Golf Ball Drill.** Another good drill that takes place on the tennis courts or on pavement is a golf ball drill. Hit golf balls, not at high speed, but where the player has to work on getting the short hop and being aggressive going for the ball. The ball's a lot smaller, so it provides an overload.

**Hard Charge.** In the "hard charge ground ball drill," you start the infielder about 30 or 40 feet behind his normal position, have him run to his position, and hit the ball while he's on the run. He has to read the hop and get himself in a good balance position to play through the ball.

**21 Outs.** This is an excellent team defensive drill. Set your entire defensive team in the field, or just the infielders, and have a coach or pitcher throw batting practice strikes to a group of hitters. Let your pitchers hit. Direct your hitters to swing at every pitch and hit balls on the ground. You can create any one of a number of base running situations. Keep the drill going until you get 21 outs. When you use the outfielders, it can create backup, cutoff and relay, and pop-up priority situations. For the infielders, this is a good drill for developing first step quickness by reading body and bat angles.

**Kamikazes.** The kamikaze infielder drill is a multipurpose, multifungo drill. It must be carefully organized and closely supervised because there is a lot of activity. One man is fungoing to the third baseman, who is throwing to a pitcher or first baseman covering first. The shortstop is playing a ball off a fungo, and throwing to second. The second baseman is throwing to first, to a fielder just behind first base and on the foul line. It is important to have a protective screen between the person taking throws at first from the third baseman and the person taking throws from the second baseman. The first baseman is throwing his fungoed ball to second base, to a receiver who is just to the right field side of second base.

You need a protective screen between the person catching the throws from the shortstop at second and the person catching the throws from the first baseman at second. The fungo men hitting the second basemen and first basemen, need to alternate their fungoing so that the first basemen and second basemen don't field and throw at the same time. The same is true when you switch the shortstop to throw to first and have the third baseman throw to second. The possibilities of this multipurpose drill are endless. You can mix in slow rollers, emphasize forehands or backhands, throw to any base, and play the infielder at any depth. This drill provides an opportunity for a number of infielders to get a lot of balls in a short period of time and also involve throwing. It is important that this does not become a rush, rush drill to just get lots of ground balls, while the quality of this technique or effort suffers. This drill also cannot replace one-on-one instructional drills.

**Striped Ball.**  Throwing the ball quickly and accurately is as important as catching the ball. The throwing phase of the fielding process is also a learned skill. It all starts with the ability to throw the ball with good rotation (6 to 12 - backspin) to ensure carry and direction. The best way to teach rotation is to use a striped ball for all throwing drills. Take a black marking pen and make a wide stripe around the entire four seams of the baseball. If the player throws with good spin, the stripe will be clearly visible throughout the flight of the ball. Any off-center spin will distort the stripe on the ball.

**Throwing on Your Back.**  Throwing off his back with his hand above his head is a drill that puts the ball above the player's hand and forces backspin rotation.

**Down the Line.**  Playing catch down the foul line is another technique that will help the player monitor the spin of the baseball. If the ball deviates off the foul line, off-center rotation is indicated. The longer the distance, the better, as long as the ball is thrown on a line.

**Knee Throwing.**  Knee throwing, where the players are on both knees squared away to the person they are throwing to, is not only a good arm-strengthening drill, but it also emphasizes getting the ball out of the glove in front of the body to load up to throw.

**Four-Person Catch.**  Four-person catch is a drill designed to work on quick transfer and release of a thrown ball. The fielder must catch the ball in to the body, get it loaded quickly by getting the ball separated and gripped quickly, and release it. On thrown balls, the ball is going to move faster than his hands. So, rather than reach out for this ball, he should let it get to him.  You want your player catching the ball in to his body and "throwing it out of his shirt pocket." On balls outside his body, he should catch the ball with one hand, while keeping his momentum going towards his target. Four players pair off, with one ball and two players on either side. The ball is quickly thrown between the four players. As each player is catching the ball, he is stepping with his left foot (right-handed thrower) and then taking a short, quick shuffle step with his right foot as he is closing his front shoulder to step and throw. Having four players involved in this drill gives each player a chance to set up to receive and throw without being rushed.

**Four-Corner Catch.**  Four-corner catch is a drill that can be done on the field from home, first, second, and third, or at a shorter distance in the outfield. Divide all the infielders and catchers up between the four corners, and throw. They can throw in any direction: clockwise, counterclockwise, or across. It develops body position to catch and throw, as well as hand and foot quickness. It also forces accurate quick release throwing. The player can incorporate tags, force plays, double play footwork, and arm fakes and reversals into this drill.

In the second part of this drill, you shorten the distance to 45 feet or less, and throw clockwise without any movement of the feet. Have them preset their feet so that when they catch the ball, they are in a position to throw without taking a step (feet staggered with right foot forward). This is especially good for double-play feeds and turns by your middle infielders, but also has application for the catchers and corner infielders who have to make snap throws without moving their feet at times.

The third part of the drill is throwing counterclockwise at 45 feet or less without moving the feet. All throwers would stagger their feet with the left foot forward. On part four of this four-corner drill, close the gap to 25 feet or less. Start off counter-clockwise. This gives your right-handers a chance to work on their backhand flip, and the left-handers a chance to work on their underhand toss. As they get more proficient, the players can increase the distance. The last part of the four-corner drill is clockwise throwing. The right-handers work on their underhand toss, and the left-handers on their backhand toss.

This entire four-corner throwing sequence can be done in 5-10 minutes. Every now and then use wet balls for this drill for rainy days or days when there is a lot of dew on the ground. Remember, the player can't throw a wet ball hard.

## THE LITTLE THINGS IN INFIELD PLAY

Everything in baseball is important. There are no little things. Teach your infielders to watch the base runners touch the bases from the inside of the diamond. By watching, the infielders force the base runner into wider turns and increase his distance around the bases. The infielders must be far enough inside that they don't obstruct the runner.

***Covering Bases and Tag Plays.*** When covering the steal at second or third, make sure the players are positioned close enough to the base that the players get to the base in time to adjust to the throw but not so early that a player vacates his position before the ball passes the hitter. If the player vacates his position early and the hitter makes contact, the player is extremely vulnerable. In making tags on throws from the catcher, another infielder, or an outfielder, should make every effort to have his glove side to the base, so that the player can go straight down and make a tag. He needs to let the ball come to him and tag straight down—no reaching out to catch the ball or reaching across his body to make a tag. Both techniques are too slow.

At second base, your shortstop or second baseman may feel comfortable taking the throw straddling second base or with his left foot at the front corner of second base. But the best position is to start at the front corner, and when the player sees it is an accurate throw, he straddles as he catches the ball. This is especially good if it is going to be a close play at second. If he is going to get the ball early or if his catcher throws tails, he is probably best on the front corner of the base. Any time he is waiting for a throw, it is best to be in an athletic position—knees bent, back straight, and head up—anticipating a bad throw. The only exception would be when he is deking a base runner by being in a more upright and relaxed position.

***Infield Pops and Fly Balls in the Outfield.*** Infielders must help the outfielders on balls hit in the air because outfielders many times do not get a read off the bat. When the ball is hit, the infielders will yell, "Line, line," or "Alley, alley." This will help the outfielder to open up to the side that the ball is hit, and visually pick up the ball.

Photo 7-4

On pops between the infielder and the outfielder, you want the infielder to call for the ball late. He should call after the ball reaches the top of its arc, and he should make big arm circles so the outfielder can see the arm action as he is closing on the ball. This ensures understanding if the outfielder can't hear the infielder because of wind, crowd noise, or intense concentration. If the infielder calls late and the outfielder hasn't called for the ball, let the infielder catch the ball over the outfielder, even if he is drifting to catch the ball. The outfielder just peels off and doesn't say anything. This eliminates the possibility of collisions, and also keeps both players from pulling up and the ball dropping between them.

When the infielder has to dive for a ball in the outfield, he dives high, and the outfielder (PHOTO 7-4) slides low to catch the ball. Have them practice this in some kind of toss drill.

Windy days are great times to practice pop-ups. They also should be practiced in the sun with flip downs or sunglasses.

# DEFENDING THE HIT AND RUN

You need to recognize the situations in which the hit and run will be used. Generally it will be a close game or when the offensive team is behind, most often with one out. Usually the pitcher is behind or even with a hitter on the count, and all three ball counts. In general, the hitter is one who has a low strike-out ratio and is not a long ball threat. The base runner is usually not of blue-chip caliber, and the hitter usually has average to less-than-average speed. This will vary from team to team. It is also important to know each team's or individual's approach to the hit and run. Is it just to hit the ball on the ground, or do they try to stay inside all pitches and hit them the other way in hit and run situations? Does their strategy vary early in the game and late in the game?

***Modified Pitch Out.*** The modified pitch-out—an eye-high fast ball just off the outside corner—is one way of dealing with the hit and run and has three advantages: 1) It conceals the pitch-out so the hitter and base runner can't read it, 2) it gives the catcher an excellent pitch to handle, and 3) it is an extremely hard pitch for the hitter to handle.

***Switching Coverage.*** Switching coverage with the shortstop and second baseman is another way of defending the hit and run. Cover second with the shortstop when right-handed hitters are up, and with the second baseman when left-handed hitters are up. You need to be careful of covering with your second baseman with a left-handed hitter because with the first baseman holding the runner on base and the second baseman covering, a large hole is created. However, if you expect hit and run and your pitcher is throwing a fast ball out, it's not a bad gamble. The player can also switch coverages each pitch to confuse the offense. This is effective against hitters with extremely good bat control who try to figure who is covering and direct the ball to the vacated area. On straight away hitters, alternating coverage on fast balls is not a bad strategy either.

***Confusing Runners.*** Faking out or deking (pronounced "deek") the base runner on batted balls is a big part of defending the hit and run. If the ball is hit on the ground or it is a base hit shadow fielding a pop fly. The player has to be a good actor to sell this deke, part of which is to verbally say, "Up, up," in this situation. As important as the fake is, it is more important to play the ball first. Too often, infielders become so preoccupied with confusing the runner that they don't go after balls they should catch. If the ball is hit into the air, the infielders should deke, turning a double play initiated from the side of the field where the ball is hit. Everyone's verbal on balls hit in the air is "stay down," to make the base runner think the ball is on the ground.

A good way to confuse the base runner on routine fly balls to right field is by simulating an extra base hit to left field. Both the shortstop and second baseman go out in tandem to left field, as if it's over the left fielder's head, and the left fielder turns his back and runs for the ball. Most of these dekes work only if the base runner does not roll his head and pick up the ball off the bat.

As a catcher, with a hit and run and runners on first and second, the receiver has the option of throwing to second or third. If there is a blue-chip runner on second and he has a good jump, the catcher may throw to second to get the trail runner, who may be slower or will get a poor jump because he has to be sure the runner from second is going before he goes. The catcher has to be careful that it is truly a hit and run, and that both runners are going, so he doesn't pass up an opportunity to throw the runner out at third.

# SOME THOUGHTS FOR THE THIRD BASEMAN

Here are some strategies to consider for your third baseman.

**_Playing the Bunt._**  Have him take the bunt away from sure bunters by playing in their face. Tell him to start back and move up on the pitch. The key is to be in their face when they're bunting and at maximum depth when they're swinging the bat.

**_Playing in the Hole._**  Play the third baseman as deep as his arm will allow and as far off the line as possible without giving up routine ground balls down the line. Most third basemen play too shallow and too close to the line. Have him move closer to the line in no-double situations; for example, two outs, no one on, late in game, one run lead.

**_Starting the Double Play._**  The third baseman should lead the second baseman to first on double play throws, unless the ball's hit softly and it's not a double play ball. Then the third baseman can give him the ball at the base or behind it, depending upon the second baseman's preference.

**_Positioning._**  Have your third baseman charge the mound on all come-backers hit to the pitcher so he's in a position to field the deflection. Make sure he's getting off-speed pitches from the shortstop so he can anticipate or adjust his prepitch positioning.

# SOME THOUGHTS FOR THE FIRST BASEMAN

You'll want to give the following tips and suggestions to your first baseman.

**_Playing off the Line._**  You want your first baseman to play as far off the line as he can and still get to the base to receive the throw. The farther off the line of play, the closer to the hitter the player should position himself. Communicate and check the position of the second baseman on each hitter. With a runner on first, he should go and get as many balls as he can because he has the force play at second base. As soon as second baseman sees that he can field the ball, he's got to let the first baseman know.

**_Rounding First Base._**  Your first baseman should round into first base when he's taking throws on ground balls. This enables him to have better body control when he has to adjust to errant throws to the right or left. He should get to the base early and stay soft with his right foot touching the base (if he's right-handed).

**_Anticipating Bad Throws._**  Train your first baseman to anticipate a bad throw. If the throw is straight and it's a close play, he will come straight off with a throw. For any throw to his right or his left, he should keep his right foot against the base, stay on the base, and catch the ball. He should always catch the throw at full extension. On high throws, he should get on top of the base before he jumps for the ball, since he gains three or four inches before he jumps.

You want him to try to short-hop balls in the dirt. If the ball is at his body or to his backhand side, the player's going to sweep at the short hop with his glove in a backhand position, with his thumb parallel to the ground.

If he gets caught with an in-between hop, he should try to stay off to the side of the hop and draw his glove back in line with the ball. He should let his body go soft on all bad or in-between hops at his body, and remember that the ball is more important than the base.

He should cross the base line, and try to tag the runner from behind on all wide throws in the base line, rather than leave his hand out in front where he can be spun around and maybe take his shoulder out of joint.

***Improving Footwork Around the Bag.*** Fungoing ground balls to your first baseman at the base is an effective way to work on footwork around the bag. The first baseman should hold runners on from the home plate side of first base, and tag straight down. Left-handed first basemen will set up with their right heel on the inside corner of the base (corner closest to the pitcher) and their shoulders square to the pitcher. Right-handed first basemen will set up with the toes of the right foot pointed to the inside corner of the base and the left shoulder pointed to the pitcher. The right-handed first baseman will give a backhanded target to the pitcher. For pitchers with erratic throwing patterns to first, the first baseman may come in front of the base a little (toward the pitcher) so he can free his feet up and keep from getting blocked off by the runner.

***Positioning on the Pitch.*** Tell the first baseman to cross over and shuffle off on the pitch. He can cross back behind the runner and shuffle off with a left-handed hitter up. The key is to get as far off the line as he can because there are many more balls hit to his right than his left. When the ball passes the hitter, he needs to be ready to break back to the base for a catcher's pick. This is an automatic on missed bunts, and swings and misses.

***Taking Catcher's Picks.*** Have him take catcher's picks with his glove between his body and the base, wait for the throw—no reaching—and tag straight down. Do not let him reach for the ball because the ball moves faster than his hand can move, so he should wait for the ball and go straight down to tag. Whenever the runner is picked and running, he should go out and meet the throw to clear a lane for the throw to second base.

***Trailing or Beating the Runner to a Base.*** On base hits or extra base hits, he should break to the inside of first base to watch the tag, and force the runner into a wider turn. Trail the runner to second on sure doubles. In some cases, he should try to beat the runner to second base. This is good when the shortstop and second baseman misread the batted ball and vacate second. If the first baseman trails, the runner walks into second. This is also good on a sure double, when the runner is indecisive or trips rounding first base. With second base covered, he will retreat to first. The trailing first baseman gets an out once every 20 years. The first baseman arriving first will stop five or six extra bases a year.

Here are a few additional quick tips:

◆ The first baseman should give a sideways target to the outfielders on throws to home. He needs to be on the move before he catches the ball when he's relaying the ball to home. Fake cut the ball on throws that are to go through to home.

◆ The hidden ball is a great play, and the best time to use it is after an error or a double play that is not made. Make sure you alert the umpire before the game.

◆ When the pitcher's covering first base, the first baseman should give him the ball when he calls for it. He should be moving toward the pitcher after he catches the ball unless it is hit way to his right. He must follow all throws to first base.

◆ On certain hitters, with a runner on third base, the player can cheat his positioning up and to the line. If the ball is hit towards the line, the player can step on first and throw home for the tag out. This play must be practiced. It can become part of his pregame infield routine.

# THE DOUBLE PLAY

With the double play in order, both the shortstop and second baseman must position themselves closer to the hitter and closer to second base. How much they change their position depends upon the score, the hitter, his speed, the inning, the count, the pitch, and the quickness of the infielder, as well as the quickness of the field. Good infielders know the scoreboard. The scoreboard will dictate everything that the players do in the game. In terms of prepitch strategy, all infielders must be thinking ground ball, double play on every pitch, but realize that every ground ball is not a double play. The basic job of the infielder on a double play is to get one out. Once the player gets that one out, his job is done. If it is not a double play ball and there are multiple runners on base, he should use an arm fake and look for guys rounding third base.

*General Thoughts—Double Play Feeds.* Your infielder must find his target before he releases the ball, and attempt to keep the ball above his hand at release, to keep the ball from tailing. It is important to get to the base early with his knees bent, and anticipate a bad throw. Don't let him hide the ball from the pivot man. He should lower his glove as he feeds the ball. This is especially true for the shortstop and second baseman. Rounding the ball allows the pivot man to see the ball better. Let the receiver know when the player's going to underhand the ball by saying "flip," so the receiver is better able to focus on the release point. He must throw the ball chest high to the pivot man, and lead the second baseman toward first. This depends on the second baseman's preference, as well as the situation.

***Shortstop—Double Play Feeds.*** When the shortstop's moving toward the base, he's going to underhand the ball. If he's close to the base, he's going to take it unassisted as often as possible, so that he has a chance to step on the base and throw to first base. On balls that are hit at him and to his left, he's going to try to catch the ball with his right foot forward, so that he can see the ball and so that his hips are open to throw. He needs to get his right foot perpendicular to second base so that he's not throwing across his body.

If the shortstop ends up catching the ball with his left foot forward and he's in a position to be throwing across his body, he can take that extra step to open up so that the second baseman can see the ball when the shortstop drops his glove and throws the ball out of his shirt. The shortstop is throwing three-quarters with a relatively low elbow. Most of the time, he can pivot and unpivot his hips without taking a step. This is a quick short-arm throw with lots of forearm and wrist action.

***Shortstop—Turning the Double Play.*** The shortstop should get to the base early and get into an athletic position with his knees flexed, head up, back straight, and hands up, with his elbows bent. He should anticipate a bad throw by squaring his shoulders to the infielder initiating the feed. When taking a throw from the second baseman, he should keep his right toe in contact with the back side of the base. The direction and accuracy of the throw will dictate his footwork. If he gets a good feed—one that is within his body or a short distance to his glove-hand side—he should catch the ball close to his body, take the ball up out of his glove, close his front shoulder, and step and throw to first. Teach him to throw through the runner directly to first.

After the player releases the ball, have him get up in the air to avoid the double play slide. If the throw is farther to his glove-hand side, or if the base runner is on top of the player, he should swing more toward right center field to initiate his throw. Have him close his front shoulder on his throw to maximize velocity and minimize ball movement. If the second baseman's throw takes him to his throwing-hand side, he has to fight to catch the ball and get an out. Occasionally, he'll be able to turn two on this poor feed, if he is dealing with poor runners. The key is not to start his momentum until he reads the direction of the throw. It helps if he reinforces the second baseman by saying, "outside, outside," as he is making his throw. On bad throws, the ball is more important than the base. He should come off the base to catch the ball and go back for the force. At worst, this keeps the runners from advancing on balls that elude the shortstop.

When taking throws from the first baseman playing behind the runner at first, the shortstop should square up to the first baseman and place his right foot on the base. The sequence is to catch the ball, push with his right foot behind his left foot, and step and throw to first. When the first baseman is holding the runner on first, the shortstop should square up to the first baseman with his left foot on the base. On a good throw, he will push off to his right foot, step with his left foot, and throw to first. Bad throw adjustments are the same as on feeds from the second baseman.

In taking double play feeds from the pitcher on come-backers, the shortstop should square up behind second with his right toe on the base. The sequence is as follows: take the throw, slide the right toe across the back of the base, and step down the

**Photo 7-5**

line to first. He may have to swing out a little if the base runner is close or is an aggressive slider. Being straight behind the base puts the shortstop in a position to catch throws that tail from right-handed pitchers. This happens frequently because many pitchers tend to guide this throw.

Occasionally, the shortstop's going to be playing up the middle and have to take a double play feed from the third baseman. He turns this double play in the same way that the second baseman would turn a double play from the third baseman. If he is a little late, he may have to make this 5-6-3 double play from behind the base by stepping on the base with his left foot as he steps to throw to first.

*Second Baseman—Double Play Feeds.* In feeding the shortstop, the second baseman should underhand the ball if the ball is directly at him or if he is moving toward second, and throw three-quarters if the ball is slightly to the left. Some infielders are comfortable dropping down on their right knee as they uncoil to throw. It's best to field the ball to the left, with the left foot forward. He should be in a position where his shoulders are open to throw the ball to the shortstop, and he can easily see it. On balls hit way to his left, he's either going to go to first base, or he will make a full turn to his glove-hand side, and plant his right foot perpendicular to second base in order to make that throw. In most cases, the second baseman should go to first base on a ball that's hit way to his left. On balls that are in the line, he should tag the runner or backhand flip the ball to the shortstop. (PHOTO 7-5) If the ball is hit inside the base line, but too slow to get two, and the runner stops, he should either run the runner to first and throw to first, or fake the backhand flip, tag the runner as he runs, and then throw to first. When making the 4-3 double play on balls over the bag, he must let the shortstop know that he has the bag.

*Second Baseman—Turning the Double Play.* These tactics should help you train your second baseman for the double play.

♦ Footwork. The tempo of the footwork for the second baseman to turn the double play is fast/slow/fast. He should adjust his prepitch positioning so that he gets to second base before the ball is released by the feeder. If he goes hard to get to the base and gather as he approaches the base, he doesn't have to cheat his positioning so drastically, thus increasing his range. He must anticipate a bad throw on every play by setting up just behind second base with his left foot on the base. His left foot should be pointed towards the pitcher's mound. His knees should be bent with his ankles flexed, and his knees centered over the balls of his feet. His back is straight, with his upper body squared to the infielder making the feed. His arms are bent at the elbows to approximately 45 degrees with hands relaxed and either facing the feeder or facing one another. The second baseman must let the throw come to the player and catch it toward the heel of the glove if it is within his body. If the throw is outside his body, he can catch it with one hand. Catching wide throws with two hands makes it difficult to get his feet going toward first. If it is a very wide throw, he must get his out at second. If there are runners on first and second, he can arm fake to first and look for the runner rounding third base.

◆ **Good Feeds.** A good feed from the third baseman or shortstop will lead the player toward first base. On a good feed, he should step toward first with his right foot just before he catches the ball, and then step straight to first with his left foot. Have him hop in the air to avoid the runner. This technique gives him momentum going to first, a shorter throw, plus a clear lane to throw. Care must be taken not to step toward third with his right foot, which kills his momentum and leads to throwing across his body. Teach him to throw through the runner if he is in his throwing lane, and release the ball above his hand to keep it from sinking. He must take the ball out of the top of the glove and throw out of his shirt pocket to ensure a quick release. On a bad throw, he must get an out for sure. If the throw is behind the base, he can step back with his right foot, step on the base with his left foot as he throws. He can adjust down to a low throw by bending his knees. The ball is more important than the base on extra bad throws. He should come off the base and get the ball.

◆ **Balls Hit Up the Middle.** On the ball hit up the middle to the shortstop, the second baseman must square up to the shortstop with his left foot on the base as he will receive the throw. Then he must push off the base with his left foot, and step toward first as he throws. Finally he should get up in the air after he releases it to get out of the runner's way. If it's a bang-bang double play ball, and he gets his left foot on the base and gets the throw quickly from the third baseman or shortstop, he can just step and throw to first base without coming to the inside of the base line. This is also true if there is a very slow runner on first. He can get the feed right on the base and work his momentum right down the base line without clearing inside.

◆ **Come-backers.** On come-backers to the pitcher, where the second baseman's not covering, he should not break to the bag. He should stand still, kneel down, and point toward second base, so that the pitcher throws to the shortstop and doesn't get confused by having two guys break to the base. (PHOTO 7-6)

On rare occasions, on come-backers with runners on first and third and no outs, the second baseman will take the pitcher's feed and throw home. This could happen late in a close game where the runner on third does not break for home until the pitcher throws to second. The second baseman will pick this up out of the corner of his eye, or get a verbal from the third baseman.

Photo 7-6

# DRILLS FOR DOUBLE PLAY TECHNIQUES

Double play techniques should be practiced by starting with the ball in the glove. The player should work on the "fast/slow/fast" footwork and use all his techniques. Have him throw into a catch net or large screen 30 to 45 feet away. The emphasis is on footwork and body control.

Next, introduce a feeder and do the same thing. Help him work his way into a 90-foot throw. The emphasis is on catching every feed and making an accurate throw to first. Mix in good and bad feeds.

After that, time his double play turns from the time the ball hits his glove until the time the ball hits the first baseman's glove. His goal is to be 1.3 or better. If the throw to first is not accurate, do not record the throw. The tendency is for the pivot man to rush his throw. The focus is on being quick, but not rushing.

Later, mix in batted and/or fungoed balls so the middle infielders have to judge the speed of the ball and make a decision as to whether it is a double play ball and, if it is, how fast they have to turn it. You can set the scene beforehand by detailing the inning, score, and running speeds. The player can carry this drill out one step further by going out in the outfield with a couple of throw-down bases. Put some runners on first without their shoes, and have the pivot men take their shoes off. Now they can practice the double play pivot with live sliders.

The four-corner throwing drill found earlier in this section under "Drills to Develop Ground Ball Skills" is an excellent drill to practice the double play feed.

# OUTFIELD PLAY

In a typical nine-inning game with 250-300 pitches and potential plays, three or four pitches or plays will decide the outcome of the entire game. In this context, playing the outfield is the most difficult position. The outfielder is far away from the action—usually around 300 feet. It's easy to lose the intense mental focus that it takes to be at their best on every pitch. Infielders are close to one another and there is a lot of communication between pitches. This adds to their focus and readiness. Outfielders do not have this advantage. They have a lot of dead time, which allows their focus to waver. It's OK for outfielders to relax between pitches, but they must be in their defensive circle, fully focused for each pitch.

## THINKING BEFORE THE PITCH

As further proof that baseball is a cerebral game, the following discussion highlights the importance of the outfielder's mental set in being effective.

*State of Readiness.* Outfielders don't see as much action as infielders. The high state of readiness that infielders have as a result of the number of plays or potential plays is not present for the outfielders. The outfielder gets infrequent reinforcement for his pitch-by-pitch focus because there are so few plays, and most are routine. The discipline of the pitch-by-pitch focus pays dividends when the play is not routine, or the play is routine and something out of the ordinary happens. This usually manifests itself in a backup situation where the play is made 95 out of 100 times. Without reinforcement, many outfielders will not go hard on all 100 situations, and will not make the play as often as they would with a routine play. If an outfielder has good speed, he may not focus well because he knows that his running ability will save him. This mentality keeps him from getting to all the balls he could.

Offense is emphasized for outfielders other than the center fielder. When on defense, outfielders should focus on defense. The individual defensive practice time spent with the outfielder pales in comparison with the time spent one-on-one with infielders. Also, outfield practice time is more physically demanding than infield practice time because of the amount of running involved.

For all these reasons, it takes a special person to play the outfield. The outfield is the last line of defense, and defensive breakdowns in the outfield cost the multiple bases, runs, and games.

***The Psyche of a Great Outfielder.*** Great outfielders want to play defense. They understand that taking runs away is as important as driving them in. They get as much satisfaction taking hits away as getting them. They work as hard with their glove as they do with their bat.

A great outfielder does not know what it means to be stationary. He flinches on every swing and movement by the opponent. A great outfielder is a thinking out-fielder. He is always in the right spot, whether it's backing up a play or his prepitch positioning of the hitter. He runs his best speed on every play or potential play, and he runs his best speed on and off the field.

Outfielders need exceptional decision-making capabilities. In the infield, the deci-sion making is routine, but in the outfield, it's not as clear-cut. This is evident in the number of bases advanced as a result of outfielders throwing to the wrong base.

***Determining Position.*** A good outfielder expects the ball to be hit to him. He knows the count; he knows the outs; he knows the scoreboard. He knows his pitcher. This is really key. Everything is predicated on prepitch preparation. The outfielder has to play the pitcher first, because where he pitches and where the batter hits the ball is usually the most important factor in determining where the outfielder should position himself. In general, if there are two strikes on the hitter, the outfielder should move more to the opposite field side and shorten up his position.

***Additional Positioning Considerations.*** The field is also a factor in determin-ing positioning. How long is the grass? How strong is the wind? Where is the sun? These conditions should be assessed before the game. The ideal time to do this is dur-ing pregame batting practice, when the emphasis should be on playing the ball live off the bat. If there is no pregame batting practice, then the outfielder must walk the field before the game and really focus on pregame infield.

An outfielder should not position himself right in the sun because he probably won't be able to see the ball. Getting a jump on the ball is really critical. Sound and bat angle are also important, but the bottom line is that the outfielder has to be totally focused on each pitch. He can't be focused 100% of the time while he stands out there defensively. But when the pitch is being made, he has to be in his defensive circle of concentration so that he's totally focused on the pitch. The center fielder can follow the pitch and read the bat angle or the hitter's body position. Unless they're playing way in the gaps, the off outfielders (left field and right field), need to focus on the strike zone area out in front of home plate and read the bat and body angle.

The count is a factor to consider because hitters will pull more when they are ahead in the count. Obviously, the type and location of the pitch are factors. For this reason, it is helpful if the infielders can relay pitches and picks to the outfielders. This has to be done subtly so the offensive team does not pick up on the pitches. As far as location is concerned, in general, the low ball is pulled more often than the high ball.

This varies from hitter to hitter and pitcher to pitcher, and must be practiced by playing more balls off the bat during batting practice than the fungo in practice.

***Prepitch Setup.*** The outfielder's prepitch setup is much like that of the infielder. His hands are up, much like a boxer's position. His feet are not far apart—a shoulders' width or slightly closer. The shoulders should be square to home plate. The outfielder should keep his body moving a little bit because a body in motion tends to stay in motion. He should creep a little on the pitch, and if he strongly anticipates that a ball is going to be hit in a certain area, he might move toward that area. It's a short right-left-right or left-right-left step on the pitch.

# REACTING TO THE BALL

***Playing the Outfield.*** Prepitch anticipation based on the pitcher, hitter, count, and depth at setup will prepare the outfielder to make a positive first step. The outfielder's first step after contact must be directly to the spot where the ball is going to land. Young outfielders who are intent on getting a good jump tend to break on the ball before they really see where it will hit. This produces a lot of false steps, not positive first steps. He can lean or start his movement based on these factors:

◆ the flight of the pitch,

◆ the amount the hitter's body stays closed or opens up, and

◆ the hitter's bat angle.

He can't set the angle and depth of his first step until the ball is hit. The sound of the ball making contact with the bat, the force of the swing, and the trajectory of the ball leaving the bat will all factor in to the angle of the first step.

An outfielder should use the bill of his cap as a reference point. If the ball rises above the bill of the cap, he goes back on the ball; if the ball stays below the bill of the cap, he should stand still or be ready to charge a low liner. When in doubt, he must go sideways with his glove side, facing away from home plate. This usually occurs on balls hit hard right at the outfielder. The technique calls for a quick jump turn towards his glove arm side. This delays his first step, but puts him in a neutral position that will allow him to move in or back with equal effectiveness. (Left fielders and right fielders should open up to the line on balls hit hard directly at them.)

Balls that are hit to his right or left (not back) side are accessed with a lead step or a cross-over step. Some outfielders who have a little more weight on their power leg (strongest leg) will lead step to the side away from their power leg and cross over to the side of their power leg.

Many outfielders use a cross-over step to both sides. The key is to hustle to the ball and loaf under it. It is much like the fast-slow-fast action of the infielder approaching a ground ball. If the ball is hit back to the right or left, the outfielder drop steps (step straight back) with the foot closest to the flight of the ball. Then, he sets a deep angle with the foot farthest away from the flight of the ball. The depth of the first step must be deep enough to take him past where the ball will hit.

The outfielder must avoid the step that is too flat and produce an "L" route to the ball. It's inefficient because he has to run a longer distance and try to track the ball in flight. If the ball is hit straight over his head, he should drop step with the throwing arm foot, step straight back with the glove side foot, and look over the throwing arm shoulder. This technique allows for a positive first step to the ball. It puts the ball on the glove side and keeps the ball far enough away from his body so that he can get his glove to it. It also allows him to run straight for the ball rather than sideways (like running a carrioca). The exception to this technique would be for the left or right fielder who always drop steps with the foot closest to the foul line on balls hit hard straight at them. Balls hit right at the corner outfielders curve to the foul line.

He must try to get behind all fly balls and play through the ball, with the front shoulder closed. It is important to catch the ball over the throwing shoulder and have momentum through every ball. This holds true on routine fly balls with no one on base. Good technique is always important. It is not situationally dependent.

After the outfielder catches the ball, he should get rid of it quickly. An important rule of thumb: Never hold on to the ball in the outfield. On extra base hits and balls off the fence, he should throw with a lead step only, not a crow hop. He must get the ball in the hands of the relay man as soon as he can. It's the same on a ball that he catches in the air going away from the infield. He should get up in the air, jump pivot, and get rid of the ball; or throw the ball in midrun or in midair, especially if it's an extra base hit. The idea is to get rid of the ball and get it to the middle guys. Third base coaches usually hold runners at second if the relay man has the ball in his hand when the runner gets to second. They advance runners when the outfielder still has the ball or the ball is in flight.

There are situations where he jump stops. He'll go in the air and jump stop with the pivot foot perpendicular to where he's throwing the ball. The jump stop alleviates the extra steps that usually are a result of trying to stop quickly when you have lots of momentum.

***Outfield Correction.*** If the outfielder finds that he has misplayed the ball and he's facing to one side and the ball is behind him on the other side, rather than make a turn toward the infield so he can face the ball, he should make a half turn away from the infield so he gets his head and body facing the ball, similar to the way a defensive back gets beat by a receiver. Rather than crossing the feet and turning toward the quarterback, he just rotates his head and adjusts to the other side.

***Calling the Ball.*** On fly balls between the outfielder and the infielder, tell your infielder to call for the ball late and to wave his hands over his head. If the outfielder has not called for the ball and is going to have to catch the ball on the run, have him peel off and let the infielder catch the ball, even if he is drifting back to catch the ball. This eliminates the chance of a collision, as well as the chance of both the infielder and outfielder pulling up and letting the ball drop between them. If the outfielder can catch the ball standing still, he should call off the drifting infielder. If the infielder is camped under the ball, the outfielder should not call the infielder off the ball.

# COMMUNICATION

Communication is important not only in playing the outfield successfully but avoiding injury as well.

**Center Fielders.** The center fielder is the captain of the outfield. He has priority on all balls in the air between outfielders. However, you don't want the center fielder to make the play on the run when another outfielder is camped underneath the ball. The center fielder must make sure that the left and right fielders are in position and that they adjust their position when necessary. When the center fielder moves, he must take the off outfielder with him. In other words, if the center fielder moves to play a right-handed hitter more opposite, he must move the left fielder more into the alley in left field.

**Off Outfielders.** On balls hit over the outfielder's head, the off outfielder can direct the outfielder going for the ball so he doesn't have to look at the ball while he's running. The off outfielder can yell, "Run, run, run!" and "Look!" when the outfielder approaches the ball.

The off outfielder is also of great help on fly balls that are carrying an outfielder on a collision course with the fence. Most warning tracks are too small or nonexistent, so we use the verbal, "Three, two, one." "Three" indicates that he is 20 feet from the fence; "two" means 15 feet; and "one" means 10 feet. This technique gives the outfielder enough time to stop before he runs into the fence, but enough confidence to run hard until he hears "one." Most teams will say, "You're all right, you're all right," and then, "Fence!" just before the guy hits the fence. Once this has been used, however, no one is going to trust that call and most players will shy away from the fences.

A player can get to the fence, feel for it with his throwing hand or glove, and then work back off the fence. On balls that are hit to the fence and are to the right or left, the player can go to the fence and run parallel with the fence so that he doesn't run a collision course with the fence.

Here's a way to fake the runners: If a ball is hit over the outfielder's head and he can't catch it, but there are runners on base, the outfielder should put his glove up as if he is going to catch the ball. This has a tendency to freeze the base runners. If there is a player on second base and the outfielder is going for a ball in the alley, the outfielder should put his glove up as if he is going to catch it. Especially if there are no outs, the runner is likely to go back and tag, and the outfielder may play the ball off the wall and maybe hold him at third base.

He can also deke base runners on fly balls that he is coming in on. On balls that he is moving towards home plate to catch that he knows he can't catch, if he calls for the ball and waves his hands like he is going to catch the ball, base runners will hold up or retreat. At worst, he can keep the base runner from taking an extra base. The best case scenario will allow him to force the base runner. He'll want to make sure his deke verbal is different from the verbal he uses when he is going to catch the ball. This allows another player, usually an infielder, to go hard for the ball without fear of being run into.

# PLAYING THE HIT

Here are a couple of indispensable techniques for playing the hit in the outfield.

*Diving.* For balls in the air that a player must dive to catch, he should use a figure four slide. (PHOTO 8-1) This is for balls that the player is coming in on or for balls close to side fences. This type of sliding diving catch greatly reduces the chance of injury. It's best to avoid diving and just try to run through and catch the ball whenever possible to avoid injuries. However, the figure four slide will reduce the possibility of injury when an infielder is going back on the same ball that the outfielder is coming in on. You want your infielder to dive high on this ball to avoid the outfielder who is sliding low.

For balls hit in the gaps (side-to-side) that the player can only catch by diving, the player should dive and bring his hands into his chest after he catches the ball, and roll away from his glove hand. This prevents the ball from being jarred out of the glove on impact if he breaks his fall with his forearms and elbows. As soon as he hits the ground, he should bounce up and show the umpire the ball. A catch involves a voluntary release, so the player should take the ball out of the glove as he is showing the umpire the ball. If he really sells the catch, some short hops that he picks will be called catches.

**Photo 8-1**

On balls that are hit in the gap equidistant from the outfielders, only one outfielder should dive for the ball. The questions of who will dive should be decided before the game, usually on the basis of who catches the ball best when diving. The outfielder who is not diving must take a deeper angle and assume a backup responsibility.

*Ground Balls.* A player catches ground balls three different ways. He fields it in front of his body like an infielder, uses a do or die technique off to the side of his body, or fields it off to the side of his body and reverse pivots and throws (glove side turn).

He should play the ball like an infielder when he doesn't have to make a quick throw after he catches the ball. This occurs on a routine base hit or on a base hit where there is no play on the lead runner. This is the technique that gives him the best chance to catch the ball and not allow the batter runner to take an extra base. Generally, the ball is hit at the outfielder or a short distance to the outfielder's right or left. He must adhere to the "fast-slow-fast" technique. The player hustles to the ball, gathers and widens his base three or four steps before he gets to the ball to gain body control, and then plays through the ball aggressively. He moves to the ball with his stride leg, catches the ball (glove at 7 o'clock and throwing hand at 1 o'clock, for a right-hand thrower), takes a short shuffle step with his pivot leg with his foot perpendicular to the direction of the throw, and takes the ball down out of the glove and back to throw. This technique is essential on poor fields because it keeps him in an athletic and controlled position, and gives him a chance to adjust to bad hops.

# THROWING FUNDAMENTALS

Throwing fundamentals for outfielders are the same as throwing fundamentals for all positions. The outfielder must generate positive momentum towards the target. The front shoulder should be pointed towards the target as he initiates the throw. The weight should be loaded on the back leg with the pivot foot close to perpendicular to the direction of the throw. He should separate his hands with the thumbs down while loaded on the back leg, and get the throwing arm up into a power position (an "L" position with the fingers pointing up and the ball facing the outfield fence). The ball should be gripped across the wide seams to allow for four-seam rotation. The ball should have backspin (6 to 12 rotation) to insure carry. For this to happen, the fingers must be pointed at 12 o'clock at the time of release.

As the front foot plants, he should initiate the throw by rolling the laces of the pivot foot down. The head is level at release and follows the hand to the target. The chest finishes over the stride leg knee. The lead arm pulls down and towards the glove side hip, and the glove should not pass the hip. The lead arm remains flexed. An outfielder with a slow release generally has poor footwork and slow feet. The pivot foot is usually the problem because the player tends to take too long a step with the pivot foot after he catches the ball, and that prevents him from getting his stride foot down so that he can initiate the throw. The outfielder can't start to throw until he has planted his stride foot. The key is a short momentum step with the pivot foot.

*Targets.* In order to throw accurately, the outfielder must have a final destination—the place he wants the ball to end up. His target is what he aims at to get the ball to his final destination, somewhere between the waist and knees of the receiver. The player should not throw it above the waist because it takes too long to get to the tag zone; if he throws it below the knees, he will be fighting the base runner. When in doubt, he should throw it lower because low throws travel 10% faster than high throws. For example, on a 270-foot throw, a low throw will travel 297 feet in the time that a high throw will travel 270 feet. (A high throw is one that has an arc in it.) If it is a short throw or if the outfielder has an exceptionally strong arm, his final destination may be the target. However, most of the time, since outfield throws are more than 200 feet, the ball is going to lose linear carry.

In these cases, he has to aim higher to carry the ball to the target in the air. The ball must be high enough to get it to his final destination, but low enough so that it can be cut off in case it's off line or late. If he doesn't have enough arm strength to carry the ball in the air, he should one hop the ball to his final destination. The target will vary depending on arm strength. He should look at the base and adjust his point of aim according to his arm strength and distance from the base. He may use the cutoff man as a target, but he must realize that the cutoff man is not always going to be in the same spot (the base is always in the same spot) and the tendency is to throw to the cutoff man rather than through him. If the ball is off line or does not have enough on it to reach the base, a relay does not generally get runners out.

*Accuracy.* The most important factor in outfield throwing is accuracy. Of equal importance is having the decision-making ability to throw to the correct base. The key here is for the outfielder to know his throwing range. Assume that most runners will run 90 feet with a running start somewhere between 3 and 4 seconds. The outfielder has to know from what spot on the field he can throw the ball to second, third, or home in less than 3.5 seconds.

In general, the ball will travel somewhere between three and four times the speed of the runner, depending on arm strength and running speed. Hypothetically, let's say the runner from second is trying to score on a base hit to left field and he runs 3.0 seconds for 90 feet. The outfielder throws 270 feet in 3 seconds. The outfielder would have to catch the ball at 270 feet or closer and release the ball before the runner gets to third base to have a chance to get him out, if you assume it is a perfect throw and allow 1/10 second for the tag.

How does the outfielder know where 270 feet is? He walks it off on the foul line before the game and looks for a reference point on the side fencing. At home, there should be a mark on the fence. The outfielder knows his initial depth relative to the 270-foot mark, and how far back or forward he has come to catch the ball, as well as his momentum. This gives the outfielder a good base of information as to where to throw the ball.

All too often, outfielders give trail runners extra bases because they try to throw out lead runners when they don't have a chance to throw them out. Testing the outfielder's throwing times and measuring distances on the field gives the outfielders a realistic reference point for throwing to the correct base. You also have to factor in the outfielder's ability to throw accurately when he is on the move. If he can't throw accurately on the move, then he is probably better trying to keep the trail runner from advancing.

The scoreboard will also dictate where to throw the ball (inning, score, outs). With two outs in the ninth inning, and a two-run lead, with a runner on second, he may choose to disregard the runner trying to score and throw directly to second to keep the batter runner from reaching second where he can score on a simple hit. How the ball is hit is also a critical factor. If the ball is hit way to the outfielder's right or left, the priority should be to keep the trail runners from taking extra bases. A simple rule might be to attempt to throw the lead runner out only when he is moving directly towards the base to which you are throwing. If he fields the ball moving right or left at all, throw to second base.

Giving up free bases by throwing to the wrong base or right base poorly leads to big innings. For example, suppose there are runners on second and third and a fly ball is hit with one out. If the outfielder gambles and throws home when he doesn't have a play, he allows the runner on second to move up to third. Or, in the same situation, he should throw to third unless it's the winning run on third. The reason for this approach is that with one out, if the runner from second goes to third on the throw home, the next hitter must get a hit to drive the runner in. With no outs, the chance of a multiple run inning is increased, because if the runner from third is safe at home and the runner from second goes to third, the hitter can score the runner on an out. Multiple run innings get you beat.

***Do or Die Technique.*** The do or die technique is used when the base runner is trying to advance on balls that the outfielder is moving in on with his momentum going towards his target. This may happen, for example, with a ground ball base hit and a runner going to third or home. The outfielder should play this ball to the glove-hand side of his body. (PHOTO 8-2) This gives him a chance to have the maximum amount of momentum with the best opportunity to catch the ball consistently. When he catches the ball in front of his body, he has to slow down to gain control so that he doesn't knock the ball out of his glove.

**Photo 8-2**

As the outfielder catches the ball, he should have his glove side leg forward. He takes a quick shuffle step with his throwing arm leg and tries to get his throwing arm foot perpendicular to the target. As this is occurring, he brings his glove up to his throwing hand, separating the ball from the glove, and closing up his front side to throw. When his stride leg plants, he moves his throwing arm forward by rolling the laces of his pivot foot. The ball/glove separation is thumbs down. If he can't master the do or die technique or he is playing on an unusually rough outfield, he can play it like an infielder and just speed everything up.

For ground balls that are hit a long distance to his glove-hand side that he has to extend to catch, he should catch the ball and turn to his glove side (reverse pivot) to throw. The key is to plant his pivot foot perpendicular to his target and to make sure that his lead shoulder does not rotate prematurely off the intended line flight. This technique gives him the needed leverage and momentum to make a quick, accurate, and forceful throw. The option would be a clockwise turn to throw, which tends to be slower and less forceful. The clockwise turn takes longer to set up because it takes longer to stop the player's momentum away from the play and he ends up with less momentum in the direction of the throw. Remember, this is not for every ball hit to the player's glove-hand side; only those that really extend him with momentum going away from the play.

## ADDITIONAL TIPS

Here are some other tips for the outfield.

**Sun Flies.** If the outfielder is playing in the sun without glasses, he should block the sun with his bare hand, step to the right or the left, or start lower to get a different angle so he's not dealing with the sun. There's no sense in playing in an area where he can't catch the ball because of the sun. If he is playing with glasses, he should get them down as soon as he locates the ball. He must keep the glasses down until after he's thrown the ball. He needs to work with glasses. With the new technology where you can wear your glasses down all the time, it eliminates some of the problems of flip down glasses. Not all outfielders can see well enough with sunglasses down at all times.

**Positioning with the Infield in.** When the infield is in, the outfield needs to take up the slack and play shallower. They should also play shallower when way ahead to take away the base hit. There are more of these than extra base hits.

## THROWING DRILLS

The following drills, some with accompanying photos, are good skill builders for your outfielders.

**Long Catch.** Long catch down the foul line is another good guide for throwing the ball. Long catch is between 150 and 250 feet. You want a trajectory of this throw to be the same as the trajectory of the throw to any base.

One hopping the ball over a long distance is also productive. You want the ball to skip hard and straight which indicates good spin and rotation. Distance magnifies poor rotation. You can have a good carry at 150 feet, but the same throw might sink and tail at 250 feet because arm strength will carry bad rotation at shorter distances. A little tail or sink at short distances may not show up, but as you increase the distance, it really affects the flight of the ball. It's good to initiate the long toss with a crow hop, a step behind, or a combination of the two. This helps keep the front side closed and takes a lot of stress off the throwing arm.

**Back Throwing.** Asking a player to throw flat off his back with his head tilted up also fosters backspin throwing. This is also best executed with a striped ball down the foul line, with his arm aligned with the foul line. This is a good drill for players who throw with a lot of side-to-side arm action with lots of tail (9-3 spin) on their throws. (PHOTO 8-3)

**Fence Throwing.** Throwing with the throwing arm next to a fence also prevents the outfielder from dropping down and throwing from the side. (PHOTO 8-4)

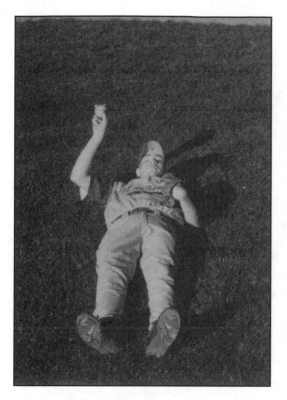

Photo 8-3

Photo 8-4

***Knee Throwing.*** Throwing off the knees with the shoulders square to the target also fosters arm strength. But more than that, it emphasizes separation of the ball from the glove in front of the body and not once the ball is loaded up to throw. (PHOTO 8-5)

***One-Knee Throwing.*** Throwing off one knee is also beneficial. Put the right knee down with the foot pointed straight back. The left leg is bent with the left foot slightly closed and pointed at the target. This leads to proper shoulder rotation and forces the elbow into an up and forward position at release. (PHOTO 8-6)

***Three-Man Throwing Drill.*** Three outfielders throwing on the field is a drill that allows outfielders to throw simultaneously to second, third, and home from their spots on the outfield. The left fielder will throw to second, the center fielder to third, and the right fielder to home. The outfielders switch bases until they get work throwing to all three bases. The outfielders can

Photo 8-5

actually warm up on the field throwing to bases. This drill gives the outfielders a chance to establish the point of aim for their throws. Carry this drill one step further by fungoing balls to the outfielders after they get loose.

***Bat Angle Drill.*** Put the outfielders in their respective positions in left, center, and right field. Have a pitcher shadow pitch to a hitter (alternate left and right-handed hitters). The hitter swings at the simulated pitch, and the three outfielders move in consort as a response to the hitter's body position and the angle of his club head. This is a drill that gives the outfielders a chance to practice their ready position, their momentum steps, and their first step and route to the ball.

***Toss Drill.*** This can be a two-man drill where one outfielder is tossing to another, or the coach is tossing and work-

**Photo 8-6**

ing with one player at a time. The drill starts with the outfielder creeping in preparation for the pitch. The toss man will work the outfielder right, left, back, back right, back left, with the outfielder focusing on his footwork. Work looking into or away from the sun. You can also bring the fence into play, as well as work on dive techniques. Tell the outfielder where you will toss the ball before you toss it.

***Outfield Correction Drill.*** This drill can be tossed or fungoed with the purpose of the drill being to learn the footwork for correcting the head position when he is looking over one shoulder and the ball is hit over the other shoulder. The outfielder breaks back, looking over his right or left shoulder. The fungo or toss man hits or throws the ball over the opposite shoulder. The outfielder turns his head and reroutes to get to the ball. The emphasis is on a quick head turn and an efficient route to the ball. It is important to keep the outfielder moving away from home plate and running hard (not side stepping) with a slight head turn. This drill can be enhanced by using two outfielders going back on the ball together. With two outfielders, you have to make one the center fielder before they break on the ball, so if they have equal chance to catch the ball, they know who has priority. The two-man outfield correction becomes a competitive drill that rewards the outfielder with the best technique.

***Line Drill.*** Line the outfielders up and start them running one at a time (work both right to left and left to right). The fungo man will lead the running outfielder with his fungos. Hit it to the outfielder on the run, or really lead the outfielder and force him to extend himself. The ball can be fungoed short or deep to force the outfielder to adjust his route. All of the above gives the outfielders lots of work catching balls on the run.

***Live Fungo.*** This is a simple little drill that gives the outfielder a chance to work on reading the ball off the bat, much like during batting practice. A feeder will soft toss the ball to the hitter. The outfielder will read the flight of the pitch and the hitter's body position to enable the outfielder to get the very best jump on the ball.

# DEFENSIVE STRATEGY AND POSITIONING

The focus of defensive strategy is staying away from the big inning and minimizing the damage. Most baseball games are lost, not won. In most games that are lost, one team scores more runs in one inning than the other team does in the whole game.

A good defensive strategy includes eliminating the following:

1. The base-on balls, and other free base situations.

2. Runners advancing on wild pitches and on passed balls.

3. The stolen base.

4. Runners taking extra bases in cut-off and relay situations.

5. Errors and compound errors.

6. Throwing to the wrong base.

It's the hidden things that really don't show up in the runs, hits and errors column, but do add to big innings because you're giving people free bases. Sometimes you have to concede that they're going to get a run this inning, but you may be able to keep them from getting two runs this inning. For example; if the opposition gets a runner on second base or third base with nobody out, you may try to keep them from scoring instead of concentrating on getting the hitter out. This heavy concentration forces you to try to get a perfect pitch on every pitch, which results in bases on balls. Or in your plan to get out of the inning, you alter your regular defense to try to get the perfect play.

## POSITIONING

Here are some positioning tips for infield and outfield as well as other general positioning ideas that can make a difference.

***Positioning the Outfielders.*** Play your outfielders as shallow as you can play them. With two strikes, go a little more opposite, and then bring the off outfielder up a little. Obviously game situations in the outfield are a factor. The information you have on opposition is important.

***Infield Positioning.*** Make sure that each infielder is positioned so that when he picks up a routine ground ball, he is in a position to throw the runner out. It doesn't help a bit if he gets to the ball but doesn't have enough arm strength to throw the guy out. You'd rather have him throw the runner out on all the balls that he gets to and get to fewer balls in terms of infield position. If he's too deep, he may get to more balls but may not be able to throw the batter/runner out.

***General Tips on Positioning.*** Bunch your defense with the outfielders more toward the alleys to protect the big part of the ballpark where most of the balls are hit. Play your third baseman farther off the line. There are more balls hit to the third baseman's left than there are to his right, and third basemen have a tendency to play too close to the line too shallow. He may have to play where he can accommodate his arm strength. It's the same thing at first base. First basemen play too shallow, and they play too close to the line.

When the third baseman plays too close to the line, the shortstop is forced to field more balls to his right, and most shortstops don't have enough arm strength to throw people out on balls to their right. Make sure your shortstop's position is shallow enough and have your third baseman off the line so he can cut balls off to the shortstop's right, which would be the third baseman's left. Playing the infield in and back or halfway is a decision based on personnel.

With no outs, teams have a tendency to play the infield in too much. If you play halfway, most managers will make the ball go through anyway with their base runner on third base, so you can gain some range by playing halfway. Or you can start deep and move up to halfway. Or you can start up and move back. A lot of times that base runner will look at the infield, and if they're in to start with, they're not running. If you back off on the pitch, in their mind they think you're in.

# DEFENSIVE FOCUS

Defensively the focus is on making the average or the routine play. Prepitch communication is very important in terms of alerting people to what they need to do before the pitch. You'll never make mistakes because there's too much communication.

Prepitch preparation is a real key to overall defensive strategy. Knowing the pitch, knowing the situation, and knowing your pitcher in terms of positioning helps you to win. Playing the pitcher before the pitch, and then adjusting according to the pitch, the count, and the hitter is how good teams win. The most important thing is knowing your pitcher and in general where batters are likely to hit the ball against this particular pitcher. Then you factor in the count and the situation, and that will also help you in terms of positioning.

In general, where a defense breaks down is when players try to do too much. For example, outfielders try to make the throw that's never been made before, or infielders try to go so fast that they're out of control. Teach them to be under control and make the average play. The defensive team that makes the average play the most is the team that's going to be the most efficient defensive team.

***Pitching.*** The best way to maximize the efficiency of your defense is to teach your pitchers to throw strikes. Statistics show that when pitchers get above the 15 or 16 pitch count in an inning they tend to be scored on. Part of this is because of errors that are created because the defense doesn't stay focused. The eight other players on defense can't help your pitcher if he doesn't let the other team's offense put the ball in play. A perfect inning would be three outs on three pitches.

***Avoiding the "Inevitable Two Runs" in the First Inning.*** The "inevitable two runs" occur for a number of reasons:

1. The pitcher does not really know what kind of stuff or command he has coming out of the bullpen.
2. The hitters are super-adrenalized and energized.
3. The umpire is searching for his strike zone and generally starts out with a small and tight zone.

In amateur baseball, it's usually only an inevitable two runs because the opposition runs out of talent. The sixth through ninth hitters in a line up can't help the offense no matter how adrenalized they are. The pitchers also tend to settle down once they have given up two runs.

To avoid the two runs situation, follow these guidelines:

1. Keep it simple for the pitcher. Minimize the types of pitches he will throw in the first inning. Don't let him pitch too fine—don't be a nibbler. But he also shouldn't over pitch. He doesn't need to use every one of his pitches right away.
2. Make sure the defense is super-focused and aware that it's going to take a great play to get out of the first without giving up any runs. Someone is going to have to throw a runner out, make a diving catch, pick someone off or throw a runner out attempting to steal.

## DEFENSIVE POSITIONING

To maximize chances for success you'll want to control everything you possibly can. Positioning fielders before the pitch is thrown is one of those. Championship teams do their homework, and always seem to be in the right spot at the right time. The following is a list of the often used terms in positioning players. In terms of feet, one walking step is equivalent to three feet.

***Opposite.*** Outfielders shift toward the right field line for a right-handed hitter, and to the left field line for a left-handed hitter. The opposite outfielder will be approximately 20 feet from the foul line; The center fielder, 100 feet from the opposite foul line; and the pull-side corner outfielder, 100 feet from the pull-side foul line.

The infield should have the opposite corner infielder playing close enough to the line so that a ball can't get between him and the line. The opposite middle infielder should play 45 feet from the foul line. The middle infielder on the pull side should be four or five steps away from being directly behind second base. The corner infielder on the pull side should be 25 feet off of the line for the third baseman, and the first baseman should play as far away from the base as he can while still being able to get to the base in time to take the throw.

**Slight Opposite.** The opposite outfielder should play 40 feet from the foul line. The center fielder should be half way between straight away and opposite, and the outfielder on the pull side should be 80 feet from the foul line. The opposite corner infielder should be ten feet from the line. The opposite middle infielder should be 50 feet from the foul line, while the middle infielder on the pull side should be 70 feet from the foul line. The pull side corner infielder should be 20 feet off of the foul line.

**Straight Away.** Both corner outfielders should play 60 feet from the foul line, while the center fielder should play one step to the left or right of second base. The center fielder should not be directly in line with the pitcher because he will not be able to see the ball being hit. The corner infielders should be seven steps from the base, and seven steps back. The first baseman may play a little bit deeper if he can still get to the base in time to receive a throw at first base. Both middle infielders should be 11 steps from second base, and 16 steps behind the base line.

**Slight Pull.** The opposite corner outfielder should be 80 feet from the line, and the center fielder should be half way between straight away and pull. The pull-side outfielder should be 40 feet from the line. The opposite corner infielder should be 20 feet from the line. The opposite side middle infielder should be 75 feet from the line, while the pull side middle infielder should be 55 feet from the line. The pull side corner infielder should be ten feet from the line.

**Pull.** The opposite corner outfielder should be 100 feet from the opposite side line, the center fielder should be 100 feet from the pull side foul line, while the pull side outfielder should be 20 feet from the line. The opposite corner infielder should be 25 feet off the line for the third baseman, and the first baseman should play as far from the base as he can while still being able to get to the base on time to take the throw. The opposite middle infielder will be four or five steps from second base, while the pull side middle infielder should be 45 feet from the foul line. The pull side corner infielder should be close enough to the line so that a ball cannot be hit between him and the line.

**Caution.** Be careful not to overlap your defensive coverage. You don't want to have a player playing where he can catch balls that are out of play. For example, the right fielder can't play 20 feet from the foul line when the out-of-play fence is only five feet from the foul line. The outfielder should be only 25 feet away from the fence. This would be wasting the outfielder's range. If the out-of-play fence was 30 feet from the foul line, the outfielder should have 50 feet of playing field to cover. This should be an acceptable position for the outfielder. Also avoid positioning two players too close to each other, as well as having outfielders play too close to the outfield fence.

***Straight-Away Depth.*** The straight-away depth of outfielders should be approximately 290 feet. Adjustments up and back can be made accordingly. Outfielders shouldn't be so deep that they're going to catch balls that are hit out of the park. Infielders should have three basic depths to position themselves. The straight-away depth is seven steps behind the base line for the third baseman, and 16 steps behind the baseline for the middle infielders. The first baseman plays as deep as he can while still being able to get to the base in time to take the throw. This positioning is referred to as the "three" position. The "two" position should be a half-way position. The corner infielders should be three or four steps behind the base line; the middle infielders, eight behind the base line. The "one" position should have all infielders on the edge of the infield grass.

# MAKING ADJUSTMENTS

These definitions are loose. They're starting points from which our fielders can base their positioning. Adjustments can be made from these positions. Middle infielders will have to adjust for double plays. Third baseman, shortstop, and the second baseman will have to adjust so that they can cover the base on stolen base attempts, and the corner infielders will have to adjust according to the possibility of a base hit bunt attempt.

***Number System.*** With the number system for infield depth, the coach may give out a number or use a hand signal designating the playing depth. For the flexibility to change the look of your depth, you may tell a player to play at the "thirty-one" depth. This means the player should start at the three depth, and then come up to the one position on the pitch. You could use any combination of these depths. It will give you the flexibility to play one side of the infield at one depth, and the other side at another depth.

***Third Baseman.*** The third baseman has to play the base hit bunt game. To win this game, he must be playing back when the hitter swings away and be in the hitter's face when he bunts. To do this, the third baseman must move up and back. He may start in the hitter's face, and then back up on the pitch. If the hitter is a definite base hit bunter, the third baseman should stay up in front of the base line for the entire at bat. He has to be careful he does not end up in "no man's land." This is the position directly in the base line. From this position, the third baseman can't defend a base hit bunt, and he has cut off his range to his left and right.

***First Baseman.*** The first baseman doesn't adjust as much as the third baseman does on bunts. Play the first baseman up in the base line and off the foul line if you think that a base hit bunt to second base is a possibility. You should do this only if there wasn't a runner on first base. The first baseman should come off the line one step for every step he takes toward the plate. This will help him maintain his range.

*Pitcher.* The number one criteria for defensive positioning is the pitcher. A particular pitcher can make a pull hitter a straight away hitter, or an opposite hitter a pull hitter. After the pitcher is evaluated, the hitter is evaluated. When these two factors are combined, the basic positioning can be found. For example, if you have a right handed pitcher with an over powering fast ball and an effective slider pitching against a right handed hitter that is a straight away hitter, you should probably adjust and play this hitter slight opposite or opposite.

## INDIVIDUAL SKILLS

A defensive player's skill level, strength, and speed will also help to determine his positioning. A shortstop who doesn't throw very well can not play very deep; he will out play his arm strength. Middle infielders who can run exceptionally well do not have to cheat as close to second base in a double play situation.

From your basic positioning, you'll want all fielders to adjust to the particular pitch being thrown. The players on the field should have a flexible system for relaying pitches. Three or four different systems should be used to avoid giving the pitches away. Make sure fielders don't make their adjustments so early that the hitter can tell what pitch is coming.

## OTHER FACTORS

You'll want to consider other factors when deciding the proper positioning. The count is one of these. Hitters tend to be more pull conscious with less than two strikes. With two strikes, hitters tend to shorten their swings and hit the ball the other way. Outfielders should adjust opposite and up with two strikes. With two outs and no one on base, make sure that you don't let balls go over the outfielders' heads. You may give up a base hit, but you want to defend against the extra base hit. A base hit will require two more hits to score the runner, while an extra base hit will require just one more hit to score a run.

Consider the score and the inning. With a big lead, you may bring the outfielders in and force the offense to hit balls over your heads. Remember, too, that weather conditions such as the wind and sun will affect positioning. Don't position a player where the sun is going to blind him. A wet field will require infielders to play a couple of steps in because the ball will travel slower on a wet field. Even the length of the grass can be a determining factor.

This information is flexible. Players will constantly make adjustments off of the basic positioning. Encourage position players to take responsibility to position themselves, leaving the coach only to fine tune the positioning.

# Section 10

# TEAM DEFENSE

Baseball games are lost, not won. A breakdown in team defense gives the opposition a chance to score. Once a batted ball is put in play, a perfectly executed team defense will prevent runners from reaching base or advancing to an undeserved extra base. Properly executed defense surrenders to the offense only what they earn and nothing more. Every defensive player has a role on every play. No one stands and watches. If a defensive player does not have a ball hit to him, he must be prepared to backup, cover or relay. This section discusses where each individual belongs in each situation. For each situation, you will find diagrams and explanatory charts that you can copy and hand out to players.

## CUTOFFS AND RELAYS

The goal of your cutoff and relay efforts is to keep base runners from advancing to bases that the batted ball does not entitle them to. It is imperative that all nine of your defensive players be prepared for each pitch. Before the pitch is made, each player needs to run down a mental checklist of what needs to be done on different types of batted balls. The factors that go into this mental checklist include how the ball is hit, the depth, the ball's velocity, the distance to the right or the left of the fielder, field conditions, arm strength and release of the fielder, the game situation, and finally, the base runner's speed. Most of these factors can be evaluated before the pitch is made. This limits the amount of information that needs to be processed after the ball is hit.

Coaches and players must realize that all nine players have an effect on every batted ball and that no player's role is any more important than another player. For example, when a batter hits a base hit to right field with a runner on first base, many would say that the most important aspect of this cutoff and relay situation is the right fielder's throw to third base. While this throw is important, there are many other "little things" that go into this play. For example, the second baseman should position himself on the inside of second base while watching the runner from first base hit second base. This should cause the runner to take a slightly wider turn around second base which makes the runner run an extra two or three feet to third base. Those two or three feet become real important on a "bang-bang" play.

The shortstop's job on this particular play is to line up to third base to be the cut-off man. If the shortstop does this correctly, he will be no more than 45 feet from the third baseman, preferably closer. By positioning himself in this manner, the shortstop has made it very difficult for the batter/runner to recognize whether or not to attempt to advance to second base. The runner can not make a decision on this until the ball has either passed the shortstop or has been cut by the shortstop. By being positioned within this 45 foot radius, as opposed to a sixty foot radius, the batter/runner's decision is delayed, which is an advantage for the defense. Also, it is easier to cut off poor throws from a position closer to the base because the player can come up to cut or relay a throw while still having more range in the handling of the high throw. With the above situation in mind, it becomes obvious that there are no "little things" when it comes to cutoffs and relays.

See the reproducibles in Figures 10-1 through 10-13 for defensive plays regarding cutoffs and relays.

## Figure10-1: SINGLE WITH NO RUNNERS ON BASE OR A RUNNER ON THIRD BASE

| | BALL HIT TO LEFT | | BALL HIT TO CENTER | | BALL HIT TO RIGHT |
|---|---|---|---|---|---|
| P | BACKUP THROW BEHIND 2B | P | BACKUP THROW BEHIND 2B | P | BACKUP THROW BEHIND 2B |
| C | BACKUP FIRST BASE | C | BACKUP FIRST BASE | C | BACKUP FIRST BASE |
| 1B | WATCH RUNNER TOUCH 1B, THEN COVER 1ST BASE | 1B | WATCH RUNNER TOUCH 1B, THEN COVER 1ST BASE | 1B | BE READY TO TAKE THROW FROM RIGHT FIELD |
| 2B | BACKUP THROW TO 2B | 2B | BACKUP THROW TO 2B | 2B | RECEIVE THROW AT 2B |
| 3B | COVER THIRD BASE | 3B | COVER THIRD BASE | 3B | COVER THIRD BASE |
| SS | RECEIVE THROW AT 2B | SS | RECEIVE THROW AT 2B | SS | BACKUP THROW TO 2B |
| LF | THROW BALL TO 2B | LF | BACKUP CENTER FIELD | LF | BACKUP 2B, SS, P |
| CF | BACKUP LEFT FIELD | CF | THROW BALL TO 2B | CF | BACKUP RIGHT FIELD |
| RF | BACKUP SS, 2B, P | RF | BACKUP CENTER FIELD | RF | THROW BALL TO 2B |

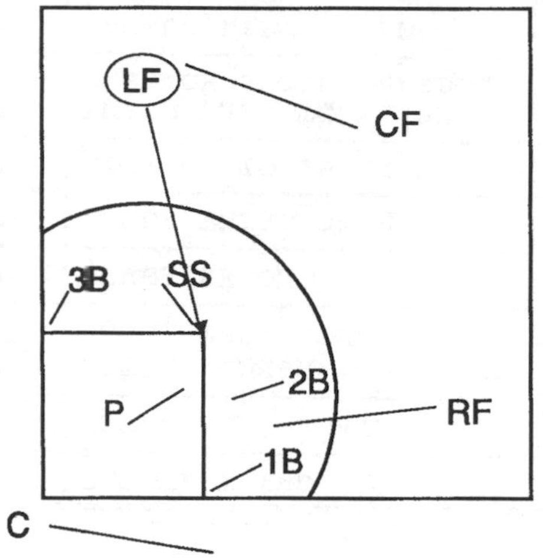

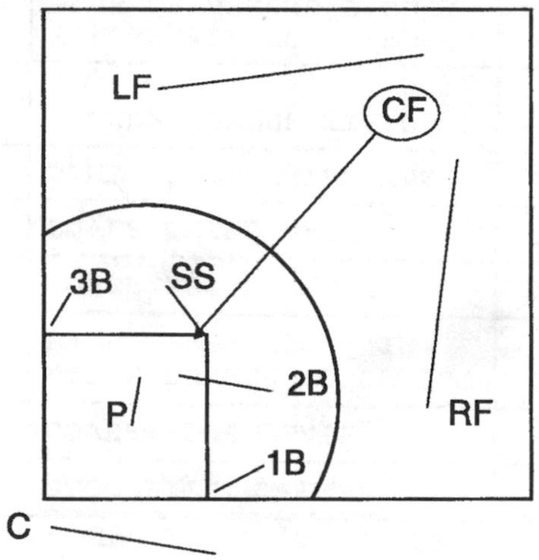

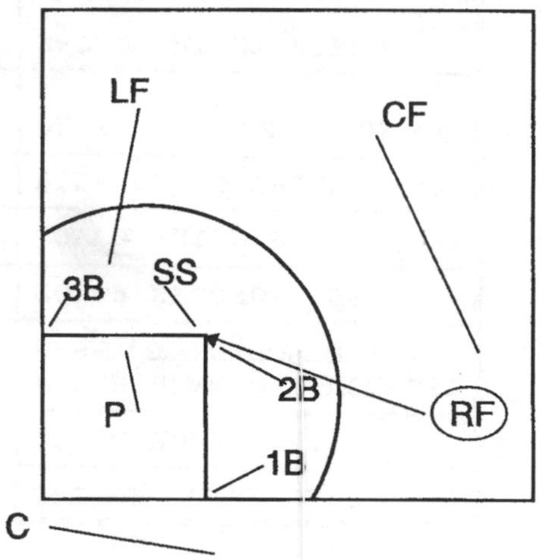

Figure 10-2: **SINGLE WITH A RUNNER ON FIRST BASE OR RUNNERS AT FIRST AND THIRD**

| | BALL HIT TO LEFT | | BALL HIT TO CENTER | | BALL HIT TO RIGHT |
|---|---|---|---|---|---|
| P | BACKUP THIRD BASE | P | BACKUP THIRD BASE | P | BACKUP THIRD BASE |
| C | COVER HOME PLATE | C | COVER HOME PLATE | C | COVER HOME PLATE |
| 1B | WATCH RUNNER TOUCH 1ST BASE, THEN COVER 1ST | 1B | WATCH RUNNER TOUCH 1ST BASE, THEN COVER 1ST | 1B | WATCH RUNNER TOUCH 1ST BASE, THEN COVER 1ST |
| 2B | COVER SECOND BASE | 2B | COVER SECOND BASE | 2B | COVER SECOND BASE |
| 3B | COVER THIRD BASE | 3B | COVER THIRD BASE | 3B | COVER THIRD BASE |
| SS | LINE UP TO THIRD BASE | SS | LINE UP TO THIRD BASE | SS | LINE UP TO THIRD BASE |
| LF | THROW BALL TO THIRD BASE OR SECOND BASE | LF | BACKUP CENTER FIELD | LF | BACKUP SECOND BASE |
| CF | BACKUP LEFT FIELD | CF | THROW BALL TO THIRD BASE OR SECOND BASE | CF | BACKUP RIGHT FIELD |
| RF | BACKUP SECOND BASE | RF | BACKUP SECOND BASE | RF | THROW BALL TO THIRD BASE OR SECOND BASE |

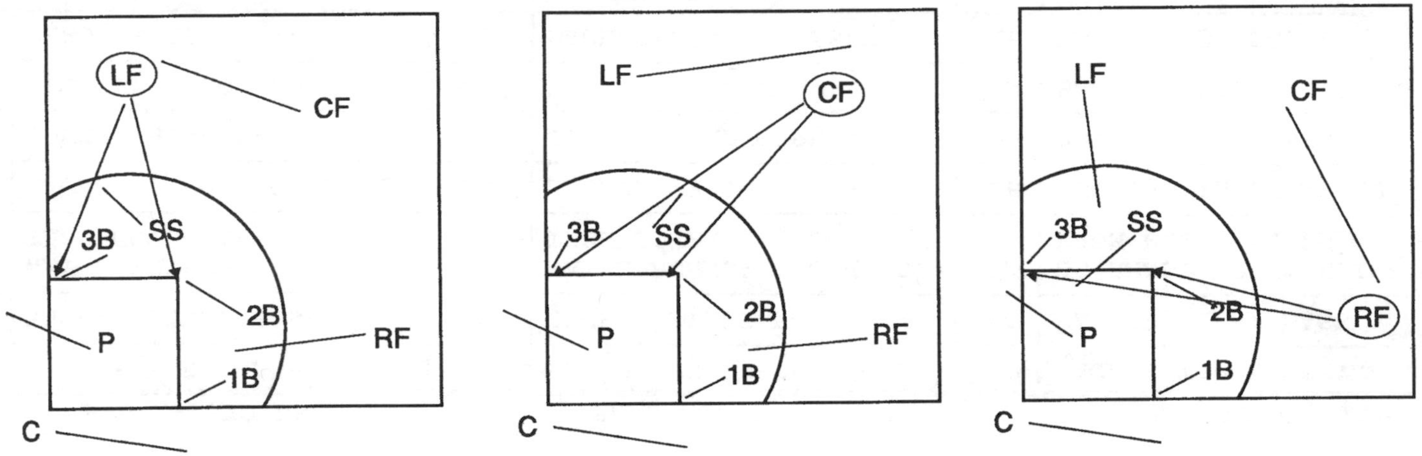

Figure 10-3: **SINGLE WITH A RUNNER AT SECOND BASE OR RUNNERS AT SECOND BASE AND THIRD BASE**

| | BALL HIT TO LEFT | | BALL HIT TO CENTER | | BALL HIT TO RIGHT |
|---|---|---|---|---|---|
| P | BACKUP HOME PLATE | P | BACKUP HOME PLATE | P | BACKUP HOME PLATE |
| C | COVER HOME PLATE | C | COVER HOME PLATE | C | COVER HOME PLATE |
| 1B | LINE UP TO HOME PLATE | 1B | LINE UP TO HOME PLATE | 1B | LINE UP TO HOME PLATE |
| 2B | COVER FIRST BASE | 2B | COVER FIRST BASE | 2B | COVER FIRST BASE |
| 3B | WATCH THE RUNNER HIT THIRD BASE, COVER BASE | 3B | WATCH THE RUNNER HIT THIRD BASE, COVER BASE | 3B | WATCH THE RUNNER HIT THIRD BASE, COVER BASE |
| SS | COVER SECOND BASE | SS | COVER SECOND BASE | SS | COVER SECOND BASE |
| LF | THROW TO HOME PLATE OR SECOND BASE | LF | BACKUP CENTER FIELD | LF | BACKUP SECOND BASE |
| CF | BACKUP LEFT FIELD | CF | THROW TO HOME PLATE OR SECOND BASE | CF | BACKUP RIGHT FIELD |
| RF | BACKUP SECOND BASE | RF | BACKUP CENTER FIELD | RF | THROW TO HOME PLATE OR SECOND BASE |

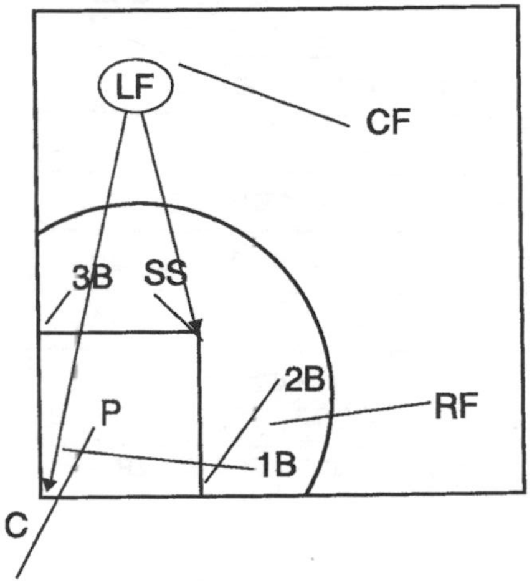

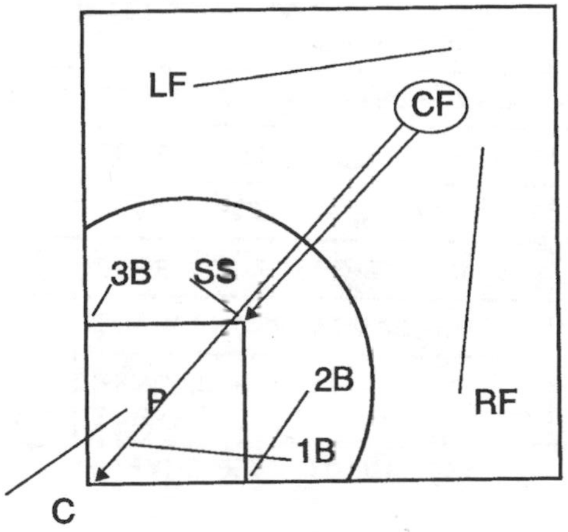

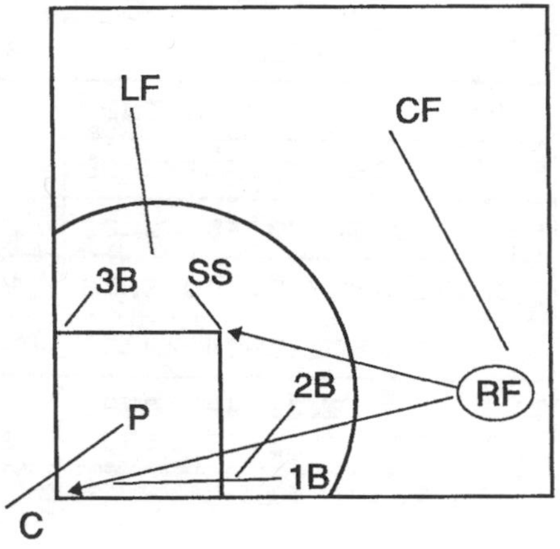

Figure 10-4: **SINGLE WITH RUNNERS AT FIRST AND SECOND BASE OR THE BASES LOADED**

| | BALL HIT TO LEFT | | BALL HIT TO CENTER | | BALL HIT TO RIGHT |
|---|---|---|---|---|---|
| P | BREAK TO 3B DUGOUT AND READ THE PLAY | P | BREAK TO 3B DUGOUT AND READ THE PLAY | P | BREAK TO 3B DUGOUT AND READ THE PLAY |
| C | COVER HOME PLATE | C | COVER HOME PLATE | C | COVER HOME PLATE |
| 1B | LINE UP TO HOME PLATE | 1B | LINE UP TO HOME PLATE | 1B | LINE UP TO HOME PLATE |
| 2B | COVER SECOND BASE | 2B | COVER SECOND BASE | 2B | COVER SECOND BASE |
| 3B | COVER THIRD BASE | 3B | COVER THIRD BASE | 3B | COVER THIRD BASE |
| SS | LINE UP TO THIRD BASE | SS | LINE UP TO THIRD BASE | SS | LINE UP TO THIRD BASE |
| LF | CAN THROW TO SECOND, THIRD, OR HOME PLATE | LF | BACKUP CENTER FIELD | LF | BACKUP SECOND BASE |
| CF | BACKUP LEFT FIELD | CF | CAN THROW TO SECOND, THIRD, OR HOME PLATE | CF | BACKUP RIGHT FIELD |
| RF | BACKUP SECOND BASE | RF | BACKUP CENTER FIELD | RF | CAN THROW TO SECOND, THIRD, OR HOME PLATE |

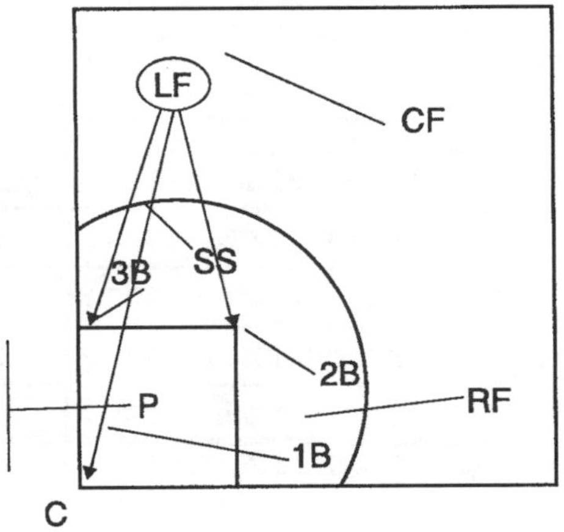

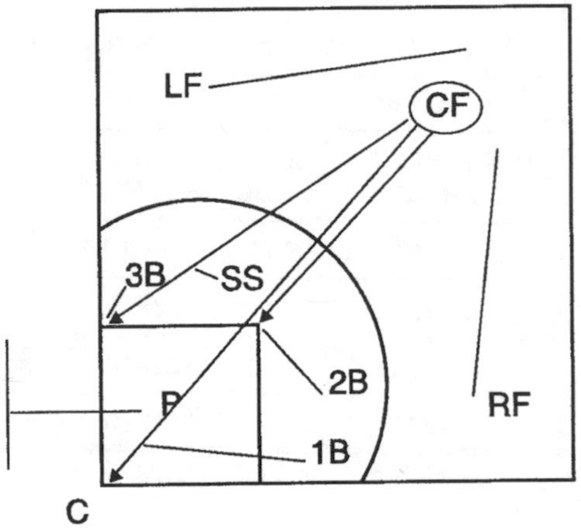

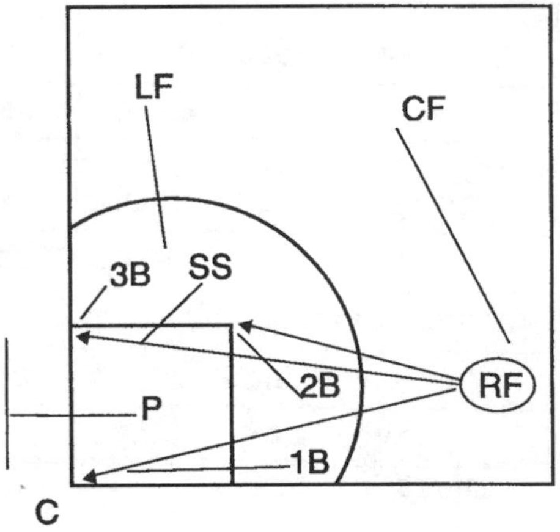

Figure 10-5: **SURE DOUBLE WITH NOBODY ON BASE, A RUNNER ON SECOND BASE, OR RUNNERS ON 2ND AND 3RD BASE**

| | BALL HIT TO LEFT | | BALL HIT TO LEFT CENTER | | BALL HIT TO CENTER |
|---|---|---|---|---|---|
| P | BACKUP THIRD BASE | P | BACKUP THIRD BASE | P | BACKUP THIRD BASE |
| C | COVER HOME PLATE | C | COVER HOME PLATE | C | COVER HOME PLATE |
| 1B | BEAT THE RUNNER TO 2B | 1B | BEAT THE RUNNER TO 2B | 1B | BEAT THE RUNNER TO 2B |
| 2B | BACKUP TANDEM RELAY | 2B | BACKUP TANDEM RELAY | 2B | BACKUP TANDEM RELAY |
| 3B | COVER THIRD BASE | 3B | COVER THIRD BASE | 3B | COVER THIRD BASE |
| SS | LEAD TANDEM RELAY | SS | LEAD TANDEM RELAY | SS | LEAD TANDEM RELAY |
| LF | THROW BALL TO TANDEM RELAY (SS,2B) | LF | GO FOR THE BALL, THROW BALL TO TANDEM RELAY (SS,2B) | LF | BACKUP THIRD BASE |
| CF | BACKUP SECOND BASE | CF | GO FOR THE BALL, THROW BALL TO TANDEM RELAY (SS,2B) | CF | THROW THE BALL TO TANDEM RELAY (SS,2B) |
| RF | BACKUP SECOND BASE | RF | BACKUP SECOND BASE | RF | BACKUP SECOND BASE |

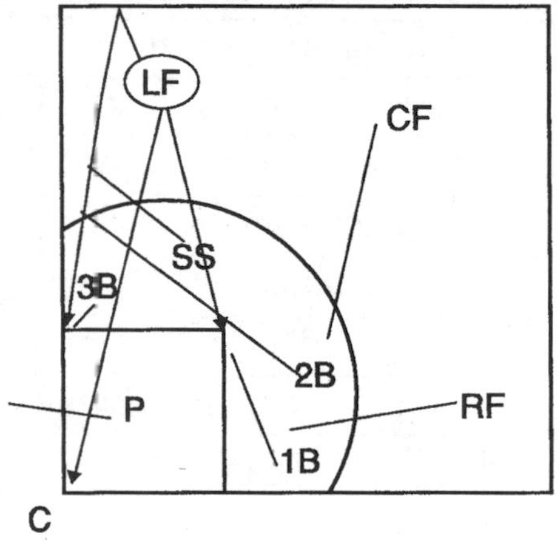

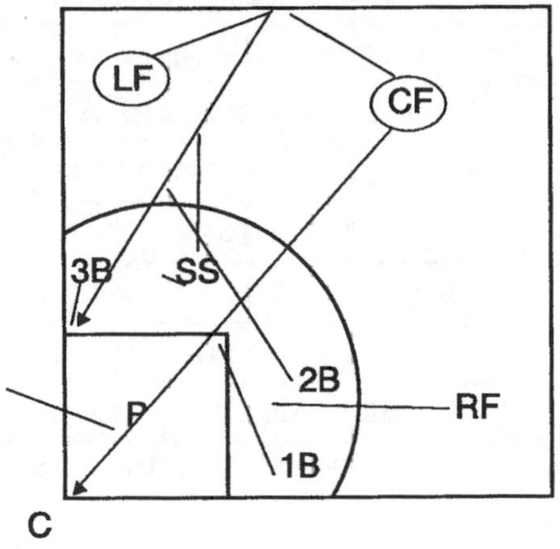

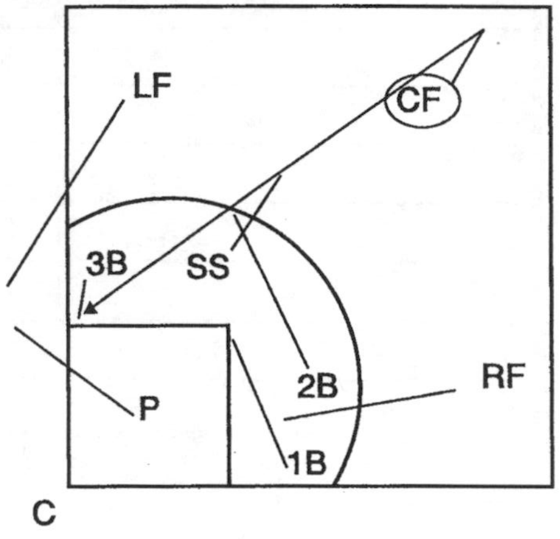

## Figure 10-5: Sure Double with Nobody on Base, a Runner on Second Base, or Runners on 2nd and 3rd Base (continued)

| | BALL HIT TO RIGHT CENTER | | BALL HIT TO RIGHT | | |
|---|---|---|---|---|---|
| P | BACKUP THIRD BASE | P | BACKUP THIRD BASE | | |
| C | COVER HOME PLATE | C | COVER HOME PLATE | | |
| 1B | BEAT THE RUNNER TO 2B | 1B | BEAT THE RUNNER TO 2B | | |
| 2B | LEAD TANDEM RELAY | 2B | LEAD TANDEM RELAY | | |
| 3B | COVER THIRD BASE | 3B | COVER THIRD BASE | | |
| SS | BACKUP TANDEM RELAY | SS | BACKUP TANDEM RELAY | | |
| LF | BACKUP SECOND BASE | LF | BACKUP THIRD BASE | | |
| CF | GO FOR THE BALL, THROW BALL TO TANDEM RELAY (2B, SS) | CF | BACKUP SECOND BASE | | |
| RF | GO FOR THE BALL, THROW BALL TO TANDEM RELAY (2B, SS) | RF | THROW THE BALL TO TANDEM RELAY (2B, SS) | | |

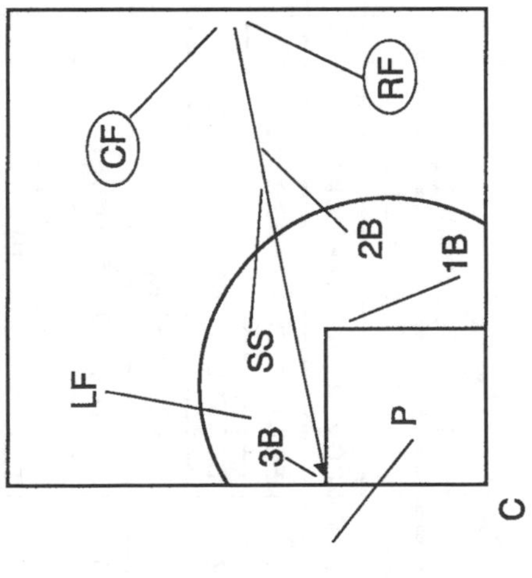


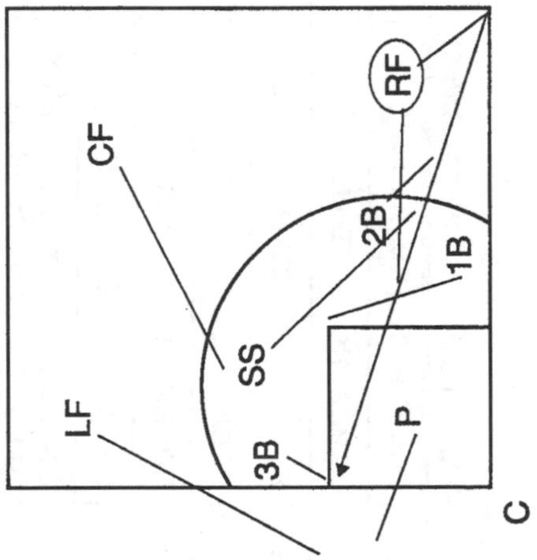

Figure 10-6: **SURE DOUBLE WITH A RUNNER ON FIRST BASE, RUNNERS ON FIRST AND SECOND, RUNNERS ON FIRST AND THIRD, OR THE BASES LOADED**

| | BALL HIT TO LEFT | BALL HIT TO LEFT CENTER | BALL HIT TO CENTER |
|---|---|---|---|
| P | BREAK TO 3B DUGOUT AND READ THE PLAY | BREAK TO 3B DUGOUT AND READ THE PLAY | BREAK TO 3B DUGOUT AND READ THE PLAY |
| C | COVER HOME PLATE | COVER HOME PLATE | COVER HOME PLATE |
| 1B | LINE UP TO HOME PLATE | LINE UP TO HOME PLATE | LINE UP TO HOME PLATE |
| 2B | BACKUP TANDEM RELAY* | BACKUP TANDEM RELAY | BACKUP TANDEM RELAY |
| 3B | COVER THIRD BASE | COVER THIRD BASE | COVER THIRD BASE |
| SS | LEAD TANDEM RELAY* | LEAD TANDEM RELAY | LEAD TANDEM RELAY |
| LF | THROW BALL TO TANDEM RELAY (SS,2B) | GO FOR THE BALL, THROW BALL TO RELAY (SS,2B) | BACKUP THIRD BASE |
| CF | BACKUP SECOND BASE | GO FOR THE BALL, THROW BALL TO RELAY (SS,2B) | THROW BALL TO TANDEM RELAY (SS,2B) |
| RF | COVER SECOND BASE | COVER SECOND BASE | COVER SECOND BASE |

*Tandem relay must stay in fair territory so that a throwing lane is created to home plate. If the tandem team is in the baseline or foul territory, the runner that is trying to score may screen the catcher from the ball.

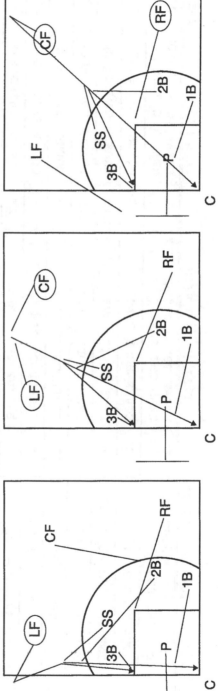

Figure 10-6: **SURE DOUBLE WITH A RUNNER ON FIRST BASE, RUNNERS ON FIRST AND SECOND, RUNNERS ON FIRST AND THIRD, OR THE BASES LOADED (CONTINUED)**

| | BALL HIT TO RIGHT CENTER | | BALL HIT TO RIGHT | | BALL HIT DOWN RF LINE |
|---|---|---|---|---|---|
| P | BREAK TO 3B DUGOUT AND READ THE PLAY | P | BREAK TO 3B DUGOUT AND READ THE PLAY | P | BREAK TO 3B DUGOUT AND READ THE PLAY |
| C | COVER HOME PLATE | C | COVER HOME PLATE | C | COVER HOME PLATE |
| 1B | LINE UP TO HOME PLATE | 1B | LINE UP TO HOME PLATE | 1B | BACKUP TANDEM RELAY |
| 2B | LEAD TANDEM RELAY | 2B | LEAD TANDEM RELAY | 2B | LEAD TANDEM RELAY |
| 3B | COVER THIRD BASE | 3B | COVER THIRD BASE | 3B | COVER THIRD BASE |
| SS | BACKUP TANDEM RELAY | SS | BACKUP TANDEM RELAY | SS | COVER SECOND BASE |
| LF | COVER SECOND BASE | LF | BACKUP THIRD BASE | LF | BACKUP THIRD BASE |
| CF | GO FOR THE BALL, THROW BALL TO RELAY (2B, SS) | CF | COVER SECOND BASE | CF | BACKUP SECOND BASE |
| RF | GO FOR THE BALL, THROW BALL TO RELAY (2B, SS) | RF | THROW BALL TO TANDEM RELAY MAN (2B, SS) | RF | THROW BALL TO TANDEM RELAY MAN (2B, 1B) |

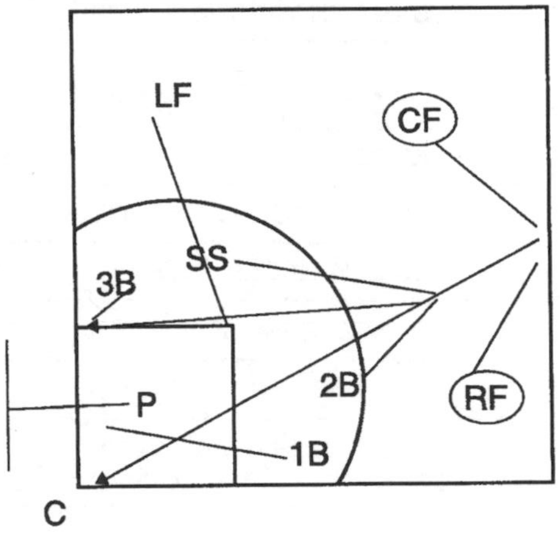

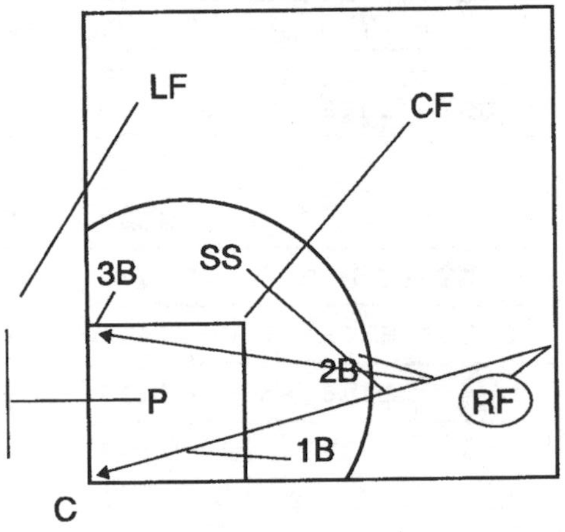

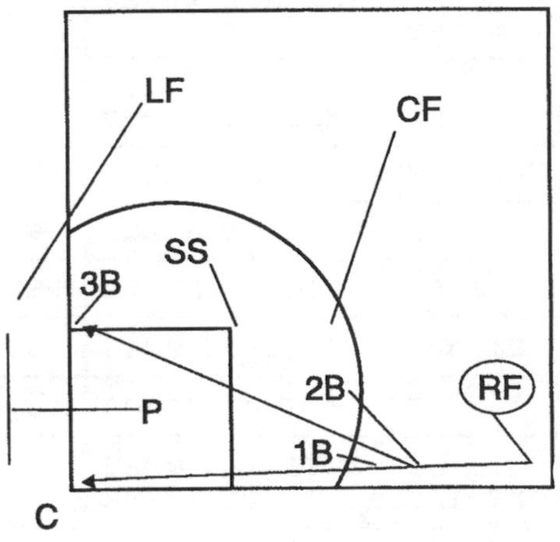

**Figure 10-7: FLY BALL WITH A RUNNER ON THIRD BASE OR RUNNERS ON FIRST AND THIRD BASE TAGGING AND TRYING TO SCORE**

| | BALL HIT TO LEFT | | BALL HIT TO CENTER | | BALL HIT TO RIGHT |
|---|---|---|---|---|---|
| P | BACKUP HOME PLATE | P | BACKUP HOME PLATE | P | BACKUP HOME PLATE |
| C | COVER HOME PLATE | C | COVER HOME PLATE | C | COVER HOME PLATE |
| 1B | LINE UP TO HOME PLATE | 1B | LINE UP TO HOME PLATE | 1B | LINE UP TO HOME PLATE |
| 2B | COVER FIRST BASE | 2B | COVER FIRST BASE | 2B | COVER FIRST BASE |
| 3B | COVER THIRD BASE | 3B | COVER THIRD BASE | 3B | COVER THIRD BASE |
| SS | COVER SECOND BASE | SS | COVER SECOND BASE | SS | COVER SECOND BASE |
| LF | THROW TO HOME PLATE OR SECOND BASE | LF | BACKUP CENTER FIELD | LF | BACKUP THIRD BASE |
| CF | BACKUP LEFT FIELD | CF | THROW TO HOME PLATE OR SECOND BASE | CF | BACKUP RIGHT FIELD |
| RF | BACKUP SECOND BASE | RF | BACKUP SECOND BASE | RF | THROW TO HOME PLATE OR SECOND BASE |

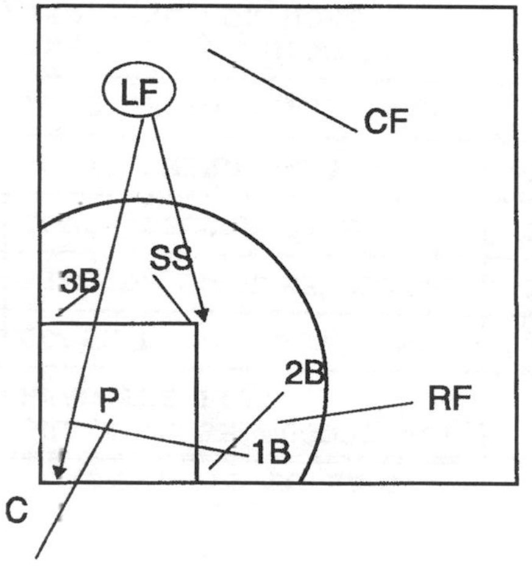

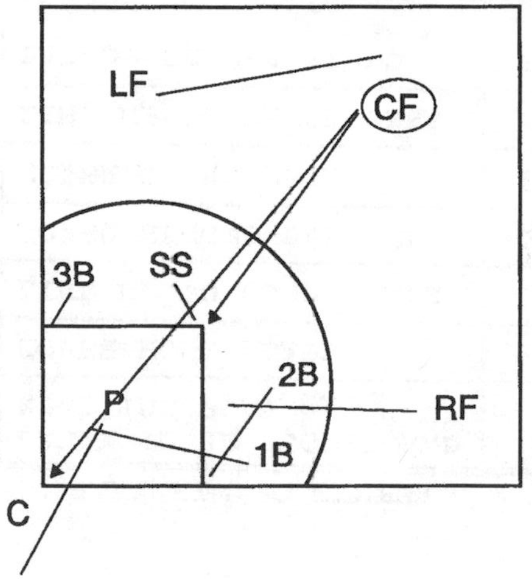

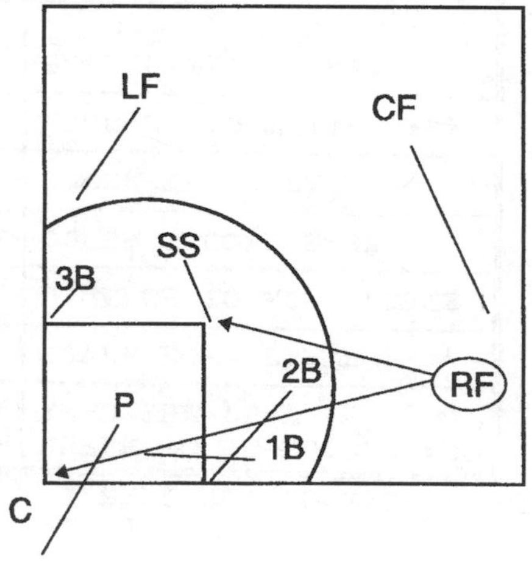

Figure 10-8: **FLY BALL WITH RUNNERS ON SECOND AND THIRD BASE OR THE BASES LOADED, RUNNERS TAGGING**

| | BALL HIT TO LEFT | | BALL HIT TO CENTER | | BALL HIT TO RIGHT |
|---|---|---|---|---|---|
| P | BREAK TO 3B DUGOUT AND READ THE PLAY | P | BREAK TO 3B DUGOUT AND READ THE PLAY | P | BREAK TO 3B DUGOUT AND READ THE PLAY |
| C | COVER HOME PLATE | C | COVER HOME PLATE | C | COVER HOME PLATE |
| 1B | LINE UP TO HOME PLATE | 1B | LINE UP TO HOME PLATE | 1B | LINE UP TO HOME PLATE |
| 2B | COVER SECOND BASE | 2B | COVER SECOND BASE | 2B | COVER SECOND BASE |
| 3B | COVER THIRD BASE | 3B | COVER THIRD BASE | 3B | COVER THIRD BASE |
| SS | LINE UP TO THIRD BASE | SS | LINE UP TO THIRD BASE | SS | LINE UP TO THIRD BASE |
| LF | READ PLAY, THROW TO 2ND, 3RD, OR HOME | LF | BACKUP CENTER FIELD | LF | BACKUP THIRD BASE |
| CF | BACKUP LEFT FIELD | CF | READ PLAY, THROW TO 2ND, 3RD, OR HOME | CF | BACKUP RIGHT FIELD |
| RF | BACKUP SECOND BASE | RF | BACKUP CENTER FIELD | RF | READ PLAY, THROW TO 2ND, 3RD, OR HOME |

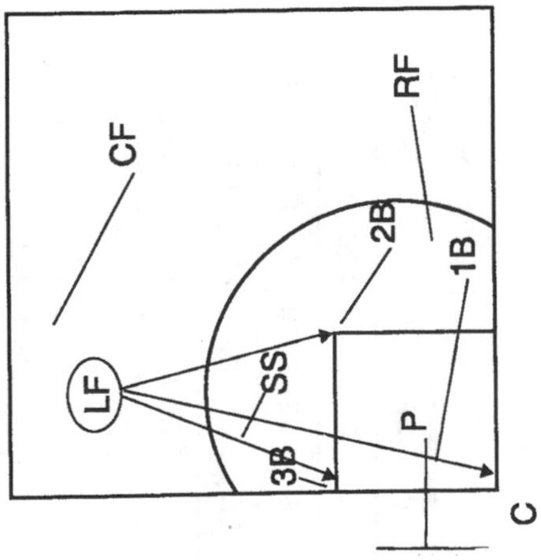

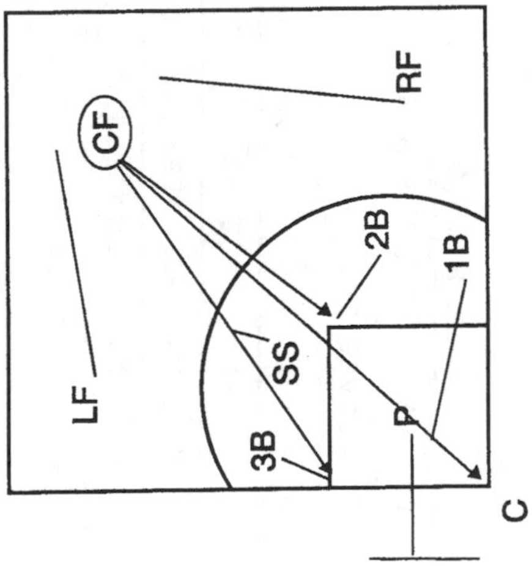

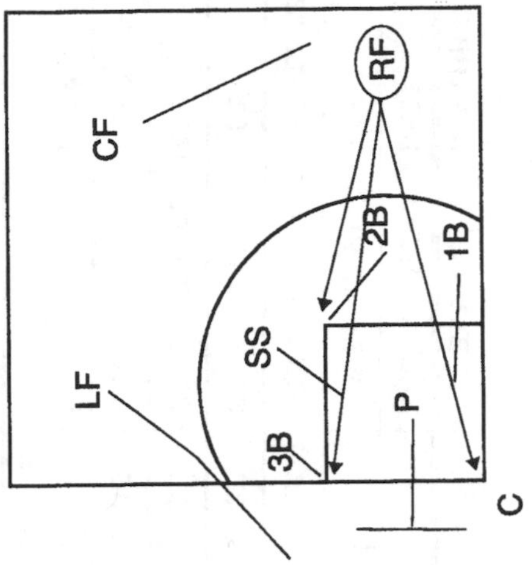

Figure 10-9: **SINGLE TO RIGHT FIELD CAUSING THE FIRST BASEMAN TO DIVE FOR THE BALL. RUNNER AT SECOND BASE OR RUNNERS AT SECOND AND THIRD BASE**

*THIS IS AN EXAMPLE OF A PLAY WHERE THE PITCHER BECOMES THE CUTOFF MAN TO HOME PLATE ON A BALL HIT TO RIGHT FIELD WITH A RUNNER SCORING. ANOTHER EXAMPLE WOULD BE A SHORT FLY BALL WHERE THE FIRST BASEMAN MUST GO FOR THE BALL.

BALL HIT TO RIGHT FIELD

| | |
|----|----|
| P | LINE UP TO HOME PLATE, YOU ARE THE CUTOFF MAN |
| C | COVER HOME PLATE |
| 1B | DIVE FOR BALL, WATCH RUNNER TOUCH FIRST BASE |
| 2B | COVER FIRST BASE |
| 3B | COVER THIRD BASE |
| SS | COVER SECOND BASE |
| LF | BACKUP SECOND BASE |
| CF | BACKUP RIGHT FIELD |
| RF | THROW BALL TO HOME PLATE |

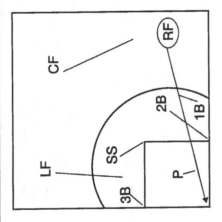

Figure 10-10: **SINGLE TO CENTER FIELD IN HOLE WITH A RUNNER AT FIRST BASE OR RUNNERS AT FIRST AND THIRD BASE**

*THIS IS AN EXAMPLE OF A PLAY WHERE THE SHORTSTOP AND THE SECOND BASEMAN MUST SWITCH
RESPONSIBILITIES DUE TO BEING OUT OF POSITION AFTER ATTEMPTING TO FIELD A BATTED BALL.

BALL HIT TO CENTER FIELD

| | |
|---|---|
| P | BACKUP THIRD BASE |
| C | COVER HOME PLATE |
| 1B | WATCH BATTER RUNNER TOUCH FIRST BASE, THEN COVER FIRST BASE |
| 2B | GO FOR THE BALL, THEN LINE UP TO THIRD BASE |
| 3B | COVER THIRD BASE |
| SS | GO FOR THE BALL, THEN COVER SECOND BASE |
| LF | BACKUP CENTER FIELD |
| CF | THROW BALL TO THIRD BASE |
| RF | BACKUP CENTER FIELD |

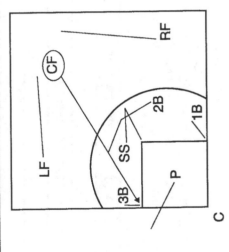

Figure 10-11:  **WILD PICK AT FIRST BASE COVERAGE**

| | |
|---|---|
| P | AFTER THE PICK, LINE UP TO THIRD BASE, YOU ARE THE CUT OFF MAN |
| C | COVER HOME PLATE |
| 1B | GO GET THE WILD THROW |
| 2B | GO GET THE WILD THROW |
| 3B | COVER THIRD BASE |
| SS | COVER SECOND BASE |
| LF | BACKUP THIRD BASE |
| CF | BACKUP SECOND BASE FOR POSSIBLE RUNDOWN BETWEEN SECOND BASE AND THIRD BASE |
| RF | GO GET THE WILD THROW |

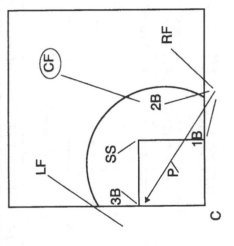

Figure 10-12: **WILD PITCH/PASSED BALL COVERAGE, RUNNER ON FIRST BASE**

| | |
|---|---|
| P | CRASH TO HOME PLATE AND HELP THE CATCHER FIND THE BALL BY POINTING AND USING VERBALS |
| C | GO GET THE BALL, LOOK FOR A POSSIBLE PLAY AT THIRD BASE |
| 1B | CRASH TO HOME PLATE AND HELP THE CATCHER FIND THE BALL BY POINTING AND USING VERBALS |
| 2B | COVER SECOND BASE |
| 3B | COVER THIRD BASE |
| SS | BACKUP THIRD BASE |
| LF | BACKUP THIRD BASE |
| CF | BACKUP SECOND BASE FOR A POSSIBLE RUNDOWN BETWEEN SECOND BASE AND THIRD BASE |
| RF | BACKUP SECOND BASE FOR A POSSIBLE RUNDOWN BETWEEN SECOND BASE AND THIRD BASE |

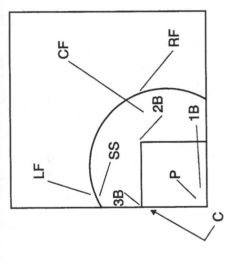

Figure 10-13: **WILD PITCH/PASSED BALL COVERAGE, RUNNER ON SECOND BASE AND/OR THIRD BASE**

| | |
|---|---|
| P | CRASH TO HOME PLATE AND HELP THE CATCHER FIND THE BALL BY POINTING AND USING VERBALS, COVER HOME PLATE |
| C | GO GET THE BALL, THROW TO THE PITCHER COVERING HOME PLATE |
| 1B | BACKUP THE THROW TO HOME PLATE |
| 2B | COVER SECOND BASE |
| 3B | COVER THIRD BASE, BACKUP THROW TO HOME PLATE IF THE BALL IS SUCH THAT THE FIRST BASEMAN CAN NOT MAKE IT IN TIME |
| SS | BACKUP THIRD BASE, COVER THIRD BASE IF THIRD BASEMAN IS FORCED TO BACKUP THE THROW TO HOME PLATE (SEE ABOVE) |
| LF | BACKUP THIRD BASE |
| CF | BACKUP SECOND BASE FOR A POSSIBLE RUNDOWN BETWEEN SECOND BASE AND THIRD BASE |
| RF | BACKUP SECOND BASE FOR A POSSIBLE RUNDOWN BETWEEN SECOND BASE AND THIRD BASE |

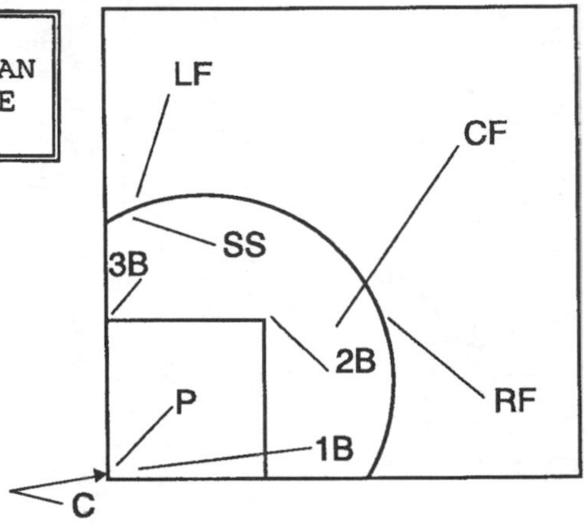

AN EXAMPLE OF THE 3RD BASEMAN BACKING UP THE PITCHER

AN EXAMPLE OF THE 1ST BASEMAN BACKING UP THE PITCHER

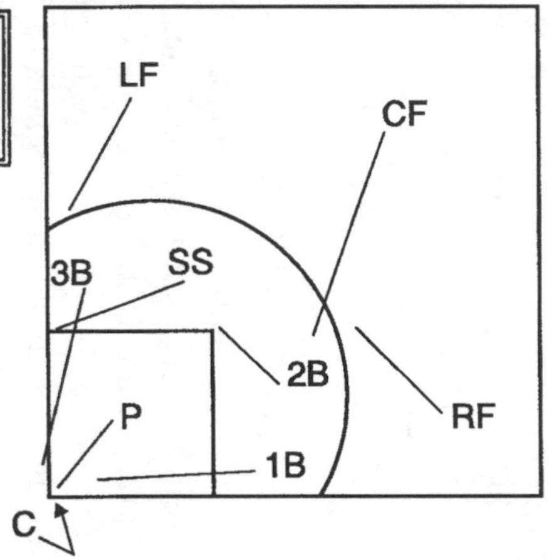

# OUTFIELDER'S ROLE

Most cutoff and relay situations begin with the outfielder fielding a batted ball. It is critical that the outfielder throws the ball low. As a rule of thumb, a low thrown ball will gain ten percent over a high thrown ball. This means that in the time that a player throws a ball 225 feet if they throw high, they can throw the same ball with the same arm strength 250 feet if they throw low.

Emphasize to your outfielders to throw through their target. This is more of a mental aspect, but it will lead to stronger throws. Avoid having the ball touch the ground. Cutoffs and relays work more effectively when the ball stays in the air.

When an outfielder throws a ball in a cutoff and relay situation, the ball is being thrown to a relay man, a cutoff man, or to an end receiver, such as a catcher at home plate, a third baseman at third base, and so on. Relay men are players that are on the outfield grass and that are going to relay the ball to the base that they are lined up to. A cutoff man is a player that is positioned on the infield grass. This player is referred to as a cutoff man because generally, balls are not relayed on the infield grass. Percentages tell us that balls that are relayed on the infield grass do not result in outs. The cutoff man's main job is to take throws that are late or off line and either hold the ball or throw the ball to another base. The cut-off man should be no more than 45 feet from the base.

*The Relay Man.*  Relay men must keep their heads on a swivel when they are lining themselves up. They're constantly looking back at the base runner to decide where to throw the ball. On an extra base hit, relays should look back at the base runner three different times. The first time is immediately after their first step to the outfield. The second look is when the ball passes the outfielder. The third and final look takes place just as the outfielder reaches to pick up the ball.

When infielders go out to be relay players, have them call out the outfielder's last name and give arm movement. This will allow the outfielders to pick up the target with their eyes as well as their ears. The verbal is also important because it will enable outfielders to pick up their targets when they are running to pick up a ball with their backs to the target.

Infielders must also make a decision as to how far they go out to relay a ball. This is determined by the arm strength of the players involved. You want to maximize the arm strength of the better arm. This means that one throw will be longer than the other. If for example, the players are attempting to throw the ball 200 feet, you want the stronger arm throwing 110-120 feet, and the weaker arm throwing 80-90. You want your relay players in the sideways position with movement towards the target when receiving the throw. This is the most efficient manner in which to relay a baseball.

*Tandem Relay.*  In an extra base hit situation, use a tandem relay, also known as a Double Cut. A tandem relay is when you have two players going out, such as the shortstop and the second baseman, or for an extra base hit down the right field line with a runner on first base, the second baseman and the first baseman. This tandem relay team is divided into a lead man and a backup man. The lead man is the player that is closest to the throwing outfielder. Make sure that your outfielders aim for the lead man.

The backup man in a tandem situation is there for exactly that reason: to backup the lead man. The backup man should be approximately 45 feet behind the lead man and slightly off center. By being off center, he will not have his vision shielded off by the lead man. Lead men should not jump for a ball unless they are 100 percent sure they can catch it. You do not want to risk deflecting the ball so that neither player can make the play. Let the back up man take the throw in that case. The same holds true for a ball that hits the ground and is going to give the lead man an in between hop. The lead man should let the back up man relay this ball.

### *Cut Off and Relay Verbals.*

**Cut Off and Relay Verbals.** A key to a successful cutoff and relay effort is a consistent use of verbals. When a relay man or a cutoff man is lining up to receive a throw he should use the thrower's last name. For the end receiver of the throw, you will use numbers if you want the ball cut to another base. For example, on a base hit with a runner on second base trying to score, your catchers will yell "three-three" if they want the throw cut and thrown to third base. "Two-two" would be the verbal to second base, "one-one" would be the verbal to first base. If your end receiver wants the ball to come straight through, untouched, he will say "leave-leave." In an incredibly rare situation, the end receiver may use "relay-relay."

This differentiation is critical because, now, your relay/cutoff men will be able to recognize sooner whether or not they need to close up and prepare to throw to another base. If the infielder hears a number, he now knows that he will be receiving his throw on this throwing arm side, and will then be throwing the ball to another base. If the infielder hears a non-number, he knows that he is letting the ball go or possibly relaying the ball, so he will be handling the ball on his glove side.

**Confusing the Baserunners.** You also want to be able to confuse base runners by saying nothing at all. If the end receiver says nothing, that is the same as "leave-leave." This is most likely to occur when you are deking the base runner. For example, the catcher may stand at home plate with his hands on his hips, trying to appear like the baseball has not been thrown to home plate. At the last second, the catcher will catch the ball. Giving a verbal in this situation would defeat the attempt to confuse the base runner.

Cutoff men should also know when throws should be cut before they get a verbal as a result of an off line throw or a throw with no velocity. The position of the runner when the ball leaves the outfielder's hand will also prepare the cutoff man to leave or cut the outfielder's throw.

The cutoff man needs to be able to effectively fake cut a ball that is being thrown through to a base or home plate. A fake cut involves slapping the palm or outside of the glove with an open hand. The sound that the hand makes against the glove can confuse a backside runner into thinking that the ball has been cut. This may result in the base runner not advancing an extra base that they normally would. A good fake cut should be followed up by either an arm fake or by running directly at the base runner that the fake cut was intended for.

Base runners should be forced into wide turns whenever possible. An example of this was given earlier with the second baseman on a base hit to right field with a runner on first base. There are many opportunities for this to occur at first, second, and third base. Remember, when base runners are forced into wider turns, it is just like making them run 100 feet rather than the 90 feet that they should be running. When a runner rounds third base, the third baseman should force a wide turn while watching the runner touch third base. This same technique is used by the shortstop and second baseman at second base, as well as the first baseman at first base. Infielders need to be careful that they do not obstruct the base runner's path by being too close to the base.

**Backing Up.** Backing up is another major part of cutoffs and relays. The back up player needs to go full speed to the proper position. A good back up drill is to simply have the infielders purposely let balls get passed them for the sole purpose of checking to see if the outfielder was in the correct position. Players who take pride in their game will be in their assigned position waiting for an overthrown ball. Players with no pride will be late and will then join in the chase of the ball.

The one fairly unique aspect our cutoff and relay system at Sacramento City College that you can use is that the first baseman is the cutoff man to the plate on base hits to left field as well as left center field. The reason for this is that it eliminates any confusion that may arise from a ball hit that both the first baseman and the third baseman think they are the cutoff man for. It is much easier if these players do the same thing on every base hit. The major drawback on this is that the first baseman may be late getting to the proper position on hard hit balls to left field or ground balls that the shortstop or third baseman has a chance of fielding. When this happens, you just have to hope that you get an accurate and intelligent throw from your left fielder.

# SHORT MAN

In addition to the regular cutoff and relay system, you can switch to another system that we call "short man." The short man system is designed to keep the ball from touching the ground and to keep backside runners from advancing bases in situations where there is a base hit and a runner attempting to score. The regular system tries to do the same thing, however the short man system makes it easier to execute. It is particularly useful when the middle infielder's arm strength and accuracy exceeds that of the outfielder's arm strength and accuracy.

Anytime the short man is on and the batter hits a potential extra base hit, or there is not a play at home plate, you switch back to your regular system. Short man can be used for some fields and not others. An example of this would be to use regular in right field with short man in left and center. Any combination of these variations is possible.

The short man defense is centered around the middle infielders. The shortstop and the second baseman become relay men to the plate. The short man will line himself up to the plate directly in line with the throwing outfielder while staying on the infield dirt. The shortstop is the short man for balls hit to left field and center field, while the second baseman is the short man for balls hit to right field. The player that is not the short man will cover second base. The first baseman will cover first base, while the third baseman will cover third base.

There is a situation where the second baseman will become the short man on a ball hit to center field. This coverage switch takes place with runners on first and second base or the bases loaded. You switch coverage in this situation so that the short-stop can line up to third base.

The following is a list of the most common three situations where you might use short man.

1. When you absolutely can't let the batter/runner advance to second base.

2. When the arm strength of the middle infielder is greater than the outfielder.

3. When there are poor field conditions that are not conducive to strong, accurate throws.

Look at Figures 10-14 and 10-15 for diagrams of defensive plays.

Figure 10-14: **SHORT MAN RUNNER ON SECOND BASE, RUNNER ON THIRD BASE TAGGING ON A FLY BALL, OR RUNNERS ON SECOND AND THIRD BASE**

| | BALL HIT TO LEFT | | BALL HIT TO CENTER | | BALL HIT TO RIGHT |
|---|---|---|---|---|---|
| P | BACKUP HOME PLATE | P | BACKUP HOME PLATE | P | BACKUP HOME PLATE |
| C | COVER HOME PLATE | C | COVER HOME PLATE | C | COVER HOME PLATE |
| 1B | COVER FIRST BASE | 1B | COVER FIRST BASE | 1B | COVER FIRST BASE |
| 2B | COVER SECOND BASE | 2B | COVER SECOND BASE | 2B | LINE UP TO HOME PLATE |
| 3B | COVER THIRD BASE | 3B | COVER THIRD BASE | 3B | COVER THIRD BASE |
| SS | LINE UP TO HOME PLATE | SS | LINE UP TO HOME PLATE | SS | COVER SECOND BASE |
| LF | THROW TO HOME PLATE | LF | BACKUP CENTER FIELD | LF | BACKUP THIRD BASE |
| CF | BACKUP LEFT FIELD | CF | THROW TO HOME PLATE | CF | BACKUP RIGHT FIELD |
| RF | BACKUP SECOND BASE | RF | BACKUP CENTER FIELD | RF | THROW TO HOME PLATE |

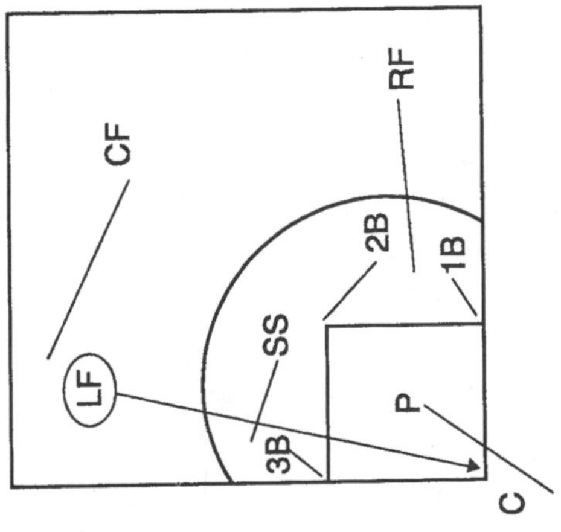

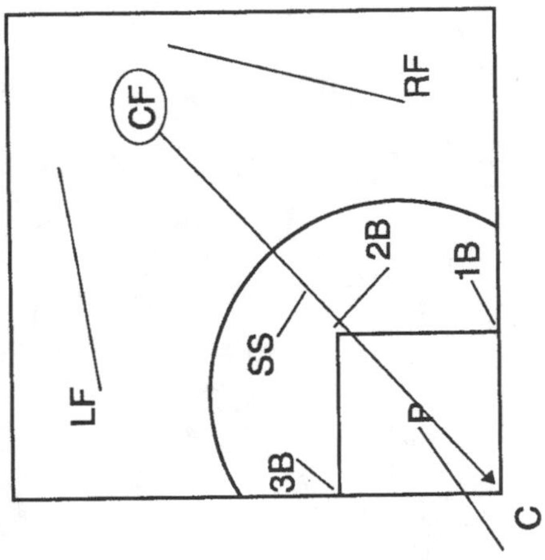

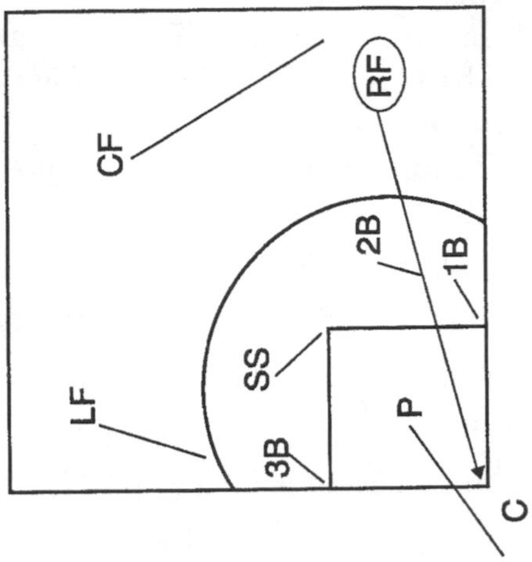

Figure 10-15: **SHORT MAN RUNNERS ON FIRST AND SECOND BASE OR THE BASES LOADED**

| | BALL HIT TO LEFT | | BALL HIT TO CENTER | | BALL HIT TO RIGHT |
|---|---|---|---|---|---|
| P | BACKUP HOME PLATE | P | BACKUP HOME PLATE | P | BACKUP HOME PLATE |
| C | COVER HOME PLATE | C | COVER HOME PLATE | C | COVER HOME PLATE |
| 1B | COVER FIRST BASE | 1B | COVER FIRST BASE | 1B | COVER FIRST BASE |
| 2B | COVER SECOND BASE | 2B | LINE UP TO HOME PLATE | 2B | LINE UP TO HOME PLATE |
| 3B | COVER THIRD BASE | 3B | COVER THIRD BASE | 3B | COVER THIRD BASE |
| SS | LINE UP TO HOME PLATE | SS | LINE UP TO THIRD BASE | SS | COVER SECOND BASE |
| LF | THROW TO HOME PLATE | LF | BACKUP CENTER FIELD | LF | BACKUP THIRD BASE |
| CF | BACKUP LEFT FIELD | CF | THROW TO HOME PLATE | CF | BACKUP RIGHT FIELD |
| RF | BACKUP SECOND BASE | RF | BACKUP CENTER FIELD | RF | THROW TO HOME PLATE |

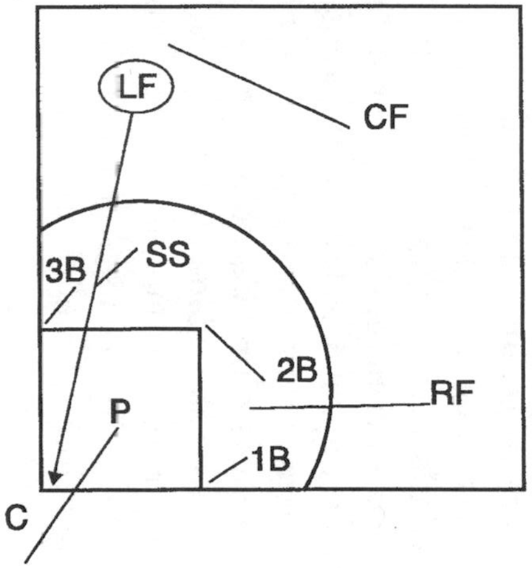

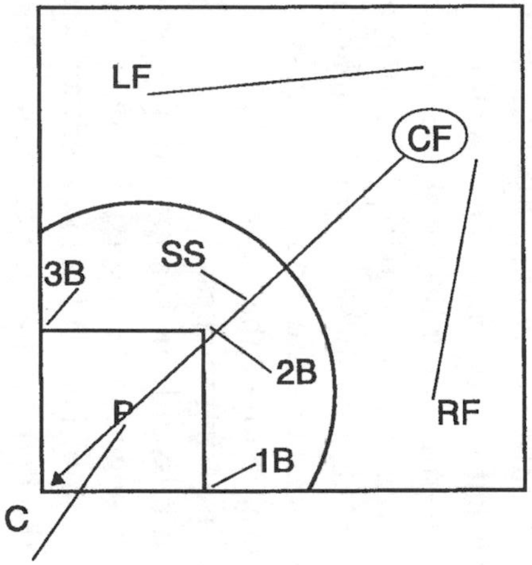

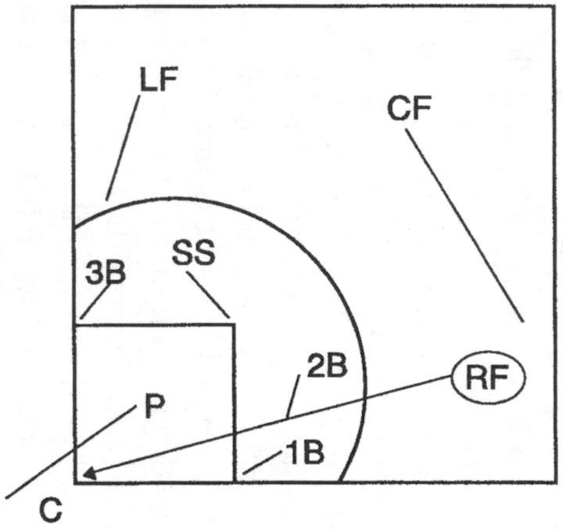

# BUNT DEFENSE

The main goal of any bunt defense is to get an out. Each of your bunt defenses is designed to get an out at a certain base, but if that out is not available, you must get the batter/runner out. Too many "big innings" are created when the defensive team does not get an out in a sacrifice bunt situation.

The key to running a successful bunt defense is having the fielder make the correct decision as to where to throw the ball. This decision has to be made by the fielder. You don't want your other position players, or coaches, or players on the bench using verbals to tell the player where to throw. Avoid situations where the fielder wants to throw one place, the catcher tells him to throw to another place, and the next thing you know, you did not get an out because of the hesitation caused by the confusion. If your players are prepared before the pitch, the bunted ball will dictate which base to throw to. All bunt defenses should be put on by the catcher, who gets the play from the coach.

Bunt defenses start with the pitcher throwing a low-mid strike to home plate. This strike should be thrown on the low end of the strike zone because it is difficult for a bunter to go down to bunt a ball. A large percentage of pitches thrown up in the strike zone are not called strikes, so pitching up in the strike zone tends to create a lot of walks in bunting situations. Also, the ball up in the strike zone is more vulnerable to being hit hard, which becomes a factor if the bunter pulls back to hit. A strike is critical in this situation because if the bunter takes the pitch, the offense will see your defense. They may change the direction of their bunt, they may hit and run, or any number of things. You want your pitcher to throw his highest percentage strike pitch in a sacrifice bunt situation. If the pitcher's highest percentage strike pitch happens to be something other than a fast ball, that is an advantage. Most teams do not practice bunting breaking pitches.

The missed bunt is a great opportunity to pick off a base runner. Many runners, especially aggressive ones, tend to over extend with their secondary leads in a sacrifice bunt situation. They get complacent and expect the bunt to be executed and are caught off guard when it is not. Catchers and infielders should look for these opportunities.

When you feel that the other team is going to bunt, try to find out for sure by picking at first base with a runner on first base, or at second base with a runner on second base or runners on first and second. Often, the hitter will flinch with his hands on the pick if he is going to bunt. Use the inside move when picking at second base because the initial move of this pick looks like the initial move of a pitch to the plate.

The most critical aspect of different bunt defenses is that they all look the same as far as the set up. This is important because you can not allow the offense to recognize which defense you are using before the pitch is thrown. You have two bunt defenses with a runner on first base only, the basic bunt defense, and the crash bunt defense. These defenses should look identical until the pitch is delivered. With a runner on second base, or runners on first and second base, you have four bunt defenses. The basic defense, the drive defense, the pick defense, and the rotation defense all appear to be the same before the pitch is made.

***Runner on First Base.*** The first baseman begins bunt defense at first base by going to the mound and talking to the pitcher. With the crash bunt defense, the first baseman must know how many times the pitcher is going to pick. You also have him go to the mound on the basic bunt defense so that the offense cannot tell which defense you are running. The shortstop will cover second base, while the second baseman will shuffle towards first base. When the second baseman sees the ball bunted, he will break to either cover first base, or backup first base depending on what the first baseman does. The third baseman will start 15 to 20 feet in front of third base and equidistant between the mound and the third base line. Being off the line puts the third baseman in the best position to cut off hit and run ground balls or balls that are slashed.

The left fielder will backup a possible throw from first base to second base, the center fielder backs up a possible throw to second base off of the bunted ball, then breaks to back up a possible throw from first base to second base. The right fielder is backing up the throw to first base off of the bunted ball. The catcher must be sure to cover third base if the third baseman fields the bunt. The pitcher and the first baseman will have different roles depending on which defense you are using.

***Runner on First Base, Basic Bunt Defense.*** The basic bunt defense is a fairly conservative defense. With this defense, the pitcher breaks straight off of the mound favoring the first base side of the infield. The first baseman shuffles straight off of the base after the pitch. If the ball is bunted hard towards first base, then he will go and get the ball. If the third baseman or the pitcher field the ball, the first baseman covers first base.

The main advantage of this bunt defense is that the first baseman takes most of the throws at first base. The possibility of the second baseman being late to cover the bag is decreased. The other big advantage of this play is that the first baseman is at first base for a catcher's pick on a missed bunt attempt. By having the first baseman stay at first base, you have decreased the number of holes in the infield in the event of a fake bunt hit and run, a straight hit and run, or a fake bunt hit.

The biggest disadvantage of this defense is that if the ball is bunted to the first base side, you will rarely have a chance to get the runner at second base. Also, the offense will be able to get away with popping the bunt up if it is popped up on the first base side of the infield.

***Runner on First Base, Crash Bunt Defense.*** The crash bunt defense is an aggressive bunt defense. On this defense, the first baseman goes to the mound to tell the pitcher how many times to throw over to first base. This is done so that the first baseman will know when to crash to the plate. After the pitcher has picked at first base for the last time, he pitches to the plate.

***Off and Back Pick.*** You can also use an off and back pick at first base with this bunt defense. With this pick, the first baseman takes two steps towards home plate as if he is breaking to the plate, then reverses back and takes a throw at first base.

After the pitcher's last pick the first baseman will crash to the plate on the pitcher's first movement. The pitcher will break straight off of the mound, while all of the other position players will do exactly the same thing as they did on the basic defense. The first baseman never returns to first base to receive a throw in a bunt defense.

With the crash defense, you have given yourself a chance to force the lead runner at second base on a ball bunted to the right side of the infield. You also will have a chance to catch popped bunts to the right side. The ball and runner's speed will tell the fielder where to throw the ball.

The disadvantages of the crash defense are having the second baseman covering first base, and the fact that your catcher will not be able to pick at first base on a missed bunt attempt.

***Runner on Second Base or Runners on First and Second Base.*** All four of your bunt defenses in this situation will look the same to begin with. The first baseman will start 10-15 feet in front of the baseline, with your right handed first baseman 10-15 feet off of the first base line. Your left handed first basemen will start 5-10 feet off of the first base line. The second baseman will start from the straight away position. The second baseman's positioning will vary slightly from defense to defense. The short-stop will start directly on the runner's butt, while the third baseman will start three steps in front of the base line and 10 feet off the third base line. The outfield backups will differ from defense to defense.

***Basic Bunt Defense.*** The basic bunt defense is your most conservative bunt defense. You are completely conceding third base to the offense. This is important because you have to remember that you will not be able to throw the ball to third base on this defense. You will not have a player there to take the throw. The pitcher breaks to the cut of the circle on the third base side. The first baseman starts from the position described above, and then reads the bunt. If he can field the ball, he will go and get it. If he can not field the ball, he simply gets out of the way. The first baseman does not back track to cover first base.

The second baseman begins by cheating a couple of steps towards first base. When the batter shows bunt, he shuffles towards first base until the ball is bunted. He then breaks to cover first base. The shortstop starts on the runner's butt and bluffs the runner back if he has a long lead or momentum towards third base. If the runner does not retreat the shortstop can continue to second with an open glove as a signal for the pitcher to pick at second. When the ball is bunted, the shortstop covers second base. The third baseman starts from his previously described position and goes after the bunted ball. He must be careful that he doesn't release from his position until the ball is bunted so that the runner on second base can not steal third base behind him. Also, if the ball is not bunted, the third baseman must retreat to cover third base.

The left fielder will backup a possible throw to third base off of a bunted ball, although this should not happen, then back up a possible back door throw from first base to third base. The center fielder will back up the possible throw to second base off of the bunted ball, then back up a possible back door throw from first base to second base. The right fielder will back up the throw to first base off of the bunted ball.

The emphasis of this bunt defense is to get the out at first base. You can force the runner at second base if the ball is bunted in a manner that allows it. There will not be a player to take a throw at third base unless the ball is bunted one hop on a line back to the pitcher.

***Drive Bunt Defense.*** The drive bunt defense is more aggressive than the basic defense. All position players with the exception of the pitcher, shortstop, and the third baseman have exactly the same duties as on the basic defense. The shortstop drives the runner back to second base with an open glove. After he does this, he covers second base. When third base coaches see this open glove, they generally will tell their runners to go back to second base. The pitcher pitches through this fake open glove and breaks straight to the third base line.

The third baseman starts in the same position as he did on the basic defense. He gets the ball if it is bunted hard towards the third base line while loudly calling the pitcher off or directing him to throw to first base. If the ball is bunted to any other part of the field, he covers third base.

The left fielder will backup the possible throw to third base on the bunted ball. If the ball is not thrown to third base, he will backup a possible back door throw to third base. The center fielder will backup a possible throw to second base off of the bunted ball. If the ball is thrown to first base, he will backup a possible back door throw to second base from first base. The right fielder will backup a possible throw to first base on the bunted ball.

The philosophy behind this defense is that the runner on second base will be driven back to second base on the pitch, causing him to get a bad jump towards third base. If the pitcher can field the ball, he can get an out at third base.

If the pitcher has to come up to field the baseball, he will have to throw to first base. If the catcher or first baseman fields the ball, they can go to either first base, second base, or third base, depending upon the bunted ball and the baserunner's jump. The play at second base is unlikely since the runner was not held on first base.

***Rotation Bunt Defense.*** The rotation bunt defense is the most aggressive defense in this situation. Use this defense when you are sure that the offense is bunting. The play is designed to get an out at third base. The initial set up for this defense is identical to the drive and basic defense with the exception of the second baseman. The second baseman must cheat close enough to second base (10-15 feet) so that he can pick the runner on the pitcher's look.

The play begins when the pitcher looks to second base and focuses on the second baseman. When the pitcher looks to second base, the shortstop takes three shuffles off of the runner at a 45 degree angle. The shortstop takes two long leaps to third base on the pitch, and then breaks to cover third base while the pitch is in flight and the hitter is in a bunting stance. When the shortstop breaks, the third baseman crashes to home plate. The second baseman breaks to second base when the shortstop begins his initial shuffle. If the runner extends with the shortstop, the second baseman can call for the pick by signaling with an open glove.

If the pitcher doesn't pick at second base, the second baseman continues through the base and positions himself two steps to the third base side of second base. When the ball is bunted, the second baseman covers second base. The first baseman covers first base on this play. If the ball is bunted hard towards the first base line, the first baseman gets the ball and tags the runner out. The pitcher breaks straight off of the mound favoring the first base side. The outfield backup assignments for the rotation defense are the same as the drive bunt defense.

The rotation bunt defense is an outstanding defense if the offensive team bunts the ball. The negative side to this defense is that you are left wide open for the offense to pull back and hit. If they do this, you will be out of position. This is particularly true with a left handed hitter at the plate. Just like the drive defense it is critical for the pitcher to throw the first pitch for a strike. If he doesn't the offense will adjust and be better able to attack your defense.

**Pick Bunt Defense.** The pick bunt defense is a take off of the rotation bunt defense. The defense sets up just like the rotation defense. On the pitcher's look, the shortstop breaks directly to third base. He does not shuffle off like he does on the rotation defense. When the shortstop breaks, the second baseman breaks to second base and receives a pick from the pitcher. The pitcher does not have an option on this play, he must pick. The first and third basemen crash to the plate when the shortstop breaks. There will not be a pitch to the plate on this defense. The left fielder will back-up a possible rundown between third base and home plate, while the center fielder and the right fielder will backup a possible rundown between second and third base.

You will usually run this defense on the pitch before you run the rotation bunt defense. You can run it twice in a row to set up your rotation defense or run it after you run the rotation play.

**Squeeze Bunt Defense, Runner on Third Base.** This defense begins with the third baseman going to the mound to tell the pitcher how many times to pick at third base. The pitcher will be in the stretch position. The third baseman starts either ten feet behind the base and on the base line, or in front of the base. When he starts behind the base, with the pitcher picking, the third baseman breaks to the base on the pitcher's leg lift. When he starts in front of the base, he tries to draw the runner off of third base. The third baseman should creep towards the plate as long as the runner keeps trailing him. The third baseman drives the baserunner back to the base on the pitcher's leg lift.

After the pitcher has picked for the last time, the third baseman will key the pitcher to pitch by breaking to third base. This will result in the runner going back to third base on the pitch. The third baseman trails the runner down the line if the batter turns to bunt the ball. This is important because on a missed bunt attempt you want to have a player in a position to take a throw from the catcher. The pitcher breaks straight off of the mound, favoring the third base side of the infield. The first baseman starts in front of the base, and crashes towards the plate when he reads the squeeze play. The second baseman covers first base, and the shortstop covers second base (option to have the shortstop go to third base and the center fielder cover second).

If the squeeze play is not on, the third baseman must break off of the line and field his position. When you are picking at third base, the third baseman breaks to the base on the pitcher's leg lift. When you are pitching to the plate, the pitcher pitches when the third baseman breaks to the base.

See Figures 10-16 through 10-22 for play diagrams on bunt defense.

## Figure 10-16: BASIC BUNT DEFENSE RUNNER ON FIRST BASE ONLY

| | |
|---|---|
| P | THROW LOW MID STRIKE, BREAK STRAIGHT OFF THE MOUND FAVORING THE FIRST BASE SIDE |
| C | PUT ON THE BUNT DEFENSE, REACT TO THE BUNTED BALL, COVER THIRD BASE IF THE THIRD BASEMAN FIELDS THE BALL |
| 1B | GO TO THE MOUND TO MAKE THE BUNT DEFENSE LOOK LIKE OUR CRASH DEFENSE, BREAK STRAIGHT OFF THE BAG ON THE PITCH, GO GET THE BALL IF IT IS BUNTED TOWARDS THE LINE AND TAG THE RUNNER OUT, OR THROW TO THE SECOND BASEMAN AT FIRST BASE |
| 2B | WHEN THE BATTER SHOWS BUNT, SHUFFLE TOWARDS FIRST BASE UNTIL THE BALL IS BUNTED READY TO COME UP ON A PUSH BUNT, THEN BRAKE TO COVER FIRST BASE OR BACKUP FIRST BASE DEPENDING ON WHAT THE FIRST BASEMAN DOES |
| 3B | START FIFTEEN TO TWENTY FEET IN FRONT OF THIRD BASE AND EQUIDISTANT BETWEEN THE LINE AND THE MOUND, READ THE BUNT |
| SS | COVER SECOND BASE AFTER THE BALL IS BUNTED |
| LF | BACKUP POSSIBLE THROW FORM FIRST BASE TO THIRD BASE |
| CF | BREAK TO BACKUP THROW TO SECOND BASE ON BUNTED BALL, THEN LINE UP TO BACKUP BACKDOOR FROM FIRST BASE TO SECOND BASE |
| RF | BACKUP FIRST BASE, LINE UP DIRECTLY WITH THE THROW TO FIRST BASE |

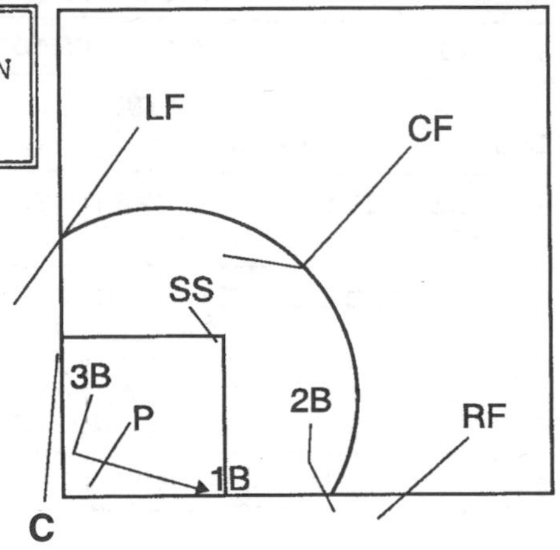

AN EXAMPLE OF THE 1ST BASEMAN FIELDING THE BALL

AN EXAMPLE OF THE 3RD BASEMAN FIELDING THE BALL

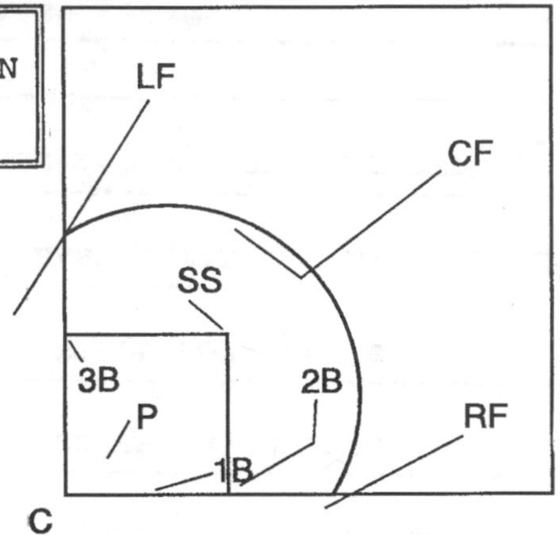

## Figure 10-17: CRASH BUNT DEFENSE
## RUNNER ON FIRST BASE ONLY

| | |
|---|---|
| P | THROW LOW MID STRIKE, BREAK STRAIGHT OFF THE MOUND |
| C | PUT ON THE BUNT DEFENSE, REACT TO THE BUNTED BALL, COVER THIRD BASE IF THE THIRD BASEMAN FIELDS THE BALL |
| 1B | TELL PITCHER HOW MANY PICKS AT FIRST BASE, BREAK TOWARDS HOME PLATE ON THE PITCHER'S FIRST MOVEMENT HOME PLATE |
| 2B | WHEN THE BATTER SHOWS BUNT, SHUFFLE TOWARDS FIRST BASE UNTIL THE BALL IS BUNTED, THEN BREAK TO COVER FIRST BASE |
| 3B | START FIFTEEN TO TWENTY FEET IN FRONT OF THIRD BASE AND EQUIDISTANT BETWEEN THE LINE AND THE MOUND, READ THE BUNT |
| SS | COVER SECOND BASE AFTER THE BALL IS BUNTED |
| LF | BACKUP POSSIBLE THROW FORM FIRST BASE TO THIRD BASE |
| CF | BREAK TO BACKUP THROW TO SECOND BASE ON THE BUNTED BALL, THEN LINE UP TO BACKUP BACKDOOR FROM FIRST BASE TO SECOND BASE |
| RF | BACKUP FIRST BASE, LINE UP DIRECTLY WITH THE THROW TO FIRST BASE |

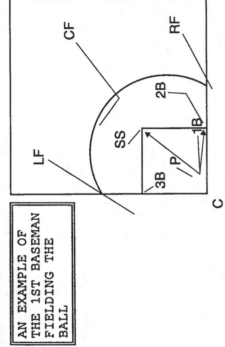

AN EXAMPLE OF
THE 1ST BASEMAN
FIELDING THE
BALL

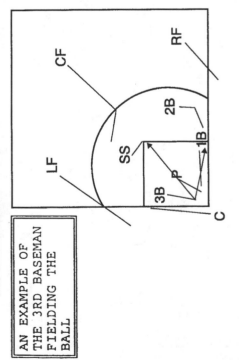

AN EXAMPLE OF
THE 3RD BASEMAN
FIELDING THE
BALL

# Figure 10-18: BASIC BUNT DEFENSE
## RUNNER ON SECOND BASE OR RUNNERS ON FIRST AND SECOND BASE

|  |  |
|---|---|
| P | PICK ON OPEN GLOVE FROM THE SHORTSTOP, THROW LOW MID STRIKE TO HOME PLATE, BREAK STRAIGHT OFF THE MOUND TO THE CUT |
| C | PUT ON THE BUNT DEFENSE, REACT TO THE BUNTED BALL |
| 1B | START 10-15 FEET IN FRONT OF BASELINE AND 10-15 FEET OFF LINE FOR RIGHT HANDERS, 5-10 FEET OFF THE LINE FOR LEFT HANDERS, READ THE BUNT |
| 2B | WHEN THE BATTER SHOWS BUNT, SHUFFLE TOWARDS FIRST BASE UNTIL THE BALL IS BUNTED, THEN BRAKE TO COVER FIRST BASE |
| 3B | START THREE STEPS IN FRONT OF THE BASELINE AND 10 FEET OFF THE LINE, TAKE A RIGHT AND A LEFT STEP ON THE PITCH, WHEN THE BALL IS BUNTED, GO AND GET IT |
| SS | START ON THE RUNNER'S BUTT, BLUFF THE RUNNER BACK IF HE HAS LONG LEAD OR MOMENTUM, COVER SECOND BASE |
| LF | BACKUP POSSIBLE THROW FROM BUNTED BALL TO THIRD BASE, THEN FROM FIRST BASE TO THIRD BASE |
| CF | BREAK TO BACKUP THROW TO SECOND BASE ON BUNTED BALL, THEN LINE UP TO BACKUP BACKDOOR FROM FIRST BASE TO SECOND BASE |
| RF | BACKUP FIRST BASE, LINE UP DIRECTLY WITH THE THROW TO FIRST BASE |

AN EXAMPLE OF THE 3RD BASEMAN FIELDING THE BALL

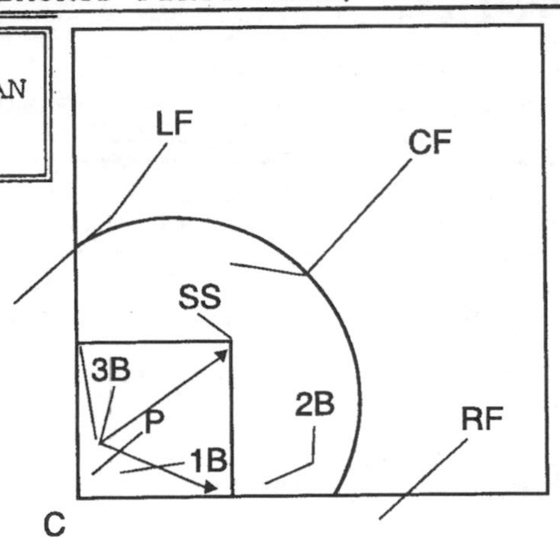

AN EXAMPLE OF THE 1ST BASEMAN FIELDING THE BALL

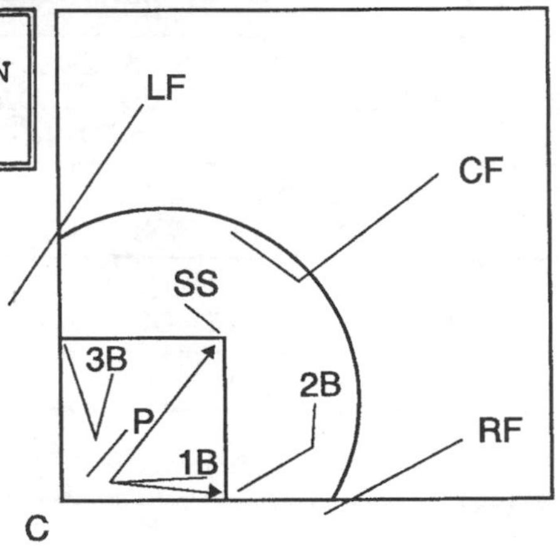

# Figure 10-19: DRIVE BUNT DEFENSE
## RUNNER ON SECOND BASE OR
## RUNNERS ON FIRST AND SECOND BASE

| | |
|---|---|
| P | PITCH THROUGH FAKE OPEN GLOVE FROM THE SHORTSTOP, THROW LOW MID STRIKE, BREAK STRAIGHT TO THE THIRD BASE LINE |
| C | PUT ON THE BUNT DEFENSE, REACT TO THE BUNTED BALL |
| 1B | START 10-15 FEET IN FRONT OF BASELINE AND 10-15 FEET OFF THE LINE FOR RIGHT HANDERS AND 5-10 FEET OFF THE LINE FOR LEFT HANDERS, READ THE BUNT |
| 2B | WHEN THE BATTER SHOWS BUNT, SHUFFLE TOWARDS 1B UNTIL THE BALL IS BUNTED, THEN BREAK TO COVER 1ST OR BACKUP 1ST DEPENDING ON WHAT THE FIRST BASEMAN DOES |
| 3B | START THREE STEPS IN FRONT OF THE BASELINE AND 10 FEET OFF THE LINE, TAKE A RIGHT AND A LEFT ON THE PITCH, COVER THIRD BASE IF THE PITCHER OR FIRST BASEMAN FIELD THE BALL, GO GET THE BALL IF BUNTED HARD TOWARDS THE THIRD BASE LINE |
| SS | DRIVE RUNNER BACK WITH A FAKE OPEN GLOVE, COVER SECOND BASE |
| LF | BACKUP POSSIBLE THROW FROM BUNTED BALL TO THIRD BASE AND THEN A POSSIBLE BACKDOOR FROM FIRST BASE TO THIRD BASE |
| CF | BREAK TO BACKUP THROW TO SECOND BASE ON BUNTED BALL, THEN LINE UP TO BACKUP BACKDOOR FROM FIRST BASE TO SECOND BASE |
| RF | BACKUP FIRST BASE, LINE UP DIRECTLY WITH THE THROW TO FIRST BASE |

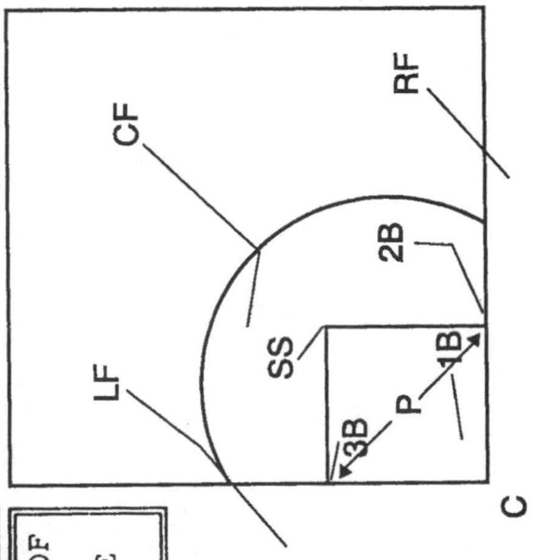

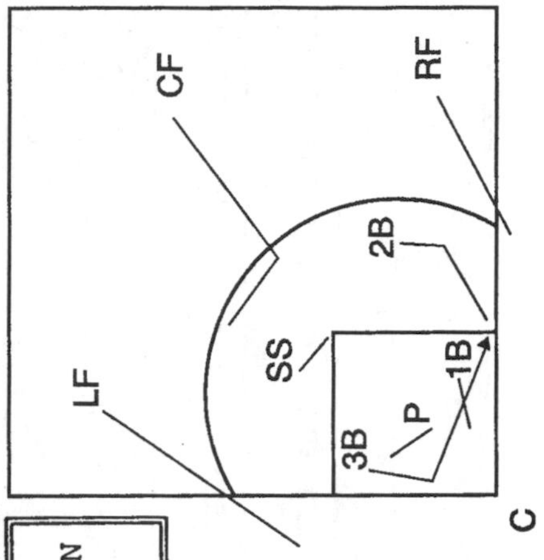

AN EXAMPLE OF THE 3RD BASEMAN FIELDING THE BALL

AN EXAMPLE OF THE PITCHER FIELDING THE BALL

# Figure 10-20: ROTATION BUNT DEFENSE RUNNER ON SECOND BASE OR RUNNERS ON FIRST AND SECOND BASE

| Pos | Instruction |
|---|---|
| P | LOOK FOR OPEN GLOVE FROM THE SECOND BASEMAN, THROW LOW MID STRIKE, BREAK STRAIGHT OFF OF THE MOUND |
| C | PUT ON THE BUNT DEFENSE, REACT TO THE BUNTED BALL |
| 1B | START 10-15 FEET IN FRONT OF BASELINE AND 10-15 FEET OFF THE LINE FOR RIGHT HANDERS AND 5-10 FEET OFF THE LINE FOR LEFT HANDERS, COVER 1B UNLESS THE BALL IS BUNTED TOWARDS THE LINE IN WHICH CASE YOU GO GET THE BALL AND TAG THE RUNNER |
| 2B | START 10-15 FEET FROM SECOND BASE AND DRIVE TO THE BASE GIVING OPEN GLOVE IF YOU CAN PICK THE RUNNER, IF YOU DO NOT PICK THE RUNNER, CONTINUE THROUGH TO THE SHORTSTOP SIDE OF SECOND BASE, COVER SECOND BASE ON THE BUNTED BALL |
| 3B | START THREE STEPS IN FRONT OF THE BASELINE AND 10 FEET OFF THE LINE, CRASH TO THE PLATE WHEN THE SHORTSTOP BREAKS |
| SS | ON THE PITCHER'S LOOK SHUFFLE THREE STEPS OFF OF THE RUNNER AT A 45 DEGREE ANGLE AND THEN BREAK HARD TO THIRD BASE TO TAKE THROW |
| LF | BACKUP POSSIBLE THROW FROM BUNTED BALL TO THIRD BASE, AND THEN A POSSIBLE BACKDOOR FROM FIRST BASE TO THIRD BASE |
| CF | BREAK TO BACKUP THROW TO SECOND BASE ON BUNTED BALL, THEN LINE UP TO BACKUP BACKDOOR FROM FIRST BASE TO SECOND BASE |
| RF | BACKUP FIRST BASE, LINE UP DIRECTLY WITH THE THROW TO FIRST BASE |

AN EXAMPLE OF THE 3RD BASEMAN FIELDING THE BALL

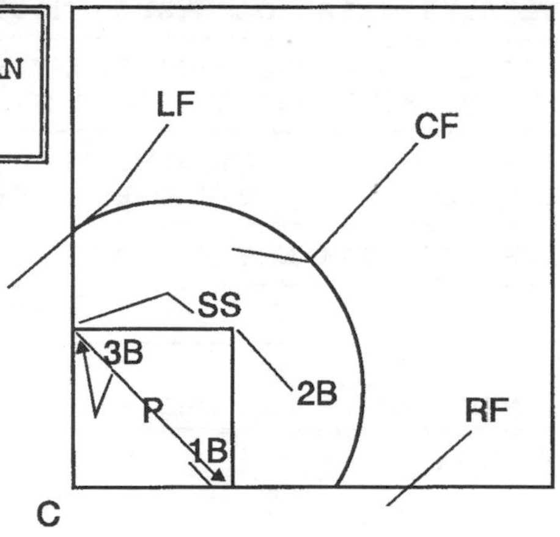

## Figure 10-21: PICK BUNT DEFENSE
### RUNNER ON SECOND BASE OR RUNNERS ON FIRST AND SECOND BASE

| | |
|---|---|
| P | PICK AT SECOND BASE WITH THE SECOND BASEMAN, THE PLAY IS KEYED BY THE SHORTSTOP BREAKING TO THIRD BASE |
| C | PUT ON THE BUNT DEFENSE |
| 1B | POSITION YOURSELF TEN TO FIFTEEN FEET IN FRONT OF BASELINE |
| 2B | START 10-15 FEET FROM SECOND BASE AND BREAK TO THE BASE WHEN THE SHORTSTOP BREAKS TO THIRD BASE. THE PITCHER IS PICKING |
| 3B | START THREE STEPS IN FRONT OF THE BASELINE AND 10 FEET OFF OF THE LINE, CRASH TO THE PLATE WHEN THE SHORTSTOP BREAKS TO THIRD BASE |
| SS | ON THE PITCHER'S LOOK, BREAK TO THIRD BASE BRINGING THE RUNNER WITH YOU |
| LF | BACKUP THIRD BASE FOR THROW FROM SECOND BASEMAN |
| CF | BACKUP PICK TO SECOND BASE |
| RF | BACKUP POSSIBLE RUNDOWN BETWEEN SECOND AND THIRD BASE |

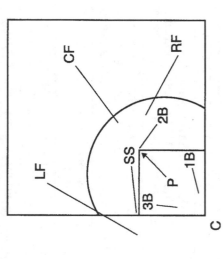

# Figure 10-22: SQUEEZE DEFENSE
## RUNNER ON THIRD BASE

| | |
|---|---|
| P | GET THE PICK SEQUENCE FROM THE THIRD BASEMAN, PITCH TO THE PLATE AND CRASH STRAIGHT OFF THE MOUND, IF THE HITTER OR THE RUNNER ON THIRD BASE SHOW EARLY, PITCH OUT |
| C | COVER HOME PLATE |
| 1B | PLAY "INFIELD IN" POSITION, DO NOT BACK TRACK TO COVER FIRST BASE |
| 2B | PLAY "INFIELD IN" POSITION, COVER FIRST BASE |
| 3B | ALERT THE PITCHER AS TO THE NUMBER OF PICKS AT THIRD BASE, START FROM EITHER IN FRONT OF THE BASE OR BEHIND THE BASE, TRAIL THE RUNNER DOWN THE LINE |
| SS | PLAY "INFIELD IN" POSITION, IF YOU DON'T FIELD THE BALL, BREAK TO THIRD BASE FOR A POSSIBLE RUNDOWN |
| LF | BACKUP POSSIBLE RUNDOWN BETWEEN THIRD BASE AND HOME PLATE |
| CF | COVER SECOND BASE |
| RF | BACKUP THROW TO FIRST BASE |

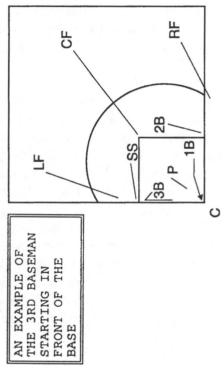

AN EXAMPLE OF THE 3RD BASEMAN STARTING IN FRONT OF THE BASE

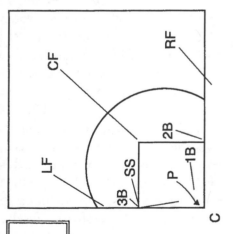

AN EXAMPLE OF THE 3RD BASEMAN STARTING BEHIND THE BASE

# FIRST AND THIRD DEFENSE

The most important aspect of a first and third defense is that the defense understands the game situation. The number of outs, the score, the arm strength of your players, and the runner's speed are the primary conditions that should be evaluated before the pitch. If your defense is executed properly, the offense will rarely score a run. All first and third defenses are put on by the catcher, who gets the defense from the coach.

*Straight to Shortstop.* This first and third defense is designed to keep the runner on third base from scoring. After the ball passes the hitter, the shortstop comes straight up towards home plate. The catcher throws straight to the shortstop without looking the runner back at third base. The second baseman covers second base after the ball passes the hitter, while the first baseman trails the runner from first base to a position midway between first base and second base. The third baseman covers third base and alerts the shortstop and the catcher when the runner breaks for home plate. He does this by yelling, "YES, YES!"

The shortstop throws the ball back to home plate after he catches it, or may possibly back door the runner at third base. The pitcher backs up home plate via the first base line after he pitches to the plate. The left fielder backs up a possible throw from the catcher to third base, the center fielder backs up the throw from the catcher to the shortstop, and the right fielder backs up a possible rundown between second and third base. This defense concedes second base to the offensive team.

*Look Him Back and Throw Him Out.* This first and third defense is designed to get an out at second, preferably without giving up a run. This would be the one defense where the offensive team could score a run even if your team executes. This should only occur if there is a premium runner at third base, and in that situation, you should not use this defense unless you are willing to give up a run.

When the pitch passes the hitter, either the shortstop or the second baseman covers second base. The player that does not cover the base backs up. The first baseman trails the runner from first base, while the third baseman covers third base. In some cases, you might not look the runner back at third base. By doing this, you are conceding the run to get an out. This may happen late in the game with a big lead. The catcher comes up and looks the runner back at third base. If the third baseman raises his glove, the catcher arm fakes to second and throws to third base. If the third baseman does not raise his glove, the catcher throws through to second base.

The middle infielder who is taking the throw comes to a position one step in front of second base and square to home plate. If the runner on third base breaks for home plate, the middle infielder receiving the throw comes up and gets the ball and throws the runner from third base out at the plate. The third baseman helps the middle infielders with this by yelling "YES, YES!" The infielder can also read this play by keeping his head on a swivel and checking the runner himself. If the runner on third base does not break, the infielder steps back to second base with his left foot and makes the tag. After the tag, the infielder continues around with a 360 degree turn in case the runner from third base breaks late.

The pitcher fake cuts the catcher's throw to second base in an attempt to confuse the runner on third base. After the fake cut, the pitcher breaks to back up home plate via the first base line. The left fielder backs up a possible throw to third base from the catcher, the center fielder backs up the possible throw to second base from the catcher, and the right fielder backs up a possible rundown between first and second base.

In the event that the runner from first base has such a good jump that you can not throw him out at second base, the catcher arm fakes to second base and looks for the runner to break off of third base.

***Arm Fake and Throw to Third.*** This defense is designed to keep the runner on third base from scoring. You are conceding second base to the offense. After the pitch passes the hitter, the third baseman covers third base, the shortstop backs up third base, the second baseman covers second base late, and the first baseman trails the runner toward second base.

With a right handed hitter at the plate, the catcher comes up and arm fakes to second base and then throws directly to third base. With a left handed hitter at the plate, the catcher closes his left shoulder to second base and then throws to third base. The pitcher backs up home plate via the first base line after he pitches to the plate. The left fielder backs up the throw from the catcher to third base, the center fielder backs up a possible throw from the catcher to second base, and the right fielder backs up a possible throw to second base from third base.

The catcher may also throw directly to third to pick the runner who is trying to get a good jump to score.

***Early Break Defense.*** The early break defense is the only first and third defense that is not put on by the catcher. This defense is a reaction to the offensive team sending the runner from first base to second base before the pitcher pitches to the plate. The pitcher steps off of the rubber and freezes the runner at third base by turning directly to the second baseman via third base. The pitcher throws the ball to the second baseman who comes straight up to the inside of the base line. He then backs up home plate by way of the third base line. The third baseman covers third base and alerts the infielders if the runner breaks to home plate by yelling "YES, YES!" The shortstop covers second base, the second baseman comes straight up into the base line to receive the throw from the pitcher, and the first baseman trails the runner to second base.

When the second baseman receives the throw from the pitcher, he begins to run the baserunner back to first base with his head on a swivel, constantly checking the runner at third base. If the runner breaks to home plate, the second baseman turns and throws to the catcher. Ideally, you would like to have the second baseman run the runner back until the first baseman calls for the ball. Allow for one arm fake from the second baseman to freeze the baserunner to allow the second baseman to tag the runner or make a short darting throw to the first baseman. The first baseman should call for the ball when he knows he can catch the ball and tag the runner out as he is passing the first baseman. He is then ready to throw the ball to home plate. Avoid having the first baseman running with the ball towards second base.

If the pitcher is late stepping off of the mound, the second baseman goes to a knee and points to second base. This signals the pitcher to throw the ball to the shortstop, who is covering second base.

The left fielder backs up a possible rundown between third base and home plate, the center fielder backs up a possible rundown between third base and second base, and the right fielder backs up the throw to second base from the pitcher.

See Figures 10-23 to 10-26 for first and third defense diagrams.

## Figure 10-23:  FIRST AND THIRD DEFENSE
### "STRAIGHT TO SHORTSTOP"

| | |
|---|---|
| P | PITCH TO THE PLATE, BACKUP HOME PLATE VIA THE FIRST BASE LINE |
| C | PUT ON THE FIRST AND THIRD DEFENSE, COME UP AND THROW DIRECTLY TO THE SHORTSTOP WHO WILL BE CHARGING STRAIGHT TOWARDS HOME PLATE, DO NOT LOOK THE RUNNER AT THIRD BACK, ARM FAKE IF YOU HEAR "YES!,YES!" FROM THE THIRD BASEMAN BEFORE YOU RELEASE |
| 1B | HOLD RUNNER ON FIRST BASE, TRAIL THE RUNNER AFTER THE BALL GETS PAST THE HITTER |
| 2B | COVER SECOND BASE WHEN THE BALL GETS PAST THE HITTER |
| 3B | COVER THIRD BASE WHEN THE BALL GETS PAST THE HITTER, ALERT THE SHORTSTOP AND THE CATCHER WHEN THE RUNNER BREAKS TO THE PLATE, ("YES!,YES!") |
| SS | WHEN THE BALL GETS PAST THE HITTER, BREAK DIRECTLY TOWARDS HOME PLATE AND RECEIVE THE THROW FROM THE CATCHER, READ THE PLAY |
| LF | BACKUP POSSIBLE RUNDOWN BETWEEN THIRD BASE AND HOME PLATE |
| CF | BACKUP THROW FROM THE CATCHER TO THE SHORTSTOP |
| RF | BACKUP POSSIBLE RUNDOWN BETWEEN SECOND AND THIRD OR FIRST AND SECOND |

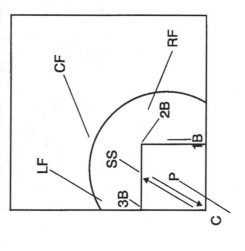

Figure 10-24: **FIRST AND THIRD DEFENSE
"LOOK HIM BACK AND THROW HIM OUT"**

|  |  |
|---|---|
| P | PITCH TO THE PLATE, FAKE CUT THE THROW TO SECOND BASE, BREAK TO BACK UP HOME PLATE VIA THE FIRST BASE LINE |
| C | PUT ON THE FIRST AND THIRD DEFENSE, COME UP AND LOOK THE RUNNER BACK AT THIRD BASE LOOKING FOR OPEN GLOVE FROM THE THIRD BASEMAN, IF THERE IS NO OPEN GLOVE, THROW TO EITHER THE SHORTSTOP OR THE SECOND BASEMAN AT SECOND BASE, BE READY TO RECEIVE A RETURN THROW FROM THE MIDDLE INFIELDERS |
| 1B | HOLD RUNNER ON FIRST BASE, TRAIL THE RUNNER AFTER THE BALL GETS PAST THE HITTER |
| 2B | IF TAKING THE THROW, AFTER THE BALL PASSES THE HITTER, COME TO A POSITION IN FRONT OF SECOND BASE AND SQUARE TO HOME PLATE, READ THE RUNNER ON THIRD BASE, IF HE SQUARES HIS SHOULDERS TO HOME PLATE, COME UP AND GET THE BALL AND THROW HIM OUT AT THE PLATE. (THIRD BASEMAN YELLS "YES!" "YES!") IF THE RUNNER ON THIRD BASE DOES NOT BREAK, STEP BACK TO SECOND BASE WITH YOUR LEFT FOOT AND MAKE THE TAG, CONTINUE AROUND TO MAKE THE 360 DEGREE TURN IN CASE THE RUNNER ON THIRD BASE BREAKS LATE |
| 3B | COVER THIRD BASE WHEN THE BALL GETS PAST THE HITTER, ALERT THE CATCHER IF THE RUNNER IS TOO FAR OFF OF THIRD BASE BY GOING OPEN GLOVE, THEN ALERT THE SHORTSTOP IF THE RUNNER BREAKS TO THE PLATE, ("YES!,YES!") |
| SS | SAME AS SECOND BASE, ONE PLAYER TAKES THE THROW, THE OTHER BACKS UP |
| LF | BACKUP POSSIBLE THROW TO THIRD BASE FROM THE CATCHER |
| CF | BACKUP POSSIBLE THROW FROM THE CATCHER TO SECOND BASE |
| RF | BACKUP POSSIBLE RUNDOWN BETWEEN FIRST AND SECOND BASE |

Figure 10-24: **FIRST AND THIRD DEFENSE**
**"LOOK HIM BACK AND THROW HIM OUT"**
(CONTINUED)

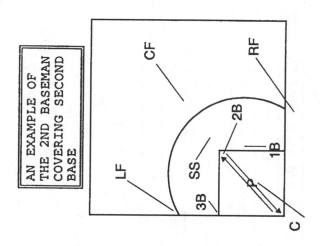

AN EXAMPLE OF THE 2ND BASEMAN COVERING SECOND BASE

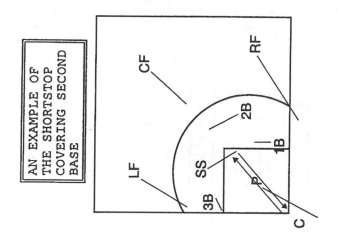

AN EXAMPLE OF THE SHORTSTOP COVERING SECOND BASE

## Figure 10-25: FIRST AND THIRD DEFENSE
## "ARM FAKE AND THROW TO THIRD"

| | |
|---|---|
| P | PITCH TO THE PLATE, BREAK TO BACK UP HOME PLATE VIA THE FIRST BASE LINE |
| C | PUT ON THE FIRST AND THIRD DEFENSE, COME UP AND ARM FAKE TO SECOND BASE THEN THROW TO THIRD BASE WITH A RIGHT HANDED HITTER, WITH A LEFT HANDED HITTER, COME UP AND CLOSE YOUR LEFT SHOULDER UP TO SECOND BASE AND THEN THROW DIRECTLY TO THIRD BASE |
| 1B | HOLD RUNNER ON FIRST BASE, TRAIL THE RUNNER AFTER THE BALL GETS PAST THE HITTER |
| 2B | BREAK TO COVER SECOND BASE AFTER THE BALL PASSES THE HITTER |
| 3B | COVER THIRD BASE WHEN THE BALL GETS PAST THE HITTER |
| SS | BREAK TO BACKUP THIRD BASE |
| LF | BACKUP THROW TO THIRD BASE FROM THE CATCHER |
| CF | BACKUP POSSIBLE THROW FROM THE CATCHER TO SECOND BASE |
| RF | BACKUP POSSIBLE THROW FROM THIRD BASE TO SECOND BASE |

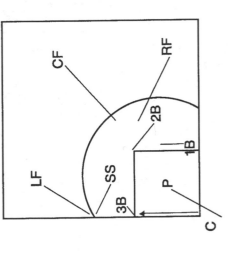

Figure 10-26: **FIRST AND THIRD DEFENSE**
**"EARLY BREAK"**

| | |
|---|---|
| P | STEP OFF AND FREEZE THE RUNNER AT THIRD BASE BY TURNING DIRECTLY TO SECOND BASE VIA THIRD BASE, THROW THE BALL TO THE SECOND BASEMAN DIRECTLY IN THE BASELINE, THEN BACKUP HOME PLATE VIA THIRD BASE |
| C | COVER HOME PLATE |
| 1B | TRAIL THE RUNNER AT FIRST BASE |
| 2B | COME STRAIGHT UP INTO THE BASELINE AND RECEIVE THE THROW FROM THE PITCHER |
| 3B | COVER THIRD BASE, HELP THE SECOND BASEMAN OR FIRST BASEMAN WITH ("YES!, YES!") |
| SS | COVER SECOND BASE |
| LF | BACKUP POSSIBLE RUNDOWN BETWEEN THIRD BASE AND HOME PLATE |
| CF | BACKUP POSSIBLE RUNDOWN BETWEEN SECOND BASE AND THIRD BASE |
| RF | BACKUP THE THROW TO THE SECOND BASE |

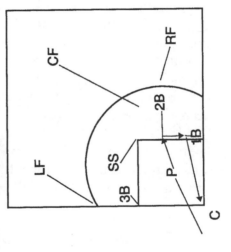

# POP-UP PRIORITY

Pop-up priority is the area of team defense that is concerned with the fielding of pop-ups and fly balls. Fielding a popped up baseball is relatively easy compared with fielding a ball that is hit on the ground. The problem is that many times, three, four, or as many as six different fielders could possibly catch the same ball. For these reasons, a system of priority has been developed. This system preassigns which position has priority over another position. The pop-up priority system is presented below.

1. The pitcher has priority over the catcher.
2. All infielders have priority over the pitcher and the catcher.
3. The second baseman has priority over the first baseman.
4. The third baseman has priority over the first baseman.
5. The shortstop has priority over all infielders.
6. All outfielders have priority over all infielders.
7. The center fielder has priority over the left and right fielders.

The pop-up priority system doesn't mean that the player who has priority should catch balls that another player clearly is going to catch. For example, the shortstop is not going to run the third baseman off of a ball that is right over third base if the third baseman has called for the ball. If the fielder who does not have priority has called for the ball and is camped out beneath the ball, the fielder with priority does not call the other fielder off of the ball.

To verbally call for a ball, the fielder should yell, "Ball, Ball!" and wave his arms with a circular action. By calling for the ball both verbally and physically, the fielder communicates more effectively.

If a fielder feels that he should catch the ball, he should call it after the ball has reached its highest point. This will help to ensure that the player's decision to attempt to catch the ball is an accurate decision. It's better to have the player call the ball slightly late, rather than early. If two players call for the ball, the player who has priority should catch it.

***Avoiding Infielder/Outfielder Collisions.*** One of the most dangerous plays in baseball is when a ball is hit between an infielder and an outfielder and neither player calls for the ball because neither player is sure he can catch it. To avoid a collision, your outfielders should slide feet first in a figure-four position. The infielders must dive high to minimize the amount of contact between the two fielders. It is impossible to completely erase the risk of a collision, but if the players call for the ball and follow the dive/slide rule, they can reduce the risk of injury.

If an infielder is moving for a ball in the outfield and has called for the ball late, and the outfielder is going to have to make the catch on the run, the outfielder should peel off and let the infielder make the play. This will help avoid dangerous collisions and keep both the infielder and the outfielder from pulling up and letting the ball drop between them. Pitchers should cover any base that is left vacant on a pop fly or shallow fly ball.

***Designated Divers.*** There should never be a collision between two outfielders, if neither fielder leaves his feet, one of the fielders should be able to call for the ball. The danger comes into play when neither fielder knows if he can catch the ball. For saftey, preassign a designated diver. The designated diver is usually the center fielder. The other outfielder that is involved in the play backs up the diver. If at all possible, avoid having two outfielders dive for the ball.

Be prepared for the possibility that your communication system may break down at times. Breakdowns occur most often on infield pop-ups between two positions. The breakdown occurs because two players are looking straight up into the sky, and may not see what the other player is doing. Sometimes, these players are so focused on catching the ball that they won't hear the other player call for the ball. If a collision is imminent, the closest player—usually the pitcher—should grab one player and pull him out of the way. Once the pitcher grabs one of the players, he should call out the position of the remaining fielder.

It is important to get all of your players involved in the pop-up communication. When a ball is hit in the air, have all of the players that are not involved in the play point to the ball. After a player has called for the ball, the other players yell out that player's position. They should not call out a player's position if he has not called for the ball.

See Figure 10-27 for 12 examples of pop-ups. In each diagram, the circled position has priority when the ball is popped up. The ball will come down where the lines converge.

Figure 10-27:  **EXAMPLES OF POP-UPS**

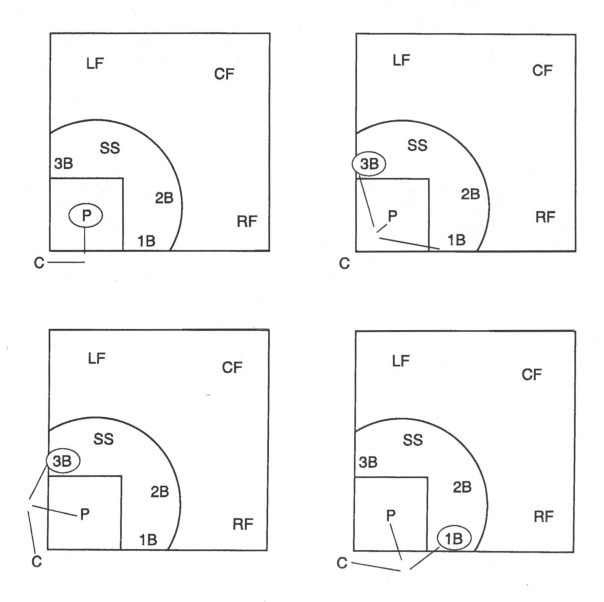

Figure 10-27: **EXAMPLES OF POP-UPS (CONTINUED)**

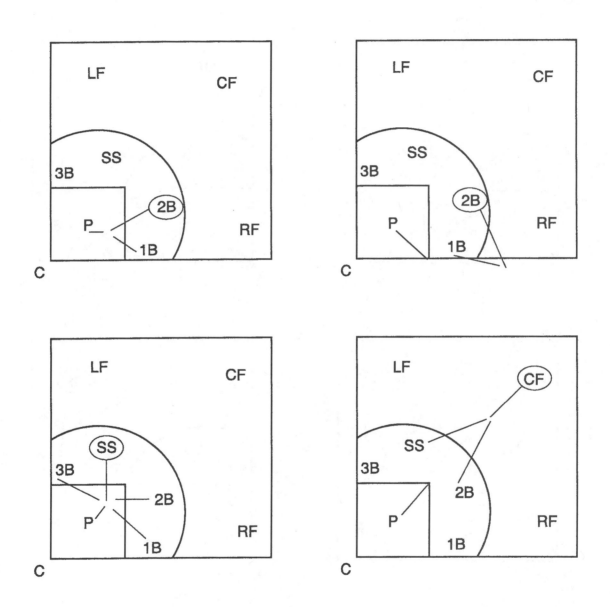

Figure 10-27:   **EXAMPLES OF POP-UPS (CONTINUED)**

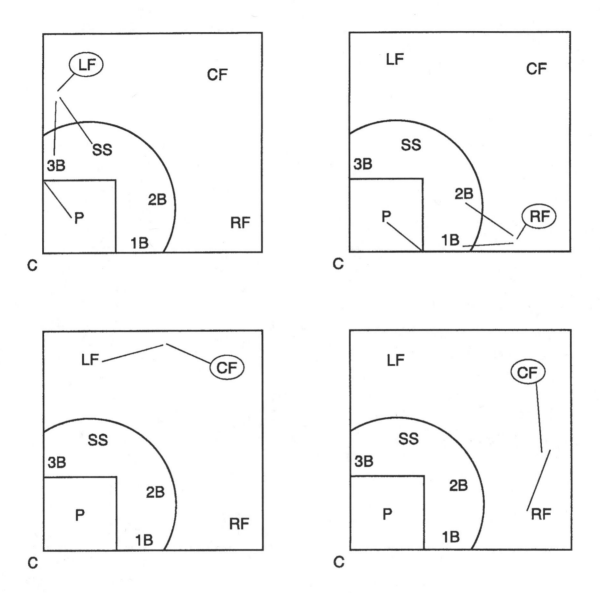

# HITTING

Some of the main topics covered in this section are stance, positioning, momentum, stride, swing contact and follow-through. Also included is additional information for advanced hitters and drills for all levels of expertise.

## THE STANCE

The mechanics of hitting begin with the stance. The stance should be square or slightly closed. The tendency now is a more open stance so the hitter can see the pitcher a little better. These hitters start open and then stride closed, which has a tendency to block their hips out. It hurts them on the inside pitch.

Photo 11-1

***Setting the Feet.*** When the hitter sets up, his shoulders should be level or slightly down and his weight evenly distributed or with a little more weight on the back side. Some hitters set up a little bit pigeon-toed. Turning the back foot slightly facilitates the hip turn, and turning the front foot in keeps the front side closed. (PHOTO 11-1) As long as he strides properly, he won't block himself out. Both knees must be flexed and centered over the balls of the feet. The ankles must also be flexed for this to happen. The front knee should be turned into the plate. To facilitate rotation, the back should be straight. The batter should then set his feet slightly wider than his shoulders and position himself in the middle of the batter's box. Adjustments can be made according to the pitcher.

267

Balance is very important in the stance and in the setup position. A bad start may create a bad finish. Some coaches don't care how a hitter sets up as long as he is in a good position at the time of contact. Of course, a coach has to allow for individual differences, but in general, a good setup gives a hitter the best chance to consistently produce a good swing.

***Setting the Head.*** If a hitter sets his head before he sets his hands, he should be able to get his head and eyes in a position where he can see the pitcher with both eyes. That's important in tracking the ball and for depth perception.

The head should be set with the bat on his shoulder. It's easier to set his head because he has a lot more flexibility in his neck if he has the bat on his shoulder. If he gets his bat up first and then tries to set his head, he may have tightness in his neck and shoulders. If he sets his head first and then gets his hands off his shoulders, he'll be able to set his head full face at the pitcher so he has both eyes on the pitcher. He must set his head with his chin above the front shoulder, so that his back shoulder does not knock his chin and eyes off the point of contact on the follow-through. He first sets his feet, then sets his head with his bat on his shoulder, and then sets his hands.

***The Hands.*** The hitter holds the bat in the base of his fingers, not in the palm of his hand (PHOTO 11-2), with the second line of knuckles aligned. Both hands should be loose and tension free, but the bottom hand should be a little tighter than the top hand. When the swing starts, the hands should be at or slightly behind the rear shoulder. Hands too far back bar out (stiffen) the lead arm and cause a stiff arm swing.

When the hitter sets his hands, he should have his bat at about a 45 degree angle. Some hitters may start with a vertical bat, and some may start with the club head a little bit down. It is preferable to have that bat somewhere between 45 degrees and flat, because it's in a hitting plane where the hitter doesn't have to make any adjustments to change the angle to hit.

This angle has a tendency to lock his wrists and load up his hands. The club head should be tilted slightly towards the pitcher just before the start of the swing. This puts the bat at approximately 11 o'clock, relating to the right-hand hitter's helmet. (PHOTO 11-3) The top hand will be closer to the pitcher and closer to the hitter's body at the start of the swing. Letting the club head hang forward in this manner will strengthen the hitter's grip and produce a more forceful and quicker swing.

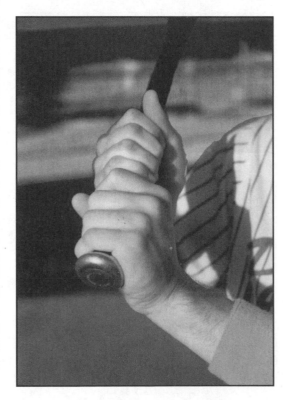

Photo 11-2

Photo 11-3

Photo 11-4

***Elbows.*** The elbows point down as the swing is initiated. However, the back elbow may start in the up position before the starts of the swing. At contact, the back elbow must be down and pass in front of the body. (PHOTO 11-4) If the hitter jams his elbow against his side, he will be forced to open up his front shoulder to hit.

## POSITIONING IN THE BATTER'S BOX

Against some one-sided pitchers—that is, pitchers who are effective to only one side of the plate—the hitter may choose to move into the plate on the pitcher who is effective away, and move off the plate against the pitcher who is effective inside. He may choose to move farther up the box against a breaking ball pitcher and deeper in the box against a pitcher with a power fast ball and no breaking ball. Some hitters make no physical adjustments, but mentally look for pitches in certain areas.

Starting in the middle of the batter's box is advantageous. If the hitter is way up in the front of the batter's box, it cuts down his reaction time. If he is deep in the batter's box, he's vulnerable to lateral breaking balls that hit the outside part of the plate, and by the time they get to him, he can't reach them. The hitter needs to have plate coverage, but he is not going to be able to cover the whole strike zone. He will have to give up certain parts of the strike zone in different situations. The best approach is to position himself in the batter's box where he can cover the strong area of his strike zone.

If they stand too close to the plate, hitters have a tendency, especially young hitters, to pull away because they're directly in line with the flight of the ball. Then the fear factor comes into play because every pitch is going to be close to him.

If the hitter sets up where he can reach the inside corner with the end of the bat, he can achieve plate coverage on everything but the low and out pitch. Being off the plate reduces the hitter's fear factor and allows him to have a better angle to read the pitch. It's like a car coming straight at you, and it's hard to judge its speed. If you're off to the side, you have reference points to determine the speed and direction of the car and you don't feel threatened.

A hitter has to adjust if the pitcher is consistently working away for strikes. He must either move into the plate and make the outside pitch a middle pitch, or make no adjustment relative to the plate and take the outside strike. Conversely, if the hitter is constantly getting jammed, he should move off the plate or take the inside strike with less than two strikes.

# THE EYES

Once the hitter establishes his stance, he must be mentally and physically prepared to attack the pitcher on each pitch. The eyes play a large part in this preparation. The eyes must track the ball from the pitcher's release point as far as possible. In order for this to happen, the hitter must first identify the pitcher's release point. This can be done while the pitcher is warming up in the pen between innings or while he is pitching to hitters early in the game.

It is best to start with a soft broad focus and switch to a hard, narrow focus before the ball is released. The switch from soft to hard focus should occur just as the pitcher starts his arm up to his power position. If the hitter gets to the pitcher's release point too early, he may get transfixed on the release point and be unable to react to the stimulus. Some hitters use the pitcher's front shoulder as a key. He soft focuses until the pitcher starts to close his shoulder and then transfers to the release point with a hard narrow focus. This eye movement and change of focus also helps to clear the brain of outside interference.

It is best to keep the head and eyes at the point of contact after contact to ensure that the eyes were there on contact. (PHOTO 11-5) Head and eye discipline can neutralize many physical deficiencies. Hitting is a half-second window of opportunity. The great hitters slow the half second by having great focus and using their vision efficiently.

***Eye Tests.*** The eyes are extremely important in baseball. One of the first things we recommend you do for your

Photo 11-5

players is to arrange for eye tests. With the help of your local sports vision specialist, you should make sure tests cover the following items:

1. Static visual acuity—for clarity of eyesight and the ability to see fine detail.

2. Depth perception—to measure the ability to see the change of speed of a moving object and the distance between two distant objects.

3. Refraction—to determine the amount of nearsightedness, farsightedness, or astigmatism in each eye. This is a basis for the recommendation of using glasses or contact lenses.

4. Eye alignment to check for the posture of the two eyes to see if the eyes turn inward or outward.

5. Binocularity of fusion flexibility—the ability to coordinate the 14 muscles of the two eyes for maximum ability to track a moving baseball.

6. Player's ability to accurately recognize the height of an object.

7. Speed of recognition and speed of eye movements—the ability to shift the eyes quickly from one target to another.

8. Eye-hand coordination speed to check the ability to quickly and accurately move the hands in response to a visual target.

9. Eye-foot coordination—for the ability to quickly and accurately pivot or move the foot in response to a visual target.

## HITTER MOMENTUM

As the pitcher is getting ready to come at the hitter, the hitter needs to be getting ready to come back at the pitcher by generating some momentum and rhythm by coiling. It is something that he must be doing as the pitcher is getting ready by winding up and getting his weight back to ready himself to pitch. The hitter can do one of many different things to coil so that he can get in rhythm with the pitch. As the pitcher is winding up, he is rocking his weight back slightly. He may start with an indiscernible rocking action. When the pitcher gets back, just before he releases, the hitter's weight goes back onto his backside so that he can initiate his stride.

## STRIDE

The stride occurs shortly before the pitcher releases the ball. The timing of the stride depends on the velocity and the type of pitch he's looking for. Just before the pitcher releases the ball, the hitter strides. The stride is on the inside part of the hitter's front foot on his big toe. (PHOTO 11-6) When he strides, his weight is centered between his feet. His hands push back and up slightly just as, or just before, he strides. He should keep the front arm bent and not barred out as he pushes his hands back. The stride, like the coil, is a preparatory movement to hitting the ball. Both help the hitter time

Photo 11-6

the pitch and give him some inertia. He can't start the swing until his stride foot hits the ground. He doesn't step and swing at the same time. A slight time lag occurs between that front foot hitting and the actual start of the swing.

Photo 11-7

The stride is a slow, easy, casual sliding in his front foot with a soft landing on the inside of the big toe. If he is on the inside part of his front foot and his front foot is closed, he'll be able to open up his hips. If he strides flat-footed, he's going to block himself out and make it very difficult to make a positive turn through the pitch, as opposed to rotating off the pitch.

***Flat-Foot Stride.*** Striding flat-footed gives the hitter the advantage of getting his weight out on his front foot before he initiates his swing. (PHOTO 11-7) But this greatly lessens his leverage and power. The flat-footed stride will jar his vision and disrupt his ability to get visual information from the ball. It also stiffens the front leg too soon, which forces his weight back and leads to upper cutting.

**Short Stride/No Stride.** A shorter stride is better because it involves less head and body movement, keeps his hands back, and allows him to get ready for the pitch earlier. Nothing says a hitter has to hit with a stride (e.g., Paul Molitor). Good two-strike hitting many times is no-stride type hitting. Against an off-speed breaking ball pitcher, the hitter may be better with a wide base, no-stride approach because many hitters tend to jump out at the off-speed pitches. The no-stride approach makes it easier to time the off-speed pitches.

# THE SWING

The hitter starts the swing mentally. He must be thinking "hit" on every pitch. He must think, "Hit, hit, hit," not, "Is it a strike? Is it a strike?" Every pitch is a strike. The pattern is to stop on balls, not start on strikes. The hitter should be thinking, "This is my pitch. I'm going to hit this pitch," as opposed to, "Is it my pitch? Is it my pitch?"

The swing is down to level. The high ball (above the waist) is "tommy hawked" by swinging down on the ball and making contact with the bat barrel above the hands. On the waist-high pitch, the barrel of the bat comes down to the ball and contacts the ball with the barrel almost parallel to the ground. On the low ball, the barrel comes down to the ball and contacts the ball on the upswing, with the barrel of the bat below the hands.

A deeper flex in the back knee helps the hitter get down to the low ball. Really exceptional runners try to work over the ball and overemphasize the downswing, so that they can keep the ball on the ground to give them a chance to use their running ability to beat out ground balls. Conversely, the big strong players who can carry fly balls out of the park try to lift the low and waist high balls with an uppercut motion. The majority of batters are best served by trying to hit line drives and ground balls. If they are going to err, they'd like to work *over* the ball rather than under. It should be a hard ground ball, as opposed to a swing and a miss or a pop-up.

Few hitters can carry fly balls out of ball parks consistently. Most cannot live in the air. With the ball coming to the plate on a downhill plane from a mound 10″ above the ground and a release point 12-18″ above the pitcher's head, it is important that the bat closely approximates the trajectory of the pitch at impact and stays on line with the pitch as long as possible. As Wade Boggs reportedly said, "Get to the ball late and stay with it long." For this reason, the swing is more down through the high ball and up through the low ball. Be sure to swing down and pick up the low ball.

**On Contact.** Once the hitter makes contact, he should continue his bat through the ball on the same plane as the flight of the pitch. Tell your hitters to try to hit the ball twice by keeping the bat on the ball as long as possible. This prevents premature wrist rolling which produces top spin instead of backspin.

The head and eyes should be right at the point of contact. On contact, the hitter's top hand is palm up, and his bottom hand is palm down with both hands on the bat. (PHOTO 11-8) The top hand may release once the hands have interchanged. The back leg is an "L," maybe a little bit deeper "L" on the low ball because hitters have a

**Photo 11-8**

tendency to go down to that low ball a little bit. The front leg and foot are firm on contact. His front foot is the power foot once the swing starts. He shouldn't spin out or rotate over the front foot before contact.

The back hip starts the swing and the bottom hand starts the bat. The bat will lag behind the hands. Hitting is a two-handed action, but the swing is initiated by a knob down inside the ball, pulling action with the lead hand. He must get his hands inside the flight of the ball so he can get approximately 24″ of handle between his hands and the ball. His back elbow passes close to his side, not against it. The approach to the ball is short to it and long through it. At the start of the swing, his lead arm is the directional arm and the back arm is the power arm. At contact, the lead arm is the power arm and the back arm is the directional arm.

**Hands Inside the Ball.** There's a great misconception about the swing that is called an inside-out swing. The hitter must be inside the ball to be effective. If he starts the bat with his top hand and starts outside the ball, he is going to end up hooking the ball. He'll be in a nonleverage position when he makes contact, because he'll have his hands around the ball, and he'll end up rolling over and hitting a lot of balls with top spin. (PHOTO 11-9) It would be tough to hit a line drive. Balls don't carry. They tend to be top spin line drives or weak ground balls. The longer he can stay inside the ball with his hands, the longer he can keep the club head on the ball.

Where the term inside-out hitter comes into play, is when a hitter takes an inside pitch and basically fights the ball off and hits it the other way. He should hit the ball where it is pitched by keeping his hands inside the ball. The ball will be contacted more

Photo 11-9

in front of the plate and with more pivot and extension when he pulls, and more at or behind the plate with less pivot extension when he hits the ball the other way (an

exception is the low, outside pitch that is hit deep in the zone with full extension).

If the hitter is inside the ball, he has three chances to hit it. He can hit it to left, center, or right. If he top hands the pitch and surrounds it, he can hit it only to the left side (right-handed hitter). If he is going to make a mistake in any way, he wants to err by staying inside the ball too long and slice the ball, as opposed to panicking and pulling out with his front side or being too quick with his hands and rolling over the ball. Being inside the ball gives him a better chance to hit the ball on the fat part of the bat.

***Point of Contact.*** At the point of contact follow these five guidelines: (PHOTO 11-10)

1. The eyes are focused on the point of contact and the head is down.

Photo 11-10

2. The top hand is palm up and the bottom is down, palm down.

3. The bat is at or close to 90 degrees with the flight of the ball (outside more than 90 degrees and inside less than 90 degrees) with the arms not fully extended (exception—ball low and away).

4. The front leg is firm, with the front foot slightly closed.

5. The back leg forms the letter "L."

***The Follow-Through.*** The follow-through is dependent upon the position of the pitch. If it's a low ball, the hitter is going to follow through a little bit higher. If it's a high ball, he's going to follow through a little bit lower. He should keep both hands on the bat on the follow-through. It is imperative to maintain balance throughout the swing. The hitter shouldn't fall across the plate, and he shouldn't fall back away from the plate. Balance is critically important in hitting. If he has a good start and a good setup, and all his mechanics are good, chances are his balance will be good after the swing.

***Comfort.*** Hitting comes down to comfort. Anything can be comfortable as long as it's practiced. Generally, what's comfortable to hitters is what they're familiar with what they've practiced. Even if it's the most unorthodox technique in the world, they may be comfortable with it. The criteria is performance as it relates to the future. The proper question for all your hitters is: "Do you use a technique that is going to allow you to be as good as you can be in the future?" Usually this relates to maximizing a hitter's bat speed, power, plate coverage, and the consistency of his swing.

# THE HITTING GAME PLAN

Here's advice for hitters in watching the pitch and deciding on location.

***One Pitch, One Location.*** When a hitter has no strikes, he should visualize a specific pitch in a specific location that he hits best. This means if it's not his pitch, he is taking the pitch. This does not mean he is not aggressive or that he is just waiting for something to happen. He is thinking "hit" on every pitch, and stopping his swing on balls rather than starting on strikes. A lot of hitters get in trouble when they get into that "Is it a strike?" mentality. Hitting is timing. If he is looking for an off-speed pitch and he gets a fast ball, then the ball is by him. A hitter has 2/10 of a second to determine whether he's going to hit or not, and if he's not aggressively thinking "hit" on every pitch, then he's got a problem.

***Deciding on Location.*** Many hitters have success looking for a ball down and away that is a strike. They do this because it's easier to adjust from this pitch area to other areas in the strike zone. If a hitter is looking outside and the ball is inside, all he has to do is stay inside the ball and be quick with his hands to pull the ball. If he's looking inside and starts the bat around the ball, he's defeated on the outside pitch. If he is looking fast ball and gets an off-speed pitch, he can adjust by keeping his hands back. But, if he's looking off-speed and gets a fast ball, the ball is by him. In nonsituational at bats, the other school of thought says look for the ball over the middle of the plate. If he does this, he can handle a pitch two ball widths in or out.

Normally a hitter can't hit the quality pitch low and away and he can't cover the whole strike zone by looking away and adjusting inside. The quality fast ball in on the hands is not a hittable pitch, even when he is looking for it. If he looks for the fast ball inside, he is giving up too much of the strike zone. There is also the consensus that he can't look for one speed pitch and hit another. The key is to have a hitting game plan that he has practiced and is committed to. Keep it simple and err on the side of being overly aggressive rather than too selective. No one ever walked to the Hall of Fame. He can't hit the ball if doesn't swing the bat. Game situations will dictate the amount of aggressiveness or selectivity he will need.

***Hitters, Do Your Homework!*** Give the following reminders to your hitters: Watch the pitcher warming up in the pen. What does he throw? What does he get over? Watch the pitcher between innings. Check the tendency chart during the game and observe how the pitcher pitches with runners on base. Pitchers are creatures of habit. Hitters should pay attention. Every pitch is a strike. Help your hitters remember: "Stop your swing on balls; don't start it on strikes. Hit, hit, hit, and stop on balls."

## TWO-STRIKE HITTING

There are two key points to two strike hitting:

1. Don't get beat away.
2. Don't be out in front.

With two strikes, a hitter must adjust since he has much more of the strike zone to cover. The key to hitting with two strikes is developing the ability to wait and then being quick with the bat. He should choke up on the bat, move into the plate, and think about hitting the ball back through the middle. The hitter must cover the entire zone and swing at marginal pitches. He must know the umpire's strike zone. He can't worry about being jammed with two strikes. His job is to make hard contact with two strikes.

Widening his stance will help because then he doesn't have to get his body in motion so early. A wide-base, no-stride concept similar to the Paul Molitor approach is a viable alternative in hitting, especially with two strikes. A batter can't hit until he gets his front foot down anyway, and the stride is just a timing mechanism. He can effect that lateral weight shift without taking a stride. The stride gets a lot of hitters in trouble. With hitters who are having problems, you can work from a no-stride situation and work back into a stride.

# SITUATION HITTING

Situation hitting is part of the hitting game plan and is something that is preplanned. A batter goes up to the plate with a different situation, maybe on every pitch. Maybe he's a left-hand hitter, there are no outs, there's a runner on first base, and his team is down a run. The situation calls for him to try to pull the ball and use the hole between first and second base. On the first pitch, the base runner may steal second base, so now he's got a runner on second base and nobody out. It's a 1-0 ball game, so now he's looking for a ball that he can pull, not necessarily in that hole, but something that he can pull in on the right side to get the guy to third base. The next pitch may be a wild pitch, and now he has a runner on third base, and the infield's back, and so now all he's trying to do is hit a ground ball to short or second to score that run. The infield may come in with one strike on him, and now his game plan is to drive the ball back through the middle to score that guy, or hit a fly ball. You have to practice all these situations, as well as the two-strike and less-than-two strike approach.

Part of a hitter's preparation is being aware of the situation. He has to look at the base running situation, the setup of the infield, and the outfield. Now he gets a game plan, steps in the batter's box, and gets a pitch on which he can execute his game plan. That happens with prepitch preparation, but it also happens with practice preparation. All your batting practice can't be stroke development. Much of your batting practice must be situational in nature.

The young hitter who doesn't have a consistent swing should work on stroke development. For the hitter who has a consistent swing, the emphasis should be on situational hitting.

A hitter has control over two things when he steps into the batter's box: his swing and which pitches he swings at. The situation determines which pitches he swings at. If he's done enough stroke development, he'll have a consistent or groove swing so that no matter what the situation, he's going to put the right swing on the pitch.

Situation hitting is knowing his strike zone and what he can do in certain situations. If, for instance, the infield is back, what type of pitch is he looking for to hit a ground ball? Is he more skilled hitting ground balls on balls up, or is he more skilled in hitting ground balls on balls down? However, he doesn't want to be so selective that he puts himself in a hole and is always hitting with two strikes.

# FIVE HITTING ZONES FOR THE ADVANCED HITTER

There are five hitting zones for the advanced hitter:
1. The zone when he's ahead in the count.
2. The zone when he's behind in the count.
3. The situational zone used given a situation where he wants to execute something specific.

4. The pitcher's zone, which he has to hit when he's got an exceptional pitcher who's got exceptional command. The hitter has to make adjustments and hit his zone.

5. The umpire's zone; he has to hit the umpire's zone, especially with two strikes.

You have to adjust your game plan to the skills of the individual. And most skills are going to change. When they become more refined, they can do different things. But you're trying to teach them the skill that's going to give them the highest probability of executing in any situation.

## TAKING PITCHES

How a hitter takes pitches is important. He should sink under the high ball by bending his knees. Sometimes hitters stand up tall, like a statue while taking pitches, and the umpire will widen the strike zone. They need to take every pitch as if they're going to hit it. This means they should keep eye contact on the ball all the way into the catcher's mitt.

Hitters with the take sign on 3-0 should not fake bunt or do anything bizarre. The umpires don't like it, and it usually gets the pitch called a strike. They should assume their normal stance and roll their head and eyes into the mitt with the pitch. The body language tells the ump that the hitter was watching the pitch all the way.

***Pitch Counts.*** Seeing lots of pitches is helpful. The more pitches a hitter sees, the more information goes into his hitting computer. He should learn something from every pitch. Seeing lots of pitches may not help him on that at bat, but it may help his team later in the inning because pitchers tend to lose velocity and location after they have thrown 16 pitches in an inning. The more pitches he forces a starter to throw early in the game, the more apt he is to get to that pitcher later in the game. Also, early high pitch counts gets his team into second line pitching sooner. Care must be taken that he doesn't get so fine with his zone that he loses his aggressiveness. It is good to see lots of pitches but it is better to hit the ball hard.

***Rolling on the Inside Pitch.*** It is important for the hitter to be able to get out of the way of a ball inside, and to protect himself on a ball on the inside part of the plate, by rolling his front shoulder in towards the plate. (PHOTO 11-11) If he doesn't play "dodge ball" on the inside pitch and get hit by balls in off the plate when pitchers are trying to throw in for

**Photo 11-11**

strikes, the pitchers will end up throwing more hittable pitches out over the plate. Care must be taken not to be so geared up to roll into the inside pitch that he is not ready and able to hit the inside strike.

***Acting in the Box.*** If a ball is hit close in the batter's box and the ump can't tell if the batted ball hit the batter, and it's not hit hard, it's generally ruled a fair ball if the hitter runs. If he doesn't run, generally it's ruled a foul ball. The hitter calls that play, so he has to be a good actor. If he jumps up and down and doesn't run, chances are it's going to be called a foul ball.

# BATTING PRACTICE

It's wise to take equal amounts of two types of batting practice. First, the hitter should take batting practice knowing what each pitch will be and not against game speed pitching. The hitter should concentrate on stroke development here, especially going with the pitch during the first part of batting practice. After he's completed this type of stroke development batting practice, you should have some batting practice under live conditions. The pitcher can throw his best stuff, and he doesn't have to tell the hitter what's coming.

***Working on the Hitter's Weakness.*** The hitter must work on his weaknesses in practice. If the curve ball, for example, is the toughest pitch for him to hit, then he should not hesitate to ask the pitcher to throw a lot of breaking balls. Too many hitters try to be impressive during batting practice by practicing only their strong points. This kind of batting practice eventually takes its toll over a long season.

***Pitching Machines.*** Taking batting practice off the pitching machine is helpful, especially at the beginning of the season. Another thing that is especially helpful during batting practice is taking high-speed batting practice, where you move the machine or the pitcher up and hit at high velocity. It forces that hitter to be quick. It eliminates all the wasted movement in hitting. Use some over speed training every day. It can be live or off the machine.

***Establishing Good Habits.*** A hitter should be selective even in batting practice. If the pitcher isn't throwing strikes, he should swing at pitches just to speed things up. He must get into the habit of swinging at nothing but his strikes. This should start from the very first day of practice so he doesn't have to break a bad habit later on. You should always have a count when your hitters take batting practice. Their zone will change with two strikes compared with when they have less than two strikes.

Hitters should mix up their hitting with three forms of batting practice:

1. Against the machine.
2. Stroke development against moderate pitching, knowing what the pitch is.
3. Against live pitching without knowing what pitch is coming.

Hitters should try to put some pressure on themselves when taking batting practice.

They should think of some imaginary situations before each pitch, such as two outs in the bottom of the ninth, two strikes, with a winning run on second base; or runner on second base, nobody out, trying to hit a grounder to the right side. Anything like this will help a hitter hit under pressure, and that's when it counts the most.

Good hitters are always swinging the bat. They swing it in rooms in front of a mirror, they swing off the batting T, they swing along the sidelines. But they swing with a purpose, not carelessly. They think about their form and pick out imaginary pitches to hit.

Proper timing for a hitter is not an automatic process. It's a result of coordination between the eyes, ears, muscles, and brain. The only way to develop that is through hours and hours of practice. A great place to practice is in the bullpen before the game or when the pitchers are getting their work in. But he needs to check with the pitchers first.

# HITTING DRILLS

There are countless hitting drills, but they are only as good as their application. There is a progression for utilizing drills. First, you must establish the purpose and goal of each drill, and show how it relates to better performance. To do this, demonstrate the end result of the drill performed correctly, diagram it, walk through it, and then practice it until you perfect it.

1. Show it.
2. Chalk it.
3. Talk it.
4. Walk it.
5. Do it.

Practice only makes permanent. Perfect practice makes perfect.

***Stance Check.*** Everything starts with an effective stance. The first drill should be a one-on-one stance check. The coach and player evaluate the player's stance, starting with the base (foot position) and finishing with the grip, bat angle, and head and eye position. Take special care in evaluating balance and weight distribution.

***Mirror Drill.*** The mirror drill is another good drill to evaluate the stance and setup. The hitter takes his stance in front of the mirror, both straight on and sideways. Take this drill a step further by taping the strike zone on the mirror. You can also tape baseballs in and out of the strike zone. You can further enhance this drill by putting a pitcher 15-20' behind the hitter. Both the hitter and pitcher will be facing the mirror. The pitcher will work on his stretch and windup delivery, and the hitter will work on his setup, his coil (timing mechanism), and his swing. Care must be taken that you have a wide open area in which to swing. This drill has endless situational possibilities, especially when you use the taped strike zone, balls taped in and out of the zone, and a pitcher. This is a good rainy day hitting station as well.

Photo 11-12

Photo 11-13

***K Board.*** The kinesthetic board (K board) is a great device to improve balance and to build adductor leg strength. It is a 1″ plywood board 18″×24″ with a 2×4 centered underneath the board. The player assumes his setup position with his bat, and tries to balance on the board. This drill heightens the hitter's feel for his body, as well as improves his ability to control his center of gravity, which is critical to being a successful hitter. (PHOTO 11-12)

***Balance Beam.*** The balance beam is another tool to aid in the development of dynamic balance, which is important in hitting because the hitter needs to be able to be balanced while he is on the move. Use a 10′ long 4″×4″ beam. The hitter starts at one end of the beam in his hitting stance, with a bat. He raises his stride leg and balances on his back leg for a three count, and then stride, retaining his weight on his back leg. He then must move his back foot up and reestablish his stance, and repeat the one leg balance and stride. He continues to do this until he reaches the end of the beam. Then he assumes the opposite side stance and comes back up the beam with the balance and stride drill. This is good for switch hitters, but it also helps right or left-handed hitters because it helps them control their bilateral balance and increases body balance awareness. (PHOTO 11-13)

***Self Toss.*** Self toss is a drill done with a fungo bat or regular game bat and a ball. It is best performed on the field from the batter's box, but it can be done inside the cages. The hitter tosses the ball up with his back hand (hand furthest from the pitcher), grabs the bat with both hands, draws his bat back, strides, and hits the ball. The toss is predetermined (in, out, up, or down) so the hitter has a target to hit towards. This is more than just fungoing the ball. The goal is to hit backspin line drives to a specific area using the best mechanics he can.

This drill puts an emphasis on a rhythmic coiling action of the body, with the hands going back just as the stride is taken. Make sure to keep the eyes at the point of contact and to finish the swing out in front. He can utilize a partner to give him feedback on the direction and trajectory of the ball after contact, so he resists the temptation to follow the flight of the ball.

***The Batting T.*** The batting T can be used in numerous drills. The key points in utilizing the T most effectively is to hit towards a target and to use a home plate with the T. A good place to use the T is in a long tunnel cage. Set the T up over the middle of the plate and teach the hitter to drive the ball on a line to the far end of the cage. You can use two T's and set one T low and inside, and the other up and away. (PHOTOS 11-14 & 11-15) This demonstrates that the hitter can hit balls away and in with the same basic swing. It also gives the hitter a clear visual picture of how deep in the strike zone he hits the ball away and how far in front of the plate he hits the ball inside. This is a good drill to do on the field because he really has to have the correct swing to keep the low inside pitch fair.

Two T's can also be used to create a short, more direct (A to B) approach to the ball. Set two T's mid, in, or out, with one T in front of the other. The front T should be in the correct contact position for the location of the pitch, and the back T should be 12-18″ behind along the route the bat will take to hit the ball off the front T. The back T should be 3-6″ higher than the front T. (PHOTO 11-16) This setup reinforces a straight line approach to the ball, and does not allow the hitter to loop the bat and drop

Photo 11-14

Photo 11-15

the club head before he starts into the ball. If he loops, he will hit the back T before he is able to make contact with the ball on the front T.

**Two-Man Soft Toss.** Two-man soft toss also allows for numerous drill possibilities. The following are a few of the many toss drills. Front toss, where the tosser is directly in front of the hitter and behind a screen is the basic toss drill. This position is much more realistic than the side toss position where the tosser is at a 45 degree angle to the hitter. It is important that there are targets either on the net or in the form of cones to reinforce that each pitch is hit to the correct part of the field. If there is distance between the targets and the hitter, that is even better because it gives the coach and hitter a chance to evaluate the quality of contact. When he hits into a screen or fence that is quite close to the tosser, the contact may feel correct, but the

Photo 11-16

ball will be sliced or have top spin, rather than be a true backspin line drive. The close distance doesn't allow you to evaluate the flight of the ball.

It is important on all toss drills to incorporate a rhythm component into the drill. As the tosser brings his hand back to toss the hitter should be loading his back side with a coil. Just before the ball is released the hitter should stride. The tosser can hold the ball occasionally to check the hitters balance and hand position. The weight should be centered between the feet on the stride and the hands should remain cocked behind the back shoulder. Some hitters like a rapid fire toss drill but the quality of the swings deteriorate when this happens. A moderately paced toss drill is good at times to work on the rhythm of the swing. Make sure to let the hitter follow through on his swing and get back to his base position before you toss the next ball.

**Soft Toss from Behind.** Soft toss from behind is an excellent drill to keep the hitter inside the ball with his hands, and to keep him from jumping out on his front foot. It also promotes extension after contact. The tosser is directly behind home plate and tosses the ball out in front of the plate. It can be tossed in, out, up, or down. The hitter watches the tosser and reacts to the ball.

**Toss off One Knee.** Hitting toss off one knee is helpful in developing hand action. Work on the high ball for this drill. Use a fungo bat or a dowel with tennis or whiffle balls. The lighter bat does not fatigue the hitter as readily, and it gives him a chance to experience higher speed hand and bat action. The hitter is on his back knee with his front leg slightly flexed. On this drill, the tosser is at a 45 degree angle and

Photo 11-17

tosses the ball eye high or higher. (PHOTO 11-17) The hitter must really "tommy hawk" this pitch by keeping the barrel of the bat above his hands and "dropping the club head" on the ball. The emphasis is on knob down and barrel up, and cutting the ball in half.

***Fence Swing.*** Fence swing toss is a drill to work on hitting the inside pitch with a short compact approach. The hitter stands a little more than his bat length from the fence, with his shoulders parallel with the fence line. (PHOTO 11-18) A cone is set out where third base would be. This can also be performed on the field with a protective screen the bat's length from the hitter. The tosser positions himself directly in front of the hitter and tosses the ball to the inside corner of the plate. If the toss is not inside, the hitter does not swing at it.

The hitter tries to line drive the ball to the pull side without any hook or top spin.

Photo 11-18

He needs to be short to the ball and long through it. If the hitter is too long to the ball, he will hit the fence or screen. Care must be taken that the hitter steps directly toward the pitcher and does not pull off the plate with his stride or fall back on his heels. Also make sure that the hitter's back elbow passes in front of his body and doesn't jam against his side. When this happens, the front shoulder really flies open. As the hitter gets more efficient in his approach to hitting the inside pitch, he can move closer to the fence.

***Two-Ball Toss.*** Two-ball toss is exactly what it says. From a front position, the tosser is tossing two balls from one hand. One ball will be above the other ball. This takes some practice to get both balls on the same trajectory. After the toss, the tosser calls out top or bottom, and the hitter hits that ball. This is an excellent concentration and focus drill that came from Ernie Rosseau, who was the Minor League Hitting Coordinator for the Chicago Cubs.

# HITTING DRILLS WITH THE AID OF EQUIPMENT

Hitting aids have long been a part of drill work. The key is that there is a transfer of skills from the drill done with the hitting aids to actual game hitting.

***40-Inch, 40-Ounce Bat.*** The 40-inch 40-ounce bat is an aid to develop an efficient short stroke. The weight of the bat is a constant factor when the club head drops below the hands as the swing is initiated. It is difficult to control the bat when the arc is too long. If the hands are started around the ball, the hitter can feel the excess weight in such a heavy bat. The bat is most efficiently swung when the club head is dropped on the ball with the hands inside the flight of the ball. The drill that best utilizes this 40-inch 40-ounce bat is short batting practice or soft toss. The 40/40 can also be used in conjunction with the T. This type of bat is hard to find, but some aluminum bat companies will customize a bat, as will certain wood bat companies that have long wood blanks.

***Short Bat.*** Short bat drills are effective for one-handed swing work. They are also helpful in reinforcing the benefits of a short arc to the ball. Hitters feel much more in control of the short bat so they become more comfortable in choking up on the bat when they have to. The short bat produces more bat speed and it gives the hitter a better feel for the relationship of the hands to the club head. The best short bat drills are performed in the short toss or soft toss mode. The short bat can be made from aluminum or wood, and should be about 25" long.

***Eye Patch.*** Head and eye discipline is the key element that determines whether a hitter is going to be successful or not. The ability to keep the head and eyes at the point of contact after contact will give him a chance to hit, even if he makes countless mistakes in other areas of his swing. On the contrary, a perfect swing without good visual technique will not produce success. Make a simple eye patch using a shoe lace and some tape. Put the eye patch over the hitter's back eye (right eye on right-handed

Photo 11-19

hitter; left eye on left-handed hitter). Then have the hitter hit against soft toss, short toss, and eventually live pitching. If the hitter pulls his head slightly, he will pull his lead eye off the ball. With the patch on the back eye, the hitter will lose sight of the ball. The eye patch is a constant reminder that the head and eyes must track the ball and remain at the point of contact.

***Side Winder.*** Hitting balance means body control during and after the stride. The hitter wants his knees and center of gravity to remain between his feet after the stride. The key is to stride on the inside part of the front foot, the big toe. There is an excellent aid to help develop this dynamic hitting balance. We use the side winder from Speed City (800-255-9930) to help develop our lateral quickness and agility. It is a piece of surgical tubing tied to two Velcro wraps that fit around the ankles. (PHOTO 11-19) This was found to be an effective aid in controlling stride length, as well as the inside of the front foot big toe stride. An added benefit is the quick back hip action as a result of the tension on the surgical tubing caused by the stride. Use this aid in any of your drills.

***Towel Drill.*** The towel drill, created by New York Yankee great Joe Gordon, is used to help keep a hitter from uppercutting, as well as to force him to take a shorter, more compact swing. Place a towel under the batter's front elbow and have him take swings against live pitching. (PHOTO 11-20) If the batter swings properly, the towel will remain between the arm and the body because the front elbow will pull down, forcing the hands down and making them quicker through the strike zone. If the batter uppercuts, the front elbow will fly upward and the towel will drop to the ground. This drill can be used in all forms of batting practice.

Care must be taken not to use the towel drill too much because it shortens the arc of the swing out in front where you want extension from the swing. Use this drill primarily for hitters who "chicken wing" the lead arm.

***Hitting Net.*** The purpose of the hitting net is to help the hitter who is having trouble by prematurely rolling his wrists, uppercutting the ball up in the strike zone, or creating too long an arc with the swing. The Swing-Rite Batting Net is a patented invention of Kenny Myers. It is similar in length to a regular bat, but it has a wide opening at the end with a net attached to it to catch balls. The net is used in the same manner as a regular bat.

Using the net as a bat, have the hitter assume his normal stance. The opening of the batting net corresponds to the hitting surface of a bat. The hitter starts with the

Photo 11-20

edge of the net facing the pitcher, and then swings, trying to catch the thrown ball in the net opening. If the hitter swings correctly, he will catch the ball in the net. But, if he rolls his wrists too soon, uppercuts the high ball, or surrounds the outside pitch, the net will go over, under, or around the ball (depending upon the direction of the roll), and the ball will be missed or hit on the edge of the net. (PHOTOS 11-21, 11-22, 11-23, 11-24) This drill may be practiced daily using plastic balls, tennis balls, or regular baseballs. Soft toss with hard balls or short batting practice with tennis or whiffle balls are the best type to utilize with the hitting net.

## LIVE BATTING PRACTICE

Live batting practice is the final part of the drill in the development of the hitter. The following are schemes that you can utilize during live batting practice to add variety and to develop skills that will lead to performance success in the game.

***No Stride Drill.*** The first of these drills is no-stride batting practice. The hitter assumes his post stride base, with his feet spread wider than shoulders' width. As the pitcher is winding up getting ready to pitch, the hitter is coiling and readying himself to swing. No stride is taken. The hitter starts his swing with his back hip and then his hands. This drill focuses on post stride balance, as well as correct hip and hand action. The no-stride drill emphasizes the timing function of the stride. It shows how soon after the stride foot hits that he must start the swing. It reinforces the benefits of

Photo 11-21

Photo 11-22

Photo 11-23

Photo 11-24

getting the stride foot down early so that he has more time to react to the pitch. Some hitters will get their weight out on their front foot before they start their swing. In the no-stride drill, the hitter will be able to feel this premature weight transfer. It is important to stay linear and not get rotational too soon on this drill.

***Off-Center Opposite Drill.*** The second live drill is off-center opposite batting practice. The pitcher stations himself 45′ from home plate and midway between the mound and the first base line for right-hand hitters or, for left-handed hitters, between the mound and the third base line. The pitcher throws to the outside corner, and the hitter tries to drive the ball hard on the ground or on a line between the pitcher and base line. The ball must be away. If it is mid or in, the hitter should not swing at it. This drill teaches the hitter how to use the whole field and the whole strike zone. Hitters that can handle balls away will compete against better pitchers, especially ones who can throw their breaking balls for strikes. This off-center opposite drill also teaches the hitter the correct relationship of the hands, bat, and plate to achieve the best leverage on balls away.

# THE SHORT GAME

Bunting is an important offensive strategy for advancing runners who ae already on base. It is used in place of a base hit. Because effective bunting can be a winning tactic in close ball games, serious players will want to add it to their list of skills.

This section discusses the two types of bunts—the sacrifice bunt and the bunt for a base hit—along with some other bunting strategies.

## SACRIFICE BUNT

The purpose of the sacrifice bunt follows its definition: the batter gives himself up to advance the runner or runners. If this is going to happen, you must put the bunter in the best possible position to get the bunt down consistently. Timing is the most critical factor in consistent execution. Early setup is imperative; it gives the bunter a chance to set the bat angle and stabilize his stance before the ball is in flight. "Early" is defined as when the pitcher comes to his set position. This gives the bunter a chance to adjust to different types of pitches and pitches in different locations in the strike zone. If the defense overcharges the hitter when he assumes his stance early, the hitter must be able to slash (fake bunt hit) the ball through the vacated area. The on-deck hitter can verbally signal the slash when he reads an aggressive crashing defense.

With just a runner on first, if the first baseman breaks hard and early, the base runner may steal second base and yell, "No, no!" so the bunter knows not to slash or bunt the pitch. The base runner must be sure that the first baseman does not break hard toward home for two steps and then break back to receive a pick from the pitcher. This steal action is based on how early the first baseman breaks and how well the runner on first runs.

The early turn can be modified to a later in-between turn or a late turn, based on the defense and the skills of the bunter. However, the basic sacrifice bunt is executed off an early turn. If your basic technique is the early turn sacrifice, the in-between (once the pitcher starts his delivery) or late turn sacrifice (just before the pitcher reaches his release point) will catch the defense asleep, and many times they do not react and first base will be uncovered or they will not get to the bunt in time to make a play.

***Sacrifice Bunt to First Base.*** With just a runner on first base, make the first baseman field the ball. (Exception would be vs. a team with a very poor fielding third baseman, in which case you want him to touch the ball as much as possible.) Bunt the ball softly to the first base line close enough to the line to make the first baseman field it, or one that the pitcher must field moving away from second base. Know how close you can bunt the ball to the line and not have the ball roll foul (check the foul lines before the game). Make sure that the bunt is not so fine that it is forever rolling foul.

The basic setup to sacrifice bunt is all the way to the front of the batter's box and as close to the plate as possible. This gives the bunter full plate coverage and the maximum amount of fair territory in which to bunt. Just as the pitcher reaches his set position, the hitter assumes his bunt stance by pivoting his hips out of his hitting stance. The front foot is 3-4″ further away from home plate than the back foot, which is right next to the interior line of the batter's box. Both feet are pointed at the pitcher (the front foot can be slightly closed) with the lead foot flat and back foot up on the toe. Some players bunt to their pull side (right-handed bunter to third base and left-handed bunter to first base) with the front toe more closed and the bat a little further back. In this way they feel that they can get out of the way of the inside pitch better than being full face at the pitcher. They also feel that they can reach the outside corner more easily. (PHOTO 12-1)

**Photo 12-1**

This gives the bunter a solid base. The knees are bent with the weight on the front foot, so the back knee can control the up/down adjustment to the pitch. The knees are bent so the barrel of the bat starts at the top of the strike zone. The bat is held at eye level at the top of the strike zone with elbows bent down and into the body, but with enough extension so the barrel of the bat is in front of the line of sight. The angle of the bat is preset to bunt the ball to first, with the barrel of the bat slightly above the hands. Approximately 30 degrees tilt up eliminates the chance of pop-ups. This angle is retained through contact.

Poor bunters drop the club head and pop balls up because the elbow of their bottom hand "chicken wings" (PHOTO 12-2). The bat is held loosely in the hands so the ball is bunted softly, which forces the pitcher or first baseman to have to go get the ball. The bottom hand is on top of the bat 4-5″ up from the knob. The top hand is a loose fist under the bat, with the thumb on top. There should be space between the web of the thumb and the bat so the thumb is not exposed to the ball and so the bat can ride

**Photo 12-2**

**Photo 12-3**

back into the web of the thumb on contact and absorb some of the force of the contact. The top hand should be at the label or a little higher. The closer the hitter holds his top hand to the end of the bat, the softer the ball will be bunted, especially if he bunts the ball more toward the end of the bat away from the sweet spot. With a wooden bat, turn the label to the ball to expose the weakest part of the barrel to the ball.

To bunt the top half of the ball, merely catch the ball on the bat—no pushing or giving at contact. The back knee lowers the club head to the ball. Once the back knee touches the ground, lower the chest to the front knee to get the bat to knee height. (PHOTO 12-3). The bunter continues to sight the ball over the top of the bat. The relative position of the bat and eyes remain constant throughout the entire process. Ideally, the club head never drops below eye level to reach the low ball. If the ball is above the barrel of the bat, it is a ball. Just pull the bat back before the ball arrives.

A great way to learn how to sacrifice bunt is to start the bunt with your back knee on the ground. After the hitter learns how to control the bat from that position, start up and put the back knee on the ground after he bunts the ball. Both these drills help the bunter stabilize his stance and keep him from bunting the ball on the run, which is the number one culprit in botched execution of the sacrifice bunt.

***Sacrifice Bunt to Third Base.*** In general, bunt the ball to the third base side when you are trying to advance a runner from second to third. One exception would be against a team with an agile and quick pitcher (especially a left-handed pitcher) and a poor fielding and throwing first baseman. In that case, try to make the first baseman field a softly bunted ball. The second exception would be against a wheel (rotation) defense where the third baseman is charging and the shortstop is rotating to third base. In that situation, slash (fake bunt hit) a ball hard on the ground to the third base side (pitch selection is important here). This is one benefit for the early setup. It gives the bunter a chance to read the defense and react to the rotation play. Being in a hip pivot stance makes it easy to get back into an efficient hitting position to slash.

A second option against the rotation defense would be to steal third base if the runner on second thinks he can beat the shortstop to third base, and the second baseman was not breaking to second to pick. The hitter must read this so that he doesn't slash or bunt the ball. The runner can help with that "no, no," verbal. Some teams will rotate and break their second baseman to second. Against that defense, a soft sacrifice bunt to first or a push bunt to second will be effective. If the first baseman is going to cover first, the soft sacrifice is best. If the first baseman is charging, the push to second is best. Good preparation through scouting is the key here.

The difference between the sacrifice to first and the sacrifice to third is twofold. The club head is angled to third by being more extended with the top hand while the pitcher is in his set position. If the bat is almost parallel to the first base line, the ball will be bunted close enough to the third base line to be effective. The ball has to be bunted close enough to the line that the pitcher can't cut the ball off and so that the third baseman does not have momentum going towards second. This reduces the chances of forcing a runner at second when bunting with runners on first and second. In this situation, the runner on first must maximize his lead and jump, especially when the first baseman is playing in front and closing on the bunter. This ball must be bunted hard enough to get it by the pitcher to force the third baseman to come up and field the ball. To bunt the ball hard, the bat must be held tight. This is especially true for the

top hand, which should be placed at the label. The bottom hand should be rolled back so the palm of the bottom hand is facing the field. This stiffens the wrist and reduces the amount of give by the bat at contact. (PHOTO 12-4)

All sacrifice bunts must be over practiced, especially at game speeds or above. The pitching machine is an especially good teaching aid for bunting. Remember to mix breaking balls and fast balls off machines and live pitching. The sacrifice bunt to third for the right handed hitter and to first for the left handed hitter are tougher and need more practice time. The angle is more critical on these bunts, and there is less margin for error.

***Squeeze Bunt.*** The squeeze bunt is a late turn sacrifice bunt. The key here is to bunt the ball fair and not to give the bunt away too soon. The bunter should pivot

Photo 12-4

just as the pitcher reaches his point of release. This is another advantage of the hip point method of bunting. It involves a minimum amount of movement to set up, thereby allowing the bunter to conceal the squeeze longer. As the hitter is assuming his bunting stance, he should slide up in the box slightly to maximize the amount of fair territory in which to bunt. He can cheat his pre-pitch position in the box a little, but care must be taken not to alert the defense when squeezing. The bunter must "stand taller," in a more upright position because he must cover balls up out of the strike zone. It is much easier to go down to balls and bunt them on the ground than to start flexed out and try to rise up and bunt balls on the ground.

When the pitcher is out of the windup, the hitter should bunt the ball directly back to the pitcher. When the pitcher is out of the stretch, he bunts the ball to the first base side. In either case, you want the ball bunted softly, so he holds the bat loosely with the bottom hand on top of the bat and the top hand past the label. Out of the windup, the base runner from third base has a longer primary and secondary lead, so you can afford to bunt the ball directly back at the pitcher without fear of being thrown out at home. This also prevents balls from rolling foul. Out of the stretch, the runner from third is going to have a shorter primary and secondary lead. If the ball is bunted directly to the pitcher, especially if it is bunted firmly, there is a chance to be thrown out at home. Bunting the ball to the first base side, about half way between the first base line and the mound, creates enough lateral movement by the pitcher to insure that the runner from third will be able to score even with a shortened primary and secondary lead. Also, the bunting angle is not so critical that lots of balls will roll foul.

***Safety Squeeze.*** The safety squeeze is an in-between turn sacrifice bunt, when the pitcher's hand reaches the bottom of his throwing arc, to first base. The runner from third does not break until the ball goes down off the bat, and the runner only bunts pitches that he can direct softly at the first baseman. This is especially effective with runners on first and third and a left-handed pitcher pitching. The first baseman is going to shuffle off with the pitch and not charge, and the left-handed pitcher is going to fall off to the third base side. Neither are going to be in position to throw the runner out at home. It is also a very low risk play.

# BASE HIT BUNT

You should use the terms "base hit bunt to third" or "base hit bunt to second," as opposed to "push" or "drag," because of the confusion of terms when you are talking with left and right-handed hitters. A push for a left-handed hitter is a drag for a right-handed hitter, and visa versa. When you use base hit bunt to third, second, first, or short stop, everyone is on the same page.

Placement of the bunt is much more important than getting out of the box quickly. The key to placement is to assume the base hit bunt stance early enough so you can consistently place the bunt effectively. Even your worst runners can be productive base hit bunters with good placement.

You'll find that with certain players you are going to be able to base hit bunt more effectively in sacrifice situations (rather than sacrificing.) If you can successfully base hit bunt in sacrifice situations it increases your chances of scoring runs because you are less apt to give up an out to advance a runner. Adept base hit bunters improve their batting average because the infielders have to cheat their positioning up toward the hitter thereby cutting down the infielders range. (Rule of thumb: up one step you lose two—one to each side.)

# BASE HIT BUNT TO THIRD BASE

There are different techniques, particularly in movement, for right-handed and left-handed hitters.

*Right-Handed Hitter.* Keeping in mind that placement is key to successful base hit bunting, the hitter must get the bat out in front early enough to insure consistent placement, but not so early that the defense gets too early a read on the bunt. When he shows depends on the depth of the defense, the bunter's bunting skills, and the bunter's speed. With placement in mind, it is better to be early than late. In general, as the pitcher is starting to raise his arm on the back side of the arc, the hitter should assume the base hit bunting position. Some need to start earlier and some later. Allow for individual differences.

It is advantageous if the hitter cheats his positioning up in the box and a little further off the plate. This must be a subtle adjustment so he does not alert the defense to his intent to bunt. Up in the box gives him more fair territory in which to bunt, and off the plate allows him to lean into the bunt, which allows for positive momentum going to first after he bunts the ball. This is key. Bunt it first, then run. You can't steal first base.

As the pitcher brings his hand up to pitch, the hitter brings the club head over the top from its cocked hitting position to a position in front of the body about chest high and parallel to the first base line. (PHOTO 12-5) The knees are bent with the shoulders remaining parallel with the flight of the ball. This is critical because if the front hip or shoulder rotates, it will bring the club head around the outside of the ball. When this happens, the ball will have lots of side spin and will often roll foul. Keeping the front elbow tight against his front side about chest high and the back elbow down and in will insure proper angle

Photo 12-5

and position of the club head. He just catches the ball on the bat. If the bat is out in front of the body and set near parallel to the first base line, the ball must be bunted down the third base line. He controls the speed of the bunt by how loosely he holds the bat and how far up the club head he holds his top hand. The bottom hand should be 4"-5" off the end of the bat.

The hitter should minimize all nonessential movement; don't advocate a drop step with the back foot as he is assuming his bunting stance. This forces the head and eyes to move and bunters try to bunt the ball on the move when they drop step. Leaning to first as he bunts gives him all the momentum he needs and allows the bunter to get a better jump out of the box by striding with his back foot (right) as soon as he bunts the ball. The knees take the bunter down to the low ball and leaning in as he reads the flight of the ball allows him to reach across the plate. He should start tall and work down to the ball. He should start off the plate and work in to the plate. Successful right-handed base hit bunters to third base must learn to be bad ball bunters. If he waits for the perfect pitch, he'll never get a ball to bunt and when he does bunt, the third baseman will be right in his face.

***Left-Handed Hitter.*** Use the same basic philosophy as the base hit bunt to third base for the right-handed hitter. Placement and early setup are the keys. The base hit bunt to third base for the left-handed hitter involves more movement than it does for the right-hander, but it does not require any position adjustments in the box before the pitch.

As the pitcher is starting his throwing hand up to the pitch, the left-handed hitter steps with his rear foot (left foot) directly at the mound. This step will carry his

left foot in front of his right foot and in front of the plate. This gets the bat into fair territory and keeps the bunter from pulling out before he bunts the ball. (PHOTO 12-6) It is advantageous to get the left foot down before the ball leaves the pitcher's hand. As the batter is bringing his foot forward, he is bringing the bat into a bunting position. This position calls for the bat to be in front of the line of sight and parallel to the first base line. The elbows are flexed, and down and in to the body. After the ball is bunted, the bunter lead steps to first with his right foot. To make sure that the ball is not bunted too hard, he holds the bat loosely with the top hand in a loose fist at or above the label. Rule of thumb: The looser the grip and the closer to the end of the bat the grip, the softer the bunt.

Practicing the base hit bunt to third base is excellent for the struggling hitter because it allows him to track the ball a

Photo 12-6

longer distance than when hitting. Many times hitters are not seeing the ball well when they are not hitting because they are not doing a good job of tracking the ball. He can base hit bunt any pitch to third base except the low inside pitch.

# BASE HIT BUNT TO SECOND BASE

The base hit bunt to third base can be defended. All your opponent needs to do is play the third baseman in the hitter's face. It is much more difficult to defend against the base hit bunt to second. The first baseman would have to cheat way up and off the line to stop the bunt. This is tough, especially if there is a left-handed pitcher, because it becomes a foot race between the bunter and the pitcher, and the pitcher has to catch the feed from the first baseman at a critical angle on a dead run. The second baseman can cheat way up and take the base hit bunt away, but that seriously compromises his positioning with runners on base or when the hitter is swinging the bat.

*Right-Handed Hitter.* The base hit bunt to second for the right-handed hitter is a running sacrifice bunt. As the pitcher starts his arm up, the bunter takes a drop stop towards the back outside corner of the batter's box with his right foot. As the pitcher releases the ball, the batter steps toward the second baseman, also with his right foot. (PHOTO 12-7) As he is stepping towards the second baseman, he is bringing the bat into a bunting position. The barrel of the bat is above the top hand at eye level, with the bat in a position to bunt the ball firmly at the second baseman. The elbows are

down and in to the body with the bottom hand more extended. The bat is held tight with the bottom hand rolled back behind the bat so that the palm of the bottom hand is facing the second baseman. This reduces the amount of give by the bat at contact, and also sets the angle of the bat so the ball will be bunted right at the second baseman.

The ball must be bunted hard enough so that it gets by the pitcher, but not so hard that the second baseman can field the ball and throw the bunter out. This is especially effective against left-handed pitchers who tend to fall off to the third base line. Just like the base hit bunt to third for the left-handed hitter is a good drill for the struggling hitter, the base hit bunt to second base (also sacrifice bunt to first) is an excellent drill for the struggling right-handed hitter because it forces the hitter to better track the ball. The hitter can base hit bunt any pitch to second, except a ball down and inside.

Photo 12-7

**Photo 12-8**

***Left-Handed Hitter.*** Just before the pitcher releases the ball, the batter steps toward the second baseman with his rear foot. This is a relatively long step that will end with his left foot closer to the second baseman than his right foot. As he steps, he brings the bat forward to shoulder height or slightly below with a straight left arm. The palm of the left hand is facing the second baseman and the bat is held firmly. (PHOTO 12-8) Pitch selection is important for the proper execution. The pitch needs to be middle in to have the best chance to get the ball by the pitcher to the second baseman. If the pitcher is working you away, you can move in to the plate and turn that outside pitch into a middle pitch, but that makes it more difficult to get extended on the ball inside. The margin for error is more towards the first baseman than the pitcher. This is especially true when using this bunt with a runner on second and no one out because, at worst, you'll advance the runner to third base if the first baseman fields the ball. He can have a real chance to beat the pitcher to first if the first baseman fields the ball and has to feed the pitcher.

## BASE HIT BUNT TO FIRST BASE

This is primarily a technique for left-handed hitters, especially left-handed hitters who are above average runners. Right-handers who can run can also base hit bunt to first. In either case, the ball is bunted softly down the first base line and the bunter must beat the first baseman to the ball, which should stop about 45' up the first base line (the start of the running box). The ideal prepitch scenario has the first baseman deep and a left-handed pitcher pitching. The key is the first baseman deep, however. Many times, the pitcher and first baseman will break on the bunt and collide. Also, when the batter/runner avoids the tag, the first baseman has to turn and throw over the runner to the second baseman who is on the run. If the bunt is the correct speed and well placed, even with perfect defensive execution, it is an extremely difficult play to defend.

***Right-Handed Hitter.*** This is similar to the base hit bunt to second base as far as the initial drop step before release is concerned, but the bat is angled to bunt the ball down the first base line. The bat is held loosely like the sacrifice to first and you have less momentum going through the ball on contact. The top hand should be near the end of the bat. The pitch up in the strike zone is easiest to get consistent results. The low and in pitch is the only pitch that will not allow you to place the bunt properly.

**Left-Handed Hitter.** The footwork for this bunt is similar to the base hit bunt to second base. The exception is that the bat is angled to bunt the ball down the first base line. The bat is held loosely with the top hand close to the end of the bat.

## BASE HIT BUNT TO SHORTSTOP

This is for left-handed bunters and is an almost unstoppable technique when executed correctly. This is especially good against right-handed pitching when the third baseman is playing up to take the base hit bunt to third away from the bunter. If the third baseman plays way up and off the line, to take the base hit bunt to shortstop away, bunt the ball down the third base line.

The technique is similar to the base hit bunt to third base. The initial step before the pitcher releases the ball is toward the shortstop. The elbows are pointed down with the top hand more extended than the bottom hand and the bat held tight with the bottom wrist rolled back. If this doesn't produce enough speed to get the ball by the pitcher, a little pushing action on contact will help.

Some left-handed bunters can execute all their bunts, base hit and sacrifice, by using a hip pivot technique. No matter what technique they use, if they are having success, don't repair it. The only exceptions would be when a technique would lead to injury or could not be utilized at the next level.

## FAKE BUNT, FAKE HIT AND BUNT

The fake bunt hit and bunt is a complement to the early turn sacrifice bunt and the slash. It is a technique that is intended to take advantage of the third baseman's indecision as to whether the hitter is bunting or slashing. The hitter assumes an early hip pivot sacrifice stance by pivoting just as or before the pitcher comes set. Just as the pitcher starts to break his hands, he brings his bat back as if to slash. As the pitcher brings his arm up to pitch, the hitter gets into his base hit bunt position to third base. When the third baseman sees that early turn, he will shorten up, but he is thinking slash. When the hitter pulls back early to assume a slash position, it confirms the third baseman's presupposition and he tends to go back on his heels, thus setting up the base hit bunt to third.

**Section 13**

# BASE RUNNING

Base running starts in the dugout, and before pregame practice, when you are "making friends with the field." Follow these steps:

1. Each player should establish distance marks on the field. He needs to know where the 270-foot mark in the outfield is so he can evaluate the outfielder's arm strength during infield. An average arm, release to glove, will carry the ball 270 feet in the time it takes an average runner to run 90 feet with a running start—3 to 3.5 seconds. He should determine where the reference points on the infield are for his 12-foot and 15-foot lead at first and his 21-foot and 24-foot lead at second base. The reference points merely reinforce the fact that the measured lead was the correct distance.

2. Have each player check the distances to the backstop and side fencing so that he is prepared to advance or not advance on overthrows or wild pitches.

3. Each player should check the base lines, especially around the bases and home plate. Is it wet around the bases where he is going to have to start his slide later? Are there any ridges outside of first and third that are going to affect his turns? Will balls roll foul or stay fair?

4. Check the outfield distances. There are sure triple areas in most ballparks.

5. Check the grass in the outfield. Is it soft and/or slow so that balls are going to get to the outfielders slowly, which will allow players to take extra bases?

6. Is the outfield wet so that balls will plug, and outfielders will not be able to stop and will run by the ball? Is it wet enough to affect the outfielder's throwing once they catch the ball?

7. On an artificial surface field, are pop-ups or flies that fall in going to bounce so high that it is an automatic double?

8. Check the sun and lights. What effect are they going to have on the play?

9. Finally, check the wind. What kind of effect is it going to have on outfield play, especially throwing? This is an ongoing process since winds change periodically during the game.

# PREGAME AND DURING-GAME HOMEWORK

Before the game, do your homework during your opponent's pregame infield.

*Outfielders.* Are the outfielders right- or left-handed throwers? Balls to their glove-hand side are more difficult to field and throw. An outfielder going away from the base he is throwing to with the ball on his glove-hand side will be slower than an outfielder with momentum going away with the ball on the throwing hand side. Obviously, arm strength is important to evaluate. Use your 270-foot marker and a stopwatch. Arm strength is best evaluated when the outfielder does not have momentum to initiate the throw. How sure-handed are the outfielders? Do they catch or bobble ground balls? Are they accurate throwers?

*Infielders.* Watch the infield arms for both arm strength and carry. Teach your players to watch for the third basemen, shortstops, and second basemen whose throws tail and who throw a lot of balls up the first base line. Base runners who anticipate this will be in a position to slide to avoid the tag as the first baseman comes up the line off the base. Catchers whose throws tail a lot dictate a slide to the third base side of second base on stolen base attempts. Weak-armed third basemen are vulnerable to base hit bunts. Weak-armed middle infielders are vulnerable when they have to relay throws on extra base hits. Weak-armed first basemen can be victimized on ground balls to shortstop or third base with a runner on second. After the third baseman or shortstop throws to first, the runner on second can go to third.

Watch the double play pivots. Do the middle infielders turn the double play from inside, outside, or on the base? Do the middle infielders reverse balls to third base on non-double play balls? If they do, watch your turns at third. Does the first baseman really stretch out to catch balls? If he does the splits, you may be able to score runners from second on infield outs. This is especially true if it's a left-handed first baseman. Are the first baseman or third baseman shaky fielders? If so, you may want to direct your entire offensive short game attack toward the weakest corner infielder. Does the catcher look the runner back to third base during infield when he throws to second? This might dictate how the runner on third will attack the first and third situation. Where and how does the catcher set up to take throws from the outfield? This helps the runner from third prepare for his slide at home.

*Between Innings.* Watch the throwing actions of the infielders and catcher between innings. During the game, fatigue, injuries, and other factors may affect how people throw. Pay close attention to the pitcher between innings. What is he throwing and where is he throwing? Is he bouncing a lot of curve balls and change-ups or fast balls? Check your Opponent's Pitcher Tendency Chart (Figure 3-8) to find the counts for particular pitches so you can anticipate balls in the dirt.

In general, aggressive and intelligent base running is as much of a run scoring factor as hitting. Once you swing the bat, you become a base runner. Great base runners have the ability to advance themselves. With the exception of the home run that leaves the ballpark, base running is what scores runs. That's what the offensive side of this game is about. Aggressive and intelligent base runners can advance themselves without the aid of the hitter.

# BATTER/RUNNER TECHNIQUE

Here are a number of tips that can help a player enhance his skills as both batter and runner.

***Pre-Pitch Preparation.*** After the hitter gets the coach's signal, he should check the infield positioning and then the outfield before he assumes his position in the batter's box. He is looking for depths and shades to prepare his offensive attack. For example, a left-handed throwing left fielder is playing way off the line and he hits a ball down the line, if he prepared, he knows it's a sure double. With runners on base, don't let the hitter set himself in the box until the base runner has established his primary lead. This is especially true after a pitcher steps off the rubber or moves to a base. If the pitcher makes him wait and he calls timeout, he should be ready to hit until the umpire grants him timeout.

Aside from the preparation before he makes contact, base running starts with contact. On the first step out of the batter's box after contact, the batter should roll his head and pick up the ball. This will determine his route to first base. If the ball is going to the outfield, the batter runner can start his loop to set up his turn at first base. The turn at first starts as soon as the batter runner reads that the ball is going to the outfield. The size of the loop is dependent on the agility and body control of the batter runner. The more agile players can take less of a loop, thereby shortening the distance to second base.

***After Touching First Base.*** You want the runner to be headed on a straight line to second base after he touches first. For this to happen, the batter runner must lean into the diamond and dip his left shoulder as he hits the front edge of the first base bag (not the inside corner). He should also drive his outside arm (right arm) across his body to keep from swinging out towards right center field on the turn. Hitting the inside corner of the base puts him on line to make a wide turn. Every foot outside of a line directly to the next base adds two feet on to the distance between bases.

The front edge of the first base bag serves as a starting block to catapult the batter runner straight to second base. (PHOTO 13-1) The batter/runner should hit the base with either foot and look at the base as he touches it. If he hits the front edge of the base, there will never be a doubt as to whether he hits the base or not. The technique and route from second to third, or third to home, is the same as the route from home to first.

***Watching the First Baseman's Feet.*** If the ball is hit on the ground at an infielder, the batter runner should look at first base and focus on the feet of the first baseman. If the first baseman's feet go in the air or leave the ground and move towards home plate, the batter runner should slide at first base. This is the only time a slide is beneficial at first. If the first baseman's feet do not move, the batter runner should run through first, lean forward with his head down, and step on top of the base. This keeps the runner from sustaining the ankle and heel injuries that are associated with the leg

**Photo 13-1**

hyperextension that occurs when a player hits the front edge of the base. After the bat-ter runner hits first base, he should square his shoulders to second base and look back over his left shoulder to pick up a wild or missed throw. Squaring up stops the batter runner close to first base, thereby putting him closer to second in case of an errant throw. (PHOTO 13-2) It also puts him in the best position to run to second without any wasted movement.

This is especially important if he hits a ground ball in the infield with a runner on third base, and the ball beats the runner from third to the plate. The runner from third is probably going to stop and get in a rundown, and the batter runner has to be ready to go to second base. Occasionally, the batter runner is going to start to run through and the ball will end up in the outfield. For example, a ground ball to the shortstop or third baseman will roll through his legs, or take a bad hop and get by him. In that case, the batter runner may have to pick up the first base coach and make a late flat turn towards second.

***Making the Turn.*** The base runner should look at the base as he is making his turn, and then pick up the outfielder. Aggressive turns are a must. Every single is a double until the outfielders stops him by catching the ball and making an accurate throw. The farther the ball is hit from first base, the more aggressive the turn at first. If the outfielder tries to throw behind him to first base, he should go to second. The only exception would be the ball that is hit sharply to right field. Once the outfielder has caught the ball and thrown accurately, the batter/runner has to stop quickly and hus-tle back to first. He must keep his eyes on the ball and stay in the throwing lane between the ball and the first baseman in case the middle infielders try to throw to first.

**Photo 13-2**

The jump stop is the fastest and most efficient way to turn aggressively and stop momentum quickly. After the outfielder fields the ball cleanly and throws the ball accurately to second, the runner should drive off his left foot and become airborne. He should stay sideways and land on the inside of his right foot to stop his forward momentum. This technique stops the momentum better than a sliding stop, or three or four extra small steps to stop.

## LEADS AT FIRST BASE

The following tips for when and how to take the primary lead, or expand it, will help players become more successful base runners.

*Primary Leads.* Before he takes his lead at first base, the runner must get the coach's signal. Then he must check the infield, check the outfield, and check the scoreboard, in that order. This is all done rapidly after he gets the signal and before he initiates his lead. Before he takes his primary lead, he must make sure the pitcher has the ball (no hidden ball outs). It is a must to get his primary lead in before the pitcher gets set. This is so the pitcher doesn't quick set and catch the runner with a short lead, or pick while he is gaining momentum to second.

The runner gets the primary lead while the pitcher is on the rubber and looking in for his signal. He should take his lead straight off the middle of the base or slightly behind a line running down the middle of the base line. This will create a direct path to second. He may lead deeper behind a line directly to second when you want him to draw a pick. Poorer runners should force more picks because the wild pick is one of his best method of advancing himself. The deep lead makes it look to the pitcher that the runner is further from the base.

The base runner may also use the deeper lead when the count is 3-2 with two outs. This will facilitate the turn at second since he'll be running on the pitch. If he is going to steal on a pitcher's first move, especially a left-handed pitcher, the runner should take his lead on the inside of the base so that if he is picked, he can take the throwing lane away from the first baseman.

The primary lead should be 12 feet. This means that the right foot is on the 12-foot mark. This will vary according to physical ability. Players who are slow to react may have to shorten their primary leads unless they are trying to draw a pick. Each runner needs to have a specific technique to get that 12-foot primary lead so that he can look at the pitcher while taking his lead. Start with a crossover step, which gets him out to 6 feet. There is little chance of getting picked on the crossover because he is so close to the base. If that is a concern, he can start with a shuffle by bringing his left foot to his right foot, and then moving the right foot 3 feet towards second. He follows the crossover or the shuffle with two more shuffle steps to reach 12 feet. He always initiates the shuffle by bringing the left foot to the right foot. If he initiates the shuffle with the right foot, he gets too wide a base and is vulnerable to being picked. He should slide his feet low to the ground when he is shuffling to his primary lead. He should not leap or jump into the primary lead. When he is airborne, he is vulnerable to being picked. Depending on his quickness, he can get 13, 14, or 15 feet on his primary one step at a time by the left-to-right shuffle technique.

**_Expanding the Primary Lead._** Expand his primary lead while the pitcher is looking away. When pitchers see movement, they pick. When the runner establishes his maximum lead, his right foot should align right toe to instep of his left foot, with the right foot open to second base. This allows the base runner to get into the correct running position on the first step without the need for a jab step to open up the front side. If he starts with his feet parallel (perpendicular to a straight line to second), he has to take a jab step with the right foot to initiate a crossover with the left. If he doesn't jab step, but tries to cross over with the feet parallel, it will take him two to four steps for him to regain efficient running form. If he chooses to lead step with the right foot (not advisable) and his feet are parallel, he has to pick up the right foot and spin it open. Keep the shoulders parallel to the base line, with his left arm bent at 45° and the right hand at the right hip. (PHOTO 13-3)

Photo 13-3

The weight is on the balls of the feet, with more weight on the right foot when stealing and more weight on the left foot when trying to draw a pick. When stealing, the first step is a crossover with the left foot, while the right hand drives from the right hip to the lips. This technique puts the arms and legs in synchronization with the opposite arm and leg forward. The arms drive from the hips to the lips.

## RETURNING TO FIRST BASE

There are three ways to return to first base: dives, crossovers, and the feet first standing technique.

**Dives.** If it is going to be a close play, the runner must dive head-first back to the base. He'll go back with a "spoking" technique that involves a crossover step with his right foot and a spoking action with the left arm. This spoking involves a cartwheeling action over the planted left arm. (PHOTO 13-4) It is fast and eliminates the friction created by the body skimming across the ground. To spoke, after the crossover, he must plant his hand and fingers parallel to the first base line and pop over the firm left arm to the front of the base. It is important to push back towards second base with the left hand to accelerate the body to first and keep it in alignment. Essentially, he can cover 15 feet by taking one step with the legs (the crossover) and one with the arm (the spoke).

Photo 13-4

***Crossover.*** If the return to first does not require a dive, he should return to the front edge of first with a crossover, and bring the left foot to the front edge of the base. He must keep his butt up and head down. (PHOTO 13-5) This action gives him several advantages—It is quick, stops his momentum, puts him in a position to see a wild pick, and protects him from serious injury. Never allow him to put his hands on his helmet. If his fingers get hit by the ball while they are pressed against his helmet, there is a greater chance of injury.

***Feet First Standing.*** A third way to return to first is the feet first standing technique, but more towards home plate. He should avoid contact with the first baseman. This is a technique that is reserved for a first and third situation against a left-

Photo 13-5

handed pitcher whose picks tail and end up on the right field side of first. This is especially good if the first baseman is also left-handed. Taking more of an inside route to the base cuts off the first baseman's route to a poor throw down the line. This technique should be used sparingly.

The accepted belief is that if the runner doesn't have to dive back to first, his lead is not long enough. In general, this is true, but there are many base stealers who feel threatened by a long lead and would rather run with a shorter lead and momentum. The problem with the short lead and momentum is that pitchers who can hold runners do not pitch when a runner has momentum, and the runner gets stuck running with a short lead and no momentum, or not running at all. Some base stealers with premium speed still prefer to run with a short lead and no momentum because they feel safe since there is no threat of being picked off. The ideal is to time the runner to second on his short lead and his long lead (so he can see the benefit of a longer lead), drill the spoking technique until he feels confident in his ability to get back to first safely, and teach him how to recognize his keys at first so that his reaction time to steal is the same with a long lead as a short one.

## USING THE STOPWATCH

Time the pitcher from his first move until the ball gets to the catcher. Time the catcher from the time the pitch hits his glove until it arrives at second base, and add 1/10 of a second for the tag. Add them all together and compare them with your runner's time with a 12-foot and 15-foot lead. Give this information to your runner so he knows what type of lead and jump he should use if everything is perfect on the defensive side.

The runner must also factor in the catcher's throwing accuracy and the type of pitch he expects. The curve ball and change-up are going to be slower to the plate. For every 1 mph of difference in velocity, add 1/100 of a second onto the release time. For example, if the pitcher is 1.3 seconds to home on an 80 mph fast ball, he's going to be 1.45 seconds on a 65 mph change-up. Also, remember that lots of breaking balls end up in the dirt. Have runners check the tendency charts to anticipate breaking balls or look at the catcher's signals when taking their lead.

You may be able to pick up the breaking ball by reading the pitcher's grip or how he is holding his wrist. More flexion or a hooked wrist usually indicates a breaking ball. Extra time to grip or asking the umpire for a new ball also indicate a breaking ball.

## SECONDARY LEADS

The base runner should take an aggressive two-sidewards hop secondary lead when he is absolutely sure the pitcher is going home. This lead should take him right to the edge of his safety zone. If the pitch is not hit on the ground, in the air to the outfield, a hit on a line, missed by the catcher, or in the dirt, he must put the brakes on and quickly return to first. If his secondary leads are long and aggressive enough, the catcher should feel that he has a chance to pick him off. In bunt situations (either base hit or sacrifice), his secondary lead should be softer and less aggressive to avoid being picked. All too often, base runners tend to break just as the ball is to be bunted, without reading the ball going down off the bat. This softer lead helps reduce that false break.

If he thinks the ball is going to be in the dirt, he should run. This is a learned technique. If it is not practiced correctly, the tendency is to wait to run after the ball has hit the ground. If executed properly, the base runner breaks before the ball hits the ground. The premise is that the catcher is going to his knees to block the ball, and he will not have enough time to get up, retrieve the ball, and throw him out if he runs early, before the ball hits the dirt. When you are competing against catchers who try to pick the ball out of the dirt, he can wait until the catcher misses the ball and it rebounds away from him.

The base runners that are proficient anticipating the ball in the dirt do their homework before they get on first base. Number one, they pay close attention to the game to see the counts that breaking balls are being thrown, or they check the Pitcher Tendency Chart. Number two, before the game, preferably during batting practice, they must establish a reference point midway between the pitcher's mound and home plate where, if the ball passes below that point, it's going to end up in the dirt.

To develop this skill, place two large ($10' \times 10'$) protective screens on a line to home plate, between the pitcher and the runner at first base. Cover the screens with a tarp so that the runner at first sees the pitcher's release, but does not see the ball again until it's 30 to 40 feet from the plate. At this juncture, and a little more forward, the base runner must learn to judge whether it will be in the dirt or not. He has to be able to read balls in the dirt off a regular secondary lead, as well as a fake break. This is a skill that is especially important for non-base stealers to master because it is a way to advance themselves without stealing the base which they can't accomplish.

# FAKE BREAK

The fake break is a type of secondary lead that can force the defense to move out of position prematurely, thereby cutting down their range. The shortstop and second baseman break towards second when they believe that the runner is stealing. This movement, no matter how slight it is, cuts down on the range of the middle infielders going away from second base. The fake break can also bring the catcher into a more upright position in preparation to throw out the runner. When the catcher starts his momentum early, especially if he raises up, he can block the umpire out and cost the pitcher strikes. This can put the hitter in a leveraged count situation where he normally would not have one. This technique also helps indicate which infielder will cover the steal. This helps the hitter direct his attack in a hit & run situation. The base runner merely squares his shoulders to second by taking a crossover step with his left foot, and then squaring up the shoulders to the base line by taking a shuffle with the right foot.

# STEALING SECOND BASE

A runner should only steal second with his best jump. If he gets thrown out anywhere, it's going to be at first base. In other words, it's okay to get picked at first, but it's not okay to get thrown out at second base. The only exception would be the three ball steal of second base, which should be treated like a hit and run. In this situation, he cannot get picked at first. Give a steal sign here, rather than hit and run, because it takes the pressure off the hitter. Many young hitters lose the count or get too defensive in a three ball hit and run situation, and swing weakly or at balls out of the strike zone. By giving the runner steal, it takes much of the thought process away from the hitter and he is allowed to swing the bat aggressively at his pitch.

If the base stealer gets picked while attempting to steal second, he should keep going to second and try to stay in the first baseman's throwing lane. He should run for the middle infielder's glove, stay up as long as he can, and slide late and tough, feet first. With just a runner on first who is picked, it is better to force the quick throw and tag, as opposed to a rundown. Good teams do not let a player escape from rundowns. However, if a rundown does ensue, he should stay in the rundown as long as he can and try to make contact with a fielder who does not have the ball or is not in the act of catching a throw. If he is about to be tagged, he should fall down flat to the ground and perpendicular to the base line. As the tagger jumps over him (in most cases, if he is perpendicular and pancaked, he will not be able to tag him), he should go back in the opposite direction to the base. The tagger will not be able to stop in time to reverse his throw and, many times, no one will be there to receive it.

# STEALING AGAINST A RIGHT-HANDED PITCHER

The key to a good break from first base is good timing, rhythm, and knowledge of the pitcher. In stealing second against a right-handed pitcher, there are three main keys to look for in deciding whether the pitcher's going to the plate or to first.

***Front Shoulder.*** The first key is the pitcher's front shoulder. If the pitcher's front shoulder is open up toward first base, he must close it before throwing to the plate. (PHOTO 13-6) This means as soon as his front shoulder moves away from first, the runner can get his break. Some pitchers do not leave their front shoulder open, but take a big coil backward before pitching. Again, the key is the pitcher's front shoulder. The straight-over-the-top pitcher will greatly elevate his front shoulder and/or lift his chin, which also gives the base runner a little extra advantage.

Photo 13-6

***Anticipation.*** A second important factor is anticipation. First, the runner must establish the maximum number of picks the pitcher will make, or the spot from where he will pick or not pick. For example, never when he's set, or only on his way up or on his way down. Then, establish the time lapse between the set and his pitch. For example, two picks maximum, and then he pitches home after coming set for two counts. He may be able to run on a pitcher's tempo alone. He should take a sideways leap one-half a count before the anticipated delivery. If the pitcher moves when he lands, he should steal second. If he does not move, stop, leap back, and be ready to dive back to first. This is a technique that's used against pitchers who are very quick to home and against catchers who are quick and accurate.

***Reading the Front Foot.*** A third important point, and the one that is used most frequently, is reading the front foot. The runner should zero in on the front foot. As soon as it moves, he should go. Any movement not involving the front foot movement indicates a pick.

Every pitcher has some key that your runners can use to help them steal second. If it is not one of the basic three, don't give up. They can only find out what to use as their body keys by observing the pitcher in the stretch. Have them make the pitcher throw to first by getting an extended one-way lead. This is especially good early in the game. If your runner leads off from deeper behind the base, it appears to the pitcher that you're farther off. If one key is not there, then go to the next until they find one that will help. Start with the pitcher's head, work down. The dugout can help them by focusing on different body parts to see what moves first.

Photo 13-7

As the coach, evaluate the total situation when you're putting on the steal. If the opposition has a bad throwing catcher, either he doesn't have arm strength or he's not accurate, then there's no reason in the world to be picked at first base. The same is true if they have a pitcher who is slow to home. You can be more conservative then, and your runners can get less of a jump than they would have to get when they have a good throwing catcher and a pitcher that's quick to the plate. The runner should roll his head and look to home on his second step, and read balls in the air.

The pitch-out should not be a problem since he's running on his best jump. The runner should choke off his break if he gets a quick slide step where the pitcher changes the tempo, or he reads that he doesn't have his best jump.

***Reading the Pitch Out.*** On the hit and run, the runner should look on his first step to read the pitch-out. (PHOTO 13-7) If it's a pitch-out, he must shut down his break and scuffle back to first base. Teach your hitters to not swing at pitch-outs or balls in the dirt. If a line drive is hit in the infield, the runner should keep on running, because he is not going to be able to get back anyway, and he might as well give himself a chance to go to third if the ball gets through the infield. If a line drive is hit to the outfield, he should stop and read it unless he is sure it's going to land safely.

# PRIMARY LEADS VS. LEFT-HANDED PITCHERS

Against a left-hander you have not seen before, have your base runner take an extended one-way lead going back. He may have to adjust the length of his leads until he knows if the left-hander has a good step-off move or not. This means he takes a long lead, but returns to first base on the first move by the left-hander. If, after he sees the left-handed pitcher's move, he finds that he has a good move, not a great one, he can take a normal leaning lead back to first base or jab step back on the pitcher's first move. When he's sure he's going to deliver, he'll shuffle off. A shorter lead with a momentum is better than a longer lead with no momentum. A safe lead with momentum is preferable to a longer two-way lead where he's not sure where he's going. It's better to have a little shorter lead and gain the distance that he lost on the shortness of the lead, with the momentum and the confidence to know that he can always get back. It is imperative that the first base runner to first force the left-handed pitcher to pick. This way you get a chance to study his move.

## STEALING AGAINST LEFT-HANDED PITCHERS

Most left-handed pitchers predetermine whether they will throw home or to first. Study them, and they will give you some indication as to what they will do before they do it. Watch for these signs:

***The Head.*** They look home and throw to first; they look to first and throw to home. (PHOTOS 13-8, 13-9)

Photo 13-8

Photo 13-9

***Upper Body.*** They lean back and throw to first; they lean forward and throw to home. (PHOTOS 13-10, 13-11)

Photo 13-10

Photo 13-11

***Lead Leg.*** Open thigh, they throw to first; closed thigh, they throw to home. (PHOTOS 13-12, 13-13)

***Hands and Legs.*** If they move their hands first, they're going home; if they move their leg first, they're going to first base.

The player runs on the first move of a left-handed pitcher with a high leg kick and a slow move to first. The player runs all the way to second, staying in the throwing lane as long as he can, and sliding late. He must be a good actor and convince the left-handed pitcher that he's not running, and he will not throw to first. He can do this

Photo 13-12

Photo 13-13

by varying the length of his primary lead and using an early jab step back to first, and then running on his first move. Good runners must be observant and creative. Some pitchers will read the runner at first base. This is the guy that he has to convince that he's not running. An early jab step on his first move, the pitcher reads him, then the runner can break before he's really initiated his move to the plate. On the other side of the ledger, the runner can feint a break to second to force a pick at first. If he does it enough, the pitcher will tire of picking when the base runner is not stealing.

Once the base runner sets the pitcher up, he can break to second instead of feint, or follow the feint with a break to second. If he has done a good enough job with his jab back or feint to second, the pitcher will not pick and he'll be able to run early in the pitcher's delivery. If a left-hander uses a glide step or slide step, and he doesn't get a good jump when he's stealing, he chokes it off and be ready to go back to first base.

Many left-handers will have a maximum number of picks to first. Few throw over three times consecutively, and almost none will pick four times. Until you observe differently, you can gamble and run on the pitcher's first move after two or three picks.

# DELAY STEAL

The delay steal is intended to catch the middle infielders or catcher sleeping. When a runner from first does not break immediately, the middle infielders focus on the hitter and have a tendency to relax. The shortstop and second baseman do not cover second, or they cover it late. Then, the catcher double-clutches in throwing to second base. The coach should look for middle infielders who play far from second base and don't break to cover second base after the ball passes the hitter. He can also look for catchers who throw from their knees back to the pitcher, or who do not get their body started and anticipate a steal on every pitch.

In the delay steal, the runner takes a safe primary lead at first, and when he's sure the pitcher is going home, takes two long, low shuffles to second, then makes his break to second base. Against left-handed pitchers with low leg kicks, he may get only 1½ leaps before running.

# THE SHADE—AN AID TO STEALING SECOND

Protect the runner in some stealing situations by shading the ball from the catcher. The hitter executes the shade by starting deeper in the batter's box to force the catcher to throw extra distance. As the ball is delivered, he checks his swing, drags the bat back toward the catcher, and covers the ball. It is important to pick the bat up at the last minute. The technique is distracting, cuts down the catcher's momentum to second base, and disrupts his throwing rhythm.

Most catchers try to gain momentum to second just before they catch the ball. The rhythm is usually step, catch, throw. Catchers start their momentum forward as the bat starts forward on the swing, or as the ball approaches the plate when there is no swing.

The checked swing shade gets the catcher's momentum started and then stops it when the bat starts moving back at the catcher. If the hitter covers the ball with the bat on the checked swing until the last second, the catcher loses sight of the ball and it jumps up on the catcher. Care must be taken not to interfere with the catcher or his throwing. When he drags the bat back after the checked swing, he must pick the bat up so that no contact is made with the catcher as he moves forward.

# EXTRA INNINGS AT FIRST BASE

By following these tips, base runners can help to avoid extra innings.

*Avoiding the Double Play.* With just a runner on first and a ground ball hit to the second baseman in the base line between first and second, have your runner stop and then run right at the second baseman who will be coming towards him to tag him out. If he can knock him off balance, chances are he will not be able to get enough on the throw to complete the double play. If there are multiple runners (first, second, or the bases loaded), he should stop and force the second baseman to throw to second for the double play. Make sure he throws to second and doesn't just fake a backhand flip to second, and tags him. If the second baseman runs towards the runner, have him retreat until he is about to be tagged. As he is about to be tagged, he should fall down flat and perpendicular to the base line between first and second. If the second baseman is able to tag him, chances are he will not be able to regain his balance or get his arm up in time to complete the double play at first. If the second baseman misses the tag, he should run hard to second.

***Tagging Up on Fly Balls.*** With runners on first and third, and less than two outs in a close game, the runner on first should tag on all catchable flies where there is a play at home. He must break hard on the throw to the plate and read the trajectory of the throw. If the throw is going up and will miss the cutoff man, he continues to second. If it is a low throw or is directed towards second, he puts the brakes on and hustles back to first. He must not get tagged out before the run scores. Inning and score will dictate when and if you utilize this play.

The base runners should use the base coach sparingly. The runner should find the ball even if he has to roll his head to do it. He also needs to watch the runner in front of him.

The runner should tag on all foul balls, and tag on fair balls when he is absolutely sure they will be caught and he is going to run on the catch. This can occur on a deep fly to left or left center field against a team with a poor throwing let fielder. Runners should go back to the base on line drives. This is a general rule at all bases.

When there are two outs, the runners should go hard and slide to beat the force. Keep the pressure on the defense. Don't let the runners call themselves out. Make the umpire chase them off the base no matter how obvious the out. If a runner obviously misses first base, he should go back and tag it. Even two-man umpiring crews usually see it when someone misses first.

## LEADS AT SECOND BASE

The following discussion focuses on the 7-step primary lead and a number of options to it.

***Primary Lead.*** The runner must get his signal on the base, check the infield, check the outfield, check the scoreboard, and, finally, take his lead. He must get his safe primary lead in early while the pitcher is looking in for a signal. A safe primary lead is 7 steps (21 feet), which allows him to return to second with 2 steps with his legs and 1 with his arm (spoke). This 7-step lead would enable him to safely return to second even if the pitcher was facing second with the ball in his hand and the shortstop or second baseman standing on the base.

If he cannot reach second safely under these conditions, using a one-way going back to the base mentality, shorten up his primary lead. He should watch only the pitcher and catcher after the pitch. They are the only ones who can pick him off. He must not retreat to second base on movement by the shortstop or second baseman. This way, he'll always have momentum to third on the pitch. He should only return to second if the pitcher or catcher picks, or if the ball is caught by the catcher. He should take his secondary lead at second when he is 100% sure the pitcher is going home. The secondary lead is two sidewards hops that takes him to the absolute edge of his safety zone (the catcher cannot pick him off).

*Shuffle Lead.* An option for the 7-step primary lead is to start behind the base line and walk straight up at the pitcher, and to shuffle on the pitch. This is a different look and gives him a little momentum on his primary lead. It also will enable him to set the pitcher up so he can steal third base with momentum.

*Give and Take Lead.* The give and take lead at second is another type of momentum lead at second. When the pitcher looks at him, the runner jabs back to second. When the pitcher looks away, the runner tries to gain momentum by shuffling. He must stay inside his safe return zone until the pitcher commits to the plate or he commits to steal third. This give and take action is a distraction to the pitcher, and pinches the shortstop and second baseman more to the middle, which cuts down on their defensive coverage. The give-and-take action is good for many base runners because it also gives them rhythm to steal third.

*Two-Out, Deep Lead.* With two outs, the runner starts his lead 7 steps from second, but 2 steps back from the base line. This facilitates his turn at third because it eliminates the question mark turn that requires two quick turns in a short distance. It allows the runner from second to make a high speed, more efficient turn at third because the runner will have better body control. This lead does increase the distance between second and third a little, but the increase in body control allows the runner to have greater acceleration as he hits the base and shortens the distance between third and home. Some runners will have to shorten their leads to $5^{1}/_{2}$ or 6 steps when they back off the base line.

With two outs, the jump at second should be good because there is little decision making. He runs on contact, making sure not to run into a tag at third. He must make the third baseman throw across the diamond. The only exception might be late in the game with two outs and his team down two or more, he wants a ball in front of him to go through so that the shortstop is not able to field a ball in the hole and throw him out at third base. With two outs and two strikes, if the bat goes, he goes.

*Avoid Making the First or Third Out at Third Base.* You may gamble to try to get your runner to third with two outs when you are facing a pitcher who throws lots of wild pitches (e.g., hard sinker baller, split, or knuckle ball pitcher). With runners on second and third, the runner at second should go to third on a ball hit to the shortstop or the third baseman, only after they throw to the plate.

Tag your runners with zero outs as long as they have a chance to advance. With one out, only on sure deep outs to center or right field, occasionally left field with a poor throwing left fielder. Make the ball hit hard through the middle go by the pitcher. If a shortstop or third baseman does not stop your runner, he may be able to go to third on the throw to first, especially with a first baseman who has a poor arm.

The fake break at second is a technique that can break down the defensive positioning of the catcher and third baseman. Catchers tend to raise up and take strikes away from the pitcher in response to the fake break at second, and third basemen vacate early to cover third and open up the hole for the hitter. The fake break technique at second is the same at first. On the pitch, the runner squares his shoulders to third base and shuffles. A fake break while the pitcher is looking at second and the shortstop and the second baseman are not close will often cause the pitcher to flinch and balk.

Reading the ball in the dirt as the runner goes into his secondary lead is easier at second base than it is at first. This is a technique for the average to above average runner in a zero or one out situation (more often with one out). It starts with prepitch preparation and anticipation. He can look for breaking ball counts, or read the catcher's signals or pitcher's grip. More breaking balls are in the dirt than any other pitch. He must read the trajectory of the pitch. If he thinks it's going to be in the dirt, he should run. It's a much easier read from second than first, because his eyes are lined up with the flight of the pitch. If the catcher goes to his knees to block the ball and it kicks away from him, he'll be safe. The runner must keep his eyes on the catcher so if he picks the ball cleanly, he can put the brakes on and scuffle back to second. With two outs, he must make sure the ball kicks to the first base side, back, or way to the third base side before running.

## THREE METHODS OF STEALING THIRD BASE

There are three methods for stealing third that are similar, in that the runner at second is going to have momentum going to third before or just as the pitcher starts his delivery. The truly exceptional runner can steal third base without momentum.

***Leap Steal.*** Before anything happens, the runner needs to prepare by doing his homework. He must study the pitcher before he gets to second, or once he gets there if he is the first runner. Find out three things: (1) What are the maximum number of looks to second by the pitcher? (2) Does the pitcher look to second and throw home, or does he look home and throw home? (3) After the pitcher's last look to second and his hands set, how long does he take before he delivers to home? He can count or use the letters of his school. For example, at Sac City, we might define the pitcher as an "SCC SC" guy, which means that once his hands come set, we are able to say "SCC SC" before he starts to pitch. Some pitchers are "bottom out" guys who start to pitch or pick as soon as their hands reach the bottom of their stretch position. If the pitcher falls into a pattern on the above three conditions, he is in an excellent position to steal third.

He should start with a safe measured primary lead of 7 steps, with his right foot on the 21-foot mark. For this to work, he has to have a good spoke technique so that he can safely return to second with that 21-foot lead. This is a still lead which does not react to movement from the shortstop or second baseman, only picks by the pitcher. When the pitcher is not looking, he should get an eighth step to get to 24 feet.

After the pitcher has made his last look to second and his head is positioned to throw home, he must take a small sidewards shuffle to third, one-half of a count before the pitcher delivers home. If his front leg moves, the runner should go to third because he will either throw home or pick at second. Either way, he'll be safe at third. If he throws home, you have approximately 54 feet to run with momentum and the pitcher is throwing the ball 60′ 6″. The catcher has to catch the ball, clear the hitter, and throw 90 feet to third base. The third baseman has to catch the ball and make a tag. If the pitcher picks at second, he has to throw approximately 66 feet with a 180° turn, and the shortstop or second baseman (usually shortstop) has to throw 90 feet with the base runner in his throwing lane. If he does not move his front leg, the runner can leap toward second and get ready to dive to the base because this lack of movement by the pitcher indicates that he has changed his focus from the hitter to the base runner.

***Give and Take Steal.*** The give and take steal works off the give and take lead. The key is to start with a short lead that is well within the runner's safety zone. He needs to shuffle off when the pitcher is looking away or thinking more about the hitter than the runner. Pitchers look at the runner at second and mentally focus on the hitter at the plate, really not seeing the base runner. The runner can jab back to second when the pitcher looks to second. When he is stealing third, he must make sure he has rhythm and momentum. The third base coach can be of great assistance in this technique. He can help the runner get momentum and locate the middle infielders for him. As the third base coach raises or lowers his voice, he can lengthen or shorten his lead. This technique is not for everyone, and against the more accomplished defensive team, excessive movement increases the chances of being picked. Also, this is a distraction to some hitters.

***Deep Lead Walking Steal.*** The runner should start 5-7 steps off second and 3-4 steps behind a line directly between second and third. As the pitcher is looking at him, he walks directly towards the pitcher straight to the base line and shuffles into his secondary lead on the pitch. If he does this enough, the pitcher gets conditioned to seeing him walking up and not running. When he is stealing, he walks up, taking more of an angle to third base, and runs on the pitcher's first move. He must time his walking lead and break with the pitcher's looks and pitching tempo.

Runners should be more aggressive against left-handed pitchers. The runner must read the catcher for location and type of pitch. He can run on the breaking ball. He must adopt the attitude of, "Steal now; don't wait. Beat the defense before it has time to adjust." Do your homework and send the runner on the first pitch especially after a steal on second.

The best time to steal third is with one out. The runner can steal third with two outs as long as he's sure he's safe—no close plays with two outs or no outs. He can set up aggressive throwing catchers and draw a catcher's pick and go to third.

The hitter can aid the steal of third by utilizing a fake base hit bunt through the ball against teams whose third basemen are overly aggressive in defending the short game. If the third baseman over commits in defending the bunt, he won't be able to get back and cover the steal. The runner should slide to the outfield side of third in case the third baseman gets back late and receives the throw in front of the base.

## LEADS AT THIRD BASE

The runner should start with a short lead and shuffle when he is sure the pitcher is committed to throw home. He must lead off in foul territory and return in fair territory, always keeping his eyes on the ball. It is important to go back on all line drives and fly balls hit to the outfield. When tagging from third, the runner should watch the catch. If he's screened off, the coach will help. He should slide on home plate, not up to it. When he gets to third standing up on balls hit to the outfield, he should shuffle off so he can advance on a botched relay. If an infielder lobs the ball to the tandem relay man, puts his head down, or runs the ball in from 200 feet or more, then send the runner—if the score is tied, you are down one, or you are ahead with one or two outs. With zero outs, the runner needs to be more conservative because he can't have the first out of the inning at home.

In close games with less than two outs, runners on first and third tag and advance on short fly balls. If the ball is thrown home, the runner from third should stop and return to third, and the runner from first should continue to second. If the ball is thrown to second, the runner from third should score, and the runner going to second should stop and try to return to first. With two outs, the runner from first can't be tagged before the run scores.

The runner must watch the pitcher until release, and then focus on the contact zone in front of the plate. If he is running on down angle, he looks for the ball to go down off the bat, and takes as much of the inside of the base line as he can to take the throwing lane away from the shortstop and third baseman. If the ball is hit hard on the ground, he rolls his head to see (peek) if it is caught so he can stop and create a rundown to allow the other runners to advance to second or third. If he runs on contact, he breaks on contact and takes the inside of the baseline and slides late and tough.

In a squeeze situation, the runner starts short and shuffles until the pitcher gets to his release point. If the ball is popped up or bunted at and missed, he puts the brakes on and returns to third on the extreme inside of the diamond to take the throwing lane away from the catcher. He should run for the third baseman's glove and slide late.

## STEALING HOME

The steal home is accomplished against a pitcher in the windup position who does not look the runner back at third and takes a very slow windup (3.1 seconds or slower). This can be accomplished against a left- or right-handed pitcher, but it's easier against a left-handed pitcher. He can run on slow windup pitchers even if they do look him back. There is no signal for the steal home. Since he's running on his own, he must let the batter know he's coming so he will not be swinging. Have him use a verbal as he approaches the plate to let the hitter know he's coming.

The hitter should be sure not to interfere with the catcher. He should not steal when his team is way up or way down in the score or if the batter has two strikes. It is a questionable maneuver when there are no outs or one out. The key to stealing home is a still, long initial lead and an aggressive shuffle before the pitcher starts his windup. It is important for the runner at third to get his shuffle in just before the pitcher starts his windup. Time everything out in practice with all of your runners, and you'll find out who can or can't steal home and from where they need to start.

## FORCING A BALK

Forcing a balk is used with a runner on third while the pitcher's in the windup. The pitcher must be bent over at the waist or start with his hands coupled. (PHOTO 13-14) Ideally, he's bent over at the waist with his hands together. Before the pitcher starts his windup, while he's taking a signal, the runner on third should take two hard steps toward home. Hopefully, this will force the pitcher to raise up or break his hands and not pitch, which is a balk. If the pitcher does not react, the runner goes back to his safety zone. Of if he pitches, he maintains safe momentum to the plate.

## BALL IN THE DIRT AT THIRD

Advancing on a ball in the dirt is pretty routine at third base, except with two outs. With two outs or less than two outs, the runner keeps his momentum going to the plate until the ball is hit, caught, or blocked. With less than two outs, he shouldn't gamble to score. The pitch has to clearly be wild enough for him to be safe. With two outs and a close game, he should gamble to score on a short passed ball or wild pitch. Pitcher/hitter match-up is also a factor. If the ball is in the dirt, he must keep his momentum going to the plate, and if he thinks the ball is going to get outside the dirt circle, he should go. If not, he is going to have to scramble back to third in a hurry, anticipating a catcher's pick. He must take the inside, stay up, and slide late. He should gamble with two outs because of the scarcity of two out RBI's, and because most teams never practice defending the situation at game speed. You'll be amazed how many times the runner will be safe on short wild pitches because the catcher slips, cannot get a grip on the ball, or cannot get his body positioned to make a throw. Errors by the pitcher can also be costly; if for instance, arrives at home late, drops the ball, or misses the tag. The key is a "no fear" aggressive approach. If you are the least bit tentative, you're dead.

Photo 13-14

# SLIDING

A good base runner must be an aggressive slider. He should try to gain momentum on his slide. The runner should slide late and hard when the conditions allow for it. No lovey-dovey outs. Check the local rules if you are a high school coach. When in doubt, slide. Slide later on wet fields.

*Feet First Slide.* The base runner should slide straight into the base by bending either leg into a figure four position. The runner stops his forward momentum with the heel of his extended leg. To slide faster, he lands flat and keeps his body parallel to the ground with his hands on his chest or above his head. He can sit up a little and pop up as he hits the base, if he is sure he's going to be safe.

*Head First Slide.* The runner lowers himself by bending at the knees before he takes off. He can't dive high. He should land on his thighs and chest, not his knees. He must keep his head and hands up. He shouldn't slide head first to home, or while breaking up a double play, or when an infielder is blocking a base.

*The Double Play Slide.* The double play slide is a bent-leg slide favoring the right or left slide. The runner should hook the infielder with the instep of his top leg, staying in the base line so he can touch the base with his hand or foot. He must get down early if the ball arrives early to the pivot man. Be aware of the special rules in high school, college, and professional baseball with respect to the double play.

*Sliding at Home Plate.* At home, the runner must slide on the plate, not up to it. If the catcher is not in possession of the ball and blocking the plate, he should go through him. He must be lower than the catcher. If the catcher's in possession of the ball and blocking the plate, he either goes through him, or slides feet first and reaches back for the plate. Again, be aware of the specific rules for your level of play.

*Sliding Practice.* Players must practice sliding. Early in the season when you are in a teaching mode, players should practice every other day. During the season, once a week is probably sufficient to maintain their skills. Some players may go a week or more without sliding in a game. Most serious injuries occur running the bases. The majority of those occur during sliding. Practice in the outfield on wet grass and with a loose base before you move the drill to the actual field. It is imperative that you find out who can or cannot slide before you put a player into a game situation where he may have to slide.

# OTHER TIPS FOR BASE RUNNING

When two runners occupy the same base, the trail runner is only out when tagged. If the trail runner is the faster of the two runners, the lead runner should vacate the base before the trail runner is tagged.

Try to keep rundowns going as long as possible to increase the chances of mishandling errors or obstruction. When a base runner is in a rundown and about to be tagged out from behind, he should fall down absolutely flat and perpendicular to the base line. When the tagger jumps over him without touching him, he should get up quickly and go in the opposite direction as the tagger.

# OFFENSIVE STRATEGY AND TECHNIQUES

Any offensive scheme or philosophy has to be based on personnel. You can recruit people to perform within a specific offensive scheme, but there is no guarantee that they will be able to do what you want, and you will eventually have to adjust to the abilities of your athletes. These abilities change, and your offensive approach will fluctuate with the change in your athletes' abilities. The ability of your opponent will also determine what you can and can't do on the offensive side, not to mention field, weather conditions, and officiating. Umpires are a factor, especially the size of their strike zone.

## PLAN FOR TODAY'S GAME

Before a game, try to evaluate your personnel against the other team's personnel, how your team is playing at the time, and how many runs you're likely to give up. From this scenario, try to anticipate your offensive scheme on that day. For example, if you're facing a team whose offensive personnel matches up well against your pitching on this particular day, you should be less apt to sacrifice. You might gamble more to create some big innings. You might hit and run, or just hit with no outs and runners on first and second rather than sacrifice bunt. In a game where you have a favorable match-up and anticipate giving up only two or three runs, you might be more inclined to play for one run at a time. We say "might," because your whole game plan can change in the first inning. Sometimes that ace pitcher who wasn't going to give up any runs struggled with the mound in the first inning, walked people, threw low quality strikes, and gave up four runs. You may have to adjust from your conservative "one run at a time" game plan.

**Adjustments.** Go into the game knowing or having a preconceived idea of what the game is going to be like. Then based on how a particular pitcher performs early in the game, you may adjust your philosophy. It may be adjusted based on weather conditions (this might only be a five-inning game because it's going to rain in a hour) or field conditions (it's very windy today, the infield's hard, the grass is short, the wind is blowing out). When you have to change your expectations, you have to change your attack. You can't go into a game with one philosophy and say, "Okay, we're going to stick to this no matter what." You have to adjust to situations and be flexible.

No matter what the situation calls for, the key to success is to ask your players to execute only those skills that they have a reasonable probability of executing successfully. The percentage play that conventional wisdom calls for may not be good, because you don't have a guy up there who can execute the play. Remember Reggie Jackson trying to bunt in the World Series? The situation called for a bunt; but as great a player as Reggie was, the team would have been better off if he had swung the bat.

You might have one offensive game plan early in the game (i.e. play for one run early to score the first run) and have a different plan later in the game. One inning may be preplanned to be a big inning depending on the match-ups (hitter/pitcher) and where you are in the batting order, and another a one-run inning for the same reason. You can't sit back and wait for three-run homers when you are playing in a gigantic ball-park and the pitcher you are facing hasn't given up a home run since Little League.

**Broad and Flexible Game Plan.** You can't be a great offensive team and be one dimensional in your ability to score runs. You need to have an offensive game plan, but it has to be broad and flexible enough to adapt to your personnel and your opponent's personnel, as well as the changing conditions of the game. The more offensive skills each player possesses, the easier it is to situationally adapt.

In certain situations, based on the personnel that you are playing, you can do it with the bat, the short game, or the base on balls. The coach has to figure out before every inning, "How am I going to score this inning? How am I going to get that one run or more? Here I am in this part of the batting order. Am I going to use the take, which is a viable technique none of the players want to use?

Maybe you're going to use some short game action. A lot of rallies are started with base hit bunts. It should never happen defensively, but it does happen. Rallies are also started with base on balls or a hit by pitch, and you can create situations where you increase your probability of getting hit or getting a base on balls in a particular inning. You'd prefer to generate your offense by swinging the bat, because good teams have pitchers who throw strikes and they take that base on balls and hit by pitch away from you. They also get in your face and make you swing the bat, and don't let you bunt. The bottom line is to evaluate the match-ups and roll the dice, even when the odds are stacked against you. Just pick the best situation, even if it's not a good one. You may have to bunt into coverage, take pitches against guys who rarely walk anyone, or ask your .120 hitter to swing the bat to get on base. Basically, in a seven-inning game, it's seven separate games. In a nine-inning game, it's nine separate games. You have to figure out a way to score in that particular inning with your personnel and their personnel.

**Convincing Your Team to Use the Whole Inning.** Many teams psychologically are not prepared to score unless they get the lead-off hitter on. You see a lot of teams where everybody's got their glove on ready to go out and play defense. Convince your players that you have 33% of your inning left once there are two outs, and as long as the current player gets the next hitter up there, you've got a chance to score. You've just got to assume it's a one-out inning, and now you have to find a way to score.

Offense is scoring runs. It doesn't matter if you score runs on hits, errors, walks, hit batters, stolen bases, or outs. Knowing how to make outs to advance runners is a critical element in run scoring.

## THE HITTER'S PLAN

It all starts with the hitter going up to the plate with a plan to either get on base, advance runners who are already on base, or score runners who are on base. A hitter who has confidence in his ability to hit with two strikes is better at implementing his offensive plan than those who do not have two-strike skills.

***Two-Strike Hitting.*** When the hitter has confidence in his ability to hit with two strikes, he can get deeper in the count with pitchers and create more walk opportunities. He gets better pitches to hit because when pitchers get deeper in the count with more balls on the hitter, they generally pitch less fine. Nothing favors the defense more than the hitter swinging at one pitch and getting himself out. There is nothing wrong with swinging at the first pitch because, certainly, the statistics indicate that much first-pitch hitting is successful hitting. The average for first-pitch hitting in professional baseball is around .300. But if you can get players, especially amateur players and young players, to develop their ability to hit with two strikes, they'll do a better job with fewer than two strikes. Seeing lots of pitches creates a more difficult situation for defensive focus and concentration. Teams don't play defense as well when you force pitchers to throw lots of pitches. Forcing the pitcher to throw lots of pitches gets you into the secondary line of pitching sooner.

***Getting Deep in the Count.*** Sometimes teams don't get deep enough in the count before they initiate their offense. They tend to generate all their offense on the first or second pitch. Early offense is easier to defend (especially steal, and hit and run) because if the pitcher gets behind early with a pitch-out, the pitcher has some wiggle room to get back into the count. Conversely, if a team waits too long for a favorable count or pitch, it hits into a lot of double plays. In general, however, the pitcher has an advantage when you hit early in the count because he's actively involved in the game from the first pitch of the game. The hitter is on the outside looking in until he gets into the box. When the hitter sees some pitches, at least the first time up, he gets acclimated and gets some valuable first-hand information for his body's computer (velocity, movement, arm angle, assortment of pitches, sequence of pitches, and so on).

## BIG INNING OFFENSE

The big inning offensive approach that you see in most big league stadiums is predicated on the fact that in the big leagues, the team that wins a high percentage of the games, scores more runs in one inning than the other team scores in the entire game. This approach is basically a "stand back and hit" approach with little use of the sacrifice bunt and hit and run. Most runners are started when the hitters have leverage (ahead in the count with high expectation for a strike, especially a fast ball strike) or have two strikes on them with a breaking ball expected.

**Big Inning Teams.** Big inning teams do not give up outs with sacrifice bunts, defensive swings to get runners over from second to third, or ground ball only swings in hit and run situations. They do not chance stealing second base, for fear of giving up an out, or having one of their big boppers walked or pitched around. The big inning team is more inclined to base hit bunt or swing the bat in sacrifice situations, look to drive the ball the other way with a runner on second and no outs, and drive the ball in hit and run situations. They prefer to hit an extra base hit with a runner on first and try to score the runner than chance stealing second and score the runner with a base hit. Given the right match-ups and personnel, the big inning approach has some real pluses. Hitters love it because they want to hit, not make outs or be nonaggressive. It does a lot for the hitter's confidence and self-esteem when you let him swing the bat aggressively.

However, good pitching stops good hitting most of the time. There comes a time in many games where you have to get one run to win, and the big inning teams—whose players are too one dimensional—can't advance runners or get them in. Big inning teams tend to waste a lot of innings and at bats because their mentality is such that they become somewhat complacent thinking that they eventually are going to get that big inning. Big inning teams hit earlier in the count because they are more aggressive. They tend to hit more extra base hits but also strike out more and have more outs in the air. Big inning teams don't seem to have the desperation and competitiveness of the teams that have to scrap and scrape for runs every inning. That doesn't mean that you can't develop that competitiveness in the big inning team.

**Seven Strategies for One-Run Inning Offense.** The one-run inning approach is saying that if your team scores one run an inning, you'll score nine runs in a game, which will most likely win 99% of your games. It is predicated on getting runners to second base with no outs, or to third base with one out, and scoring runs on outs. The thinking is that it is a lot easier to score runs on outs than hits. The key in the "one run an inning" approach is to get the lead-off hitter on. If you do that, you have to consider the match-ups to determine what will happen next. Following are a number of schemes for scoring a run when you get the lead-off hitter on base. Any one of the options is based on the personnel:

1. Sacrifice bunt, or base hit bunt the runner to second, steal third base (help the poor runner with a screen or fake base hit bunt), score him on a hit or an out. (There are 10 ways to score from third base with less than two outs: hit, error, balk, wild pitch, passed ball, base on balls, hit by pitch, sacrifice bunt, sacrifice fly, fielder's choice.

2. Steal second base (with aid of shade), sacrifice or base hit bunt runner to third base, score him with one of your ten options.

3. Hit and run the runner to second, or possibly third; advance him to third base (without giving up an out) if the hit and run didn't get him there on a hit and you have one out; and score him from third with one out by executing your offense based on your personnel.

4. Swing the bat, with the emphasis on hitting the ball to the right side (to the left of the second baseman) to get a hit and advance the runner to second or third, or to force the second baseman to throw to first, allowing the runner to be safe at second. If he's on second with one out, get him to third without giving up an out, then score him with the right kind of out.

5. If you end up with runners on first and second with no one out, you try to get runners to second and third and you are not concerned if you give up an out. The hit and run, base hit bunt, and sacrifice are all options. If you swing the bat in this situation and do not end up with a hit, your best case scenario is to end up with runners on first and third. However, there is also the chance of a double play or a fly ball that is not deep enough to advance the runner from second. Should you end up with one out and runners on first and third, you have some options to score a run on an out. The squeeze, safety squeeze, and hit and run are all options. Should you chose to swing the bat, you need to get the ball in the air to the outfield deep enough to score the runner from third. If the hitter has running speed and there is not a big chance of hitting into a double play, a ground ball to the right side (to the left of the second baseman) is a possibility. Stay away from the ground ball to the left side because of the high incidence of double plays on these ground balls.

6. If you end up with runners on second and third with no outs, you should produce a two-run inning with two productive outs. (Ideally, with the infield back, the first out should be a ground out to the right side).

7. The bases loaded, no out situation should be a two run or more inning. However, you are somewhat limited because ground balls with the bases loaded produce a lot of double plays. You'd like to be able to drive the ball in the air to the right side so you can advance the runner from third to home, and from second to third. Short game action is a possibility with the right hitter and/or defensive alignment (first baseman and/or third baseman back).

After reading about all these offensive possibilities to advance runners and score runs, you're probably saying, "It's way too complicated for my team. Let's just swing the bat." But if you are going to be a "one run an inning team," you are going to have to execute. Remember, you can simplify and cut down the offensive options, but if you are in a one-run mode, you need an offensive scheme that the players on your team can execute. Asking people to do things that they cannot usually do does not work.

***Gambling with the Bottom Part of Your Lineup.*** You need to gamble a little bit more offensively with your lesser players. In other words, you have to start runners, bunt more, and hit and run more, or fake bunt hit and run with your down-the-line players. It's important that the players understand the offense and their role in the offense, and that they accept their role in the offense. Ask people to do things that they are confident in doing. Nothing's worse than asking a big league number three or four hitter to sacrifice bunt, and they can't do it. Plus, they don't want to do it. You have to sell your people, and they have to have the skills. You can't just say, "Well, the situation dictates that we should sacrifice bunt here," and we've got Cecil Fielder up there to sacrifice bunt when he hasn't sacrifice bunted in eight years, and he probably hasn't practiced it properly in practice. Why ask him to do it when, in your mind, you know that he's probably going to foul off the first pitch and he looks so terrible doing it that you're going to change anyway and let him hit?

**Knowing Your Personnel.** You need to know your personnel; they, in turn, need to know your offense and their role in the offense. Even though you have a "one run an inning" offensive philosophy, recognize the potential for a multi-run inning when it presents itself.

The one-run inning offense is good for the team that makes consistent contact, has base stealing and base running skills, team speed, short game skills, bat control skills, and lacks extra base power. The weakness in this approach manifests itself when you don't get lead-off hitters on base. It puts you in a position where you have to ask your players to do things that they are not adept at. In a sense, you're bucking the odds and rolling the dice. For example, you have a runner on first with two outs. Even the big inning team is going to have trouble scoring a runner. (The big inning team tends to run on 3-ball counts in this situation. They also like to run on 2-2 because the pitcher doesn't want to go 3-2 with two outs and give the guy at first a running start where he may score on a single in the gap.) The team with little extra base power will need two or more hits in a row to score that runner from first. How many times do you get two hits in a row in a game? Not very often. You've got to get the runner to second. How? Read the ball in the dirt. Take a long one-way lead to draw multiple picks, hoping that one will be thrown away. If all else fails, you have to run (straight steal or delay) early in the count with a poor runner against a pitcher who is quick to the plate and a catcher who has a plus arm. Hopefully, that runner is going to get his body going before the pitcher starts to pitch (straight steal) and the defense is going to break down by any of these means—ball in the dirt, drop by the catcher, bad ball for the catcher to handle, inaccurate throw, drop by the shortstop or second baseman, or late coverage by the shortstop or second baseman). Sometimes your options are limited and you have to go against the odds.

When the offensive game plan runs amuck, you still have to find a way to score. Adversity is something that every good team must overcome. Something bad is going to happen in every game and you must find a way to play through it. If your team folds its tent every time the lead-off hitter is an out or starts to get their gloves to play defense every time there are two outs and no one on base, you'll have a difficult time of being competitive offensively.

# BATTING ORDER

How you group your hitters is going to affect your run-scoring potential. At times, you will have to adjust your lineup based on their performance and your competition. Your order and lineup may change in response to a left or right-handed pitcher. It may change because you want to get more defense or offense into the lineup on a particular day. The order may change because you want a specific pitch for certain hitters or base stealers, and where you place them in the order will increase the possibilities of that happening.

***Setting Up Right-Handers and Left-Handers.*** If you have a mixture of right and left-handed hitters, there are advantages to alternating them. This precludes the pitcher from getting into one pattern that's effective to both right and left-handed hitters. For example, a 3/4 curve ball or slider thrown down and away to right-handed hitters is an excellent pitch. But the same pitch thrown in the same location to a left-handed hitter would be down and in, which is a hittable pitch. The right-left stagger keeps the pitcher from dominating all hitters with one pitch, location, arm slot, or release point.

***Circular, Not Linear, Batting Order.*** The actual batting order and defining the skills for each hitter in the order are greatly overrated because the lead-off hitter may lead off only once in a game, and the number four hitter may never hit fourth in an inning. Every hitter has to have lead-off skills, run-scoring skills, and advancing-runner skills. To limit certain spots in the lineup to on-base spots or run-scoring spots is overrated. Your best lineup may be based on on-base average. The guy with the highest on-base average leads off and the lowest bats ninth.

It's a plus to have the players who can use the hole between first and second behind your high on base percentage guys. The hole is wider when the first baseman is holding the runner on.

There are some general guidelines that often prove beneficial. Speed in the one and nine spots keeps your base stealers from being stopped by base cloggers on base in front of them. Also, if you can hit a left-hander behind your base stealers, it makes it tougher on the catcher to clear the left-handed hitter to throw to second. It also helps if the left-handed hitter is patient, has good two-strike skills, and can handle the fast ball.

In deciding on your batting order, you have to decide whether you want to bunch all your good hitters together or mix in some role player types in between them. When you stagger the best guys, you allow teams to pitch around them, especially with two outs. However, if you bunch your best guys, and you have only two or three, your potential for multiple run innings is limited. Ideally, you'd like to have some role players with on-base and execution skills between your productive hitters who can hit and drive people in.

# CONTROLLING THE TEMPO

The offense controls the tempo of the game. The pitcher can work only as fast as the offense allows him to work. Successful pitching and defense is usually quick paced and up tempo. Pitchers naturally want to get into a consistent tempo, but you can subtly slow down or occasionally force the pitcher to speed up, thereby destroying his tempo.

Generally, you want quick tempo when you are on defense and slow tempo when you are hitting, but it's not necessary to create three-hour marathons. You want a tempo that is most conducive to your offense. You control the tempo by not letting your batter rush up to the plate after the previous hitter is done (especially after a one-pitch out). Don't let him get in the box until he is ready to hit, and don't let the pitcher rush him into the box just because he is ready to pitch. Don't let the pitcher pitch until he is set in the box. Call time or ask the umpire to let your hitter get set before he releases the pitcher to pitch. Just expand that window between pitches by a few seconds when necessary. Pitchers like to get their signal and pitch within a certain time frame, but you want the time frame that is most conducive to your offensive attack. This is very similar to the tempo control strategy that basketball teams use.

## OFFENSIVE TECHNIQUES

Everything is dependent upon game situations and, more importantly, personnel—yours and theirs. Be careful of complicating things by over executing. First and foremost, hitters must know how to hit. When in doubt, they should swing the bat. The key is to analyze the situation and ascertain what technique is going to produce the best results for your team. Ask your players to do the things that give them a high probability of succeeding. When you start asking your players to do things for which they have little chance of being successful, they lose confidence in themselves and lose trust in you as a coach. If they can't do it in a game-like competitive practice, they're not going to be able to do it in the game.

## HIT AND RUN

You want the ball hit anywhere on the ground out of the middle of the diamond in a hit and run situation. Ground balls up the middle produce double plays in hit and run situations, because the middle infielders are breaking to cover and the ball is hit right to them. Early in the game, allow certain players to drive the ball and to hit only fastballs without being concerned with hitting the ball on the ground. These are the guys who hit a lot of line drives and have some gap power. Late in the game, get ground balls out of these hitters. Early, gamble to have a chance for a big inning.

There are no "always" or "nevers" as to the correct count to hit and run. Any three-ball count is a good hit and run count. Just give the base runner the steal signal in a three ball hit and run situation, and tell the base runners to treat the three ball steal like hit and run. The reason for this is that many times when you give the hitters hit and run with three balls, they forget the count and swing at ball four. Hit and run with less than three balls against strike throwers. Anytime you think the pitcher is going to throw a strike is a good time to hit and run. The hit and run is for hitters who make consistent contact and are not "lift power" types. It is beneficial for the below average runner types who hit lots of ground balls. It helps them stay out of the double play when you start the runner. It is generally best not to hit and run with your blue chip base stealers because you probably have a better chance of stealing bases and scoring. It is good for the guy who is in a slump or tied up mentally, because it takes all the decision making out of the pitch. He gets geared up to swing and doesn't have to judge whether the pitch is a ball or strike, a fast ball, or some other pitch. It is good in a sacrifice situation when you anticipate rotation or a crashing defense because with all that movement from the defense, lots of ground balls will roll through. It is also an option to use with poor bunters who make consistent contact swinging the bat.

***Hitter's Responsibility on Hit and Run.*** If the ball is over the middle of the plate, the batter must hit the inside of the ball so he can take advantage of opposite side coverage of second. Occasionally, the shortstop will cover second with a right-handed hitter up, and the second baseman with a left-handed hitter up. This can be picked up by looking at their prepitch positioning or by watching who moves when the base runner fake breaks. In those cases, the hitter must hook the middle pitch so he can take advantage of the hole on the pull side. He must swing at every pitch, unless he has three balls and the pitch is definitely out of the strike zone. If it is a pitch-out, or the ball is in the dirt, he shouldn't swing. If he thinks the pitch will be wild and go to the backstop, he must take the pitch. In a hit and run situation he looks for the ball up and away. This gets his swing down through the ball and provides more ground balls. From up, he can adjust down to the low ball. If he looks down, he can't hit the ball up. From away, he can hit the ball inside; but if the hitter looks inside, he's dead on the ball away. Looking up and away allows the hitter to cover more pitches in and out of the strike zone and convert them into ground balls. Spend time during practice working on your hitters' hit and run skills on balls up out of the strike zone.

***Base Runner's Responsibility on Hit and Run.*** The base runner is not trying to steal the base. He must get a jump but not get picked off. After one step, he looks to the hitter so he can avoid the fly ball double play and read the pitch-out. A runner should not run on pitch-outs but should choke off his break and scramble back to first. If it is a line drive in the infield, he keeps running because he doesn't have time to get back. He should hold up and read the line drive into the outfield.

***Fake Bunt Hit and Run (Runner on First).*** The hitter's responsibility on a fake bunt hit and run is to sell the bunt with a good believable stance. He must keep his bat angled to first base with his back elbow anchored to his side (right-handed hitter—RHH). The runner is running and the hitter must swing at the pitch regardless of where it is. Like the hit and run, if it's a pitch-out or ball in the dirt, he should take the pitch. The ball must be hit on the ground between third and short. The hitter should recoil and stay bent as the pitcher starts his arm up. He should bring the top hand down to the bottom hand (4″ off the end of the bat) and keep the bat flat. Right-handed hitters hit the ball hard on the ground between third and shortstop. This hole should be open. When the third baseman cheats up to take the bunt away, the second baseman cheats towards first on the bunt, and the shortstop is breaking to cover second base on the steal. Left-handed hitters can hit the ball anywhere on the ground out of the middle of the diamond. The advantage of fake bunt hit and run over hit and run is that you know where the hole is going to be since the shortstop is almost always covering the steal.

The runner's responsibility is to not try to steal the base. He doesn't have to get his best jump to run. He must, however, pick up the hitter after one stride to see where the ball is hit. The base runner will choke off his break on the pitch-out and continue to run on the ball in the dirt.

**Fake Bunt Hit (Slash).** The fake bunt hit is used in conjunction with the sacrifice bunt. If the defense, especially the third baseman, charges over aggressively, the bunter should recoil from the bunting position and hit the ball on the ground. As a right-handed hitter, he should hit the ball in the hole between third and shortstop. Left-handers can hit the ball anywhere on the ground. The hitter should fake-bunt-hit only the pitch that he can direct at the defense's weakness. If it is not his pitch, he must take it. The responsibility for fake bunt hitting lies with the on-deck hitter and/or the hitter. The on-deck hitter must read the defense (3B) and let the hitter know early (hit, hit). The hitter can anticipate the situation by watching how the third and first basemen have reacted in previous bunt situations.

**Suicide Hit and Run.** This is the same as the regular hit and run, except that the hitter must make ground ball contact on all pitches, including pitch-outs and balls in the dirt. The ball can be hit anywhere on the ground. The runner on third base shuffles sideways to home until the pitcher reaches his point of release. The runner on third takes a wide loop as he breaks for the plate so he doesn't get hit by a batted ball. Use this play instead of the squeeze when you have:

1. A contact hitter up, who is a poor bunter.

2. It's an important run and you have a poor runner on third base, a ground ball hitter up, and your opponents are playing the infield in.

3. With two strikes on the hitter where a ball batted foul is a foul ball, but a ball bunted foul is an out.

4. With one out and runners on first and third, or the bases loaded, starting the runner with a below average-running ground ball hitter up decreases the chance of the double play.

5. Three-ball counts with the bases loaded puts added pressure on the pitcher and gives the hitter the latitude to swing at strikes or near strikes only.

Popped up suicide squeeze bunts usually lead to double plays. Popped up swings give the runner on third time to get back, and if the ball is hit to the outfield, the runner on third may have enough time to get back to third, tag and score.

The following offensive techniques are discussed in detail in the Short Game section:

1) Squeeze vs. pitcher out of the windup (discussed under "Squeeze Bunt").

2) Squeeze vs. pitcher out of the stretch (discussed under "Squeeze Bunt").

3) Sacrifice bunt first base.

4) Sacrifice bunt third base.

5) Fake bunt hit and run.

6) Safety squeeze.

# FIRST AND THIRD SHORT GAME TECHNIQUES

Here are a number of valuable techniques for the short game:

***Early Turn Sacrifice Bunt Third Base.*** This is a play that is best run with no outs, where you are trying to trade an out for a run while still looking for a multiple run inning. The runner at first fake breaks on the pitch to influence the shortstop to cover second. As the ball is bunted to the third baseman, the runner on third trails the third baseman, and as he throws to first, the runner from third scores. The runner has to run only 45 feet and the ball is going to travel approximately 190 feet. Make sure the third baseman does not arm fake, and be alert for the shortstop rotating to third base on the bunt (pitcher also). If the shortstop does rotate to third base, bunt to first (runner at third base goes on down angle) or steal second depending on what the second baseman does. The runner from first may be able to go all the way to third if the shortstop does not rotate or the pitcher or third baseman does not retreat to cover third base.

***Early Turn Sacrifice Bunt First Base.*** This is good against the team who has prepared for the first and third early sacrifice bunt to third base by rotating their shortstop to third and covering the steal of second with the second baseman. The first baseman is committed to cover first on the bunt so the runner on third can score on contact, assuming the ball goes down off the bat. If the first baseman comes to get the bunt, the runner on third can hold and you'll end up with the bases loaded because no one will be in a position to cover first. If the first baseman crashes early, the runner at first can steal second. Utilize this with your weaker hitters who have bunting skills. The hitter assumes his bunting stance with his bat angled to bunt the ball to first as the pitcher comes set. He holds the bat loosely and bunts only strikes. The runner on third reads down angle and goes.

***Fake Squeezes.*** This is a technique used to induce the pitcher to throw a wild pitch, force a catcher's balk, or create favorable count leverage for the hitter as a result of the pitcher throwing a ball and getting behind in the count. You are trying to convince the defense that you're squeezing so that the pitcher will not throw a strike. In their haste to defend the squeeze, you may get a wild pitch and, occasionally, the catcher will balk by jumping out in front of the hitter to catch the pitch.

The runner from third and the hitter have to show early to convince the defense that it is a squeeze. It has to be late enough so that it's not an obvious fake, but early enough so that the pitcher has a chance to react.

With the pitcher out of the windup, the hitter should show bunt and the base runner should break hard for the plate when the pitcher reaches over his head. With the pitcher in the stretch, squeeze action must start as soon as the pitcher makes his first move. The runner on third base must be close to third base and be sure that the pitcher is pitching and not picking at third base.

The fake squeeze is effective with runners on first and third when you want to steal second base. The catcher usually comes up in a response to the squeeze, and loses his momentum to second. Many times, the catcher forgets that there is a runner on first when he overreacts to the potential squeeze.

*Forced Balk.* This is a base running technique that is designed to force the pitcher to balk with a runner on third base. The pitcher must pitch out of the windup for you to attempt to force the balk. Ideally, the pitcher starts with his hands coupled and is bent at the waist to get the signal from the catcher. If the pitcher is bent over, but not coupled, that is all right also. You can occasionally force the balk if the pitcher is in an upright position with his hands coupled. As the pitcher is looking in for a signal from the catcher, the runner on third breaks three steps hard for the plate. It is better to break too early, as opposed to too late. If he breaks late, the pitcher will have started his windup and will not balk. If the pitcher reacts by separating his hands, or raises up from the bent over position and does not pitch, it is a balk. The base runner has to start close to third base so that the pitcher does not step back and pick.

*Fake Break.* This is a base running technique intended to disrupt the defense. When a base runner breaks as if he is going to steal, infielders tend to break to cover bases. When the infielders do this, they lose range on batted balls. Fake breaks cause catchers to raise up to throw the runners out. When this happens, the catchers block the umpire's vision of the pitch. When the umpires don't see the pitch, they're going to call it a ball. When strikes are called balls, the pitchers have to make more pitches, and the more pitches an offense sees, the more productive it becomes. A fake break early in the count lets you know who is covering the steal, so that if you hit and run later in the count, you have a good indication who will cover second. This allows the hitter to direct his contact towards the vacated area. The fake break is good from second base in conjunction with the base hit bunt to third base. A good fake break at second ties the third baseman to third and forces the pitcher to make the play to first on the bunter. This is especially tough for the right-handed pitcher who falls off to the first base side.

*Fake Base Hit Bunt.* This is a technique for non-base hit bunters to bring the corner infielders in, thereby opening up wider holes to drive ground balls through. For each step closer to the hitter an infielder plays, he loses ability to catch balls to the right and left. The technique for the fake base hit bunt, which is normally to third base, is the same as the bunt for a hit, but the bunter pulls his bat back as the ball is approaching the plate.

This can be used by bunters and nonbunters in conjunction with the steal of third base against a team whose third baseman aggressively charges when the hitter shows base hit bunt. The base runner steals third base while the hitter base hit bunts through the ball. The base runner steals on his best jump and slides to the back side of third base.

*Shade.* The shade is a method of aiding a base stealer in his attempt to steal second or third base. The shade allows the hitter to protect the base stealer. With a runner on first, the hitter sets up deep in the batter's box. This forces the catcher deeper than normal, increasing the distance of his throw to second. As the pitch is coming to the plate, the hitter starts his swing on the same plane as the ball. When the club head reaches the plate, the hitter drags his bat back and then up, so as not to interfere with the catcher. This keeps the catcher from getting his normal momentum into the pitch. As the bat starts forward into the pitch, the catcher also starts forward. When the bat stops and starts back at the catcher, he stops or slows his momentum, which will affect his throwing rhythm. If the hitter is able to cover the ball with his bat until he draws his bat back, the catcher loses sight of the ball and the ball is on top of the catcher before he knows it.

This same technique can be used to protect the runner from second, stealing third. A second option would be for the batter to slide to the back of the batter's box as the pitch is in flight. This takes the catcher's throwing lane away if he is going to clear the hitter from behind to throw to third base. Most catchers prefer to clear behind the hitter, so you're forcing them to do something they don't want to do.

***Take.*** The take signal is a necessary evil. The players don't like it. The hitting coaches don't like it and the pro scouts don't like it, but this is a team game, and winning and performance is a goal. You have to take pitches at times to improve your chances of positive performance and winning. The consensus against the use of the take signal is that it takes aggressiveness and the decision-making process away from the hitter. The feeling is that hitters can learn their strike zones better when they, not the coach, make the decision to swing or not. There is definitely a lot to be said for that philosophy. However, there are going to be times during the season when you have hitters coming up who do not have disciplined strike zones and good pitch recognition skills, and the situation calls for the take. These same situations may call for even the disciplined hitter to take. The following are a few of the situations that may call for a take signal:

1. Early in the game and lead-off hitter in the inning is out on the first pitch.
2. The first at bat of the day so that you can get zeroed in on the pitcher's stuff and his release point.
3. The first pitch against a relief pitcher with poor control.
4. For undisciplined hitters who are better hitters late in the count. This is especially true for fast ball hitters who swing at a lot of first pitch breaking balls out of the strike zone.
5. Late in the game when the umpire is tightening his strike zone—any time you have an umpire with a tight zone.
6. Early in the game when you are down by a lot of runs. The take, along with a disciplined strike zone, forces pitchers into higher pitch counts. After 16 pitches in an inning, pitchers tend to lose stuff and command. Higher pitch counts get you into the second line pitching sooner. Longer and high pitch count innings also produce more fielding errors because the defense loses focus. However, you don't want to create higher pitch counts at the expense of aggressive hitting with a disciplined strike zone.

Encourage timid "analysis paralysis"-type hitters into a "see it and hit it" mode without too much concern for the strike zone.

Invariably, when you have the take on and the pitch is a strike, the hitter will tell you that it was their pitch and that they really saw the ball well. This is usually true because the hitter's mind is clear when the take is on because there is no decision to make.

Even the good disciplined hitters need to learn how to deal with the take signal. When the game situation calls for a take signal, hitters sometimes go to pieces and give up their entire at bat because they had to take a pitch. Also, the guys who do not have good two-strike skills have problems taking pitches.

When the hitter is taking a pitch, he should take it out of his hitting stance as if he is hitting. Umpires tend to expand the strike zone when the hitter doesn't assume a hitting posture. However, sinking under the high ball will keep the ball up from being called a strike. Against some pitchers on the 3-0 take, and if the hitter is way off or on top of the plate, the pitcher has trouble throwing strikes.

The hitter can also take out of an early turn sacrifice bunt stance. This gives a chance to read the opponent's defensive scheme. Do not do this in obvious take situations. Umpires tend to expand the strike zone if the hitter shows bunt.

Develop aggressive hitters with disciplined strike zones by judicious use of the take sign, but don't use take signs in off season practice and play, intrasquad games, or during games when player development is the goal.

## STEALING A RUN—FIRST AND THIRD OFFENSE

First and third offense starts by defining the action of the runner at third base. The runner at third has three options:

1. When the catcher's throw passes the pitcher's head, the runner should fake a break toward home. (This technique is used in conjunction with the straight steal, delay steal, or halfway straight steal from first. These are discussed at greater length in this section under "Options for the Runner at First.") The runner on third is looking for a low throw to second that's going to bounce. If the runner on third thinks the ball is going to bounce before it reaches second base, he runs. The belief is that the shortstop or second baseman will not catch the low throw cleanly, or if they do, they will not have good enough body control to make an accurate throw.

Three different rundown options are possible at this point:

◆ A rundown between first and second will ensue when the shortstop or second baseman is running the runner out of control toward first and they pass the midway point between first and second. The feeling is that the shortstop or second baseman will throw to home without momentum and with poor body control. The runner breaks from third.

◆ In the second rundown option, the first baseman runs the runner toward second with the first baseman running out of control past the halfway point between first and second. This is the better of these rundown options because the thrower is going away from home, and if the first baseman is the trigger man, his arm is generally not as strong as the shortstop or second baseman. Here's an added plus in forcing the first baseman to make the throw—many first basemen are left-handed throwers. A left-handed thrower has to make an almost 180° turn while running away from home.

◆ In the third rundown option, the runner on third breaks for home just as the runner between first and second is about to be tagged from behind. As the base runner is about to be tagged out, he falls down flat and goes perpendicular to the base line. The defensive player is going to try to tag the runner but can't reach him because he's flat on the ground, yet the tagger will not trip over him because he's perpendicular and not lengthwise in the base line. The tagger won't have enough body control to straighten up and throw effectively.

On all these plays, it is important for the runner at third to gain momentum by shuffling down the line as the ball passes the pitcher's head or as the rundown is progressing. He must have enough momentum so that he is not breaking for home from a dead start, but not so much momentum that he gets so far off of third base that he could be picked before he breaks for home.

In general, when the rundown is created between first and second, there are two outs and the hitter is overmatched by the pitcher. If that's the case and you don't feel the hitter is capable of driving the runner in, run your offense early in the count. You want the catcher to throw to second in this situation, and often when the defense gets two strikes on the hitter, they will not throw through to second base.

**2.** The runner from third base shuffles on the pitch and breaks just before the catcher releases to second, as long as the catcher does not look the runner back at third base. If the catcher looks the runner back at third base, the base runner stops and fake breaks to home after the ball passes the pitcher's head. In that case, the rundown rules apply. If the catcher does not look the runner back and the runner has shuffle momentum, it is virtually impossible to throw him out. The runner is running 75 feet or less with momentum, and the defense is going to have to execute two throws totaling approximately 250 feet. The runner from third can't be timid and should slide on the plate, not up to it. If the catcher arm fakes, throws straight to third or straight to the pitcher or shortstop, you are in trouble. The ball's going to beat your runner and he'll have to scuffle hard to get out of a rundown.

**3.** On the third technique at third base, the runner on third breaks for home before the catcher's release, whether the catcher looks him back or not. It helps to lead right in the base line on this play, so the catcher can't see how far off third base the runner is. This play works because much of the time, the catcher is looking, but not seeing when he looks to third. The catchers that look runners back at third base are almost always going to throw through to second base. The purpose is to have momentum and to create two long throws.

***Options for the Runner at First.*** The runner from first base has various options at first to initiate the first and third offense. The following are just a few of the many options for the runner at first:

**Straight Steal.** The straight steal with runners on first and third is designed to get the runner from first into scoring position. The runner from first runs with his best jump only. If the runner on first gets picked, he turns it into a rundown situation. You want your base stealer to slide to the back side of second base so the middle infielder has to stay back to receive the throw. The runner on third reads a low or errant throw to second in order to score.

**Straight Steal/Halfway.** This is the same as the straight steal, except the runner on first can't get picked and he must stop one-half to two-thirds of the way to second base. You're trying to score the runner from third base and want to make sure he will score before the runner from first can be tagged out. The runner from third will break just before the catcher's release, in response to a poor throw by the catcher, or as a result of a rundown between first and second.

**Delay Steal.** The runner should never get picked in this situation. He starts with two long low hops once he is sure that the pitcher is going home. The runner stops on the catcher's release so as not to get tagged out before the run scores. You are hoping that the catcher is surprised and forgets to look the runner back at third base, or throws wildly because he is out of rhythm. The middle infielders may arrive late and the ball could end up in center field, or they could have no momentum or body control to throw home once they catch the ball. The runner on third can run just at release, on a poor throw, or on the rundown.

***Additional Options.*** Here are some additional options for stealing under other situations:

**Long Pick at First.** This can be run against a right-handed pitcher or a left-handed pitcher. You want the runner on first to take a long enough lead at first that the pitcher will pick, but not so long that he will step off and run at him. It's okay to draw a step off pick against the left-handed pitcher. If they refuse to pick, turn it into a halfway steal, a delay, or try to force the pick from the catcher. As soon as the pitcher makes his first move to pick at first, the runner on first breaks hard to second. You want the runner from first to take the inside lane so the first baseman has to throw over him. You want the first baseman to have to throw quickly to second. When the base runner from first gets to two-thirds of the way to second, he pulls up so that he does not get tagged out before the runner on third base scores. If you run this with less than two out, the runner from first will go all the way to second and finish it off with a late tough slide. He should stay up and get into the shortstop's glove with his helmet. The runner from third shuffles hard on the pick and runs on the first baseman's release. The defense has to carry the ball 215 feet with two exchanges, and the base runner at third only has 70 feet to run and he has momentum. If the first baseman arm fakes to second, the runner from first should continue to second and the runner from third should put the breaks on and scramble back to third.

**Short Pick at First.** Run this play with less than two outs late in the game when that run will put you ahead. This is especially effective when you are working against a poor defensive first baseman. It starts out just like the long pick. The runner takes a long lead, but not so long that the pitcher steps off. After the pitcher picks, the runner from first takes a jab step back to first to encourage the first baseman to chase him. As the first baseman runs at the base runner, the base runner starts for second, all the time making the first baseman run hard, but allowing him to close the distance between the base runner and the first baseman. As the base runner going to second is about to be tagged by the first baseman, he falls down. You want him to fall perpendicular to the base line in an elevated position (on hands and knees) so the first baseman will fall over the base runner as the reaches down to tag him out. The runner on third base starts with a short lead at third and shuffles on the rundown, until the base runner from first is about the be tagged out, and then he runs.

**First and Third Double Break vs. Left-Handed Pitcher.** You're trying to force the pitcher to pick to first and break your runner from third just before the pitcher initiates his pick. A lefty with a slow move to first and a left-handed first baseman provides the best scenario for the runner from third to score easily. You'd like to have a pitcher who picks a lot (no step off moves) and has a slow leg lift. The reader type left-handed pitcher who picks his leg up and reads the runner on first is perfect. As the pitcher picks his leg up, the runner from third breaks and then the runner on first breaks. It's almost a simultaneous break, but the runner on third initiates the action. In the event that the pitcher throws home, you're looking for the hitter to base hit bunt the ball to second. This is generally a two strike, two out play, so you have to do your homework and make sure the timing is correct so the pitcher will pick to first.

### Gimmick Plays to Steal a Run.

**Hollywood Play at Second.** This calls for the base runner at second to be a good actor. Therefore, the name "Hollywood." This play can be run with the bases loaded or just runners on second and third. The runner at second takes an aggressive two-hop secondary lead that takes him right to the edge of his safe return zone. When the play is on, the base runner at second takes himself out of his safe return zone with his secondary lead and trips. He gets up quickly to make an attempt to get back to second base. You want the catcher to have to come up and throw quickly to get the runner out at second. The runner on third base starts close to third base and slowly shuffles up the line on the pitch. As the catcher is about to release this throw to second, the runner on third breaks for home. The runner on second stops before he reaches second base, so as not to get tagged out before the runner on third scores. If the catcher hesitates or looks the runner back at third, the runner at second goes back to second and the play is off. This is an effective play versus a team with a catcher who likes to pick.

**Hollywood Play at First.** This can be run with the bases loaded or with runners on first and third. The runner on first is the actor and tries to draw the pick from the catcher just like the runner at second did on the previous play. This play is designed to take advantage of a poor throwing first baseman. If you have a plus runner on third, the abilities of the opponent's first baseman are not a factor. The runner at third must get an aggressive secondary and run just before the catcher releases the pick.

# SCHOLARSHIPS AND PROFESSIONAL BASEBALL

When an athlete and his parents are trying to decide between a college education and signing with major league baseball, they need to consider the situation from the same viewpoint they would use when evaluating any career choice. First, the student should decide what he wants to do for a living and then prepare for that career.

Certain skills will apply across the broad spectrum of multiple career paths. The ability to compete, for example, can be transferred from sports to many other fields. The persistence a player learns from baseball will overcome many obstacles later in life. These skills really count. If a player has these skills, he can accomplish anything.

The key to a successful life is passion. Students need to understand that if they do the things they have a passion for, their lives will be fulfilling. Remember that Cal Ripken said on the night he broke Gerhig's record that the keys to his success were, "Love for the game, passion for his team mates and dedication to being the best he could be every day of his life." If a career choice matches a purpose in life, it will never seem like work. Athletes who are passionate about baseball find it easier to work at the job of baseball. Those who see baseball merely as a vehicle to accomplish something else often struggle with their career choice unless they connect the "something else" to their purpose in life. Baseball players who enter the game just for the money may be disappointed—no matter how much they earn. In considering any other career choice, students can easily see that they can substitute "engineering" for "baseball" and the results will be similar.

## APPROACHING A CAREER IN BASEBALL

Once a player has it fixed in his mind that a career in baseball is like any other career choice, he must consider the peculiarities of an athletic career. Most careers don't limit how long someone can participate, but the average baseball career, as a player, is less than ten years. Unless the player considers his playing career an entry level position to a management, administration or broadcasting career, he may not have a secure future. If an athlete wants only to "play" the game and doesn't want to be involved in any other capacity, he and his parents should consider carefully the steps to achieving a career path that doesn't end the career when he is still a young man.

The athlete who is considering a professional offer versus going to college should keep in mind the value of all his assets. If he has a college scholarship, he has more leverage with a professional team in terms of commanding a greater bonus. The more money he gets from professional baseball, the more opportunities he has to fail because the team doesn't want to give up on a major investment. If he goes right out in professional baseball, and he's a performer from the beginning, he should have no problem. But most young people don't step right into professional sports and excel because there's an adjustment period to the life in professional baseball. That is why each player needs to make sure there's commitment and investment toward his development. The more money invested, the more the commitment from his employer, the more chances he has to fail.

To be in that position, the player has to have good enough grades to be eligible for a scholarship. A student/athlete can't get a scholarship so that he can create that leverage in professional baseball if he's not a performer in terms of SAT scores and grades. The more options he has in life, the more choices he has, and the more chances he has to be happy. From the academic standpoint, there's life after baseball, even if he plays in the big leagues for ten years, he's still in his early thirties. Eventually he's going to have to go to work.

### Importance of Non-Baseball Skills.

When a player eventually goes out to work, he will need skills he has learned in school. When he goes to find a job, his prospective employer won't be concerned with his earned run average, wins and losses or his batting average. The only thing that matters is whether he can do the job in this field.

If a player is going to create his own job, he still has to have certain skills to manage his own money. He can gain those skills in school through business, economics, or accounting classes, but he can also get those skills by getting a job, having a checking account, and managing his own life. However, athletes usually don't have time for anything besides the game. All too often athletes who have made money in professional pursuits have lost it by turning it over to people who manage their money for them. They really didn't have any information or knowledge about money management because they didn't take the time to train themselves. So just as they train themselves for athletics, they have to train for life after athletics.

### Other Considerations in Signing or Going to School.

The average stay in the big leagues is three years. Only 5% of all the players who sign a contract ever get to the big leagues. A player can't make enough money in minor league baseball to support a family and every player needs to be prepared to get on with his life after baseball.

When he is trying to decide "do I sign?" or "do I go to school?" there are a number of factors that are important:

1. Is the player ready to go out in the business of professional baseball? It's a tough business.

2. Does he have the skills? Or is he ready to acquire the skills?

3. Is he mature enough to go out there and compete? Many young people have never had to compete, and they're not ready to go out and compete in professional baseball.

4. Has he truly evaluated the bonus structure in professional baseball? If he breaks up a bonus over a five-year period and takes the taxes out, it may not amount to much. He should also consider the training time it's going to take to get to the big leagues. It is from four to six years. If he gets a $100,000 bonus and amortizes that over five years, it's really only $20,000 a year because the salary he earns in the minor leagues barely covers expenses. For the other six months of the year, the player has to support himself. An outstanding player may go to instructional leagues for two years and then play in Mexico, Puerto Rico, or the Dominican Republic. He may make some money there, but he's not going to get rich.

5. Has he been offered an amount that makes it impossible not to sign a professional contract? He may have to consider going into pro ball before he is completely ready, because if he waits till he's ready, it may be too late.

6. Is he thinking about age as a factor in professional athletics? Players have a window of opportunity during a short period of time in their lives, and they have to take advantage of it then.

7. Has he considered the possibility of getting hurt in professional baseball? If he doesn't have another career to fall back on, that also can be a problem.

***Returning to School After Baseball.*** Most players don't go to school after they're done with professional baseball, even if they have a school program tied into their contract. If they sign as a high school player at 17 or 18 years old and then play five or six years of professional baseball and never get to the big leagues, chances are they don't go back to school because they have commitments. Many of them get married and have families. At 23, they're not ready to go back to school with 17 and 18-year-olds. They've been out of the academic mode for so long, they just can't get back into that scheme.

This is the chance an athlete takes when he opts for the pro contract. Advise your players in the presence of their parents of the pitfalls that are possible. Care for them as you would your own children. Be adamant about making sure they are prepared for life after baseball.

## EVALUATING A PATHWAY

You may want to suggest to the majority of players, depending upon the amount of signed bonuses, that they go to a community college for a year or two years and play a hundred games in the fall. They can play 60 games during the season, and evaluate things on a year-to-year basis.

Going into a four-year situation is really difficult now. The NCAA is restrictive in terms of the contact time that college coaches can have with their student athletes. There is very little player development time because of these restrictions. The coaching staffs are greatly reduced. The real plus, especially the first two years for a four-year college, is social development. Generally when a player attends a four-year college, he moves away from home unlike the typical junior college athlete who stays in his local community and still lives at home. This is a time to develop responsibility.

Academics are relatively comparable in terms of the classes players take and the type of instruction that they get in the community college as opposed to the four-year school. Psychologically, it can be tough for a player to say he is going to a community college when he has been such a stand-out. But a community college is a positive alternative if

◆ he is a professional prospect,

◆ he's a high draft choice, and he's not ready to jump into professional baseball,

◆ or the bonus is not at the right level.

A player with no education and no skills outside of baseball may get in to a panic mode when he continues to fail in baseball, which can be detrimental to his development. A player who knows he has something to fall back on and knows that he has a short route to getting a degree and being marketable is more relaxed and has a better chance of performing up to his capabilities. Otherwise he can go only as far as his physical abilities will carry him.

**The Viewpoint of a Professional Organization.** Most organizations are for their players and want to do what's best for them, but the system isn't structured that way. It's a business decision. The organization has to make sure the athlete gets to the big leagues as fast as he can because the younger he gets to the big leagues, the more productive time he's going to have as a pro. They can't encourage a guy to go to school and set him back in his development as a professional player. If that's going to help him get to the big leagues a little bit better or faster because he's in a better mental state, that's fine. They want their players to be successful after baseball, but the system is stacked against that happening.

For a good player to get to the big leagues, he'll have to go to instructional league for probably two years. He'll have play during the winter, and a lot of things can get in the way in baseball. If he's going to get to the big leagues, he's got to be single-minded and focused. There are very few guys who can go to school and get their work in the off-season. The good ones tend to be super focused—100% committed, in fact. Everything is baseball, and they don't let anything get in the way of it. They can't divide that focus.

**Money in the Minor Leagues.** For a first year player, the maximum is $850 per month; after that, everything is negotiable. Generally speaking, a second-year player earns about $1,100 in an A league, and in a double A league, $1,300 or $1,400. A tremendous variation in the amount of money is paid in triple A, especially if players are the big league types.

When a player breaks down the time it takes to get to the big leagues and the costs he incurs, he needs to get a lot of money for it to be cost effective. Some players don't understand that they're not being paid year round—they're being paid only while they're playing. If a player makes $850 a month, that's only for the months he plays. Some players think they're making $850 a month for the entire year.

It's a break-even proposition for the first three years in minor league baseball. A new player may have to tap other resources, especially if he has a family to support. He may make some money down the line, but chances are slim. For the six months that he is not playing, he may not be able to find a good job. It's tough to go back to school because many schools start in August, which creates a time conflict with the minor leagues playing through the beginning of September.

# GETTING HELP WITH THE DECISION

When an athlete is dealing with professional baseball, he is dealing with professional negotiators, and he should have help. He should get advice and not necessarily from an agent. He should have an information base, or professional baseball should allow an information base for parents so that they have a base of knowledge to negotiate. The NCAA rules right now are restrictive. For all intents and purposes, a 17-year-old has to negotiate for himself, and he can't have someone negotiate for him, and that includes a parent.

The information is readily available in terms of what a draft choice got last year. A player is drafted based on his skills and the needs of that organization. Certain organizations have more money than others, but he can get a ballpark figure of how much that spot in the draft is worth.

Regarding scholarships, there are very few college scholarships now. There are almost no full scholarships because with 11.7 scholarships for each college, teams can't afford to give a full scholarship to just one player. If a school did that for everybody, they'd have 11 outstanding players on full scholarship, and the rest of their 25-man roster as walk-on-type guys. They would have a tough time winning.

Aspiring athletes need to understand scholarships vary just as pro contracts do. Some scholarships limit the number of units a player may take. Some scholarships include a meal plan that is not a full meal plan—they may get two meals a day. There are many variations. Players should scrutinize the college scholarships, especially in baseball.

***Promotion Bonuses and How They Work Against College Money.*** Bonuses in professional baseball range widely. A player may get $1,000 for moving from an A team to a double A team for 90 days, $1,500 from a double A team to a triple A team, and $5,000 from triple A to the big leagues.

A player with a college scholarship plan and an incentive bonus plan would find that they counterbalance each other. Any money that he takes out of the incentive bonus plan takes away from his college scholarship.

A player should understand that he gets only the money that he uses. If he doesn't use it, he doesn't get it. If he signs a letter of intent with an expensive school and goes back to the local junior college and/or state college, he doesn't get the money that was allocated for the expensive private school. He just gets the money that he needs for that local school.

If a player never goes to school, he will never receive that money. If he is an outstanding player and goes to the big leagues, chances are he won't see that money because he won't have time to go back to school. He should get his education money or his bonus money up front, and then do what he wants with it when he is ready to do it.

***Increasing the Player's Leverage.*** A player should not plan to go to school if he has absolutely no academic skills and no motivation to go to school. If he has the skills necessary to go out and play, that's probably what he should do. But if he doesn't, or if the bonus isn't right, he shouldn't go out and play for nothing because chances are he's going to fail.

There is a relationship between the time line of how much time he is in the organization versus how much money he got from the day he started. A player needs to do whatever it takes in his case to get the highest amount of money going in. It is vital to have his skills refined or to develop his skills even before he is drafted as a high school player to the highest level so he can command the greatest amount of money.

A player must get super committed to developing himself as a baseball player if he recognizes that he is not an academic, or he will put himself at a disadvantage.

The point here is that most young players would rather develop themselves as athletes than as scholars. But if a player puts some effort into school, he has a chance to defend himself in the academic setting. In sports, the gradient is much steeper. A player must be in the A+ category in athletics to make it. Academically, he can be a C student. There are a lot of C students and many students with a 2.0 who have college degrees. There are, however, no 2.0 baseball players. If a player is a C performer, he's not a professional baseball player.

# Baseball Terms

*Backdoor* — A breaking ball that catches the outside corner to a LHH (Left Handed Hitter) from a RHP (Right Handed Pitcher) or outside from a LHP to a RHH. Also can be a fastball that tails back on the outside corner (LHP to a LHH or RHP to a RHH).

*Bottoming Out* — When pitching out of the stretch, the pitcher does not come to a complete stop.

*Buckle* — When a hitter flinches on a breaking ball (LHP to LHH or RHP to RHH) that starts at him and is moving away. Can also occur on inside fast balls that tail back to the plate (RHP to LHH or LHP to RHH).

*Comebacker* — A batted ball hit directly back to the pitcher (abbreviation: CB).

*Deke* — In a hit-and-run situation, the acts of the defensive team to confuse the baserunner to return to first or second base.

*Double Clutch* — The act of a fielder starting to throw and then stopping as a result of losing the grip on the ball or as a result of late coverage and then restarting the throw.

*Downer* — A curveball that breaks straight down from 12 pm to 6 pm.

*Framing* — The act of the catcher tracing the frame of the strike zone to keep marginal pitches in the strike zone.

*Gapping Hitters* — When a fastball thrown inside and off the plate from a RHP to a LHH or from a LHP to a RHH forces the hitter to bend at the waist and then tails into the strike zone.

*LHH* — Left handed hitter

*LHP* — Left Handed Pitcher

*Rally Hats* — The superstitious act of wearing baseball caps inside out to generate a run scoring rally.

*RHH* — Right-handed hitter

*RHP* — Right Handed Pitcher

*Slash* — The act of the hitter from a sacrifice bunt stance, drawing the bat back and hitting the ball hard on the ground toward the space or spaces vacated by the defense as a result of their early response to a potential sacrifice bunt.

*Slurve* — A 3/4 breaking ball. A pitch that breaks down and away from the throwing arm side.

*Spoking* — A dive technique used by the baserunner to return to first or second.

*Synergy* — The team concept where the sum of the whole is greater than the sum of its parts.

# SCORE CARD (SAMPLE: FRONT AND BACK)

| SCORE CARD | umpire's name | SCORE | | | | | | | | | | DATE March 12 |
|---|---|---|---|---|---|---|---|---|---|---|---|---|
| | PLATE Bill Zephyr | Them | 0 | 0 | 0 | 1 | 1 | 1 | 3 | 0 | 0 | |
| | BASES Lew Phillips | Us | 1 | 0 | 0 | 1 | 1 | 0 | 0 | 2 | 2 | |

| # | b | name | 1 | 2 | 3 | 4 | 5 | comment |
|---|---|---|---|---|---|---|---|---|
| 2 1 6 | 1 | Crabe | ◆ sb BB | K | 2B | BD ◆ SB HBP | ◆ 1B bunt | (1) leads too short (5) Great push bunt |
| 17 R 8 | 2 | Omares | 1-3 sac | WP ◆ 2B | K | 7-2 | 1B | (2) Route to 2b bad (4) dropped bat head on bunt attempt |
| 16 R 3 | 3 | Jones | 6-3 rbi | K | K 2-3 | sb ◆ tb 8-2 1B 1 rbi | 2B RBI | "Lunger" needs to stay back |
| 18 R DH 34 | 4 1 | Goode Dagwood | 7-8 | 1-3 squeeze rbi | L-6 | BB | | (2) turned too early on squeeze |
| 3 S 9 | 5 | Devon | | | wild pitch | | | Bad body |
| | (2) | Alexander | 7-7 | 4-3 | E-6 | 1B bunt | | language |
| 11 R 2 | 6 | Edgewood | K | ◆ 1 rbi HR | 1B | 6-4-3 DP | | (2) Nice off field adj on curve (5) too anxious in rbi situation |
| 6 R 4 | 7 | Serive | L-5 | K | 2-3 | ◆ E-5 | | Think about teaching to switch hit-good speed |
| 22 L 7 | 8 | Haerge | | CIS 2-4 | 5-3 | K | | (2) bad first step on steal |
| | (2) | Darton J | 7-2 | bb | | | | (4) took strikes with bunt on |
| 27 R 5 | 9 | Pasco | K | 5-3 | 7-9 | 8-3-2 1B | | Needs to work on shortgame |

**ASSIGNMENTS**

CATCHER'S GEAR Edgewood
HELMETS Goode
FIRST AID Crabe
ICE Callahan
WIFFLES Omares
BALL BUCKET Jones
SCORE BOOK Crespi
COACHES BUCKET Dagwood
BATS & HELMETS Williams
CATCH WITH OF Jax
CHARTS Greenwald
BULLPEN
FOUL BALLS 1-2
FOUL BALLS 3-4
FOUL BALLS 5-END

**RESERVES**

| # | NAME | 14 | Williams |
|---|---|---|---|
| 9 | Crespi | 44 | Jax |
| 15 | Alexander | | |
| 26 | Gruenwald | | |
| 31 | Callahan | | |
| 13 | Darton J | | |

**POST GAME NOTES**

Remind Kids about Saturday Bull pens

Fundraising Money Due Tommorrow

To order blank score cards, call Tom Alston at 916-689-2246

## TRIPS TO THE MOUND

| | 1 | 2 | 3 | 4 | 5 |
|---|---|---|---|---|---|
| **OURS** | | 1 | 1 | | |
| **OPPONENT** | 1 | 1 | | 1 | |

| # | p | name | 1 | 2 | 3 | 4 | 5 | comment |
|---|---|---|---|---|---|---|---|---|
| 3 | 2 | Grauman | K | K | 5-3 | K | L-6 | |
| 14 | ph | Diabolato | | 111 | 121 | 112 | 11 | |
| 9 | 4 | Muster | 5-3 | ◆ HBP | K 22 | ◆ BB | K | |
| 7 | 6 | Stoner | L-5 | 1B | SB SB 1B | ◆ BB | | |
| 46 | DH | Buchmiller | 1-3 | 5-3 | K | 1B | | |
| 21 | 7 | Clayton | | | | E-9 | | |
| 24 | 8 | Harrington | K | 4-3 | Sac-8 | K | | |
| 33 | 5 | Harrington | 6-3 | K | | 6-4 | | |
| 19 | | Dorman | | | 26 | 1B | | |
| 44 | 9 | Teitz | 1B | ◆ E-6 | 4-3 | FC | | |
| 4 | 1 | Silva | UA-3 | K | ◆ 1B | 5-4-3 DP | | |
| 45 | 3 | Reed | | K | K | K | | |
| 6 | 3 | Gladden | L-6 | | | | | |

1=FB 2=CURVE 5=CHANGE-UP S=STRIKE B=BALL

| OPPONENT RESERVES | OUR # | PITCHER | 1-1 | 1-1 | 2-1 | 2-b | 5-1 | 5-b | S | B | SUB TOTAL | TOTAL | K | BB | R | ER | |
|---|---|---|---|---|---|---|---|---|---|---|---|---|---|---|---|---|---|
| Diabolato | 14 | Dagwood | 6 | 5 | | | | | 6 | 5 | 11 | | 1 | 0 | 0 | 0 | 1.0 |
| Dorman | 19 | Dagwood | 2 | 3 | 4 | 0 | 1 | 0 | 7 | 3 | 8 | 19 | 1 | 0 | 0 | 0 | 1.0 |
| Clayton | 6 | Dagwood | 6 | 3 | 3 | 0 | | | 9 | 3 | 12 | 31 | 1 | 0 | 0 | 0 | 1.0 |
| Fairbanks | 37 | Dagwood | 6 | 3 | 2 | 1 | | | 8 | 4 | 12 | 43 | 1 | 1 | 1 | 1 | 1.0 |
| Berk | 51 | Dagwood | 6 | 5 | 5 | 1 | | | 11 | 6 | 17 | 60 | 2 | 0 | 1 | 0 | 1.0 |
| | | Dagwood | 9 | 2 | 1 | 3 | | | 10 | 5 | 15 | 75 | 1 | 0 | 1 | 1 | 1.0 |
| | | Dagwood | 5 | 8 | 2 | 1 | | | 7 | 9 | 16 | 91 | 2 | 2 | 3 | 2 | .67 |
| | | Totals | 40 | 29 | 17 | 6 | | | 58 | 35 | | 93 | 9 | 3 | 6 | 4 | 6.67 |
| | | Callahan | 2 | 1 | 3 | 0 | | | 5 | 1 | 6 | 6 | 1 | 0 | 0 | 0 | .33 |
| | | Callahan | 4 | 2 | | | 1 | 0 | 5 | 2 | 7 | 13 | 0 | 0 | 0 | 0 | 1.0 |
| | | Totals | 6 | 3 | 3 | 0 | 1 | 0 | 10 | 3 | 13 | | 1 | 0 | 0 | 0 | |
| | | Crespi | 6 | 6 | 2 | 0 | 1 | 0 | 9 | 6 | | 15 | 2 | 0 | 0 | 0 | 1.0 |